CHOOSING HOMES, CHOOSING SCHOOLS

CHOOSING HOMES, CHOOSING SCHOOLS

ANNETTE LAREAU
KIMBERLY GOYETTE
EDITORS

Russell Sage Foundation · New York

The Russell Sage Foundation

The Russell Sage Foundation, one of the oldest of America's general purpose foundations, was established in 1907 by Mrs. Margaret Olivia Sage for "the improvement of social and living conditions in the United States." The Foundation seeks to fulfill this mandate by fostering the development and dissemination of knowledge about the country's political, social, and economic problems. While the Foundation endeavors to assure the accuracy and objectivity of each book it publishes, the conclusions and interpretations in Russell Sage Foundation publications are those of the authors and not of the Foundation, its Trustees, or its staff. Publication by Russell Sage, therefore, does not imply Foundation endorsement.

Library of Congress Cataloging-in-Publication Data

Goyette, Kimberly A., editor of compilation.
 Choosing homes, choosing schools / Annette Lareau and Kimberly Goyette, editors.
    pages cm
 Includes bibliographical references and index.
 ISBN 978-0-87154-496-4 (pbk. : alk. paper) — ISBN 978-1-61044-820-8 (ebook) 1. Discrimination in education—United States. 2. Segregation in education—United States. 3. Educational equalization—United States. 4. Social classes—United States. I. Lareau, Annette, editor of compilation. II. Title.
 LC212.2.C43 2014
 379.2'6—dc23
                        2013041411

RUSSELL SAGE FOUNDATION
112 East 64th Street, New York, New York 10065
10 9 8 7 6 5 4 3 2 1

Contents

List of Tables and Figures

About the Authors

Annette Lareau is Stanley I. Sheerr Professor in the Department of Sociology at the University of Pennsylvania and past president of the American Sociological Association.

Kimberly Goyette is associate professor in the Department of Sociology and director of the Center for Vietnamese Philosophy, Culture, and Society at Temple University.

Michael D. M. Bader is assistant professor in the Department of Sociology and affiliate of the Center on Health, Risk, and Society at American University.

Felicia Butts is an early childhood educator in Chicago.

Kyle Crowder is professor in the Department of Sociology and affiliate of the Center for Studies in Demography and Ecology at the University of Washington.

Lori Delale-O'Connor is a research scientist with Child Trends in Washington, D.C.

Stefanie DeLuca is associate professor of sociology at the Johns Hopkins University.

Caroline Hanley is assistant professor of sociology at the College of William and Mary.

Paul A. Jargowsky is professor of public policy and director of the Center for Urban Research at Rutgers-Camden.

Shelley McDonough Kimelberg is assistant professor of sociology at Northeastern University.

Maria Krysan is professor in the Department of Sociology and the Institute of Government and Public Affairs at the University of Illinois at Chicago.

Mary Pattillo is Harold Washington Professor of Sociology and African American Studies at Northwestern University.

Anna Rhodes is a graduate student in the Department of Sociology at the Johns Hopkins University and a predoctoral fellow at the Institute for Education Sciences.

Salvatore Saporito is associate professor of sociology at the College of William and Mary.

Amy Ellen Schwartz is director of the NYU Institute of Education and Social Policy and professor of public policy, education, and economics at the Wagner School and Steinhardt School, New York University.

Leanna Stiefel is professor of economics at the Wagner School of Public Service and professor of economics and education policy at The Steinhardt School of Culture, Education, and Human Development at New York University.

Elliot B. Weininger is associate professor of sociology at SUNY College at Brockport.

Preface

KIMBERLY GOYETTE AND ANNETTE LAREAU

Schools vary enormously in the United States. Some, particularly those serving low-income children, have decrepit buildings, limited supplies, high rates of student turnover, unqualified teachers, and other formidable challenges. By contrast, other schools have wood-paneled offices, well-stocked supply cabinets, and highly trained teachers (Anyon 1997; Ingersoll 2001; Kozol 1991). Children are not randomly distributed into these schools; low-income children are much more likely to attend challenging schools. These patterns are not simply in urban settings; suburban neighborhoods are increasingly socially stratified. In addition, despite the growth of school choice programs, the most recent data suggest that 73 percent of children continue to attend a neighborhood school (U.S. Department of Education 2009).

This volume centers on an important question that all families face: what kinds of schools will my children attend? In recent decades, attention to voucher programs, charter schools, and school transfer programs has increased. Federal legislation like the No Child Left Behind Act has given families the right to transfer schools under certain conditions. Schools, which may have once been perceived as part of the package of public goods associated with particular neighborhoods, are more often talked about as private "choices" that families make for the welfare of their children.

Advocates of school choice policies ranging from controlled choice desegregation programs to magnet and charter schools to voucher programs, contend that one benefit of expanded choice is less social inequality across schools. They contend that increasing options for school choices should lessen school inequality for two reasons. First, students who are the most dissatisfied with their schools, often those in the worst schools, are afforded the opportunity to move into other schools with better resources, better instruction, or both. Second, because schools, including public schools, have to compete to enlist and retain students, all schools are motivated to provide their students with a competitive education (Chubb and Moe 1990; Coons and Sugarman 1978; Nathan 1989; Young and Clinchy 1992). Under the vision associated with increased choice, schools operate more like the private market. Consumers, who are the primary beneficiaries of schools under this vision, choose those places that best fit the needs of their children. Schools that do not meet the needs of parents and children suffer the consequences of a lack of demand— fewer resources and less funding—and then they ultimately close.

Due to legislation like No Child Left Behind, and the increased availability of charter schools, transfer policies, and other increased school choice options, families in many locations, particularly those who live in cities, are not limited to their assigned neighborhood schools. In many places, they may choose schools outside their assigned areas or apply to charter or magnet schools. As of 2007, about 15.5 percent of school-age children attended a school of choice like a charter or magnet school, and about 11.3 percent attended a private school (U.S. Department of Education 2009). Proponents of increased school choice have applauded the expansion of these policies, arguing that families with fewer resources benefit from the separation of a family's residential location and their school choice. For other families, though, assigned neighborhood schools are the schools their children attend. In fact, most children in the United States still attend their assigned neighborhood schools (U.S. Department of Education 2009). This may be because they make a very clear choice to live in a neighborhood to attend a particular school or as a result of a host of complex factors simply wind up in a particular residential location (Goyette 2008).

The extent to which and how people make decisions about where to live and where to send their children to school (either jointly or separately) has consequences for who lives where and what opportunities they have. As many scholars before us have argued, we assert that more than the type of house or apartment they live in and more than the availability of parks, shopping, or transportation, the types of schools children attend have consequences for their later life outcomes. Elementary, middle, and high schools most immediately affect whether the students who attend them expect to and then attend some sort of postsecondary education. For those who do, schools may influence the selectivity of those schools (Alexander and Eckland 1977). Beyond their further education, children's schools may shape their future occupations, their citizenship, and their self-esteem (Alwin and Otto 1977; Banks 2008; Rowan-Kenyon et al. 2011; Simmons et al. 1979). Few scholars (and parents and students) would disagree that schools shape students, though they may disagree about the extent to which they matter compared to other influences in children's lives. Whether or not research supports it, many families seem to believe that the quality of their children's schools influences their ability to get ahead in life (Johnson 2006).

Schools in places with more resources, typically in wealthy, suburban communities, are able to provide more resources for their students. Schools in wealthier communities typically have higher per capita funding (Greenwald, Hedges, and Laine 1996; Rowan-Kenyon et al. 2011) and more highly qualified teachers (for a review, see Wayne and Youngs 2003). Whether or not funding is important (Hanushek 1997), students in these schools are often surrounded by other students from advantaged backgrounds (Engberg and Wolniak 2010). This matters because peers convey and reinforce high educational expectations and promote behaviors that aid students' academics, such as forming study groups, founding academic clubs, and so on. Although debate in the academic community still rages around whether schools really do matter for children's educational outcomes and has for decades (see Coleman et al. 1966; Jencks and Brown 1975), many families aren't taking any chances with their children's futures. Many families go to great lengths to place their children in the schools they believe are best, to the extent their resources will allow.

Beyond the effects of schools on children's and families' lives, though, where children go to school may influence larger patterns of social inequality in the United States, particularly the inequality associated with where people live. Scholars have long pondered how people separate themselves according to their choices of residence or segregation. People in the United States tend to live in neighborhoods with people who are similar to them, both socioeconomically and racially. Some segment of the population is able to choose from many options of places to live whereas others have very few options. Families who are able to may make schools a very high, or even the highest, priority in this choice. Other families may not have that luxury. Advantaged and perhaps white families may choose the same schools and concentrate in the same neighborhoods, further contributing to patterns of segregation (Goyette 2008). Families without resources may be priced out of these neighborhoods with little access to low-income or multifamily housing. And, in a vicious cycle, further residential segregation has consequences for school segregation, which leads to greater inequality in school resources and in educational outcomes.

The chapters in this book grapple with this issue. Who can choose schools? How do people choose schools? What factors are important? Does race matter and, if so, how does race matter? Who gets to choose schools through choosing homes (which is the most secure way of getting into your school of choice)? When families make these choices, we may not reflect on the larger patterns of inequality that result. The chapters in this book also take that up: how do school choices result in school and residential segregation and in turn how does residential segregation affect schools?

Common Themes

The chapters that follow approach these questions from a number of perspectives. The chapters look at both macro-level societal patterns of residential and school segregation, as well as the individual decision-making processes of families. Some use quantitative methods, others mostly qualitative analyses. Some focus more on the institutional level policies that shape choices, while others explore the decision-making that occurs within particular contexts.

Taken together, several common themes emerge from these chapters. First, the chapters as a whole suggest that the notion of choice, whether it refers to homes or schools, should be problematized. When policymakers promote increased choices in schooling or housing, they often operate with several assumptions. These assumptions include that information will be available and accessible to all choosers, regardless of their social position, that information will be used in similar ways across individuals and families, and that there are few or no obstacles to enacting preferences, or at least, that these obstacles are not systematically related to social background.

The chapters suggest these assumptions may be faulty. First, structural or policy constraints operate on choices. In some cities and regions, easily accessible choice programs that allow for transfer across schools or allow families to choose charter schools for their children do not exist. When they do, families may be limited by the number of openings they offer or by extensive application processes, some of which may require long waits, often outdoors in lines, that working parents may be less able to afford to do.

Information about schools may come from different sources depending on one's social background or race, and may be used in different ways, again depending on the social background of the parent or parents. The search process is different by social class and residential location (in the cities or suburbs, for example).

These chapters also show that choices are often bundled—housing and school, child care and transportation, these go together for many families. Families may choose schools based not only on where they live (or vice versa), but also on where their members work, who will take care of children after school hours, and how they will be able to get to all of the places they need to go in a day. Families with fewer resources often have to compromise in enacting their ideal preferences more than those with more resources do. A family that has a car and can afford high-quality, after-school programming for their children may be more easily and freely able to enact their ideal preferences for schooling than a family that has to rely on public transportation and relatives for aftercare. For these reasons, choice programs may not always reduce inequalities in school quality across families from different social backgrounds, but instead may reproduce or even exacerbate them. Those best able to take advantage of increased choice may be families with resources: access to good information from advantaged social networks, easy transportation, the ability to afford after-school care, and others.

These chapters point out that it is important to not underestimate the role that access to information plays in how people get sorted into homes and schools. They show that access to information is structured by particular policies (where, how, and how often school indicators are publicized). These chapters also show that individuals differ in whether and how they access that information. Upper-middle-class families in the suburbs, for example, do not feel the need to search extensively for schools because they rely on school reputation information from their trusted networks. Middle-class families living in cities, though, rely heavily on the Internet and other sources to get a sense of their options and how to order their preferences. It appears that for families of all social backgrounds, social networks are a key source of information. These networks, though, are stratified, with upper-middle-class families relying on networks of advantaged individuals, and working-class families often relying on other working-class families. The homogeneity of social networks limits knowledge of schooling options for many. To those who live in the suburbs, the only "option" they may consider is the school with the best reputation, whereas working-class individuals may best know the schools attended by family members and may primarily consider those.

Other chapters in this volume take up the consequences of individual-level choices in both housing and schooling for macro-level segregation. These chapters point out that the origins of preferences are difficult to determine. It could be that people want to live around those like them (homophily), want to avoid those unlike them (prejudice), and to avoid neighborhoods that they perceive to be of low quality (race proxy). They may want to maintain or increase their social status, and they may rely on homogeneous social networks as sources of information about homes and schools all at the same time. It is also difficult to determine the extent to which current residential segregation patterns are uniquely due to race or class position, as the two covary so much in the United States (though the chapters in this volume suggest racial residential segregation is stronger than segregation by poverty status). The chapters also point out that individual-level decisions that result in larger patterns of residential and school segregation are the result not only of individual-level preferences and constraints, but also of specific policies that structure the types of available options.

To a greater or lesser degree, the chapters also show how institutions and policies shape choices. Policies, decided on by actors in institutions such as school boards or superintendent offices, banks, and city or town governments, create structural constraints that limit people's individual-level preferences. School boards, superintendent's offices, or other school governance bodies decide whether and how many charter schools will operate, whether and to what extent to allow transfer and choice across district schools, whether to merge urban and suburban districts, and other types of expanded choice policies. Banks and their lending practices allow people to afford more or less expensive homes in particular areas. City councils create zoning restrictions that may prevent affordable multi-unit housing from being built. Even the governance structure of cities, counties, and schools may matter. Counties with smaller districts or townships may experience greater inequality across schools than places where counties and school districts are one and the same. These policies create structural constraints that limit people's individual-level preferences.

The chapters here question how people make decisions within these particular contexts. They point out where there are structural constraints to choice and how expanded choice policies may not take people's daily lived contexts into account. Ultimately, the chapters question whether expanded choice necessarily leads to better results, particularly reduced inequality in school resources and outcomes.

Important Differences

Despite their commonalities, the chapters provide insight into different settings and different themes. Families are included from Boston (chapter 7), Chicago (chapter 8), a large mid-Atlantic city (chapter 9), and Mobile, Alabama (chapter 5). The choice process looks very different across these areas. Boston, Chicago, and the mid-Atlantic city have many choices, of which parents seem to be aware. In Boston, those options allow some parents to remain in public schools in the city. Parents in Boston can choose the public school to which they want their children sent. In Chicago and in the mid-Atlantic city, charter schools are options that parents actively consider. In Mobile, though, parents have fewer options. Schools are largely determined by residential location, and, though some parents have found ways to try to work around the situation, where children live pretty much determines where children go to school. Parents who cannot afford to live in neighborhoods associated with high-quality schools do not have the option of going to such schools.

Another notable difference in the chapters is in the description of the choice process across those who live in the cities versus those who live in the suburbs. Families in the city, for the most part, see schools as choices and consider their options carefully. Middle- and upper-class as well as some working-class families who remain in the city seem to know that they will be actively choosing schools for their children once they decide to move to or remain in a city. In some chapters, families' searches seem frantic and fraught with importance. Families may be sensitive about their choices, hoping that they have done the right thing, and ready to change if they feel they have not.

Suburban parents, on the other hand, seem far more casual about their search for schools. In fact, the suburban parents described in this volume, seem to have less actively compared schools, but rather accepted the reputation of the schools they chose, with little corroboration from outside information or school visits. These families trust that the school quality follows its reputation, and seem far more relaxed about their choices. Some even seem to have difficulty seeing their choice of schools as a choice in which they considered options and made decisions. Choosing their suburban school seemed quite natural, and was not fraught with the same anxieties that their middle- and upper-class urban counterparts faced.

Finally, we see important differences in social class reflected in these chapters. One chapter focuses mostly on the decision-making of middle- and upper-class whites; another looks solely at low-income and poor families. Other chapters include a mixture of white and black, upper-, middle-, and working-class families. Through comparing these chapters, we see how the options of the upper- and middle-class respondents appear to be much greater than those of the working-class and poor respondents. Families with more resources can easily move between cities and suburbs, and those who choose to stay in cities have the networks and information at their disposal to manage the complex school choices that some cities afford. Middle- and upper-class families can afford those homes associated with schools with more resources. Working-class and poor families cannot afford to move to more advantaged neighborhoods and so often do not have the options to increase the quality of their children's schools that families with more resources do. In addition, for those who live in cities with increased options for choice, working-class and poor families use information resources less than do middle- and upper-class families and often rely on their homogeneous social networks for information about which schools to send their children.

Chapter Overview

The first chapter provides an overview of the literature on residential segregation, school segregation, housing choices, and schooling choices. Kimberly Goyette points out that though these topics are closely linked, most research is done within these broad categories, but very little of it looks at the connections across these processes. The next part of the volume, chapters 2 through 4, looks at the patterns of and explanations for residential and school segregation.

In chapter 2, Maria Krysan, Kyle Crowder, and Michael Bader describe recent trends in residential segregation and review the common explanations for these trends. They categorize explanations as economic, housing market discrimination, or preference-based. They note that these explanations are not disparate, but complementary, and that researchers need to understand how the explanations work together in complicated ways to shape residential preferences and behaviors. The authors also argue that we need to better understand the processes that may contribute to residential segregation. To understand these processes, we need to know how residents get their information about neighborhoods, and how people consider their options. Information networks, residential opportunity structures, and experiences of segregation or integration in neighborhoods in childhood may all be factors that affect these processes.

In chapter 3, Salvatore Saporito and Caroline Hanley provide an historical overview that tracks how enrollment in private schools among white students has been influenced by the racial composition of their neighborhoods. They follow these trends using U.S. Census data from 1970 to 2010. Although it appears that the relationship between neighborhood racial composition and the rate of private school enrollment among white students has gradually weakened since 1980, race nevertheless persists as a correlate of private school attendance. These correlations contribute to racial segregation in public schools. Saporito and Hanley argue that the persistence of these correlations suggests that white families want to avoid large shares of black students in their public, neighborhood schools, whether this is due to overt discrimination, the perceived quality of these schools, or both.

In chapter 4, Paul Jargowsky looks specifically at changes in residential segregation over the past four decades. He looks at segregation by both race and poverty status and questions the extent to which racial residential segregation is due to poverty status, and the extent to which segregation by poverty status may be due to race. He finds that, though some small amount of racial segregation is due to poverty status and a larger amount of segregation by poverty status is due to race, both work independently of each other, for the most part. Both race and economic status contribute to patterns of residential segregation.

Whereas chapters 2 through 4 focus on larger patterns of segregation, chapters 5 through 9 look at individual-level decision-making in particular contexts. Although the decisions are not often easily separated, chapters 5 through 6 explore decision making about homes, primarily, and the roles schools do or do not play in the process. In chapter 5, Anna Rhodes and Stefanie DeLuca describe the mobility of low-income African American families in Mobile, Alabama. They find that decisions to move are often not the result of calculated moves to improve school quality or to find better neighborhoods with more amenities. Instead, families move often because of situations that they have little control over: conflict with landlords, bad conditions in their apartments, lack of safety in neighborhoods, need for child care, and others. When these families do move, they cannot afford homes in the neighborhoods associated with better schools. Financial constraints, limited information about higher quality schools and neighborhoods, and the often unplanned nature of their moves, prevent them from accessing better schools. Some families try to circumvent this by using others' addresses for school registration, but most of these families wind up moving between similar low-quality schools when they move residences, which Rhodes and DeLuca show is quite frequently.

Chapter 6 explores the process of decision-making about homes, and to some extent, schools, among a very different population, one that includes not only working-class but also middle- and upper-class suburban residents of a large mid-Atlantic city, both white and black. Annette Lareau finds that, for the most privileged parents who live in the suburbs, the schools their children attend are less conscious, carefully researched choices than taken-for-granted amenities of the neighborhoods in which they live. These privileged families, rather than looking at a range of options, usually consider only a few places to live (often only one) based on the reputation of the school district. They rely on their networks for information about school reputation, and do little to either confirm or disconfirm whether the empirical data concerning the schools match their reputations. In a similar way, working-class suburban residents rely on their networks for information about schools. This information often leads them to the less prestigious suburban schools, but these families still consider only a few of the many options they may have based on the information their networks of family and friends provide. These families, though in less prestigious schools, report being happy to "escape" the schools in the city.

In chapter 7, Shelley Kimelberg looks at very different choices from those made by the respondents in chapter 6. She analyzes the choices made by middle- and upper-middle-class parents who choose to stay in the city and send their children to Boston city public schools. Because of the choice policies in Boston, families can apply for children to attend a wide range of public city schools. The parents in chapter 7 carefully research the elementary schools their children attend. However, Kimelberg shows that this choice feels tentative to most parents. Parents in her study report choosing public schools (for elementary school only) to "see how it works." These parents believe that they can supplement their children's elementary education such that the children will have the tools they need to do well academically. However, parents feel less prepared to supplement the education of their children in middle or high school, and are actively prepared to leave the district if their children are not admitted to the prestigious Boston Latin exam school. This chapter vividly points out the resources that middle- and upper-middle-class parents have at their disposal. Parents can choose to stay in city schools because they have confidence in their abilities to educate their children and, when and if they feel dissatisfied with these schools, easily leave for the schools in the suburbs.

In chapter 8, Mary Pattillo, Lori Delale-O'Connor, and Felicia Butts also look at the choice of schools in an urban district, this time in Chicago. They focus on two sets of African American parents of teenagers: those whose children are attending a neighborhood high school to which most of them were assigned according to their residence and those who chose and were admitted by lottery to a charter high school. For the most part, those who chose the charter school were satisfied. Those who wound up in the neighborhood high school were often not satisfied, ambivalent, or angry about this placement. The authors point out that enacting one's "choice" depends on many factors, including, for example, access to information, overcoming significant socioeconomic barriers, initiative, and whether one is lucky enough to succeed in a lottery. Policymakers assume that when schools are choices, some families (those savvy enough or lucky enough to have made the choice) have access to better education, and when such options are expanded, more families will be able to take advantage of higher quality schools. Policymakers also assume that when enough families opt out of assigned neighborhood public schools, these schools will close down from lack of funding. However, the authors point out, this moment takes time to occur. In the meantime, students attending those schools are receiving a low-quality education. The chapter authors contend that if we decide to make a good education a right rather than a choice, we would be better motivated to provide high-quality schools to all students, regardless of the choices they and their families are shrewd enough or lucky enough to make.

Chapter 9, by Elliot Weininger, takes up the important question of how parents acquire information about schools when deciding which one to select for their children, focusing, in particular, on the use of No Child Left Behind performance data. Weininger examines parents residing in a large city that has a choice policy permitting out-of-catchment attendance; the city also has numerous charter and private schools. Weininger finds that parents of all backgrounds have considerable anxiety over the selection of a school for their children, and all rely on information provided by trusted network contacts to some degree. However, differences in whether and how parents make use of performance data are significant. Working-class parents exhibit relatively little awareness of school test score data, and instead depend primarily on advice from friends or kin. By contrast, middle-class parents frequently check district websites or sites such as Greatschools.org to complement information gleaned from their networks with test score data. Moreover, within the middle class, the weight attributed to test scores appears to vary, with parents who have few ties to other parents in their neighborhood placing significantly greater emphasis on the scores. Weininger concludes that, at least in this setting, rather than simplifying school choice for working-class families, the publicization of school performance data appears to mainly fuel middle-class anxiety about social reproduction.

Chapter 10, by Amy Schwartz and Leanna Stiefel, questions the types of housing and school policies that might make schools more equitable in an environment in which school quality is closely tied to residential choices. The authors mention several possible approaches, including increasing the ability of poor students to move not only within districts, but also across them. Schwartz and Stiefel find, however, that this is likely not to affect equity in schools because neighborhood public schools remain the default schools for most students, and students with increased choice often move from school to school within districts with few resources, not across districts with very different amounts of resources. The authors suggest that in addition to thinking about increasing choice for students, policymakers should also consider affecting the housing choices of students' families by reducing mobility through increased subsidies for housing, building educational and other types of support for students in low-income housing, and consciously locating low-income housing developments in areas where they will have access to high-quality schools. Schwartz and Stiefel contend that to improve the educational quality of low-income students we need to address both students' housing and their schools.

Acknowledgments

As the social sciences become increasingly specialized, researchers in related fields often do not engage with one another. Thus, though scholars in the fields of residential segregation and sociology of education have much in common, studies are not as engaged with one another as one might hope. We are grateful to Eric Wanner and the Russell Sage Foundation for providing an opportunity for vigorous intellectual exchange. A small conference held at Russell Sage provided a chance for the contributors to meet, critically assess the research, and provide feedback. A number of scholars, whose work does not appear on these pages, provided valuable input at that meeting. Among others, we are grateful to Pamela Bennett, Jennifer Jennings, Aaron Pallas, Lincoln Quillan, and Amy Stuart Wells for thoughtful comments. Suzanne Nichols has been an enormous help in guiding this project through the crucial steps in the process. We also want to express our gratitude for the comments of the anonymous reviewers. All errors, of course, are our responsibility and not the sponsoring agency's.

The chapters in this book suggest that parents' choices around schools and neighborhoods are structured by particular policies and enacted by individuals with preferences and constraints. Understanding how households make choices is important because these choices matter. They matter because they shape how resources are distributed in society. These resources can help maintain patterns of inequality. Hence, where families choose to live and how this relates to where children go to school may not only affect whether they go to college and what type of college they get into, for instance, but also where children believe they belong, where they are comfortable, and what they perceive as normal and desirable. Neighborhoods and schools influence children's perceptions of opportunities and of their place in the world. These effects may be hard to measure in empirical research, but are nonetheless no less important than the measurable effects of test scores, or of college attendance or selectivity. In sum, inequality in the life circumstances of families is very powerful in shaping children's life chances. Everyone agrees that the character of neighborhoods and schools where children are situated matters. This volume seeks to help unpack the key ways that parents and children end up in such different schools and neighborhoods, and highlight the kinds of policies that might weaken this important, and disturbing, pattern of continued inequality.

References

Alexander, Karl L., and Bruce K. Eckland. 1977. "High School Context and College Selectivity: Institutional Constraints in Educational Stratification." *Social Forces* 56(1): 166–88.

Alwin, Duane, and Luther B. Otto. 1977. "High School Context Effects on Aspirations." *Sociology of Education* 50(4): 259–73.

Anyon, Jean. 1997. *Ghetto Schooling: A Political Economy of Urban Educational Reform.* New York: Teachers College Press.

Banks, James A. 2008. "Diversity, Group Identity, and Citizenship Education in a Global Age." *Educational Researcher* 37(3): 129–39.

Chubb, John, and Terry Moe. 1990. *Politics, Markets, and America's Schools.* Washington, D.C.: Brookings Institution.

Coleman, James, Ernest Campbell, Carol Hobson, James McPartland, Alexander Mood, Frederic Weinfeld, and Robert York. 1966. *Equality of Educational Opportunity.* Washington: Government Printing Office.

Coons, John, and Steven Sugarman. 1978. *Education by Choice: The Case for Family Control.* Berkeley: University of California Press.

Engberg, Mark E., and Gregory C. Wolniak. 2010. "Examining the Effects of High School Contexts on Postsecondary Enrollment." *Research in Higher Education* 51(2): 132–53.

Goyette, Kimberly. 2008. "Race, Social Background, and School Choice Options." *Equity & Excellence in Education* 41(1): 114–29.

Greenwald, Rob, Larry V. Hedges, and Richard D. Laine. 1996. "The Effect of School Resources on Student Achievement." *Review of Educational Research* 66(3): 361–96.

Hanushek, Eric A. 1997. "Assessing the Effects of School Resources on Student Performance: An Update." *Educational Evaluation and Policy Analysis* 19(2): 141–64.

Ingersoll, Richard M. 2001. "Teacher Turnover and Teacher Shortages: An Organizational Analysis." *American Educational Research Journal* 38(3): 499–534.

Jencks, Christopher S., and Marsha D. Brown. 1975. "The Effects of High Schools on Their Students." *Harvard Educational Review* 45(3): 273–324.

Johnson, Heather Beth. 2006. *The American Dream and the Power of Wealth: Choosing Schools and Inheriting Inequality in the Land of Opportunity.* New York: Routledge.

Kozol, Jonathan. 1991. *Savage Inequalities: Children in America's Schools.* New York: Crown Press.

Nathan, Joe, ed. 1989. *Public Schools by Choice: Expanding Opportunities for Parents, Students, and Teachers.* Bloomington, Ind.: Meyer-Stone.

Rowan-Kenyon, Heather T., Laura W. Perna, and Amy K. Swan. 2011. "Structuring Opportunity: The Role of High School Context in Shaping High School Students' Occupational Aspirations." *Career Development Quarterly* 59(4): 330–44.

Simmons, Roberta G., Dale A. Blyth, Edward F. Van Cleave, and Diane Mitsch Bush. 1979. "Entry into Early Adolescence: The Impact of School Structure, Puberty, and Early Dating on Self-Esteem." *American Sociological Review* 44(6): 948–67.

U.S. Department of Education. 2009. *The Condition of Education 2009.* Washington, D.C.: National Center for Education Statistics.

Wayne, Andrew J., and Peter Youngs. 2003. "Teacher Characteristics and Student Achievement Gains: A Review." *Review of Educational Research* 73(1): 89–122.

Young, Thomas W., and Evans Clinchy. 1992. *Choice in Public Education.* New York: Teachers College Press.

= Chapter 1 =

Setting the Context

Kimberly Goyette

To place the chapters in this book in conversation with research done thus far, in this introduction I discuss four bodies of work that have mostly been done separately, often without a more thorough exploration of their connections. The first literature is on residential segregation, about which a vast amount has been written, but very little of the research has considered the role of schools in the process.

Residential Segregation

Although black-white segregation in American metropolitan areas remains quite pervasive, declines in such segregation have nonetheless been substantial over the past few decades (Iceland, Weinberg, and Steinmetz 2002). For example, the black-white dissimilarity score averaged across all U.S. metropolitan areas declined from 0.73 in 1980 to 0.64 in 2000. The 0.64 figure can be interpreted as indicating that about 64 percent of blacks or whites would have to move for all neighborhoods in a metropolitan area to have an equal proportion of blacks and whites. The rule of thumb is that dissimilarity scores above 0.60 are considered quite high in absolute terms. Hispanic-white and Asian-white segregation levels tend to be more modest, though they did not decline in the same fashion as black-white segregation in recent decades. For example, Hispanic-white dissimilarity remained about the same at 0.50, as did Asian-white dissimilarity at about 0.41 between 1980 and 2000 (Iceland, Weinberg, and Steinmetz 2002). From 2000 to 2010, segregation indices for some groups declined. By 2010, the black-white dissimilarity index for all areas of the country had declined to 0.59, and Hispanic-white segregation was 0.48. The segregation of Asians and whites remained almost the same at 0.41 (Logan and Stults 2011).

Dissimilarity indices generally give us an idea of how disproportionately groups are distributed in particular areas, but researchers of residential segregation also use measures of diversity and isolation to capture groups' experiences with those of other races. According to the 2010 census, whites live in neighborhoods with about 75 percent other whites, 8 percent blacks, 11 percent Hispanics, and 5 percent Asians. Blacks, though, live in neighborhoods that are about 45 percent black, 35 percent white, 15 percent Hispanic, and 4 percent Asian. Hispanics live in neighborhoods with 46 percent Hispanics, 35 percent whites, 11 percent blacks, and 7 percent Asians. Asians live in neighborhoods with 22 percent other Asians, 49 percent whites, 9 percent blacks, and 19 percent Hispanics (Logan and Stults 2011). Isolation refers to the percentage of other minorities in the neighborhood. For blacks, isolation ranges from a high of 81 percent in the Detroit metropolitan area to about 9 percent in less segregated cities such as Phoenix in 2010. Comparable percentages for Hispanics range from 96 percent in Laredo, Texas, to 12 percent in Minneapolis, and, for Asians, from 76 percent in Honolulu and as low as 6 percent in Tampa (Logan and Stults 2011).

Generally, explanations for residential segregation focus on either the structural constraints to housing choices or on individual preferences. Spatial assimilation explanations suggest that differences in socioeconomic status (SES) among racial and ethnic minority groups, and in acculturation among recent immigrants, shape patterns of segregation (Charles 2003). Whites are better able to afford neighborhoods with higher quality services and more amenities than are blacks, Hispanics, and Asians (Clark 2007). Research does show that income and education matter for segregation. Higher income families are segregated from lower ones, and though segregation by income is less stark than by race, it has grown over the last four decades (Fischer et al. 2004; Iceland, Sharpe, and Steinmetz 2005; Reardon and Bischoff 2011; White 1987). The spatial assimilation model may be important in explaining some amount of residential segregation because of the continued disparities in SES across racial and ethnic groups. Blacks and Hispanics in particular lag behind whites in terms of incomes, occupational status, and education (Harrison and Bennett 1995). Segregation by income may also be important to understand because, as Sean Reardon and Kendra Bischoff (2011) point out, growth in the segregation of higher income families from other types of families leads to neighborhoods of concentrated wealth with particularly good services and amenities, like schools.

Discriminatory policies and practices in the housing market against blacks in particular, but Hispanics and Asians as well, have contributed to patterns of racial residential segregation (Ross and Turner 2005; Turner and Ross 2003; Turner et al. 2002). Redlining policies codified the unequal access of whites and blacks to favorable mortgage rates. Discriminatory practices have included real estate agents steering racial groups to certain neighborhoods and providing less information and assistance to minority home seekers, and lenders' provision of unequal access to mortgage credit (Goering and Wienk 1996; Yinger 1995). Research has indicated a decline in discrimination in the housing market in recent years. Changing attitudes in society, the rising economic status of minority customers, and the continuing effect of the Fair Housing Act and its enforcement on the real estate industry all likely played a role in these trends (Ross and Turner 2005). Despite declining overt racial discrimination in real estate policy and practice, high (though declining) racial residential segregation persists (Charles 2005; Squires and Kurbin 2006). Many argue that individual preferences maintain these patterns.

Numerous studies show that variation in residential preferences between members of different racial groups perpetuates residential segregation (Charles 2000; Emerson, Yancey, and Chai 2001; Farley et al. 1994; Krysan 2002a; Krysan and Farley 2002; Quillian 2002). The primary debate in this literature is what drives these preferences. Racial residential preferences are argued to derive from three main sources: in-group preferences, racial prejudice or out-group hostility, or perceived status differences.

According to the in-group preferences hypothesis, members of different racial groups prefer to live in neighborhoods and associate with others who share a cultural background. Thus, whites have a strong preference to live in neighborhoods in which a significant proportion of residents are of that same race (Clark 1986, 1991). Blacks, too, have this preference, though it is stronger among whites. Maria Krysan and Reynolds Farley (2002), for example, find that blacks are willing to tolerate far higher proportions of whites than whites are willing to tolerate of blacks.

Although some evidence suggests that this *benign ethnocentrism* accounts for racial segregation, the preponderance of empirical evidence suggests that segregation is driven by out-group aversion. For example, Maria Krysan and Reynolds Farley (2002) find that it is not a preference for living near other blacks but rather fear of out-group hostility that motivates blacks' preferences. Minority group members may wish to avoid being pioneers in all-white neighborhoods for fear of hostility. In contrast, whites' avoidance of minority groups is driven by racial prejudice or a desire of racially advantaged groups to avoid those with lower social standing. Thus, the extent to which members of one racial group avoid neighborhoods comprised of members of other racial groups depends on either the social distance between the two groups or the intensity of prejudice of the superordinate group toward the subordinate group (Bobo and Zubrinsky 1996). Because blacks have historically been perceived as the group that is the most different from whites, segregation between blacks and whites is the most stark (Bobo and Zubrinsky 1996; Charles 2000; Farley et al. 1994).

Other researchers suggest that it is not that white preferences are driven by prejudice, but rather that whites prefer to avoid the real or perceived conditions associated with neighborhoods in which the majority of residents are nonwhite. Whites worry that the quality of their neighborhood services and the value of their homes will decline as blacks and other minorities move in (Clark 1992; Galster 1989). Whites say that as blacks and other minorities move in crime will go up, schools will be worse, and property values will decline (Farley et al. 1994; Krysan 2002a). Some researchers (Harris 1999, 2001; Taub, Taylor, and Dunham 1984) argue that white preferences for more segregated neighborhoods have less to do with racial composition as such, and more with the unfavorable perceptions of neighborhood quality that often accompany integration.

The evidence in support of this is mixed. For example, David Harris (1999) tests this "racial proxy hypothesis" using a hedonic price analysis and argues that "housing in neighborhoods with a high percentage of black residents is less valuable not because of an aversion to blacks per se, but rather because people prefer affluent, well-educated neighbors, and those traits are more common among whites than blacks" (476). In contrast, Michael Emerson, George Yancey, and Karen Chai (2001) find, after presenting hypothetical housing situations with varied neighborhood conditions and racial compositions, that even when public services, school quality, and housing values are held constant, whites prefer to buy houses in neighborhoods with proportionately fewer blacks, though not Asians or Hispanics. Similarly, Kyle Crowder (2000) finds that the racial composition of neighborhoods influences the likelihood of moving out of a neighborhood, net of the neighborhood social and economic conditions. Race, then, may play an independent role in the housing choices of whites, above and beyond the relationship between racial integration and neighborhood services.

A core debate in the literature is whether race remains an important factor in neighborhood choice after real housing values and quality of neighborhood services are taken into account. Maria Krysan (2002a) distinguishes between "racial reasons" and "race-associated reasons" for housing preferences. Racial reasons involve direct antipathy or hostility toward members of another race on the basis of negative stereotypes. Whites do not want to live around blacks because they distrust them or are uncomfortable around them, because they do not want to be in the minority, or because their status position is threatened by an influx of blacks into a neighborhood. Race-associated reasons include worries that public services will degenerate, crime will go up, and property values will decline (Swaroop and Krysan 2011). Maria Krysan (2002a) maintains that race-associated reasons for white preferences are not often empirically distinct from racial reasons because the prejudices of whites may inform their perceptions that services will decline, whether or not they actually do. Whites may perceive that crime has or will go up as black residents move in, even if the crime rate does not increase (Chiricos, McEntire, and Gerts 2001; Quillian and Pager 2001). Whites may perceive that housing values will decrease when black residents move in, whether they do immediately or not. Indeed, whites may use a change in the presence of blacks as an indicator of whether their neighborhood quality and housing values will increase or decrease regardless of whether other "objective" indicators of such changes are present (Wolf 1963). The perception that this will occur may, in fact, lead it to occur—whites who perceive their property values will decrease may move out of neighborhoods in large proportions, precipitating a decrease in property values.

Literature on residential segregation has found that of all household types, white households with children are among the most segregated from blacks and Hispanics (Ellen 2007; Iceland et al. 2010; Logan 2004; Logan et al. 2001). In 2000, the black-white dissimilarity index for all households averaged across U.S. metropolitan areas was 0.64, but for children it was 0.68 (Logan et al. 2001). White households with children are more segregated from and have less interaction with other racial and ethnic groups than other types of white households (Iceland et al. 2010). Because of this, black families with children are more likely to live in neighborhoods with higher poverty and crime and lower school quality than otherwise similar white families (for example, Adelman et al. 2001; Massey, Condran, and Denton 1987; Sampson and Sharkey 2008; South and Deane 1993). It is important, though, that the difference in levels of segregation between households with and without children is modest. There may be reasons why white families with children are less likely to live in integrated neighborhoods, but researchers know very little about how much of a role children play in families' decision-making about residential preferences.

One reason that these households may be modestly more segregated may have to do with schools. Hamilton Langford and James Wyckoff (2006) find that the racial composition of schools and neighborhoods are very important in school choice and residence decisions even after accounting for other school and local government characteristics in their study of white families in the New York metropolitan area. These authors suggest that prejudice against blacks and Hispanics may be motivating families' decisions, but it could also be that race is being used a proxy for school quality.

Children may influence where families decide to live because parents are concerned about social reproduction and want to guarantee their children's safety and ensure their social position in the future (Ball 2003; Lareau 2011; Lee, Macvarish, and Bristow 2010). Parents with children may more strongly want to identify with their racial or ethnic group, or may feel less trusting of other racial and ethnic groups than they did before having children. White families with children may want high-quality services and schools to maintain their social status or to enable their children's social mobility. Minority families may desire less segregated and more integrated neighborhoods for these same reasons. Integrated neighborhoods, those with a larger proportion of white families, may provide better services, amenities, and schools than minority segregated neighborhoods.

Little research has explored what, if any, role concerns about schooling play in the preferences of white and minority parents for particular types of neighborhoods, and how these preferences shape patterns of racial residential segregation. However, what appears to be clear is that schools in segregated neighborhoods tend be segregated themselves and that this has consequences for the children they serve. It is to this literature that I now turn.

School Segregation

Neighborhood and school racial change often accompany each other. For example, because school feeder areas comprise neighborhoods, as neighborhoods integrate or segregate so do schools. However, school racial change often proceeds more rapidly because those who have more recently moved into neighborhoods are often (minority) younger adults with children, while those residents least likely to move are those (whites) who are older who have finished raising children (Orfield and Lee 2006). In addition, private schools may lead to more rapid racial change in schools than in neighborhoods because advantaged white children may leave neighborhood schools for more segregated spaces (Reardon and Yun 2002).

Racial segregation, both de facto and de jure, has characterized schools in this country for more than a century. The historic Brown v. the Board of Education of Topeka, Kansas (1954) Supreme Court decision made de jure segregation unconstitutional based on the argument that separate schools could not provide equal resources to their students. However, despite this decision, the federal government had no real way to enforce it. The most it could do was to send National Guard troops to protect black students attending white schools. Not until the Civil Rights Act of 1964 and Title I of the Elementary and Secondary Education Act of 1965 could the federal government promote integration. Schools practicing de jure segregation were cut off from government Title I funding (intended to increase resources for schools with many students in poverty), and schools that did not achieve racial balance were threatened with a loss of federal funding.

Numerous policies were attempted to integrate schools, including merging urban and suburban districts, allowing interdistrict transfers of black students to primarily white schools and white students to primarily black schools, and student reassignment and busing. All of these policies met with opposition, and in 1974, The Supreme Court decided in Milliken v. Bradley that schools could not be forced to integrate if there was no intent to keep them segregated. Although racial segregation in schools declined during the 1970s and 1980s, more cases like Milliken were brought to the Supreme Court in the 1990s. During the 1990s, it was clear that no longer was the condition of segregation unconstitutional, merely the intent. If students were in segregated schools because they lived in segregated neighborhoods or because they simply chose different schools, policy had little role to play (Patterson 2001).

Historians argue that the flight of whites to the suburbs to avoid segregating schools, particularly in the South, resulted in the consolidation of the power of those who lived in the suburbs to shape policy, which contributed to patterns of de facto segregation. Suburban counties and townships control zoning in their communities, which often restricts builders from constructing multifamily dwellings, particularly those that house low-income, and possibly minority, families. Suburban communities often have more wealth and resources at their disposal. They also have control over the composition of their communities through policies that restrict housing choices. Suburban communities, particularly in the South but also in the North, are more homogeneously white than the urban areas they surround, and segregation is maintained through de facto means, or what are perceived as housing "choices" (Kruse 2005; Lassiter 2006; Sugrue 2008).

Other policies, such as the creation of **jurisdictional boundaries,** also matter for school segregation. For example, in metropolitan areas that have numerous, small school districts or highly fragmented districts, racial segregation between these districts is more likely. However, schools within these districts are more racially homogeneous and thus less likely to exhibit segregation than those schools in larger, less fragmented districts (Bischoff 2008). Kendra Bischoff (2008) argues that smaller political boundaries afford more choices for families who are looking to surround themselves with other families similar to them racially or socioeconomically. Competition for residents across these smaller districts ensues, and municipalities associated with these districts attempt to maintain a high degree of services and provide a desirable community identity for their residents, sometimes through zoning regulations that prohibit commercial real estate or high occupancy dwellings (Bischoff 2008). The segregation that results when there are many smaller jurisdictions rather than fewer and larger consolidated districts is a combination of the macro-level policies that create wealthier, desirable communities with many services and amenities, and the micro-level decisions of families to want to live in areas that include people who are racially and socioeconomically similar to them.

Although segregation in schools had declined in the 1970s and 1980s, it increased again dramatically in the 1990s. Since about 1998, though, similar to racial residential segregation, there is some evidence that school racial segregation has declined (Stroub and Richards 2013). Despite this recent decline, it is still quite apparent in many schools across the nation. Currently, about 80 percent of Latino students and 74 percent of black students attend majority nonwhite schools. The average white student attends schools where about 75 percent of his or her peers are white. (Whites currently make up only a little over 50 percent of the school-age population). The typical black student attends school with only 25 percent of whites (Orfield, Kucsera, and Siegel-Hawley 2012).

Indeed, segregation in public schools is more stark and persistent than that in neighborhoods (Orfield and Yun 1999; Rickles et al. 2001), in part because of increasing neighborhood segregation, but also because of the choices families may make to either move out of neighborhoods with integrated schools or to attend private, charter, or other schools. For decades, researchers have tried to evaluate how the racial composition of schools influences whites' attendance at these schools. These researchers have generally found that as public schools have integrated, whites have left these schools (Bankston and Caldas 2000; Clark 1987; Clotfelter 1976; Coleman, Kelly, and Moore 1975; Farley, Richards, and Wurdock 1980; Giles 1978; Giles, Cataldo, and Gatlin 1975; Hess and Leal 2001; Smock and Wilson 1991; Wrinkle, Stewart, and Polinard 1999). While some suggest this is the result of specific desegregation plans in particular districts, others argue that it is not integration of schools per se that drives white flight from integrated neighborhoods to more homogeneously white suburbs, but rather that this process would have occurred no matter the racial composition of schools (Clotfelter 2001; Coleman, Kelly, and Moore 1975; Frey 1979). This white flight from integration has occurred in inner-ring suburbs, as well. Sean Reardon and John Yun (2001) find that as minority populations in particular suburbs grow, residential and school segregation of the surrounding suburbs increases.

More recent research on the effects of school choice on school segregation finds that the proportion of nonwhite students in public schools affects the likelihood of white enrollment in private, charter, and magnet schools, even when controlling for measures of school quality, including graduation rates, test scores, safety, and student-teacher ratios (Bankston and Caldas 2000; Fairlie and Resch 2002; Hess and Leal 2001; Renzulli and Evans 2005; Saporito 2003; Saporito and Sohoni 2006; Wrinkle, Stewart, and Polinard 1999). Rather than moving from integrating neighborhoods, families may use public school choice programs to avoid neighborhood-based schools. For example, Salvatore Saporito (2003) and Saporito and Deenesh Sohoni (2006) find that white children are more likely to leave public neighborhood schools for magnet schools as the proportion of nonwhite children in a school increases, even after accounting for school characteristics such as average test scores and poverty rates. Further evidence based on interviews suggests that white parents are averse to sending their children to schools with large numbers of black and Latino students (Saporito and Lareau 1999). Similarly, Linda Renzulli and Lorraine Evans (2005) find that whites are more likely to attend charter schools in districts with greater degrees of racial integration. Robert Fairlie (2002) suggests that this flight may not be confined to whites, but may also extend to Latino families. He finds that Latino students are also more likely to leave public schools for private schools the greater the percentage of blacks in their neighborhood public schools. Studies such as these cause concern for educators and policymakers who had hoped that choice programs such as magnet and charter schools, "schools within schools," and voucher programs would serve to integrate schools.

It is difficult to discern families' motives for leaving integrated schools because the racial composition of neighborhoods, schools, and their "quality" vary together, though the mechanisms that lead to this covariation are unclear. Black adolescents in racially segregated neighborhoods may have fewer institutional resources, particularly lower quality schools (Bennett 2011). It could also be that schools in predominantly black neighborhoods have less qualified and less experienced teachers, and this leads to lower test scores for students attending those schools (Bennett 2011; Orfield, Kucsera, and Siegel-Hawley 2012). These schools have high dropout rates and a smaller proportion of their student body attends four-year schools (Guryan 2004; Teranishi et al. 2004). Research suggests that even controlling for various other school and individual characteristics, minority students in predominantly minority segregated schools have less access to information about college than those attending integrated schools do (Hoelter 1982). Students who attend predominantly minority schools, both white and black, appear to have lower educational expectations and test scores, even controlling for social background characteristics, compared with their peers at more integrated schools (Bankston and Caldas 2000; Bennett 2011). Attending a predominantly minority school appears to have negative effects on students' school outcomes, whereas integrated schools positively influence the outcomes of minority students (Mickelson 2005). Attending a school that experienced court-ordered desegregation (versus one that did not) seemed to increase the educational attainment and earnings of adult blacks, and reduced incarceration rates (Johnson 2011) and desegregation appears to have reduced the dropout rates of blacks (Guryan 2004), suggesting that at least de jure segregation is detrimental to black students' outcomes. There are some exceptions, however. First-generation, Hispanic immigrant students tend to benefit from a large presence of Hispanics at their schools

(Klugman, Lee, and Nelson 2012). Other scholars have noted that segregated charter schools are often able to achieve great success with their students (Stulberg 2008).

There appear to be consequences to attending noncharter, predominantly minority public schools and these schools seem to have fewer resources than those with larger proportions of whites generally. What is less clear is whether and to what degree families rely on racial composition as a proxy for school quality, and how this and other characteristics of local, assigned neighborhood schools weigh into their decisions to find a home. Housing choice is the next topic I address.

Housing Choices

Research on the motivations of people who decide to change residences is widespread and multidisciplinary. Much of the literature on residential movement considers the decision-making process of potential movers from an economic standpoint (Phe and Wakely 2000). This market-based approach theorizes that people decide to move based on an analysis of how the move will maximize their housing investment. Households seek to reach a "locational equilibrium" that maximizes the value of their property in relation to other amenities such as distance to the urban center, the provision of public goods, the cost of taxes, and other locationally related expenditures (Alonso 1964; Cho 2001). Although much of this market theory is based strictly on price analyses, some revisions include other measures of community quality in analyses of residential choice (Cho 2001; Phe and Wakely 2000). For example, the physical environment, housing quality, and public expenditures have been associated with residential location (Phe and Wakely 2000).

Community public policies also matter for attracting residents. Public expenditures, particularly service quality and tax rates, have been linked to municipalities' ability to attract residents (Tiebout 1956). Those towns with better services and lower tax rates should attract residents because they offer better value for their consumers (Logan and Schneider 1981). This has led to the notion that by providing high-quality services while controlling the cost of service by restricting increases in taxes, towns can positively influence the in-migration of residents (Margulis 2001). This model has also been used to determine how educational quality affects residential locational choices. Harry Margulis (2001) found that smaller municipalities that could deliver a quality education while maintaining relatively low property tax rates could successfully attract higher income families over the short term, at least until the cost of providing those services begins to rise.

Sociologists and demographers added noneconomic factors to research on who moves and who stays (Landale and Guest 1985). These include life-cycle factors such as age (Lee, Oropesa, and Kanan 1994; South and Deane 1993), marital status (South and Deane 1993), and the presence of children (McHugh, Gober, and Reid 1990), as well as household factors such as the source of a household's income (Kasarda 1988) and the receipt of public housing assistance. Other research incorporated these life-cycle–demographic explanations of residential mobility into research that assesses the role of people's residential satisfaction in their decision to move.

Building on the work of Peter Rossi (1955), who proposed that moves resulted when there was stress between the needs of a household and what its environment could provide, Alden Speare (1974) added residential satisfaction with the current neighborhood as a mediating variable between individual household characteristics, neighborhood characteristics, and the likelihood of a move. Among the survey items used to construct an index of residential satisfaction were housing characteristics (age, size, presence of a yard), satisfaction with the surrounding neighborhood and section of town in which the house is located, and the distance of the home to schools, shopping, and work. Attachment to the community, indicated by the number of relatives the respondent had in the neighborhood and whether the respondent felt a bond with his or her neighbors, was also measured. Speare (1974) found that residential satisfaction was a significant factor in determining whether an individual was motivated to move. He posited that when dissatisfaction reached a threshold of intolerability, the resident was prompted to move.

The residential satisfaction theory of mobility has been revised and extended several times. In their reevaluation, Nancy Landale and Avery Guest (1985) stressed the importance of subjective measures of community bonds. In fact, a strong connection to neighbors was found to be nearly as important as any other measure. Another addition to the Speare model was neighborhood context, which can be conceptualized in different ways. Objective indicators of neighborhood character can be used to describe the context: income, racial mix, density, change in population, and length of tenure of its residents. Another aspect of the neighborhood context is the residents' perceptions of neighborhood conditions. Barrett Lee and his colleagues (1994) added both "objective" measures of neighborhood context and residents' perceptions of the neighborhood to the traditional Speare model. To model perceptions, they used questions about neighborhood problems such as crime and traffic congestion, measures of attachment, thoughts about physical and demographic changes in the neighborhood, and whether the neighborhood was improving.

The common perception among the public is that schools influence the locations to which people move. Realtors prominently place the school districts associated with particular houses on their websites. Economists suggest that a neighborhood high school's SAT scores are desirable because they are positively associated with prices across otherwise comparable homes (Barrow 2002). Families may choose to rent strategically so that their children are able to attend particular schools. These perceptions about the draw of quality schools to potential home-buyers or renters are *pull* factors; those characteristics that draw people to more desirable neighborhoods. Research on *white flight* also suggests that school racial change, and perhaps consequently school quality, is also a *push* factor. People may leave neighborhoods where school quality is perceived to have "gone downhill" (Goyette, Farrie, and Freely 2012), possibly due to racial change in that school. Recently, though, options for attending non-neighborhood schools have increased in the United States. These increased choices could weaken the connection between residences and schools for some families, and perhaps make it stronger for others. The next section focuses on the research on school choice.

School Choices

More research is devoted to the decision to buy or rent a home than on where to go to school. Perhaps this is because, for a large portion of the population and for much of the past fifty years, the school that one attends is connected to the location of his or her home. School "feeder areas" or "catchment zones" show the attendance boundaries for elementary, middle, and high schools within school districts. For those who choose not to attend Catholic, other religious, or other private schools, the public school of their catchment area is often the school they attend. However, particularly in the past two decades, the connection between catchment areas and school attendance has been loosened. Magnet schools, charter schools, intradistrict transfer programs, and other schools of choice have increased the number of options for families who want their children to attend public schools, though perhaps not the ones in their neighborhoods. These choices have led to an awareness that schools are indeed choices, and families are perceived as consumers in much of the literature that explores how families decide where to send their children to school.

A variety of policy efforts and initiatives have expanded the choices that families have for schooling their children. Families, particularly wealthier families, have long had the option to choose private religious or nonreligious schools for their children. These schools may be affiliated with Episcopal, other Protestant, Quaker, or other religious traditions or secular, and may be associated with particular educational philosophies, such as Montessori or Waldorf. Catholic schools, though originally a refuge for Catholics from the Anglo Protestant public schools emerging in the United States in the nineteenth century, now often have a mission to serve less advantaged, non-Catholic students in urban areas. They offer lower tuitions and more subsidies for this population. As a result, Catholic school students make up the largest proportion of private school students (U.S. Department of Education 2012).

Though they had existed for rural students in Maine and Vermont, school voucher programs became popular in the 1990s as a way to increase school choices for families facing unsatisfactory schools. Milwaukee was one of the first districts to use vouchers in this way. Students who are eligible (come from low-performing schools, are low income, have disabilities, are from military families or other criteria, depending on the state) may receive vouchers to pay for a portion of their education at private schools. Schools must meet some standards set by states to accept vouchers.

Magnet schools are public schools that admit students based on academic talent and sometimes other criteria. Magnet schools like Boston Latin have been in existence since the seventeenth century; however, magnet schools proliferated in the 1970s and 1980s as school integration efforts expanded. Magnet schools were considered a way to retain academically talented white students who would otherwise leave integrating urban schools for schools in the suburbs. Magnet schools often specialize in a field or fields, some devoted to the arts and others to sciences. These schools generally consider the test scores of students to determine admittance, though other criteria may also be used (Goldring and Smrekar 2002).

Efforts to integrate schools also encouraged different types of policies that expanded choice for parents. In some districts, parents could opt to send children to other schools within the district, particularly if racial balance had not been achieved in schools within the district. In some places, urban and suburban districts combined (well-studied examples of this are Raleigh and Wake County, Charlotte and Mecklenberg County in North Carolina, and St. Louis City and St. Louis County in Missouri) and students from city schools could opt to transfer to whiter, suburban schools through intradistrict transfer programs. Although there were few such programs to begin with, many—such as those in North Carolina and Missouri—have been dismantled; consequently, schools have become resegregated in these areas. Urban school districts (such as Philadelphia) may offer the choice of transfer to particular neighborhood public schools, given available slots, and other districts (such as Cambridge, Massachusetts) require families to choose particular public schools that specialize in areas (such as science or art) before entering the public school system; however, the districts typically do not include suburban neighborhoods.

A more recent but rapidly expanding sector of school choice is charter schools. Charter schools operate under less supervision from the district school board, especially in manners of salary, hiring, and firing, than more traditional public schools do. Charter schools often propose a school based on some innovation, perhaps teaching style or method, organization, or theme. School district authorities then grant these schools charters to operate, providing funding usually based on the numbers of students they serve. Charter schools do not admit students based on academic talent, but rather typically students are admitted by lottery (though there may be preferences for students based on their neighborhoods or whether or not they have siblings who attend). Starting with two charter schools in Minnesota in 1991, the number of charter schools had grown to three thousand in 2004 and could be found in more than thirty-seven states (U.S. Department of Education 2004).

Government policy, in particular the No Child Left Behind (NCLB) Act of 2001, also increased awareness of school choice. This act, a reauthorization of the Elementary and Secondary Education Act of 1965, stipulated that schools must administer yearly standardized tests. Those schools that do not make adequate yearly progress (AYP), a measure defined by states, are subject to various corrective measures. After two years of not achieving AYP, schools are labeled "in need of improvement" and a plan must be made to correct the situation. Students are offered the option to transfer from the school. After another year of missing AYP, students must be offered tutoring or other educational services to improve student performance. Beyond the third year, more drastic actions must be taken, including school and personnel reorganization or school takeover by the state, charter schools, or other private school management companies. Although the implementation of these provisions has not always been straightforward, and it is often not easy for parents to navigate their new choices, NCLB increased the perception that families should have the right to choose alternative schools if their school is not judged adequate.

Most of the literature on how families make school choices is based on the preferences of parents for their ideal, hypothetical schools. Safety and academic quality are often the most important qualities of these ideal schools (Henig 1995; Lee, Croninger, and Smith 1996; Schneider, Marschall, and Roch 1999). However, few studies have looked extensively at how families choose schools across the wide range of options they may have, including private and religious schools, schools of choice, and desirable public schools associated with homes within particular catchment zones. Some of the difficulty of doing so may be because schools of choice are not evenly distributed throughout the country, and many of them are concentrated in urban areas. The proliferation of schools of choice accelerated in the 1990s, and the phenomenon is still relatively new in education research. Finally, although federal agencies like the National Center for Education Statistics and the Census Bureau routinely collect information on schools and school districts, little is known about the catchment zones schools lie within. Thus, it is difficult to know the characteristics of neighborhoods associated with particular schools. Fortunately for researchers of school choice, the effort to collect information about these catchment zones has been extensive and more data about them are forthcoming.

A few studies have explored how students choose non-Catholic private schools. They find that white, wealthier, more highly educated families in which parents themselves have gone to private schools, and those concerned with maintaining or increasing their social status are more likely to choose private schools (Ball 1997; Betts and Fairlie 2001; Persell and Cookson 1985). Tuition costs of the schools seem to matter little in these decisions (Buddin, Cordes, and Kirby 1998).

Other research that has been done on how families choose their children's schooling has focused on whether families consider schools of choice options. One way that parents' decision-making has been explored in the literature is by asking parents whether they believe they have choices. Ruth Neild (2005) finds that most of the parents of Philadelphia school students she interviewed were aware that they had some choice in the schooling of their children, but they were unaware of the constraints on these choices, such as the lack of openings in the most desirable schools.

Researchers have also asked parents about the options they considered for their children's schooling. Jack Buckley and Mark Schneider (2003) contend that some parents act as "marginal consumers" when considering several options. They gather information about potential schools to make informed decisions, but this research varies by the social and economic characteristics of the families. In other research, Mark Schneider and colleagues (1997) contend that high income parents are less likely than those families with lower incomes to use relatives to find out about schools. Middle-class parents rely more heavily on their social networks for information about schools and therefore consult fewer other sources of information than working-class parents do (Schneider 2001). Schneider and colleagues (1997) also find that blacks and other minorities have smaller networks than whites do. Other researchers note that organizations within neighborhoods, such as day-care centers and preschools, are important sources of information for parents because they provide such information, but also because they serve as sites of networking for parents (Small 2009).

Families' decision making about schools may differ according to their views on public education and by social background. For example, some working-class families may believe that a good public education is provided by the state and that student effort matters most in students' outcomes (Fuller, Elmore, and Orfield 1996; Reay and Ball 1998; Wells and Crain 1997). Amy Stuart Wells and Robert Crain (1997) find that many of the black families in their study in St. Louis do not transfer out of city schools with fewer resources to suburban schools with more resources because they believe the city schools provide their children with a satisfactory learning environment. On the other hand, middle- and upper-class families may explicitly decide to match the values and attributes of the family (perhaps race, status, or religion) and those of the child (artistically talented, scientifically inclined, and so on) to the best-fitting school (Ball 2003; Bowe, Ball, and Gewirtz 1994; Holme 2002).

Some parents feel committed to public schools, and urban public schools, in particular. Gentrification of city neighborhoods has brought many upper- and middle-class whites back to city neighborhoods, and some portion of these parents choose to send their children to their neighborhood schools. This process is fraught with difficulty, though, as Jennifer Stillman (2012) points out. Newly resident, mostly white middle-class parents face discomfort in predominantly minority schools. Styles of communication, the types of education valued (traditional versus more progressive), and perceptions of safety differ by race and class. Middle- and upper-class white parents demand resources from principals, administration, and teaching staff, which often come at the expense of attention to minority, less privileged students. Resentment between groups develops and whites, once again, leave these schools (Cucchiara 2013; Stillman 2012).

Upper- and middle-class parents may feel qualified to make complex educational choices for their children, whereas working-class families may leave much of this decision-making to their children (Lareau 1989; Reay and Ball 1998; Wells and Crain 1997). Children in the families in Amy Stuart Wells and Robert Crain's study who chose not to transfer to suburban schools desired the comfort and familiarity of their neighborhood schools. Families' school decisions are also likely influenced by the traits they consider desirable in schools and the constraints they face in their children's attendance at particular schools, which may be shaped by their social backgrounds as well. Lower-income and minority parents in Cincinnati and St. Louis are more concerned about transportation when choosing schools for their children than middle-class, white parents are, for example (Smrekar and Goldring 1999). Claire Smrekar and Ellen Goldring (1999) also find that in St. Louis 74 percent of parents with incomes over $50,000 reported academic reputation as their main reason for choosing a magnet school compared with 26 percent of lower-income parents (33).

Most research on school choice explores whether families decide to send children to schools outside their assigned neighborhood public schools. Few consider that parents choose schools by choosing their homes in particular school districts or catchment zones. One study that does so, though, is by Jennifer Jellison Holme (2002). She shows how high-status families seek homes associated with particular schools. Parents rely on high-status neighbors and social networks to find schools that match their class and racial ideologies, equating race and class with the culture and values of the schools. These parents seek to maximize the academic and social advantages schools are able to provide. Even though the school they chose was a neighborhood, public school, these parents gathered information about a variety of public schools before locating to their neighborhood, and chose that neighborhood because of its public school.

Families may also choose to opt out of formal, institutional schooling altogether by homeschooling. Only about 2.2 percent of school-age children were home-schooled in 2003 (Princiotta and Bielick 2006), but this option is often chosen by those who dislike or do not trust educational institutions for religious or other reasons, and by those who feel that these institutions cannot well serve the needs of their child or children (Stevens 2001).

School choice innovations largely occur in urban areas, so the majority of the research on school choice has been conducted in and around large cities or counties like Milwaukee, Detroit, Montgomery County in Maryland, New York, San Antonio, St. Louis, and Cincinnati (for example, Henig 1995; Lee, Croninger, and Smith 1996; Martinez, Godwin, and Kemerer 1996; Smrekar and Goldring 1999; Wells and Crain 1997; Witt and Thorn 1996). However, charter schools and other school choice programs are expanding into suburban and even rural areas (Kane and Lauricella 2001). Increasing school choices lead to the increasing perception that school is less of a public good and more of a private choice, but how that influences the link between schooling and residential decisions is unclear. As people more and more perceive school to be a family's choice, they may become more aware of how housing plays a role in this decision and choose homes to also choose particular schools. Residential segregation could increase as middle- and upper-middle-class white families cluster together around schools that they believe are of high quality. Or, as options for non-neighborhood public and private schools proliferate, families may feel more free to enact their ideal residential preferences without concern for schooling quality. This may decrease racial residential segregation and, though perhaps to a lesser extent, school segregation. Families who want to live in cities but are concerned about the quality of public schools may move to cities if they have their choice of neighborhood or charter schools across a city. Finally, it is possible that both could be occurring: Families with resources may be better able to take advantage of non-neighborhood public schools, particularly in gentrifying urban areas, and also more likely to use homes as a means of securing their ideal schools. We look at the intersections of these decisions, and the constraints upon them, in this volume.

References

Adelman, Robert M., Hui-shien Tsao, Stewart E. Tolnay, and Kyle D. Crowder. 2001. "Neighborhood Disadvantage Among Racial and Ethnic Groups: Residential Location in 1970 and 1980." *Sociological Quarterly* 42(4): 603–32.

Alonso, W. 1964. *Location and Land Use*. Cambridge, Mass.: Harvard University Press.

Ball, Stephen J. 1997. "On the Cusp: Parents Choosing Between State and Private Schools in the UK: Action Within an Economy of Symbolic Goods." *International Journal of Inclusive Education* 1(1): 1–17.

———. 2003. *Class Strategies and the Education Market: The Middle Classes and Social Advantage*. London: Routledge Farmer.

Bankston, Carl L., III, and Stephen J. Caldas. 2000. "White Enrollment in Nonpublic Schools, Public School Racial Composition, and Student Performance." *Sociological Quarterly* 41(4): 539–50.

Barrow, Lisa. 2002. "School Choice Through Relocation: Evidence from the Washington, D.C. Area." *Journal of Public Economics* 86(2): 155–89.

Bennett, Pamela R. 2011. "The Relationship Between Neighborhood Composition and Verbal Ability: An Investigation Using the Institutional Resources Model." *Social Science Research* 40(4): 1124–141.

Betts, Julian R., and Robert W. Fairlie. 2001. "Explaining Ethnic, Racial, and Immigrant Differences in Private School Attendance." *Journal of Urban Economics* 50(1): 26–51.

Bischoff, Kendra. 2008. "School District Fragmentation and Racial Residential Segregation: How Do Boundaries Matter?" *Urban Affairs Review* 44(2): 182–217.

Bobo, Lawrence, and Camille Zubrinsky. 1996. "Attitudes Toward Residential Integration: Perceived Status Differences, Mere In-Group Preference, or Racial Prejudice?" *Social Forces* 74(3): 883–909.

Bowe, Richard, Stephen Ball, and Sharon Gewirtz. 1994. " 'Parental Choice', Consumption, and Social Theory: The Operation of Micromarkets in Education." *British Journal of Educational Studies* 42(1): 38–52.

Buckley, Jack, and Mark Schneider. 2003. "Shopping for Schools: How Do Marginal Consumers Gather Information About Schools?" *The Policy Studies Journal* 3(2): 121–45.

Buddin, Richard J., Joseph J. Cordes, and Sheila Nataraj Kirby. 1998. "School Choice in California: Who Chooses Private Schools?" *Journal of Urban Economics* 44(1): 110–34.

Charles, Camille Zubrinsky. 2000. "Neighborhood Racial-Composition Preferences: Evidence from a Multiethnic Metropolis." *Social Problems* 47(3): 370–407.

———. 2003. "The Dynamics of Racial Residential Segregation." *Annual Review of Sociology* 29(1): 167–207.

———. 2005. "Can We Live Together?" In *The Geography of Opportunity*, edited by Xavier de Souza Briggs. Washington, D.C.: Brookings Institution.

Chiricos, Ted, Ranee McEntire, and Marc Gerts. 2001. "Perceived Racial and Ethnic Composition of Neighborhood and Perceived Risk of Crime." *Social Problems* 48(3): 322–40.

Cho, Cheol-Joo. 2001. "Amenities and Urban Residential Structure: An Amenity-Embedded Model of Residential Choice." *Papers in Regional Science* 80(4): 483–99.

Clark, William A. V. 1986. "Residential Segregation in American Cities: A Review and Interpretation." *Population Research and Policy Review* 5(2): 95–127.

———. 1987. "School Desegregation and White Flight: A Reexamination and Case Study." *Social Science Research* 16(3): 211–28.

———. 1991. "Residential Preferences and Neighborhood Residential Segregation: A Test of the Schelling Segregation Model." *Demography* 28(1): 1–19.

———. 1992. "Residential Preferences and Residential Choices in a Multiethnic Context." *Demography* 29(3): 451–66.

———. 2007. "Race, Class, and Place." *Urban Affairs Review* 42(3): 295–314.

Clotfelter, Charles T. 1976. "The Detroit Decision and 'White Flight.' " *Journal of Legal Studies* 5(1): 99–112.

———. 2001. "Are Whites Still Fleeing? Racial Patterns and Enrollment Shifts in Urban Public Schools, 1987–1996." *Journal of Policy Analysis and Management* 20(2): 199–221.

Coleman, James, Sara Kelly, and John Moore. 1975. "Trends in School Segregation." Working paper no. 722-03-01. Washington, D.C.: Urban Institute.

Crowder, Kyle. 2000. "The Racial Context of White Mobility: An Individual-Level Assessment of the White Flight Hypothesis." *Social Science Research* 29(2): 223–57.

Cucchiara, Maia B. 2013. *Marketing Schools, Marketing Cities: Who Wins and Who Loses When Schools Become Urban Amenities?* Chicago: University of Chicago Press.

Ellen, Ingrid Gould. 2007. "How Integrated Did We Become During the 1990s?" In *Fragile Rights Within Cities: Government, Housing, and Fairness,* edited by John Goering. Lanham, Md.: Rowman and Littlefield.

Emerson, Michael O., George Yancey, and Karen J. Chai. 2001. "Does Race Matter in Residential Segregation? Exploring the Preferences of White Americans." *American Sociological Review* 66(6): 922–35.

Fairlie, Robert W. 2002. "Private Schools and 'Latino Flight' from Black School Children." *Demography* 39(4): 655–74.

Fairlie, Robert, and Alexander Resch. 2002. "Is There 'White Flight' into Private Schools? Evidence from the National Educational Longitudinal Study." *Review of Economics and Statistics* 84(1): 21–33.

Farley, Reynolds, Toni Richards, and Clarence Wurdock. 1980. "School Desegregation and White Flight: An Investigation of Competing Models and their Discrepant Findings." *Sociology of Education* 53(3): 123–39.

Farley, Reynolds, Charlotte Steeh, Tara Jackson, Maria Krysan, and Keith Reeves. 1994. "Stereotypes and Segregation: Neighborhoods in the Detroit Area." *American Journal of Sociology* 100(3): 750–80.

Fischer, Claude S., Gretchen Stockmayer, Jon Stiles, and Michael Hout. 2004. "Geographic Levels and Social Dimensions of Metropolitan Segregation." *Demography* 41(1): 37–60.

Frey, William. 1979. "Central City White Flight: Racial and Nonracial Causes" *American Sociological Review* 44(3): 425–48.

Fuller, Bruce, Richard F. Elmore, and Gary Orfield. 1996. "Policy-Making in the Dark: Illuminating the School Choice Debate." In *Who Chooses? Who Loses? Culture, Institutions, and the Unequal Effects of School Choice,* edited by Bruce Fuller and Richard F. Elmore. New York: Teachers College Press.

Galster, George. 1989. "Residential Segregation in American Cities: A Further Response to Clark." *Population Research and Policy Review* 8(2): 181–92.

Giles, Michael W. 1978. "White Enrollment Stability and School Desegregation: A Two-Level Analysis." *American Sociological Review* 43(6): 848–64.

Giles, Michael W., Everett F. Cataldo, and Douglas S. Gatlin. 1975. "White Flight and Percent Black: The Tipping Point Re-examined." *Social Science Quarterly* 56(1): 85–92.

Goering, John, and Ron Wienk. 1996. *Mortgage Lending, Racial Discrimination, and Federal Policy*. Washington, D.C.: Urban Institute Press.

Goldring, Ellen, and Claire Smrekar. 2002. "Magnet Schools: Reform and Race in Urban Education." *The Clearing House* 76(1): 13–15.

Goyette, Kimberly, Danielle Farrie, and Joshua Freely. 2012. "This School's Gone Downhill: Racial Change and Perceived School Quality Among Whites." *Social Problems* 59(2): 155–76.

Guryan, Jonathan. 2004. "Desegregation and Black Dropout Rates." *American Economic Review* 94(4): 919–43.

Harris, David. 1999. "'Properties Values Drop When Blacks Move in Because . . .' Racial and Socioeconomic Determinants of Neighborhood Desirability." *American Sociological Review* 64(3): 461–79.

———. 2001. "Why Are Whites and Blacks Averse to Black Neighbors?" *Social Science Research* 30(1): 100–17.

Harrison, Roderick J., and Claudette Bennett. 1995. "Racial and Ethnic Diversity." In *State of the Union: America in the 1990s*, vol. 2, edited by Reynolds Farley. New York: Russell Sage Foundation.

Henig, Jeffrey R. 1995. "Race and Choice in Montgomery County, Maryland, Magnet Schools." *Teachers College Record* 96(4): 729–35.

Hess, Frederick, and David Leal. 2001. "Quality, Race, and the Urban Education Marketplace." *Urban Affairs Review* 37(2): 249–66.

Hoelter, Jon W. 1982. "Segregation and Rationality in Black Status Aspiration Processes." *Sociology of Education* 55(1): 31–39.

Holme, Jennifer J. 2002. "Buying Homes, Buying Schools: School Choice and the Social Construction of School Quality." *Harvard Educational Review* 72(2): 177–205.

Iceland, John, Kimberly Goyette, Kyle Anne Nelson, and Chaowen Chan. 2010. "Racial and Ethnic Residential Segregation and Household Structure: A Research Note." *Social Science Research* 39(1): 39–47.

Iceland, John, Cicely Sharpe, and Erika Steinmetz. 2005. "Class Differences in African American Residential Patterns in U.S. Metropolitan Areas: 1990–2000." *Social Science Research* 34(1): 252–66.

Iceland, John, Daniel H. Weinberg, and Erika Steinmetz. 2002. *Racial and Ethnic Residential Segregation in the United States: 1980–2000*. U.S. Census Bureau special report no. CENSR-3. Washington: Government Printing Office.

Johnson, Rucker C. 2011. "Long-Run Impacts of School Desegregation & School Quality on Adult Attainments." *NBER* working paper 16664. Cambridge, Mass.: National Bureau of Economic Research.

Kane, Pearl Rock, and Christopher J. Lauricella. 2001. "Assessing the Growth and Potential of Charter Schools." In *Privatizing Education: Can the Marketplace Deliver Social Choice, Efficiency, Equity, and Social Cohesion?* edited by Henry M. Levin. Boulder, Colo.: Westview Press.

Kasarda, John D. 1988. "A Tale of Dual Cities." *New Perspectives Quarterly* 5(3): 19–22.

Klugman, Joshua, Jennifer C. Lee, and Shelley L. Nelson. 2012. "The Role of Co-ethnic Communities in Hispanic Parent Involvement in Schooling." *Social Science Research* 41(5): 1320–337.

Kruse, Kevin Michael. 2005. *White Flight: Atlanta and the Making of Modern Conservatism.* Princeton, N.J.: Princeton University Press.

Krysan, Maria. 2002a. "Whites Who Say They'd Flee: Who Are They and Why Would They Leave?" *Demography* 39(4): 675–96.

———. 2002b. "Community Undesirability in Black and White: Examining Racial Residential Preferences Through Community Perceptions." *Social Problems* 49(4): 521–43.

Krysan, Maria, and Reynolds Farley. 2002. "The Residential Preferences of Blacks: Do They Explain Persistent Segregation?" *Social Forces* 80(3): 937–80.

Landale, Nancy S., and Avery Guest. 1985. "Constraints, Satisfaction, and Residential Mobility: Speare's Model Reconsidered." *Demography* 22(2): 199–222.

Langford, Hamilton, and James Wyckoff. 2006. "The Effect of School Choice and Residential Location on the Racial Segregation of Students." In *Advances in Applied Microeconomics,* vol. 14, *Improving School Accountability: Check-Ups or Choice,* edited by Timothy J. Gronberg and Dennis W. Jansen. Amsterdam: Elsevier.

Lareau, Annette. 1989. *Home Advantage: Social Class and Parental Intervention in Elementary Education.* Lanham, Md.: Rowman and Littlefield.

———. 2011. *Unequal Childhoods: Class, Race, and Family Life.* Berkeley: University of California Press.

Lassiter, Matthew D. 2006. *The Silent Majority: Suburban Politics in the Sunbelt South.* Princeton, N.J.: Princeton University Press.

Lee, Barrett A., R. Salvador Oropesa, and James W. Kanan. 1994. "Neighborhood Context and Residential Mobility." *Demography* 31(3): 249–70.

Lee, Ellie, Jan Macvarish, and Jennie Bristow. 2010. "Editorial: Risk, Health, and Parenting Culture." *Health, Risk and Society* 12(4): 293–300.

Lee, Valerie, Robert Croninger, and Julia Smith. 1996. "Equity and Choice in Detroit." In *Who Chooses, Who Loses: Culture, Institutions, and the Unequal Effects of School Choice,* edited by Bruce Fuller and Richard Elmore. New York: Teachers College Press.

Logan, John R. 2004. "Resegregation in American Public Schools? Not in the 1990s." Albany: Lewis Mumford Center, State University of New York.

Logan, John R., Deirdre Oakley, Polly Smith, Jacob Stowell, and Brian Stults. 2001. "Separating the Children." Albany: Lewis Mumford Center, State University of New York.

Logan, John R., and Mark Schneider. 1981. "Suburban Municipal Expenditures: The Effect of Business Activity, Functional Responsibility, and Regional Context." *Policy Studies Journal* 9(7): 1039–51.

Logan, John R., and Brian J. Stults. 2011. "The Persistence of Segregation in the Metropolis: New Findings from the 2010 Census." Census Brief prepared for Project US2010. Available at http://www.s4.brown.edu/us2010/Data/Report/report2.pdf (retrieved August 2, 2011).

Margulis, Harry L. 2001. "Household Mobility, Housing Traits, Public Goods, and School Quality in Cleveland's Metropolitan Statistical Area." *Urban Affairs Review* 36(5): 646–78.

Martinez, Valerie R., Kenneth R. Godwin, and Frank R. Kemerer. 1996. "Public School Choice in San Antonio: Who Chooses and with What Effects?" In *Who Chooses, Who Loses? Culture, Institutions, and the Unequal Effects of School Choice,* edited by Bruce Fuller, Richard F. Elmore, and Gary Orfield. New York: Teachers' College Press.

Massey, Douglas S., Gretchen A. Condran, and Nancy A. Denton. 1987. "The Effect of Residential Segregation on Black Social and Economic Well-Being." *Social Forces* 66(1): 29–56.

McHugh, Kevin E., Patricia Gober, and Neil Reid. 1990. "Determinants of Short- and Long-Term Mobility Expectations for Home Owners and Renters." *Demography* 27(1): 81–95.

Mickelson, Roslyn Arlin. 2005. "The Incomplete Desegregation of Charlotte-Mecklenburg Schools and Its Consequences." In *School Resegregation: Must the South Turn Back?* edited by John Charles Boger and Gary Orfield. Chapel Hill: University of North Carolina Press.

Neild, Ruth Curran. 2005. "Parental Management of School Choice in a Large Urban District." *Urban Education* 40(3): 270–97.

Orfield, Gary, John Kucsera, and Genevieve Siegel-Hawley. 2012. "E Pluribus . . . Separation: Deepening Double Segregation for More Students." Los Angeles: The Civil Rights Project, University of California.

Orfield, Gary, and Chungmei Lee. 2006. "Racial Transformation and the Changing Nature of Segregation." Cambridge, Mass.: The Civil Rights Project, Harvard University.

Orfield, Gary, and John T. Yun. 1999. "Resegregation in American Schools." Cambridge, Mass.: The Civil Rights Project, Harvard University.

Patterson, James T. 2001. *Brown v. Board of Education: A Civil Rights Milestone and Its Troubled Legacy.* Oxford: Oxford University Press.

Persell, Caroline, and Peter Cookson. 1985. *Preparing for Power: America's Elite Boarding Schools.* New York: Basic Books.

Phe, Hoang Huu, and Patrick Wakely. 2000. "Status, Quality, and the Other Trade-offs: Toward a New Theory of Urban Residential Location." *Urban Studies* 37(1): 7–36.

Princiotta, Daniel, and Stacey Bielick. 2006. "Homeschooling in the United States, 2003." *NCES* report no. 2006–042. Washington: U.S. Department of Education, National Center for Education Statistics.

Quillian, Lincoln. 2002. "Why Is Black-White Residential Segregation So Persistent? Evidence on Three Theories from Migration Data." *Social Science Research* 31(2): 197–229.

Quillian, Lincoln, and Devah Pager. 2001. "Black Neighbors, Higher Crime? The Role of Racial Stereotypes in Evaluations of Neighborhood Crime." *American Journal of Sociology* 107(3): 717–67.

Reardon, Sean F., and Kendra Bischoff. 2011. "Income Inequality and Income Segregation." *American Journal of Sociology* 116(4): 1092–153.

Reardon, Sean F., and John T. Yun. 2001. "Suburban Racial Change and Suburban School Segregation: 1987–1995." *Sociology of Education* 74(2): 79–101.

———. 2002. "Segregation in Church and State? Vouchers and Racial Enrollment Patterns Among Public and Private Schools." *Teachers College Record* (July 15, 2002).

Reay, Diane, and Stephen J. Ball. 1998. "'Making Their Minds Up': Family Dynamics of School Choice." *British Educational Research Journal* 24(4): 431–48.

Renzulli, Linda, and Lorraine Evans. 2005. "School Choice, Charter Schools, and White Flight." *Social Problems* 52(3): 398–418.

Rickles, Jordan, Paul M. Ong, Shannon McConville, and Doug Houston. 2001. "The Relationship Between School and Residential Segregation at the Turn of the Century." Los Angeles: The Ralph and Goldy Lewis Center for Regional Policy Issues, University of California.

Ross, Stephen L., and Margery Austin Turner. 2005. "Housing Discrimination in Metropolitan America: Explaining Changes Between 1989 and 2000." *Social Problems* 52(2): 152–80.

Rossi, Peter H. 1955. *Why Families Move.* New York: Free Press.

Sampson, Robert J., and Patrick Sharkey. 2008. "Neighborhood Selection and the Social Reproduction of Concentrated Racial Inequality." *Demography* 45(1): 1–29.

Saporito, Salvatore. 2003. "Private Choices, Public Consequences: Magnet School Choice and Segregation by Race and Poverty." *Social Problems* 50(2): 181–203.

Saporito, Salvatore, and Annette Lareau. 1999. "School Selection as a Process: The Multiple Dimensions of Race in Framing Educational Choice." *Social Problems* 46(3): 418–39.

Saporito, Salvatore, and Deenesh Sohoni. 2006. "Mapping Educational Inequality: Concentrations of Poverty Among Poor and Minority Students in Public Schools." *Sociology of Education* 79(2): 81–105.

Schneider, Mark. 2001. "Information and Choice in Educational Privatization." In *Privatizing Education: Can the Marketplace Deliver Choice, Efficiency, Equity, and Social Cohesion?* edited by Henry M. Levin. Cambridge, Mass.: Westview.

Schneider, Mark, Melissa A. Marschall, and Christine Roch. 1999. "Heuristics, Low Information Rationality, and Choosing Public Goods: Broken Windows as Shortcuts to Information About School Performance." *Urban Affairs Review* 34(5): 729–41.

Schneider, Mark, Paul Teske, Christine Roch, and Melissa Marschall. 1997. "Networks to Nowhere: Segregation and Stratification in Networks of Information About Schools." *American Journal of Political Science* 41(4): 1201–223.

Small, Mario Luis. 2009. *Unanticipated Gains: Origins of Network Inequality in Everyday Life.* Oxford: Oxford University Press.

Smock, Pamela J., and Franklin D. Wilson. 1991. "Desegregation and the Stability of White Enrollments: A School-Level Analysis, 1968–84." *Sociology of Education* 64(4): 278–92.

Smrekar, Claire, and Ellen Goldring. 1999. *School Choice in Urban America: Magnet Schools and the Pursuit of Equity.* New York: Teachers College Press.

South, Scott J., and Glenn D. Deane. 1993. "Race and Residential Mobility: Individual Determinants and Structural Constraints." *Social Forces* 72(1): 147–67.

Speare, Alden, Jr. 1974. "Residential Satisfaction as an Intervening Variable in Residential Mobility." *Demography* 11(2): 173–88.

Squires, Gregory D., and Charis E. Kurbin. 2006. *Privileged Places: Race, Residence, and the Structure of Opportunity.* Boulder, Colo.: Lynne Rienner.

Stevens, Mitchell L. 2001. *Kingdom of Children: Culture and Controversy in the Homeschooling Movement.* Princeton, N.J.: Princeton University Press.

Stillman, Jennifer Burns. 2012. *Gentrification and Schools: The Process of Integration When White Reverses Flight.* New York: Palgrave Macmillan.

Stroub, Kori J., and Meredith P. Richards. 2013. "From Resegregation to Reintegration: Trends in the Racial/Ethnic Segregation of Metropolitan Schools, 1993–2009." *American Educational Research Journal* 50(3): 497–531.

Stulberg, Lisa M. 2008. *Race, Schools, and Hope: African Americans and School Choice After Brown.* New York: Teachers College Press.

Sugrue, Thomas J. 2008. *Sweet Land of Liberty: The Forgotten Struggle for Civil Rights in the North.* New York: Random House.

Swaroop, Sapna, and Maria Krysan. 2011. "The Determinants of Neighborhood Satisfaction: Racial Proxy Revisited." *Demography* 48(3): 1203–229.

Taub, Richard P., D. Garth Taylor, and Jan D. Dunham. 1984. *Paths of Neighborhood Change: Race and Crime in Urban America.* Chicago: University of Chicago Press.

Teranishi, Robert, Walter R. Allen, Daniel G. Solorzano, and Renee Smith Maddox. 2004. *Separate but Certainly Not Equal: 2003 Capaa Findings.* Vol. 1, no. 2. Los Angeles: Ralph Bunche Center for African American Studies, University of California.

Tiebout, Charles M. 1956. "A Pure Theory of Local Expenditure." *Journal of Political Economy* 64(October): 416–24.

Turner, Margery A., and Stephen L. Ross. 2003. *Discrimination in Metropolitan Housing Markets: Phase 2—Asians and Pacific Islanders of the HDS 2000.* Washington: U.S. Department of Housing and Urban Development.

Turner, Margery A., Stephen L. Ross, George Galster, and John Yinger. 2002. *Discrimination in Metropolitan Housing Markets: National Results from Phase 1 of the Housing Discrimination Study (HDS).* Washington: U.S. Department of Housing and Urban Development.

U.S. Department of Education. 2004. *Evaluation of the Public Charter Schools Program: Final Report.* Washington: Office of the Under Secretary.

———. 2012. *The Condition of Education 2012.* Washington, D.C.: National Center for Education Statistics.

Wells, Amy Stuart, and Robert L. Crain. 1997. *Stepping over the Color Line: African-American Students in White Suburban Schools.* New Haven, Conn.: Yale University Press.

White, Michael J. 1987. *American Neighborhoods and Residential Differentiation.* New York: Russell Sage Foundation.

Witte, John F., and Christopher A. Thorn. 1996. "Who Chooses? Voucher and Interdistrict Choice Programs in Milwaukee." *American Journal of Education* 104(3): 186–217.

Wolf, Eleanor. 1963. "The Tipping-Point in Racially Changing Neighborhoods." *Journal of the American Institute of Planners* 29(3): 217–22.

Wrinkle, Robert D., Joseph Stewart Jr., and J. L. Polinard. 1999. "Public School Quality, Private Schools, and Race." *American Journal of Political Science* 43(4): 1248–253.

Yinger, John. 1995. *Closed Doors, Opportunities Lost: The Continuing Costs of Housing Discrimination.* New York: Russell Sage Foundation.

= Part I =

Residential Segregation Today

═ Chapter 2 ═

Pathways to
Residential Segregation

Maria Krysan, Kyle Crowder,
and Michael D. M. Bader

In a recent report for the Manhattan Institute, the economists Edward Glaeser and Jacob Vigdor (2012) offered the argument that dramatic shifts in public attitudes, changes in housing policies, and improved access to credit have ushered in a new era of residential integration, putting an end to the hyper-segregation that has characterized America's cities for more than a century. In making this case they point out that all-white neighborhoods are virtually extinct and most isolated black neighborhoods are fading away. To be sure, Glaeser and Vigdor are not alone in their optimism; other leading scholars have interpreted recent declines in aggregate patterns of segregation as a sign of emerging residential equality unlike that seen in modern America (see, for example, Farley 2011; Iceland 2009; Timberlake and Iceland 2007).

At the same time, many other authors interpret similar evidence with considerably more skepticism (for example, Crowder, Pais, and South 2012; Krysan 2011). Certainly, racially disparate residential mobility patterns and the slow pace of segregation declines, especially in areas where racial and ethnic minority populations are most concentrated, may be interpreted as a sign that residential stratification remains, and is likely to remain, a defining feature of our metropolitan areas. This residential inequality carries with it serious individual-level and collective consequences; high levels of racial-residential segregation have been linked to, among other outcomes, racial disparities in economic opportunities (Massey et al. 1991; Turner 2008; vonLockette 2010), wealth accumulation (Lipsitz and Oliver 2010), a range of individual health outcomes (Diez Roux and Mair 2010; Kramer and Hogue 2009; Kramer et al. 2012; Russell et al. 2012), and exposure to crime (Krivo, Peterson, and

Kuhl 2009) and environmental hazards (Crowder and Downey 2010). Perhaps most troubling is that with an increasing number of school districts abandoning busing and other remedies emerging from the Brown v. Board desegregation order, the persistence of residential segregation has profound implications for school segregation, interracial contact among students, and disparities in educational outcomes (Logan et al. 2008; Reardon et al. 2012).

In this chapter we provide an overview of current levels and recent trends in patterns of residential segregation by race, and then review the dominant theoretical arguments used to explain persistent residential segregation by race and some of the key evidence related to these perspectives. We focus not just on the relative support for these theoretical arguments but also on the ways that mechanisms implicated in these competing theoretical frameworks complement each other, interacting to shape racially disparate residential outcomes. We also delve into some of the forces ignored by the Big Three theoretical arguments, including information networks, residential opportunity structures, and intergenerational dynamics. Scattered research from a number of subdisciplines suggests that these forces play underappreciated roles in perpetuating segregation in the face of the apparent softening of racial attitudes, shifting racial disparities in socioeconomic conditions, and rapidly diversifying populations. The review points to new lines of research that must be explored if we are to understand the endurance of segregation across neighborhoods and schools.

Patterns and Consequences of Residential Segregation

According to all accounts, residential segregation has declined markedly in recent decades. For example, across metropolitan areas the average score on the index of dissimilarity—our most common measure of residential evenness—for blacks and whites dropped from 79 in 1970 to 59 in 2010 (Logan and Stults 2011). Thus, according to the metric offered by Massey and Denton (1993), average black-white segregation across metropolitan areas has dropped from a very high level to the top of the moderate level. The segregation of other groups from whites is even lower; while there are substantial variations across subgroups, the average Latino-white dissimilarity score across metropolitan areas is 48.5 and the average Asian-white score is 40.9. Average residential dissimilarity scores comparing most pairs of nonwhite groups are even lower (Iceland 2009; Logan and Stults 2011).

Yet, despite these signs of progress, it is difficult—though apparently not impossible—to deny that racial-residential stratification remains a defining feature of U.S. metropolitan areas. Since 1970, average levels of segregation of both Latinos and Asians from whites have actually increased. And, despite recent declines in many areas, the average black-white dissimilarity level remains near the high range (Iceland 2009) and, more importantly, remains most pronounced and most rigid in metropolitan areas containing the largest black populations (Logan and Stults 2011; Logan, Stults, and Farley 2004). Moreover, though the black-white index of dissimilarity dropped by 25 percent between 1970 and 2010, the residential contact of blacks to whites grew by just over 9 percent, with the average black-white exposure index across metropolitan areas increasing from 32 in 1970 to 35 in 2010 (Logan and Stults 2011). This pattern reflects the fact that the decreasing isolation of whites and blacks has come largely as a function of increasing contact with fast-growing Asian and Latino populations rather than with increasing exposure to each other. At the same time, the level of residential isolation has increased among these growing Asian and Latino populations. By 2010, the average Latino individual lived in a census tract in which 46 percent of the residents were also Latino. This figure stood at 38.2 percent in 1980. During this time the average tract percentage Asian for Asian individuals increased from 17.4 to 22.4 (Logan and Stults 2011).

The persistence of residential separation by race is also reflected in the durability of neighborhood composition over time (see, for example, Sampson 2012). Table 2.1 provides a neighborhood transition matrix showing changes in the composition of the country's census tracts between 1990 and 2010. To maintain comparability, we define neighborhoods using 2000 census tract boundaries and use normalized 1990 and 2010 census data distributed by GeoLytics (2008, 2012). We categorize neighborhood racial composition in 1990 and 2010 using the neighborhood classification typology developed by David Fasenfest, Jason Booza, and Kurt Metzger (2004) in their study of neighborhood diversification (for alternative but generally similar typologies, see Friedman 2008; Denton and Massey 1991; Galster 1998). This classification scheme differentiates between seven types of neighborhoods: Predominantly white neighborhoods are tracts that are at least 80 percent non-Hispanic white and in which no other racial-ethnic minority group represents more than 10 percent of the population. Predominantly black neighborhoods are those that are at least 50 percent non-Hispanic black and in which no other racial-ethnic minority group represents more than 10 percent of the population. Predominantly other race (hereafter *predominantly other*) neighborhoods are at least 50 percent Hispanic or non-Hispanic Asian and no more than 10 percent non-Hispanic black. Mixed white and other race (hereafter *white-other race*) neighborhoods are between 10 percent and 50 percent Hispanic or Asian and less than 10 percent black. Mixed white and black (hereafter *white-black*) neighborhoods are between 10 and 50 percent black, at least 40 percent white, and less than 10 percent

Table 2.1   Changes in Racial Composition of U.S. Metropolitan Census Tracts, 1990 to 2010

Neighborhood Composition, 2010	Neighborhood Composition, 1990							
	Predominantly White	Predominantly Black	Predominantly Other	White-Other	White-Black	Black-Other	Multiethnic	Total
Predominantly white	11,846	3	2	31	228	1	7	12,118
	48.17%	0.07%	0.07%	0.32%	4.59%	0.04%	0.29%	23.76%
Predominantly black	102	2,773	1	1	539	28	11	3,455
	0.41%	68.44%	0.04%	0.01%	10.86%	1.14%	0.46%	6.78%
Predominantly other	76	1	2,642	2,621	5	271	153	5,769
	0.31%	0.02%	92.80%	27.05%	0.10%	10.99%	6.40%	11.31%
White-other	9,001	2	86	5,698	227	29	273	15,316
	36.60%	0.05%	3.02%	58.82%	4.57%	1.18%	11.42%	30.03%
White-black	1,094	126	0	6	1,386	1	13	2,626
	4.45%	3.11%	0.00%	0.06%	27.93%	0.04%	0.54%	5.15%
Black-other	239	1,037	109	694	808	2,034	1,217	6,138
	0.97%	25.59%	3.83%	7.16%	16.28%	82.48%	50.92%	12.04%
Multiethnic	2,233	110	7	637	1,769	102	716	5,574
	9.08%	2.71%	0.25%	6.58%	35.65%	4.14%	29.96%	10.93%
Total	24,591	4,052	2,847	9,688	4,962	2,466	2,390	50,996
	100%	100%	100%	100%	100%	100%	100%	100%

Source: Authors' compilation based on Neighborhood Change Database (GeoLytics 2008) and 2010 SFI in 2000 Boundaries (GeoLytics 2012).

Note: Neighborhood types are defined as follows:

Predominantly white = Predominantly white tract: >= 80% white; <= 10% each black, Hispanic, Asian, other race.
Predominantly black = Predominantly black tract: >= 50% black; <= 10% each white, Hispanic, Asian, other race.
Predominantly other = Predominantly other race tract: >= 50% Hispanic or Asian; <= 10% black.
White-other = Mixed white and other race tract: between 10% & 50% Hispanic or Asian; <= 10% black.
White-black = Mixed white and black between 10% & 50% black; >= 40% white; >= 10% Hispanic or Asian.
Black-other = Mixed black and other race tract: >= 10% black; >= 10% Hispanic or Asian; <= 40% white.
Multiethnic = Mixed multiethnic tract: >= 10% black; >=10% Hispanic or Asian; >= 40% white.

Hispanic or Asian. Mixed black and other race (hereafter *black-other race*) tracts are at least 10 percent black and at least 10 percent Hispanic or Asian and no more than 40 percent white. Finally, mixed multiethnic (hereafter *multiethnic*) tracts are at least 10 percent black, at least 10 percent Hispanic or Asian, and at least 40 percent white.

The data in table 2.1 reveal strong continuity in neighborhood racial composition even as overall levels of residential segregation were declining. For example, almost half (48.2 percent) of the tracts that were predominantly white in 1990 were still predominantly white two decades later. During this same period, 272 tracts were added to the list of predominantly white neighborhoods, with tracts that had a white-black composition in 1990 exhibiting the highest (although quite small) likelihood of transition to predominantly white by 2010. Overall, the number of predominantly white neighborhoods has declined substantially in recent decades (24,559 in 1990 to 12,118 in 2010), fueling Glaeser and Vigdor's (2012) optimism about the end of residential isolation. However, neighborhoods that are overwhelmingly white—where the concentration of white folks far exceeds their representation in virtually all metropolitan areas—are still far from endangered, much less "effectively extinct," as Glaeser and Vigdor claim.

Also noteworthy is that, while many of these predominantly white neighborhoods have become more diverse over time, this diversity has come primarily through the addition of Asian and Hispanic populations, and those categorized in the other-race category (including those reporting more than one race). Of those tracts that were predominantly white in 1990 but had a different composition by 2010, almost three-quarters ($10,622 \div 14,621 = 0.73$) had transitioned to the white-other category through the increase of Latino or Asian populations, or both. As shown in figure 2.1, the representation of Asians and the representation of Latinos both increased by an average of about 2 percentage points between 1990 and 2010 in neighborhoods classified in 1990 as predominantly white. Combined, nonblack minority populations increased in predominantly white neighborhoods by a total of almost 9 percentage points. In contrast, the black share in these tracts increased by an average of just 3.5 percentage points. Overall, white residential exposure to African Americans remains stubbornly low, as evidenced by the relative rarity of black-white neighborhoods; even as of 2010, fewer than 5.2 percent of all metropolitan census tracts could be considered black-white (see table 2.1).

Also evident from table 2.1 is the compositional stability of predominantly black neighborhoods. More than two-thirds (68.4 percent) of predominantly black neighborhoods in the metropolitan America of 1990 remained predominantly black in 2010. Glaeser and Vigdor correctly note that many neighborhoods that were mostly black in the past have become more diverse over time, but figure 2.1 shows that these

Figure 2.1   Changes in Racial Composition of Metropolitan Tracts, 1990 to 2010, by 1990 Tract Type

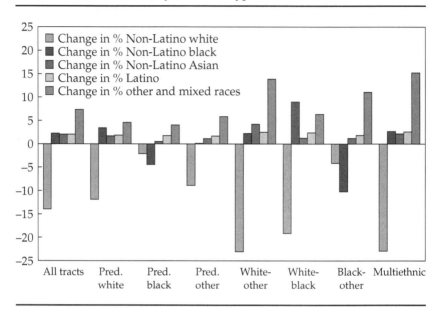

Source: Authors' compilation based on Neighborhood Change Database (GeoLytics 2008) and 2010 SFI in 2000 Boundaries (GeoLytics 2012).

places have diversified primarily through the growing share of other-race (including mixed-race) residents. Specifically, tracts that were predominantly black in 1990 saw, on average, increases of about 4.3 percentage points in the local concentration of other-race individuals. In contrast, the already low white representation in predominantly black neighborhoods declined by an average of about 2 percentage points between 1990 and 2000. As a result of these compositional changes, almost all (1037 of 1279, or 81 percent) of those predominantly black neighborhoods that transitioned to a different type between 1990 and 2010 moved into the compositionally similar black-other category (table 2.1). Moreover, more than 10 percent of the tracts that were white-black in 1990 became predominantly black by 2010, losing an average of about 20 percentage points in their white shares during this period (figure 2.1). Thus, despite declining levels of segregation in most metropolitan areas over the past few decades, relatively isolated black neighborhoods have remained an indelible feature of metropolitan America.

Persistent residential stratification is also borne out in racially disparate mobility patterns. A recent study by Kyle Crowder and his colleagues (2012) shows that black and white householders not only tend to originate in neighborhoods with very different characteristics, they tend to move into areas with high concentrations of their own group. These racial differences appear to have changed very little over time and persist even with controls for socioeconomic resources and other individual- and family-level characteristics that affect residential attainment. Moreover, neighborhoods containing sizable shares of black residents remain especially uncommon destinations for white movers, and black movers are very unlikely to end up in neighborhoods with more than a small representation of whites. Thus, though diverse neighborhoods have become more common in many metropolitan areas (see table 2.1), they are not frequent destinations for residential movers. Overall, it is clear that residential stratification has not disappeared, although it may have become more multiethnic over time.

This persistence of racial-residential stratification is problematic, if for no other reason, because it continues to drive profound racial differences in neighborhood quality, and has important consequences for opportunity structures faced by members of different races. Table 2.2 provides an indication of the magnitude of this stratification. Again, the focus here is on metropolitan neighborhoods as characterized by tract-level data from the 2006–2010 American Community Survey. Because the tract-level data used in this table are weighted by the number of members of specific racial and ethnic groups in the tract, the figures in table 2.2 can be interpreted as the average tract characteristics experienced by the members of each group. Following past research (for example, Adelman et al. 2001; Crowder and South 2003, 2011), we focus on tract-level characteristics linked to both the strength of the local tax base and to educational attainment, family-formation behavior, and other individual-level outcomes. To highlight the magnitude of racial differences in these contextual conditions, figure 2.2 displays the average tract characteristics experienced by non-Latino blacks, non-Latino Asians, and Latinos as ratios of the average conditions faced by whites in metropolitan tracts.

The results presented in table 2.2 and figure 2.2 highlight the neighborhood repercussions of persistent segregation and underlying racial differences in processes of inter-neighborhood mobility. Black and Latino residents of metropolitan areas reside in neighborhoods with substantially lower concentrations of adults with a college education and lower household income levels. Especially pronounced are racial differences in exposure to neighborhood poverty; on average, blacks and Latinos live in neighborhoods with poverty rates nearly twice that experienced by the average white metropolitan resident. On average, blacks also reside in neighborhoods with substantially lower housing values, far more vacant units, and lower concentrations of homeowners. These racial differences in census-based tract characteristics accompany sharp racial and ethnic differences in exposure to harder-to-measure neighborhood features, including collective efficacy (Sampson 2012) and the stability of local institutions (Neild and Balfanz 2006; Wilson 1987).

Table 2.2 Racial and Ethnic Differences in Average Tract Characteristics, 2006 to 2010

Tract Characteristic	Non-Latino Whites	Non-Latino Blacks	Non-Latino Asians	Latinos
Percent college educated	31.00%	21.17%	37.72%	20.48%
Median household income	$62,574.45	$44,921.41	$70,420.59	$49,987.18
Percent in poverty	11.16%	21.24%	11.81%	18.74%
Median housing value	$250,385.40	$188,363.70	$395,946.70	$256,578.50
Median gross rent	$785.16	$705.03	$1,072.95	$832.42
Housing vacancy rate	9.51%	12.83%	7.47%	9.63%
Homeownership rate	71.69%	55.59%	60.76%	56.49%

Source: Authors' compilation of data from the American Community Survey (U.S. Census Bureau 2012).
Note: All figures based on tract-level data, weighted by group population.

Figure 2.2   Racial Differences, Average Tract Characteristics, 2006 to 2010

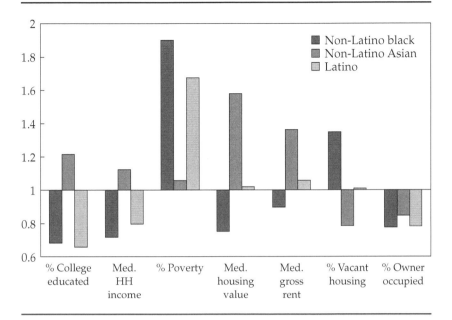

Source: Authors' compilation of data from the American Community Survey (U.S. Census Bureau 2012). All tract-level characteristics weighted by group population size.

Thus, despite declines in average levels of segregation and the increasing prevalence of multiethnic neighborhoods, members of different groups tend to remain exposed to fundamentally different opportunities as a function of their qualitatively unequal neighborhood environments. The consequences of this residential stratification for segregated minorities are vast and well documented. High levels of residential segregation have been shown to increase black poverty (Ananat 2011), concentrate overall levels of poverty in black-populated neighborhoods (Massey and Denton 1993; Quillian 2012), contribute to large racial disparities in wealth accumulation (Oliver and Shapiro 2006), and create the context for sharp racial disparities in the financial risks associated with the recent Great Recession (Rugh and Massey 2010). By concentrating blacks and some other minorities in the worst-quality neighborhoods, segregation also contributes to dramatic racial disparities in exposure to environmental hazards (Crowder and Downey 2010), access to healthy food choices (Moore and Diez Roux 2006), and exposure to crime and other sources of environmental stress (Karb et al. 2012; Peterson and Krivo 2010; Theall, Drury, and Shirtcliff 2012), thereby helping produce profound and persistent racial disparities in health (Nuru-Jeter and LaVeist 2011; Williams and Jackson 2005). Perhaps most important for this volume, residential segregation across neighborhoods also helps maintain high levels of residential segregation at the school level, which has dire and demonstrable consequences for the racial educational achievement gap (Condron et al. 2013; Massey and Fischer 2006).

The Big Three

Given the implications for racial differences in neighborhood experiences and individual opportunities, the persistence of residential segregation by race has remained a topic of intense scholarly interest. Virtually all of this massive body of research is informed by one or more of three canonical and seemingly distinct sets of theoretical arguments: economic explanations, perspectives focused on the persistence of discrimination in housing markets, and preference-based arguments. The first of these Big Three arguments draws on the spatial assimilation model (Alba and Logan 1993; Logan and Molotch 1987) in arguing that residential outcomes are primarily determined by access to economic resources. According to this argument, residential differentiation by social class emerges as individuals match their own socioeconomic status with that of their neighborhood, using their human capital and other endowments to purchase residences in the most desirable neighborhood. In emphasizing socioeconomic characteristics as the main predictors of mobility between lower- and higher-quality neighborhoods, the economic model suggests that racial and ethnic differences in residential attainment and proximity to whites reflect group differences in socioeconomic resources (Alba and Logan 1993; Charles 2003). Blacks and whites, for example, occupy separate residential spaces simply because, on average, blacks have fewer economic resources with which to buy their way into neighborhoods similar to those occupied by whites.

Support for the economic argument is not difficult to find. At the aggregate level, the highest-income members of most minority groups tend to be less segregated from whites than lower-income members of these groups are (Iceland and Wilkes 2006), which is especially apparent when the focus is restricted to experiential measures of segregation rather than to simple unevenness (Spivak, Bass, and St. John 2011). At the individual level, minority access to neighborhoods occupied by the white majority group, lower levels of poverty, and protection from high levels of pollution tend to increase with education and income (Crowder and Downey 2010; Crowder and South 2005; Crowder, Pais, and South 2012; South, Crowder, and Pais 2008). Clearly, economics matter for residential outcomes, and one of the pathways to racially disparate residential outcomes is through group differences in socioeconomic resources.

However, socioeconomic characteristics do not tell the entire story. Although spatial isolation is typically lower for high-income members of minority groups than for low-income members, this variation is least pronounced among blacks; even high-income blacks tend to be at least moderately segregated from whites (Iceland and Wilkes 2006). Similarly, segregation remains high even among those with the economic resources necessary to secure home ownership (Friedman, Tsao, and Chen 2013). At the individual level, racial differences in a variety of residential outcomes—exposure to pollution, levels of neighborhood disadvantage, the likelihood of escaping a poor or racially isolated neighborhood, and proximity to white neighbors—are pronounced even after controls for income, education, and other resources (see, for example, Charles 2003; Crowder and Downey 2010; Crowder and South 2008; Crowder, South, and Chavez 2006; Crowder, Pais, and South 2012). In other words, blacks and whites with similar levels of income and education end up in geographically and qualitatively distinct neighborhoods. Moreover, although socioeconomic resources clearly influence residential outcomes for minority households, even high-income blacks tend to live in neighborhoods with more crime, pollution, and poverty than lower-income whites do (Crowder and Downey 2010; Crowder and South 2008; Pais, South, and Crowder 2012; Pattillo-McCoy 2000).

The inability of the economic model to explain racial differences in residential outcomes, especially for blacks, reinforces the idea that residential options of minority households are constrained by discrimination in the housing market. The place stratification perspective, developed largely in reaction to the shortcomings of the assimilation perspective, posits that racially disparate residential outcomes and the aggregate patterns of segregation they inform emerge from the desire of more privileged groups to distance themselves from other racial and ethnic groups. Most notably, whites' aversion to sharing residential space with minority neighbors is said to motivate discriminatory practices by real estate agents, landlords, mortgage lenders, and neighborhood residents (Massey and Denton 1993; Roscigno, Karafin, and Tester 2009; Ross and Turner 2005; Squires 2007; Yinger 1995) that essentially block minority households from gaining access to neighborhoods occupied by whites and, more generally, from converting their socioeconomic resources into advantageous residential contexts.

A large body of literature highlights the ways in which this discrimination has become deeply institutionalized, taking the form of a range of subtle and not so subtle biases built into both historical and contemporary housing-market practices and public policies: racial steering by real estate agents (Ross and Turner 2005); physical intimidation and overt violence targeting potential minority residents (Meyer 1999; Loewen 2005); federally mandated redlining practices (Hillier 2005; Squires 1994), restrictive covenants (Gotham 2000; Satter 2010), and exclusionary zoning (Rothwell and Massey 2009); destruction of minority neighborhoods under the name of

urban renewal (Gotham 2001; Kleniewski 1986; Seitles 1998); federal funding for suburbanization and accompanying decline of central-city neighborhoods occupied by those left behind (Jackson 1985; Orfield 2002; Sugrue
2005); the concentration of public housing projects and subsidized units
in poor and minority neighborhoods (Galster 2013; Kawitzky et al. 2013;
Massey and Kanaiaupuni 1993; Schill and Wachter 1995); and persistent
racial biases in mortgage lending and foreclosure practices (Clark 2013;
Hyra et al. 2013; Pager and Shepard 2008; Rugh and Massey 2010). Most
observers agree that the common forms of contemporary housing discrimination are likely fairly subtle (Squires 2007; Roscigno, Karafin, and Tester
2009; Yinger 1995), but have the cumulative impact of restricting housing
opportunities for minority (especially black) households. In combination
with service-funding disparities, these institutional forces serve to reinforce
both racialized notions of minority neighborhoods as problematic and black
neighbors as undesirable (Anderson 2012; Charles 2006).

Direct evidence that discrimination restricts residential opportunities
for any individual minority household is scarce, however. Given the difficulty in detecting and documenting subtle forms of discrimination, support for the discrimination thesis typically comes in the form of residual
effects of race on residential outcomes. In other words, observations that
racial disparities in access to more advantageous neighborhoods and residential proximity to the white majority are often interpreted as indirect
evidence of discrimination (for example, Crowder et al. 2006; Crowder
and Downey 2010; Pais, South, and Crowder 2012).

The tendency to attribute residual racial disparities in neighborhood
outcomes to discrimination hinges on the key assumption that members
of all races seek similar residential outcomes. In fact, perhaps most popular
among the dominant three theoretical perspectives is that racial differences
in residential outcomes reflect group differences in residential preferences.
According to this argument, segregation persists because members of different racial and ethnic groups simply choose to reside in areas dominated
by their group. Certainly, available evidence suggests that, though racial
attitudes among whites appear to be softening, willingness among whites
to share residential space with members of other racial and ethnic groups
is still limited. Whites tend to rate neighborhoods that include racial
or ethnic minorities as substantially less desirable than predominantly
white neighborhoods (Charles 2006; Krysan and Bader 2007) and, consequently, the likelihood that white householders will move out of their
neighborhood increases with the size of its minority population (Crowder
and South 2008). Moreover, neighborhoods with relatively large shares of
minorities are most likely to lose white population in the aggregate (see,
for example, Rawlings, Harris, and Turner 2004).

Residential preferences of members of most nonwhite groups are a bit
more complex. Available evidence suggests that members of many Latino

and Asian groups hold negative stereotypes about blacks and express a limited willingness to move into predominantly black areas (Charles 2006). Like whites, blacks express the strongest preferences for neighborhoods with large concentrations of same-race neighbors (Clark 2009; Krysan and Bader 2007) and an increasing reluctance to be the extreme numerical minority in mostly white neighborhoods (Krysan and Farley 2002). Many black survey respondents also express somewhat negative attitudes toward Latinos and Hispanics (Charles 2006). Additionally, ethnographic research often points to black animosity toward other minority groups settling in predominantly black neighborhoods (for example, Johnson, Farrell, and Guinn 1999; Wilson and Taub 2006). However, compared with whites, blacks express considerably greater tolerance for integration, preferring neighborhoods with considerably more nonblacks than the neighborhoods blacks reside in (Charles 2006; Krysan and Bader 2007; Krysan and Farley 2002). Although the link between preferences and actual residential outcomes is rarely observed (for an exception, see Adelman 2005), group differences in stated residential preferences leave open the possibility that segregation and resulting disparities in neighborhood conditions reflects group differences in residential preferences (see, for example, Clark 2009).

Missing the Complexity

Research confirms that each of the Big Three explanations highlight forces that have important influences on processes and patterns of segregation. However, this literature typically portrays the Big Three perspectives as conceptually and empirically distinct, pitting the theoretical arguments as competing explanations for the phenomenon. In fact, these arguments are often presented as mutually exclusive and exhaustive explanations for the emergence and persistence of residential segregation, to the point that failure to support hypotheses drawn from one perspective is interpreted as support for another. For example, as noted, the failure of economic differentials to explain racial differences in residential outcomes is typically accepted as evidence of housing discrimination.

In the following sections, we offer two important counterpoints to the tendency to view the Big Three as exhaustive and mutually exclusive explanations of segregation.

Missing Interactions

We begin our discussion of the theoretical myopathy with selected examples of the interactions between the forces highlighted in the Big Three—examples that are intended to be illustrative but not exhaustive of the many ways in which these factors might operate in combination with each other.

Discrimination and Preferences Much of the scholarly debate about the role of discrimination and preferences in perpetuating segregation has been focused on which is more important, discrimination or preferences. In the late 1980s and early 1990s, W. A. V. Clark (1986, 1988, 1989) and George Galster (1988, 1989) engaged in a back and forth (four separate installments) in several issues of the journal *Population Research and Policy Review* that illustrates this either-or perspective. The framing of the discussion was centrally about gathering the evidence to establish that segregation was either caused primarily by discrimination (Galster) or mostly by preferences (Clark). The policy implications of these two explanations were quite clear: if it was discrimination, there was something to be done about it; if it was preferences, then the "free will" of the people was driving segregation, and policy interventions were either inappropriate or would likely be ineffective.

The debate between Clark and Galster typifies much of that about the relative roles of discrimination and preferences: residual racial differences in neighborhood attainment are viewed either as a direct effect of discrimination or a reflection of group differences in residential preferences. In reality, this either-or perspective does a disservice to understanding the complex interactions between discrimination and residential preferences, creating an incomplete and overly simplified story. Indeed, discrimination can have an important impact on the racial residential preferences of both majority and minority group members in at least two ways. The first is perhaps the more obvious one. One line of research has established repeatedly in metropolitan and national studies that individuals of all races and ethnicities tend to prefer to live in neighborhoods with members of their own racial-ethnic group. Groups differ considerably on the relative percentages, but nevertheless the largest group in most respondents' ideal neighborhood is their own group. The conventional wisdom or unstated assumption is that these preferences are driven by in-group favoritism—a desire to be around culturally similar people (Clark 2009). As Maria Krysan and Reynolds Farley (2002) show, however, evidence is scant among African Americans that in-group favoritism drives a desire to avoid whiter neighborhoods (see also Charles 2006).

Instead, African American residential preferences are influenced significantly by concerns about racial discrimination in whiter neighborhoods. In other words, you cannot disentangle a preference from the historical and contemporary experiences that African Americans have had with respect to discriminatory actions of whites and institutional biases firmly imbedded in the housing market. African Americans show little interest in pioneering white neighborhoods, less because of a desire to be in a culturally similar environment and more because of a desire to not stand out. As a respondent in one study succinctly explained it, "Because you either get treated as a token or you get ignored or there's this superficial niceness that is annoying. More often than not one of these three things happens" (Krysan and Farley 2002, 961). In short, discrimination and preferences are inextricably linked when it comes to African Americans.

Camille Charles (2006) provides the most comprehensive study of the impact of concerns about discrimination on the residential preferences of groups other than whites and blacks. In her study, she found that blacks, Latinos, and Asians in Los Angeles who perceive whites as being more discriminatory include fewer whites in their ideal neighborhood. Interestingly, perceptions of white discrimination decrease the number of whites in blacks' ideal neighborhood, but do not increase the number of same-race neighbors. The same pattern holds for Asians: the perception that whites are discriminatory shapes only the number of whites in their ideal neighborhood and not the number of Asians. For Latinos, perceptions of white discrimination reduce the number of white households included in the ideal neighborhood as well as the number of same-race neighbors. These analyses again highlight how perceptions of discrimination contribute to the formation of preferences—they are not an either-or proposition.

Discrimination influences residential preferences, particularly those of whites, in another perhaps more subtle way. As noted, a number of institutional actors—real estate agents, banks, local and federal agencies—have participated in a range of discriminatory actions that have resulted in barriers to the movement of individuals into neighborhoods of their choosing and have also created structurally disadvantaged minority neighborhoods. The "divergent social worlds" Ruth Peterson and Lauren Krivo (2010) document are a stark illustration of the vast disparities across white, black, and integrated neighborhoods. The abundance of such neighborhoods has no doubt fed into whites' perceptions of black neighborhoods as undesirable places to live. Indeed, Elijah Anderson (2012) argues that these perceptions constitute an "iconic ghetto" that has taken on a life of its own. Especially for white Americans, the images of the iconic ghetto follow African Americans wherever they go. Whites presume that any African Americans they meet (even outside the ghetto) are nevertheless "of the ghetto." As a result, in everyday interactions with African Americans, whites assume a range of negative characteristics about the individual, necessitating that African Americans expend considerable energy proving that they are not "from the ghetto."

Ingrid Ellen (2000) argues that these images of the iconic ghetto (Anderson 2012) or what she calls "neighborhood stereotypes" are an important factor shaping residential segregation. As others explain, these stereotypes grow and flourish out of a system of inequality. Lawrence Bobo, James Kluegel, and Ryan Smith (1997, 23) maintain that "sharp black-white economic inequality and residential segregation . . . provide the kernel of truth needed to regularly breathe new life into old stereotypes about putative black proclivities toward involvement in crime, violence, and welfare dependency." Similarly, institutional forces that perpetuate instability and disinvestment in black neighborhoods—including discriminatory lending practices, heavy subsidies for decentralized growth, and placement of public housing in poor and minority neighborhoods—simultaneously reinforce notions that black areas are to be avoided as potential destinations. That is, whites (in particular) associate negative social and economic conditions with minority neighborhoods, providing justification for the very behavior that perpetuates segregation: avoidance of minority-populated, and especially black-populated, neighborhoods.

To be clear, we are not arguing that whites' preferences are driven exclusively by perceptions about the social class characteristics of minorities and minority-populated neighborhoods. In fact, evidence is ample that race matters, above and beyond social class (for example, Krysan et al. 2009; Krysan and Bader 2007; Emerson, Chai, and Yancey 2001; Lewis, Emerson, and Kleinberg 2011). Rather, we argue that these preferences are shaped in whites' imaginations by their stereotypes and perceptions of neighborhoods with a large minority presence (see Anderson's iconic ghetto). Also, these linkages are an outgrowth of the persistent discriminatory actions of individuals and institutions that created these disadvantaged communities in the first place. Devah Pager and Hannah Shepherd (2008) make the connection between discrimination and preferences (which have stereotypes at their foundation) very explicit:

> These historical sources of discrimination may become further relevant, not only in their perpetuation of present-day inequalities but also through their reinforcement of contemporary forms of stereotypes and discrimination. As in Myrdal's (1944) "principle of cumulation," structural disadvantages (for example, poverty, joblessness, crime) come to be seen as cause, rather than consequence, of persistent racial inequality, justifying and reinforcing negative racial stereotypes. (75–78)

The perceptions whites have of neighborhoods that include black residents—their neighborhood stereotypes—were documented by Maria Krysan, Reynolds Farley, and Mick Couper (2008). In this study, whites were shown short videos of neighborhoods where the racial composition of the neighborhood was experimentally varied (either white only, black only, or a combination of white and black residents). Despite the fact that neighborhoods were identical in every way except the purported racial composition, whites were significantly more likely to rate the black neighborhood as less safe, as likely to decline in property values, and as having significantly lower quality schools.

In another study, Krysan (2002) found that many whites who said they would flee from integrated neighborhoods in Atlanta, Boston, Detroit, and Los Angeles explained their attitudes based on their perceptions of the negative characteristics (schools, safety, property values) of these areas. Clearly, these neighborhood stereotypes are prevalent. It is decades of discriminatory actions throughout the real estate industry, however, that have created the distressed neighborhoods that provide the kernel of truth for the white preference to avoid sharing residential spaces with blacks. Thus, even when the observable features of a neighborhood are of the same social class, the presence of whites versus blacks portrayed as residents results in whites' downgrading the quality of that neighborhood. This is fueled in part by racial stereotypes about blacks, but is no doubt also a manifestation of the prevalence of disadvantaged neighborhoods that characterize many—though by no means all—heavily African American neighborhoods.

Preferences and discrimination may be interrelated in another even more indirect way: it may be that perceived preferences shape discrimination. The historical record seems clear on this possibility. To take just one example, the federal government codified redlining (Yinger 1995) to keep loan funds out of particular (minority) neighborhoods; this was done in part because of the belief that whites prefer white neighborhoods and blacks prefer black neighborhoods. In more contemporary periods, we know that steering is the one form of housing discrimination documented by the U.S. Department of Housing and Urban Development's Housing Discrimination Studies (HDS) that persists (Turner and Ross 2005) and has in fact increased for some groups. This steering may be in part a function of real estate agents and landlords assuming the racial preferences of their clients, and of assuming the racial preferences of their clients' potential neighbors.

In different ways, then, we suggest that trying to determine whether preference or discrimination shapes segregation is a fool's errand. Rather, preferences themselves are in some ways shaped by discrimination and, conversely, discriminatory treatment likely reflects assumptions about residential preferences. For whites in particular, the larger discriminatory system that created the disadvantaged neighborhoods contributes to the stereotypes whites hold about neighborhoods and in turn their desire to avoid more than minimally integrated neighborhoods. For their part, racial minorities prefer to have high enough numbers of their own group in the neighborhood so as to guard against discrimination. To the extent that the preference levels of racial-ethnic groups are incompatible with each other—African Americans want more blacks in their neighborhoods than whites are willing to live with—then the preferences, steeped in a tradition of discriminatory actions, will reinforce the segregated neighborhoods that dominate our urban landscapes.

Economics and Preferences   Existing research also places too little emphasis on important interactions between preferences and economic forces shaping residential stratification. The most obvious question about the possible relationship between economics and preferences would be to ask whether people of different social classes and economic circumstances have different preferences about racial-residential composition. Relatively (and perhaps surprisingly) little research examines this question, though Charles's (2006) comprehensive study of the racial residential preferences of Los Angeles whites, blacks, Latinos, and Asians is an exception. She generally shows that for whites and blacks, social class and residential preferences are almost unrelated. The same is not true for Asians and Latinos, where immigration-related characteristics (which often include social class) do influence racial residential preferences. She finds that the immigrant's individual economic characteristics, as well as their beliefs about the social class disadvantages of blacks as a group, shape the desire to avoid having blacks as neighbors.

Social class and preferences can become intertwined in other, less direct ways, beyond the simple question of whether a person's social class position shapes openness or avoidance of particular racial-ethnic groups. The first raises questions about whether racial residential preferences and preferences related to social class can be disaggregated; the second points to the way in which social class can alter the impact of preferences on actual residential outcomes. We turn to these two examples next.

Starting in the late 1990s, growing attention has focused on the question of whether preferences that have traditionally been described as racial residential preferences are in fact driven not by racial concerns, but instead by associated social class characteristics (Crowder 2000; Crowder and South 2008; Harris 1999, 2001). This debate has been lively in the literature, largely responding to the weaknesses in the traditional measures of racial residential preferences, which typically focus on individual preferences related to neighborhood racial composition but rarely incorporate information on other neighborhood characteristics—such as socioeconomic composition—that may shape residential outcomes. One line of research examines neighborhood satisfaction as the expression of residential preferences, and demonstrates that social class characteristics of a neighborhood explain much of the effect of racial composition, per se (Harris 1999, 2001; Taub, Taylor, and Dunham 1984). In a more recent test of the racial proxy hypothesis, Sapna Swaroop and Maria Krysan (2011) find that social class characteristics of the neighborhood explain much of the effect of racial composition on neighborhood satisfaction for Latinos and African Americans in Chicago, but that the relationship is much weaker for Chicago-area whites. In particular, racial composition continues to influence whites' neighborhood satisfaction, even after objective and subjective measures of neighborhood social class characteristics are controlled. Similarly, controlling for nonracial economic characteristics of neighborhoods do not explain whites' heightened likelihood of out-mobility from neighborhoods containing larger minority populations (Crowder 2000; Crowder and South 2008).

A recent study by Kimberly Goyette, Danielle Farrie, and Joshua Freely (2012) suggests that the dynamic for neighborhoods (that racial composition factors into perceptions of quality above and beyond other class-related characteristics) also holds in the context of school quality perceptions. Using a telephone survey of whites living in Philadelphia, the authors find that increases in a local school's black student population, above and beyond changes in other school characteristics (safety, poverty level, test scores), resulted in lower evaluations of the local school. In addition, Salvatore Saporito and Annette Lareau (1999) use a different dataset and study location to demonstrate that, net of a range of other objectively measured school characteristics (safety, affluence, SAT scores, teacher experience, distance to school), a school's racial composition is a substantial and significant predictor of whether white parents selected a school as an option for their child.

A second approach to the question of the effect of race on residential preferences—as against the associated social class characteristics—is to conduct vignette studies that allow researchers to tease apart the race-versus-class debate by experimentally manipulating the racial and social class characteristics of neighborhoods (Emerson, Chai, and Yancey 2001; Krysan et al. 2009; Lewis, Emerson, and Kleinberg 2011). These studies confirm that social and economic characteristics of a neighborhood shape how people evaluate it; Valerie Lewis and her colleagues (2011), for example, show a strong effect of the quality of schools and crime levels on whether whites, blacks, and Latinos say they are willing to buy a house in a particular neighborhood. But the vignette studies have also demonstrated that race matters above and beyond these social class characteristics. Again, however, whites, blacks, and Latinos respond differently. Krysan and her colleagues (2011) report that racial composition matters more for whites than blacks in the Chicago and Detroit metropolitan areas, and that racial composition works in different ways for these groups; the presence of blacks creates lower desirability ratings for whites whereas all-white neighborhoods are downgraded among black respondents, once social class characteristics are controlled. Lewis and her colleagues (2011) report that racial composition influences evaluations of neighborhood quality for whites but not for Latinos or Asians in Houston. Overall, this body of research points to the conclusion that racial preferences are not merely social class preferences in disguise.

The second indirect way in which the story becomes more complicated when we connect social class and preferences is to ask whether the consequences of preferences differ based on the social class of the person holding the preferences. Although not fully explored in the literature, some evidence indicates that economic resources affect the ability of individuals to make moves that match their residential preferences. For example, Robert Adelman (2005) compared white and black middle-class residents of Atlanta, Boston, Detroit, and Los Angeles and found that members of the white middle class are better able to translate preferences into reality than the black middle class; like other African Americans, members of the black middle class tend to live in neighborhoods that are less integrated than they prefer. Although this analysis did not directly test the idea that people of different levels of social class have a differential ability to act on their preferences, in other research, Crowder (2000) shows that high-income whites are the most likely to leave diverse neighborhoods. Although his research does not allow for direct measures of preferences, the finding is again suggestive of the idea that whites with more resources are better able to actuate their preferences for homogeneous neighborhoods.

In short, although the evidence is not on the side of race being simply a substitute for social class (as in the racial proxy debate), we suggest that social class is implicated in the process in potentially important ways, in that it appears to modify the way in which preferences do (or do not) translate into an ability to move in accordance with those preferences.

Economics and Discrimination Most studies of housing discrimination are audit studies in which the characteristics of the tester are selected to ensure that they meet the requirements of the housing being inspected. This highlights a disadvantage of the audit study—information is relatively scant about how social class characteristics can shape the experiences of discrimination. A few clues, both direct and indirect, suggest that people experience housing discrimination differently based on their social class background. For example, audit studies typically test rental and purchase markets separately. Insofar as housing tenure is an imperfect indicator of social class, the evidence suggests higher levels of disparate treatment for those of a lower social class, renters (Turner and Ross 2005). In addition, in a detailed study of steering—the one form of discrimination that has not declined over the past several decades—Margery Turner and Stephen Ross (2005) examine three types: information steering, segregation steering, and social class steering. They find that "whites are encouraged to consider more affluent neighborhoods than comparable blacks or Hispanics. . . . This can occur when whites are recommended or shown homes in more affluent neighborhoods, or when they are told positive things about these neighborhoods" (95). They report that social class steering is more common for blacks than for Hispanics.

The previous examples are more indirect and suggestive of social class differences in the experience of discrimination. A few studies test the relationship between economics and discrimination more directly. Douglas Massey and Garvey Lundy (2001) and Mary Fischer and Massey (2004) conducted telephone-based audit tests in which both the race and the apparent social class characteristics of the tester were varied by using testers with different accents. Massey and Lundy (2001) report an interaction between race, gender, and social class: low-income black women receive the most negative treatment and middle-class white men receive the most positive.

Fischer and Massey (2004) replicate these findings, but then further explore the role of geography in shaping these results; in doing so, they draw an important linkage between discrimination and segregation. That is, if discriminatory treatment were unrelated to the racial composition of a community into which an individual is trying to move, it would be irrelevant to the perpetuation of segregation. However, as expected, the pattern of discrimination is consistent with the perpetuation of segregation. For example, blacks are less able to gain access to the suburbs and to places that were farther away from already-black neighborhoods. Thus, they find that class, race, and geography all intersect in the functioning of discrimination, implying that the economic-discrimination linkage has consequences for where people live and, therefore, for the perpetuation of segregation.

Missing Drivers of Segregation

In addition to being largely blind to the ways in which economics, preferences, and discrimination interact to shape residential patterns, current theoretical arguments are largely blind to many of the dynamic processes that perpetuate racial-ethnic residential segregation. These additional factors no doubt shape, and are shaped in part, by economics, preferences, and discrimination; if we ignore them, our story about the processes and mechanisms through which segregation is perpetuated is incomplete. Here we highlight some examples from a cluster of such factors that relate to information and knowledge.

The models and theories that generally frame the debate about the causes of racial-residential segregation assume that individuals have accurate and complete information about their residential options and, by extension, that this knowledge does not vary for different racial-ethnic groups. The research on preferences, for example, assumes that individuals have solid knowledge of the characteristics of various neighborhood options and select from these neighborhoods one that best matches their preferences. The research on the role of social class in shaping choices similarly assumes accurate information on the part of movers as to what communities they can and cannot afford to live in. Although not regularly incorporated into residential mobility and residential segregation research, a growing body of research highlights the ways in which this assumption of perfect information is unsupported.

One recent study addresses this untapped dimension most directly by focusing on the simple question of whether race-ethnicity shapes whether people know about communities. Presenting a random sample of Chicago area residents with a map of the metropolitan area, Krysan and Michael Bader (2009) asked survey respondents to identify which of the forty-one communities identified on the map they "did not know anything about." The authors found that, for the most part, blacks, whites, and Latinos in Chicago report significantly more awareness of neighborhoods in which their own racial-ethnic group is overrepresented and far less awareness about areas dominated by other groups. At the same time, the patterns across different racial-ethnic groups are interesting. For example, whites are less familiar with racially diverse communities, even communities in which whites are the majority. African Americans, for their part, are less familiar with communities that are both geographically distant and overwhelmingly white. Although many of the places that are blind spots (overwhelmingly white, outlying communities) for African Americans are explained by social class and geography (distance between a resident's community and the community asked about), these controls do not, for the most part, explain whites' blind spots. Latinos, in general, have far more blind spots than either African Americans or whites, though these differences tended to disappear when social, demographic, and geographic controls were included. Krysan and Bader (2009) argue that due to the historical and contemporary patterns of extreme segregation in Chicago, controlling for distance between a person's home and the community about which they may or may not have a blind spot is tantamount to controlling for segregation and illustrates how segregation can beget segregation through its impact on racialized patterns of community knowledge.

Although it draws attention to the possibility that community knowledge is a critical factor in shaping the mobility decisions that, in the aggregate, perpetuate segregation, Krysan and Bader's (2009) study is largely descriptive and, due to data limitations, is unable to test whether this knowledge shapes actual residential choices. Yet a range of disparate research provides indirect clues to the role that community knowledge plays in the residential choices people actually make. We turn to these studies now.

The role of residential knowledge is likely reflected, in underappreciated ways, in the strong spatial dependence of mobility. Research on migration and residential mobility consistently highlights the fact that migration flows are strongest between nearby neighborhoods, and that individuals are much more likely to move to nearer destinations than to those farther away (Crowder and South 2008; Lee 1966; Long 1988).

Following general migration theory (Lee 1966), this distance-dependence can be seen as a function of economic cost, but it is highly likely, especially in the context of inter-neighborhood mobility, that the tendency to choose nearby neighborhoods reflects differences in knowledge about residential opportunities in nearby versus more distant areas. Because housing searches are costly in terms of money and time, residents will likely consider residences they know through daily experiences or social relationships (Brown and Moore 1979), and will be most likely to search in neighborhoods they believe will satisfy their aspirations based on the conditions they perceive to exist (Brown, Horton and Wittick 1970).

For most individuals, daily activities tend to be centered on the home neighborhood; the immediate and surrounding neighborhoods encompass a good share of the daily round and those who venture greater distances in a day for work, school, church, and recreation typically return home on a regular basis (Fan and Khattack 2008; Hannes, Janssens, and Wets 2008; Holz-Rau and Sicks 2013). Through these daily activities, individuals are likely to develop the strongest knowledge of the residential opportunities—noticing rental vacancies, new construction, for-sale units, and neighborhood conditions—in those areas close to home. As a result, even when individuals use more formal search tools, including online searches, newspapers, and real estate agents, their searches are likely biased toward neighborhoods near their home "anchor point" (Huff 1986; see also Chen and Lin 2012; Rashidi, Auld, and Mohammadian 2012; Smith et al. 1979). Indeed, though not a direct test of the impact, race-matching is tremendous between housing searcher and real estate agent (between 60 percent and 100 percent), suggesting that even reliance on professionals to assist in the search may not dramatically change levels of knowledge about a variety of neighborhoods (Krysan 2008; Krysan and Bader 2009). The possible effects of these kinds of racial homophily are likely to be enhanced by any reliance on neighborhood-based social networks for information about housing opportunities. Consistent with these arguments, economic geographers point to tremendous inefficiencies in the housing-search process, noting that individuals have only limited knowledge of local real estate markets but much more about nearby communities than more distant ones (Chen and Lin 2012; Clark and Smith 1979; Huff 1986).

The result of these biases in residential knowledge is that individuals are more likely to perceive and search for housing options in and around their neighborhood of residence. Although unrecognized in extant literature on residential segregation, this tendency is likely to produce racially differentiated patterns of mobility that serve to perpetuate racial-residential stratification. Specifically, because segregation, by definition, exposes members of different races to different residential environments (Krivo et al. 2013), knowledge about residential opportunities in different parts of the metropolis is likely to be uneven across racial and ethnic groups. Moreover, given the spatial clustering of similar neighborhoods (Massey and Denton 1993; Wright et al. 2013), even when the housing search extends into surrounding neighborhoods, it is likely to encompass areas fairly similar to the neighborhood of residence. For example, because of their extreme residential isolation in many cities, African Americans are likely to know the most about residential opportunities in black neighborhoods and the least about neighborhoods that include large proportions of other groups. The same is likely to be true for members of other racial and ethnic groups.

Evidence of this dynamic is apparent in at least two findings. First, even after controlling for socioeconomic resources, lifecycle position, and a host of other factors affecting residential selection, most movers relocate to neighborhoods just a short distance from their origin. Second, these short-distance movers experience much less change in the composition of their neighborhood than the relatively rare individuals who move greater distances do (Crowder and South 2008; Crowder, Hall, and Tolnay 2011). Through these dynamics, segregation tends to perpetuate itself by funneling residential movers into neighborhoods quite similar to those they left and, on average, dominated by their own race (Crowder, Pais, and South 2012). Interestingly, this distance dependency is virtually ignored in research on residential segregation, where the underlying assumption of ongoing theoretical debates is that knowledge of residential opportunities does not vary across racial groups and across neighborhoods, so that racially disparate mobility outcomes are driven by some combination of economic resources, preference, and discrimination.

In a similar way, evidence is growing that racial segregation tends to perpetuate itself through the production of racially disparate life-course experiences. Several recent studies have shown a strong continuity in residential experiences across generations (Sharkey 2008; Sampson and Sharkey 2008) and across the life course (Marsh, Polimis, and Crowder 2013; Sharkey 2012; Swisher, Kuhl, and Chavez 2013; Wagmiller 2013). For example, a recent study by Kris Marsh and her colleagues (2013) suggests that the racial composition of neighborhoods experienced by individuals in adolescence is a very strong predictor of the composition of neighborhoods they experience as adults long after they have left their parents' homes. Moreover, about 80 percent of black-white differences in neighborhood racial composition in adulthood can be explained by group differences in the composition of neighborhoods occupied during adolescence. In other words, the racial differences in household residential location that define segregation are driven, in large part, by the continuity of racial differences in residential experiences earlier in life. Certainly, these linkages between adolescent and adult context can be viewed through the lens of dominant theoretical arguments. For example, residential loca-

tion in adolescence may shape educational and employment opportunities (Holloway and Mulherin 2004; Bennett 2011; Sampson 2012), thereby
affecting the accumulation of socioeconomic resources that, according
to economic models of segregation, are crucial for explaining neighborhood sorting. Similarly, residential experiences in adolescence may shape
neighborhood preferences such that, all else being equal, individuals
simply try to emulate, through their adult mobility choices, their neighborhood experiences from adolescence.

However, the research by Marsh and her colleagues provides only
limited support for these traditional arguments and suggests that neighborhood knowledge might instead be a key mechanism linking adolescent and adult context. Specifically, contradicting the simple economic
argument, the association between adolescent and adult context remains
pronounced even after controlling for socioeconomic characteristics, as
well as a variety of other factors thought to shape residential sorting. In
addition, the association is much weaker for individuals who move to a
different metropolitan area between adolescence and adulthood. If simple
preferences were at play, householders would presumably attempt to sort
themselves into neighborhoods matching their adolescent neighborhood
even after moving to a different metropolitan area. That a long-distance
move breaks the association between adolescent and adult residential
outcomes provides some indirect support for the importance of residential knowledge; compared with those remaining in the same metropolitan
area, intermetropolitan movers may end up in neighborhoods that look
less similar to their adolescent context because they are unable to rely on
knowledge and perceptions of specific neighborhoods developed during
adolescence as they make their adult residential choices.

The importance of residential knowledge and other mechanisms not
reflected in traditional explanations of segregation is also reflected in the
large and growing body of research focused on the mobility of individuals who participate in a range of federally funded housing assistance
programs (HOPE VI, Gautreaux, Moving to Opportunity). Our purpose
here is not to review the debates about the success or failure of these
programs. Instead, we point to how this body of research highlights the
role—and limitation of—the idea that knowledge may be an important
factor in shaping patterns of racial-residential segregation in general, and
of course individual housing outcomes in particular.

On the one hand, Robin Smith and colleagues (2002) conducted focus
groups with HOPE VI participants and suggest that program participants'
lack of knowledge about neighborhoods played an important role in shaping their housing outcomes. These participants had very little awareness
of neighborhoods outside their geographic or social spheres—and were
driven mainly by the characteristics of the housing units and less by the
features of the neighborhood (Smith et al. 2002). This draws attention to

both our general lack of knowledge about how people make housing decisions, and the important role information plays in shaping decisions.

At the same time, Stephanie DeLuca's research illustrates the severe constraints that individuals in housing mobility programs face when conducting a housing search. We know from a variety of studies that participants in these programs often end up moving to neighborhoods that look like their previous neighborhoods (for example, Sampson 2012). DeLuca, Peter Rosenblatt, and Holly Wood (2012) note the hurried nature of housing searches for this population when they point out that 80 percent of moves taken by participants in their study of very low-income African American families were involuntary: occurred because of circumstances such as a unit becoming uninhabitable due to fire or flood or structural damages. Adding to the involuntary and hurried nature of the search, DeLuca (2012) highlights how housing searches for this population are severely constrained, calling into question the very relevance of the idea of choice and preferences. For example, she questions the assertion that housing mobility program participants choose to stay in their neighborhoods rather than move to places with more opportunity. She argues that economic constraints (that influence, among other things, access to information about neighborhoods and communities) shape how we should understand housing preferences and choices. She therefore highlights the fundamental way in which knowledge constrains preferences:

> because of the legacy of segregation and discrimination, many families could never really "choose" neighborhoods in the middle class suburbs because they have never seen one and have no way of understanding the potential cost-benefit tradeoffs. Instead, they learn to accept the status quo, even though they know it poses risks, because it is "what they know" and it's possible. . . . Choices are not free if individuals do not have access to information. (2012, 25–26)

In an interesting way, this highlights the challenge with interpreting preferences, due to the severe constraints to free choice that shape mobility choices, and the fundamental role played by information in shaping those preferences. DeLuca (2012) highlights that this knowledge may not even be limited to awareness of the name of one community or another, but to a more profound difference in knowledge—about how communities can vary, what such a community would look like, and what is possible.

Conclusion

Despite evidence of some improvement members of different racial and ethnic groups operate in largely separate residential spaces. For the most part, existing efforts to explain these patterns have remained largely silent on the specific processes that result in the choices that, in the aggregate, create segregated neighborhoods. That is, the choices people make about where they will live remain profoundly undertheorized. Indeed, for the most part, researchers have tended to treat choice as unproblematic. Some who have argued that preferences are the main driver behind segregation assume, for example, that individuals have the knowledge needed to find a place that matches those preferences. Similarly, proponents of economic models assume that residential sorting operates along socioeconomic lines by actors with perfect knowledge of residential opportunities. The purpose of this chapter is to challenge many of these assumptions by problematizing the process of housing searches and the resulting residential choices people make. Although this focus is on choosing homes, as other chapters in this volume suggest, some of the same questions are no doubt appropriate when considering the question of how people choose schools.

By focusing attention on the ways in which economics, preferences, and discrimination interact to shape housing decisions, we make concrete the idea that choices are differentially constrained. An individual's economic circumstances can shape in fundamental ways even the choice set that individuals can imagine, never mind their ability to realize those preferences. As DeLuca (2012) shows, for disadvantaged black women, the economic constraints are so severe that it becomes almost irrelevant what their neighborhood preferences are—and indeed even understanding that certain kinds of choices exist is called into question. On the other hand, the mobility patterns of advantaged whites suggest that they are well positioned to move in keeping with their preferences.

We also suggest some of the many ways in which any one of the Big Three segregation factors might affect another: neighborhood social class characteristics certainly shape whether a place is considered a good neighborhood, but even independent of these features, the effect of neighborhood racial composition persists. Some evidence also suggests that one's social class position shapes the discrimination likely when trying to find housing. These are but a few examples of a range of ways in which treating the Big Three as mutually exclusive have resulted in a restricted view of the factors that shape segregation, limiting the development of policy strategies to address these challenges.

We also argue that we need to move outside the Big Three factors of economics, preferences, and discrimination to identify the mechanisms through which these and other factors operate in the housing search process. We point to racially differentiated patterns of neighborhood knowledge and perceptions as an example of one underappreciated force. We suggest that information about housing options is both cause and consequence of segregation. Through social networks that are racially segregated, from the segregated childhoods that shape adult residential outcomes, to the way in which our daily rounds shape the access to information we have, we draw attention to a number of ways in which information is implicated in the perpetuation of segregation. Again, this chapter is intended to open up a more nuanced conversation about how people choose neighborhoods.

The factors we include here are not exhaustive; and indeed, other chapters in this volume point to other ways in which choice must be problematized to enable scholars to provide policymakers with more valuable information about the processes that lead to both school and residential segregation. Both types of segregation are inextricably linked to persistent racial inequalities across numerous life outcomes.

One of the primary barriers to the exploration of a more nuanced perspective on the causes of segregation is no doubt the shortage of appropriate data. As we have demonstrated in this chapter, there are hints across a number of studies that these other factors must be considered. A more complete accounting is impossible due to data constraints, however. To be sure, progress in this regard has been tremendous. What we used to have to infer from census data about individual mobility in the face of racial turnover in neighborhoods can now be directly tested through the creative repurposing of studies originally designed for other purposes. For example, the Panel Study of Income Dynamics (PSID), originally designed to track changes in the economic circumstances of families, has provided a platform for prospective mobility studies that reveal the relative roles of race, class, and neighborhood conditions in predicting neighborhood mobility. But as rich and valuable as the PSID has proven to be, because the focus of the study is not to assess residential mobility behavior, we lack any information about the reasons people leave their neighborhoods and why they select the destinations they do. So we know that racial composition is related to moves, but we don't know how or why. For their part, attitudinal studies that tap the residential preferences of residents paint an important portrait of if and how race shapes how people evaluate neighborhoods. Original studies, which focused exclusively on a neighborhood's racial characteristics, have been improved by including a neighborhood's nonracial characteristics as controls to assess the independent effects of social class (such as school quality, taxes, property values, crime rates, and the like). Ultimately, however, these studies are limited because they mainly measure a set of preferences that are disconnected from actual mobility behavior, largely because the studies are cross-sectional. For their part, audits of discrimination are of great value as a general gauge of the prevalence of a particular kind of discrimination that occurs at a very specific point in a particular kind of housing search process. Insightful as an indicator of whether unfair treatment occurs, this research does little to shed light on the specific ways in which this kind of discrimination translates into the housing outcomes of individuals. Indeed, the more general question of how people go about searching and selecting a place to live has been the subject of little empirical work—especially in a way that allows one to link them to residential outcomes.

Finally, a clear understanding of the set of information-related factors that we highlight in our discussion of the areas that are outside the purview of the Big Three also suffer from a lack of data. Forays into this area have been made, but the data, as we noted, are very limited and only hint at the possible role that these factors play. Future research needs to identify creative and comprehensive ways to measure factors implicit in the Big Three and also outside these core explanations if we are to be able to answer in a more satisfying way important questions about how housing searches unfold and how they result in choices that either perpetuate or break down the patterns of segregation that continue to plague many of our nation's cities.

This research was supported by grants awarded to the University of Washington's Center for Studies in Demography and Ecology (R24 HD042828).

References

Adelman, Robert M. 2005. "The Roles of Race, Class, and Residential Preferences in the Neighborhood Racial Composition of Middle-Class Blacks and Whites." *Social Science Quarterly* 86(1): 209–28.

Adelman, Robert M., Hui-shien Tsao, Stewart E. Tolnay, and Kyle D. Crowder. 2001. "Neighborhood Disadvantage Among Racial and Ethnic Groups." *Sociological Quarterly* 42(4): 603–32.

Alba, Richard D., and John R. Logan. 1993. "Minority Proximity to Whites in Suburbs: An Individual-Level Analysis of Segregation." *American Journal of Sociology* 98(6): 1388–427.

Ananat, Elizabeth Oltmans. 2011. "The Wrong Side(s) of the Tracks: The Causal Effects of Racial Segregation on Urban Poverty and Inequality." *American Economic Journal: Applied Economics* 3(2): 34–66.

Anderson, Elijah. 2012. "The Iconic Ghetto." *The Annals of American Academy of Political and Social Science* 642(1): 8–24.

Bennett, Pamela. 2011. "The Relationship Between Neighborhood Racial Concentration and Verbal Ability: An Investigation Using the Institutional Resources Model." *Social Science Research* 40(4): 1124–141.

Bobo, Lawrence D., James Kluegel, and Ryan Smith. 1997. "Laissez-Faire Racism: The Crystallization of a 'Kinder, Gentler' Anti-Black Ideology." In *Racial Attitudes in the 1990s: Continuity and Change,* edited by Stephen Tuch and Jack Martin. Westport, Conn.: Praeger.

Brown, Lawrence A., Frank E. Horton, and Robert I. Wittick. 1970. "On Place Utility and the Normative Allocation of Intra-Urban Migrants." *Demography* 7(2): 175–83.

Brown, Lawrence A., and Eric G. Moore. 1970. "The Intraurban Migration Process: A Perspective." *Geografiska Annaler B* 52(1): 1–13.

Charles, Camille Zubrinsky. 2003. "The Dynamics of Racial Residential Segregation." *Annual Review of Sociology* 29(1): 167–207.

———. 2006. *Won't You Be My Neighbor: Race, Class, and Residence in Los Angeles.* New York: Russell Sage Foundation.

Chen, Cynthia, and Haiyun Lin. 2012. "How Far Do People Search for Housing? Analyzing the Roles of Housing Supply, Intra-household Dynamics, and the Use of Information Channels." *Housing Studies* 27(7): 898–914.

Clark, Bridget. 2013. "Employing Simulation Methodology to Test the Effects of Mortgage Discrimination on Residential Segregation." *Sociological Insight* 5(1): 16–30.

Clark, William A. V. 1986. "Residential Segregation in American Cities: A Review and Interpretation." *Population Research and Policy Review* 5(2): 95–127.

———. 1988. "Understanding Residential Segregation in American Cities: Interpreting the Evidence." *Population Research and Policy Review* 7(2): 113–21.

———. 1989. "Residential Segregation in American Cities: Common Ground and Differences in Interpretation." *Population Research and Policy Review* 8(2): 193–97.

———. 2009. "Changing Residential Preferences Across Income, Education, and Age: Findings from the Multi-City Study of Urban Inequality." *Urban Affairs Review* 44(3): 334–55.

Clark, William A. V., and T. R. Smith. 1979. "Modeling Information Use in a Spatial Context." *Annals of the Association of American Geographers* 69(4): 575–88.

Condron, Dennis J., Danial Tope, Christina R. Steidl, and Kendralin J. Freeman. 2013. "Racial Segregation and the Black/White Achievement Gap, 1992 to 2009." *Sociological Quarterly* 54(1): 130–57.

Crowder, Kyle D. 2000. "The Racial Context of White Mobility: An Individual-Level Assessment of the White Flight Hypothesis." *Social Science Research* 29(2): 223–57.

Crowder, Kyle D., and Liam Downey. 2010. "Inter-neighborhood Migration, Race, and Environmental Hazards: Modeling Micro-Level Processes of Environmental Inequality." *American Journal of Sociology* 115(4): 1110–149.

Crowder, Kyle, Matthew Hall, and Stewart Tolnay. 2011. "Neighborhood Immigrant Concentrations and Native Mobility." *American Sociological Review* 76(1): 25–47.

Crowder, Kyle D., Jeremy Pais, and Scott J. South. 2012. "Neighborhood Diversity, Metropolitan Constraints, and Household Migration." *American Sociological Review* 77(3): 325–53.

Crowder, Kyle D., and Scott J. South. 2003. "Neighborhood Distress and School Dropout: The Variable Significance of Community Context." *Social Science Research* 32(4): 659–98.

———. 2005. "Race, Class, and Changing Patterns of Migration Between Poor and Nonpoor Neighborhoods." *American Journal of Sociology* 110(6): 1715–763.

———. 2008. "Spatial Dynamics of White Flight: The Effects of Local and Extralocal Racial Conditions on Neighborhood Out-Migration." *American Sociological Review* 73(5): 792–812.

———. 2011. "Spatial and Temporal Dimensions of Neighborhood Effects on High School Graduation." *Social Science Research* 40(1): 87–106.

Crowder, Kyle D., Scott J. South, and Erick Chavez. 2006. "Wealth, Race, and Inter-neighborhood Migration." *American Sociological Review* 71(1): 72–94.

DeLuca, Stefanie A. 2012. "What Is the Role of Housing Policy? Considering Choice and Social Science Evidence." *Journal of Urban Affairs* 34(1): 21–28.

DeLuca, Stefanie A., Peter Rosenblatt, and Holly Wood. 2012. "Why Poor People Move (and Where They Go): Residential Mobility, Selection, and Stratification." Paper presented at 82nd annual meeting of the American Sociological Association. Las Vegas (February 23–26, 2012).

Denton, Nancy A., and Douglas S. Massey. 1991. "Patterns of Neighborhood Transition in a Multiethnic World: U.S. Metropolitan Areas, 1970–1980." *Demography* 28(1): 41–63.

Diez Roux, Ana V., and Christina Mair. 2010. "Neighborhoods and Health." *Annals of the New York Academy of Sciences,* 1186: 125–145.

Ellen, Ingrid Gould. 2000. *Sharing America's Neighborhoods: the Prospects for Stable Racial Integration.* Cambridge, Mass.: Harvard University Press.

Emerson, Michael O., Karen J. Chai, and George Yancey. 2001. "Does Race Matter in Residential Segregation? Exploring the Preferences of White Americans." *American Sociological Review* 66(6): 922–35.

Farley, Reynolds. 2011. "The Waning of American Apartheid?" *Contexts* 10(3): 36–43.

Fan, Yingling, and Asad J. Khattak. 2008. "Urban Form, Individual Spatial Footprints, and Travel: Examination of Space-Use Behavior." *Journal of the Transportation Research Board* 2082(1): 98–106.

Fasenfest, David, Jason Booza, and Kurt Metzger. 2004. *Living Together: A New Look at Racial and Ethnic Integration in Metropolitan Neighborhoods, 1990–2000.* Washington, D.C.: Brookings Institution.

Fischer, Mary, and Douglas S. Massey. 2004. "The Ecology of Racial Discrimination." *City and Community* 3(3): 221–41.

Friedman, Samantha. 2008. "Do Declines in Residential Segregation Mean Stable Neighborhood Racial Integration in Metropolitan America? A Research Note." *Social Science Research* 37(3): 920–33.

Friedman, Samantha, Hui-shien Tsao, and Cheng Chen. 2013. "Housing Tenure and Residential Segregation in Metropolitan America." *Demography* 50(4): 1–22.

Galster, George. 1988. "Residential Segregation in American Cities: A Contrary Review." *Population Research and Policy Review* 7(2): 93–112.

———. 1989. "Residential Segregation in American Cities: A Further Response to Clark." *Population Research and Policy Review* 8(2): 181–92.

———. 1998. "A Stock/Flow Model of Defining Racially Integrated Neighborhoods." *Journal of Urban Affairs* 20(1): 43–51.

———. 2013. "U.S. Assisted Housing Programs and Poverty Deconcentration: A Critical Geographic Review." In *Neighbourhood Effects or Neighbourhood Based Problems?* edited by David Manley, Maarten van Ham, Nick Bailey, and Ludi Simpson. Dordrecht: Springer Netherlands.

GeoLytics. 2008. *CensusCD Neighborhood Change Database 1970–2000 Tract Data* [Machine-readable database]. Available online at: http://www.geolytics.com/USCensus,Neighborhood-Change-Database-1970–2000,Products.asp.

———. 2012. *2010 Summary File (SF1) in 2000 Boundaries* [Machine-readable database]. Available online at: http://www.geolytics.com/USCensus,2010-Normalized-Data,Products.asp.

Kleniewski, Nancy. 1986. "Triage and Urban Planning: A Case Study of Philadelphia." *International Journal of Urban and Regional Research* 10(4): 563–79.

Kramer, Michael R., and Carol R. Hogue. 2009. "Is Segregation Bad for Your Health?" *Epidemiologic Reviews* 31(1): 178–194.

Kramer, Michael R., Lance A. Waller, Anne L. Dunlop, and Carol R. Hogue (2012). "Housing Transitions and Low Birth Weight Among Low-Income Women: Longitudinal Study of the Perinatal Consequences of Changing Public Housing Policy." *American Journal of Public Health* 102(12): 2255–261. doi: 10.2105/AJPH.2012.300782

Krivo, Lauren J., Ruth D. Peterson, and Danielle C. Kuhl. 2009. "Segregation, Racial Structure, and Neighborhood Violent Crime." *American Journal of Sociology* 114(6): 1765–1802.

Krivo, Lauren J., Heather M. Washington, Ruth D. Peterson, Christopher R. Browning, Catherine A. Calder, and Mei-Po Kwan. 2013. "Social Isolation of Disadvantage and Advantage: The Reproduction of Inequality in Urban Space." *Social Forces* 92(1): 141–64.

Krysan, Maria. 2002. "Whites Who Say They'd Flee: Who Are They and Why Would They Leave?" *Demography* 39(4): 675–96.

———. 2008. "Does Race Matter in the Search for Housing? An Exploratory Study of Search Strategies, Experiences, and Locations." *Social Science Research* 37(2): 581–603.

———. 2011. "Race and Residence from the Telescope to the Microscope." *Context* 10(3): 38–42.

Krysan, Maria, and Michael D. M. Bader. 2007. "Perceiving the Metropolis: Seeing the City Through a Prism of Race." *Social Forces* 86(2): 699–733.

———. 2009. "Racial Blind Spots: Black-White-Latino Differences in Community Knowledge." *Social Problems* 56(4): 677–701.

Krysan, Maria, Mick P. Couper, Reynolds Farley, and Tyrone Forman. 2009. "Does Race Matter in Neighborhood Preferences? Results from a Video Experiment." *American Journal of Sociology* 115(2): 527–59.

Krysan, Maria, and Reynolds Farley. 2002. "The Residential Preferences of Blacks: Do They Explain Persistent Segregation?" *Social Forces* 80(2): 937–80.

Krysan, Maria, Reynolds Farley, and Mick P. Couper. 2008. "In the Eye of the Beholder: Racial Beliefs and Residential Segregation." *The DuBois Review* 5(1): 5–26.

Lee, Everett S. 1966. "A Theory of Migration." *Demography* 3(1): 47–57.

Lewis, Valerie A., Michael O. Emerson, and Stephen Klineberg. 2011. "Residential Segregation and Neighborhood Racial Composition Preferences of Whites, Blacks, and Latinos." *Social Forces* 89(4): 1386–407.

Lipsitz, George, and Melvin L. Oliver. 2010. "Integration, Segregation, and the Racial Wealth Gap." In *The Integration Debate: Competing Futures for American Cities,* edited by C. Hartman and G. Squires. New York: Routledge.

Loewen, James W. 2005. *Sundown Towns: A Hidden Dimension of American Racism.* New York: New Press.

Logan, John R., and Harvey L. Molotch. 1987. *Urban Fortunes: The Political Economy of Place.* Berkeley: University of California Press.

Logan, John R., and Brian Stults. 2011. "The Persistence of Segregation in the Metropolis: New Findings from the 2010 Census." Census Brief prepared for

Project US2010. Available at: http://www.s4.brown.edu/us2010 (accessed November 1, 2013).

Logan, John R., Deirdre Oakley, and Jacob Stowell. 2008. "School Segregation in Metropolitan Regions, 1970–2000: The Impacts of Policy Choices on Public Education." *American Journal of Sociology* 113(6): 1611–44.

Logan, John R., Brian J. Stults, and Reynolds Farley. 2004. "Segregation of Minorities in the Metropolis: Two Decades of Change." *Demography* 41(1): 1–22.

Long, Larry H. 1988. *Migration and Residential Mobility in the United States.* New York: Russell Sage Foundation.

Marsh, Kris, Kivan Polimis, and Kyle Crowder. 2013. "Adolescent Experiences and Adult Neighborhood Attainment." Paper presented at the meetings of the Population Association of America. New York (August 9, 2013).

Massey, Douglas S., and Nancy A. Denton. 1993. *American Apartheid: Segregation and the Making of the Underclass.* Cambridge, Mass.: Harvard University Press.

Massey, Douglas S., and Mary J. Fischer. 2006. "The Effect of Childhood Segregation on Minority Academic Performance at Selective Colleges." *Ethnic and Racial Studies* 29(1): 1–26.

Massey, Douglas S., Andrew B. Gross, and Mitchell L. Eggers. 1991. "Segregation, the Concentration of Poverty and the Life Chances of Individuals." *Social Science Research* 20(4): 397–420.

Massey, Douglas S., and Shawn M. Kanaiaupuni. 1993. "Public Housing and the Concentration of Poverty." *Social Science Quarterly* 74(1): 109–22.

Massey, Douglas S., and Garvey Lundy. 2001. "Use of Black English and Racial Discrimination in Urban Housing Markets." *Urban Affairs Review* 36(4): 452–69.

Meyer, Stephen Grant. 1999. *As Long as They Don't Move Next Door: Segregation and Neighborhood Conflict in American Neighborhoods.* Lanham, Md.: Rowman and Littlefield.

Moore, Latetia V., and Ana V. Diez Roux. 2006. "Associations of Neighborhood Characteristics with the Location and Type of Food Stores." *American Journal of Public Health* 96(2): 325–31.

Neild, Ruth Curran, and Robert Balfanz. 2006. *Unfulfilled Promise: The Dimensions and Characteristics of Philadelphia's Dropout Crisis, 2000–2005.* Baltimore, Md.: Center for Social Organization of Schools, The Johns Hopkins University.

Nuru-Jeter, Amani M., and Thomas LaVeist. 2011. "Racial Segregation, Income Inequality, and Mortality in U.S. Metropolitan Areas." *Journal of Urban Health* 88(2): 270–82.

Oliver, Melvin, and Thomas Shapiro. 2006. *Black Wealth/White Wealth: A New Perspective on Racial Inequality.* New York: Routledge.

Orfield, Myron. 2002. *American Metropolitics: The New Suburban Reality.* Washington, D.C.: Brookings Institution.

Pager, Devah, and Hana Shepherd. 2008. "The Sociology of Discrimination: Racial Discrimination in Employment, Housing, Credit, and Consumer Markets." *Annual Review of Sociology* 34:181–209.

Pais, Jeremy, Scott J. South, and Kyle Crowder. 2012. "Metropolitan Heterogeneity and Minority Neighborhood Attainment: Spatial Assimilation or Place Stratification?" *Social Problems* 59(2): 258–81.

Pattillo-McCoy, Mary. 2000. *Black Picket Fences: Privilege and Peril Among the Black Middle Class.* Chicago: University of Chicago Press.

Peterson, Ruth D., and Lauren J. Krivo. 2010. *Divergent Social Worlds: Neighborhood Crime and the Racial-Spatial Divide.* New York: Russell Sage Foundation.

Quillian, Lincoln. 2012. "Segregation and Poverty Concentration: The Role of Three Segregations." *American Sociological Review* 77(3): 354–79.

Rashidi, Taha Hossein, Joshua Auld, and Abolfazl Kouros Mohammadian. 2012. "A Behavioral Housing Search Model: Two-Stage Hazard-Based and Multinomial Logit Approach to Choice-Set Formation and Location Selection." *Transportation Research Part A: Policy and Practice* 46(7): 1097–107.

Rawlings, Lynette, Laura Harris, and Margery Austin Turner. 2004. "Race and Residence: Prospects for Stable Neighborhood Integration." *Neighborhood Change in Urban America* no. 3. Washington, D.C.: The Urban Institute.

Reardon, Sean F., Elena Tej Grewal, Demetra Kalogrides, and Erica Greenberg. 2012. "Brown Fades: The End of Court-Ordered School Desegregation and the Resegregation of American Public Schools." *Journal of Policy Analysis and Management* 31(4): 876–904.

Roscigno, Vincent J., Diana L. Karafin, and Griff Tester. 2009. "The Complexities and Processes of Racial Housing Discrimination." *Social Problems* 56(1): 49–69.

Ross, Stephen L., and Margery Austin Turner. 2005. "Housing Discrimination in Metropolitan America: Explaining Changes Between 1989 and 2000." *Social Problems* 52(2): 152–80.

Rothwell, Jonathan, and Douglas S. Massey. 2009. "The Effect of Density Zoning on Racial Segregation in U.S. Urban Areas." *Urban Affairs Review* 44(6): 779–806.

Rugh, Jacob S., and Douglas S. Massey. 2010. "Racial Segregation and the American Foreclosure Crisis." *American Sociological Review* 75(5): 629–51.

Russell, Emily F., Michael R. Kramer, Hannah L.F. Couper, Sheryl Gabram-Mendola, Diana Senior-Crosby, and Kimberly R. Jacob Arriola. 2012. "Metropolitan Area Racial Residential Segregation, Neighborhood Racial Composition, and Breast Cancer Mortality." *Cancer Causes and Control* 23(9): 1519–27.

Sampson, Robert J. 2012. *Great American City: Chicago and the Enduring Neighborhood Effect.* Chicago: University of Chicago Press.

Sampson, Robert J., and Patrick Sharkey. 2008. "Neighborhood Selection and the Social Reproduction of Concentrated Racial Inequality." *Demography* 45(1): 1–29.

Saporito, Salvatore, and Annette Lareau. 1999. "School Selection as a Process: The Multiple Dimensions of Race in Framing Educational Choice." *Social Problems* 46(3): 418–39.

Satter, Beryl. 2010. *Family Properties: Race, Real Estate, and the Exploitation of Black Urban America.* New York: Metropolitan Books.

Schill, Michael H., and Susan M. Wachter. 1995. "The Spatial Bias of Federal Housing Law and Policy: Concentrated Poverty in Urban America." *University of Pennsylvania Law Review* 143(5): 1285–342.

Seitles, Marc. 1998. "The Perpetuation of Residential Racial Segregation in America: Historical Discrimination, Modern Forms of Exclusion, and Inclusionary Remedies." *Journal of Land Use and Environmental Law* 14(1): 89–124.

Sharkey, Patrick. 2008. "The Intergenerational Transmission of Context." *American Journal of Sociology* 113(4): 931–69.

———. 2012. "Temporary Integration, Resilient Inequality: Race and Neighborhood Change in the Transition to Adulthood." *Demography* 49(3): 889–912.

Smith, Robin E., Arthur Naparstek, Susan Popkin, Lesley Bartlett, Lisa Bates, Jessica Cigna, Russell Crane, and Elisa Vinson. 2002. "Housing Choice for HOPE VI Relocatees." Washington, D.C.: The Urban Institute. www.urban.org/uploadedpdf/410592_HOPEVI_Relocatees.pdf

Smith, Terence R., William A. V. Clark, James O. Huff, and Perry Shapiro. 1979. "A Decision-Making and Search Model for Intraurban Migration." *Geographical Analysis* 11(1): 1–22.

South, Scott J., Kyle Crowder, and Jeremy Pais. 2008. "Inter-neighborhood Migration and Spatial Assimilation in a Multi-ethnic World: Comparing Latinos, Blacks and Anglos." *Social Forces* 87(1): 415–43.

Spivak, Andrew L., Loretta E. Bass, and Craig St. John. 2011. "Reconsidering Race, Class, and Residential Segregation in American Cities." *Urban Geography* 32(4): 531–67.

Squires, Gregory D. 1994. *Capital and Communities in Black and White: The Intersections of Race, Class, and Uneven Development.* Albany: State University of New York Press.

———. 2007. "Demobilization of the Individualistic Bias: Housing Market Discrimination as a Contributor to Labor Market and Economic Inequality." *The Annals of the American Academy of Political and Social Science* 609(1): 200–14.

Sugrue, Thomas J. 2005. *The Origins of the Urban Crisis: Race and Inequality in Postwar Detroit.* Princeton, N.J.: Princeton University Press.

Swaroop, Sapna, and Maria Krysan. 2011. "The Determinants of Neighborhood Satisfaction: Racial Prejudice and Racial Proxy Revisited." *Demography* 48(3): 1203–229.

Swisher, Raymond R., Danielle C. Kuhl, and Jorge M. Chavez. 2013. "Racial and Ethnic Differences in Neighborhood Attainments in the Transition to Adulthood." *Social Forces.* 91(4): 1399–428.

Taub, Richard P., D. Garth Taylor, and Jan D. D. Dunham. 1984. *Paths of Neighborhood Change: Race and Crime in Urban America.* Chicago: University of Chicago Press.

Theall, Katherine P., Stacy S. Drury, and Elizabeth A. Shirtcliff. 2012. "Cumulative Neighborhood Risk of Psychosocial Stress and Allostatic Load in Adolescents." *American Journal of Epidemiology* 176(Suppl. 7): S164–74.

Timberlake, Jeffrey, and John Iceland. 2007 "Change in Racial and Ethnic Residential Inequality in American Cities, 1970–2000." *City and Community* 6(4): 335–65.

Turner, Margery Austin. 2008 "Residential Segregation and Employment Inequality" In *Segregation: The Rising Costs for America,* edited by J. H. Carr and N. K. Kutty. New York, NY: Taylor and Francis.

Turner, Margery Austin, and Stephen L. Ross. 2005. "How Racial Discrimination Affects the Housing Search." In *The Geography of Opportunity: Race and Housing Choice in Metropolitan America,* edited by Xavier de Souza Briggs. Washington, D.C.: Brookings Institution.

United States Census Bureau. 2012. 2006–2010 American Community Survey. U.S. Census Bureau's American Community Survey Office. Available at: www.census.gov/acs (accessed August 1, 2012).

vonLockette, Niki Dickerson. 2010. "The Impact of Metropolitan Residential Segregation on the Employment Chances of Blacks and Whites in the U.S." *City and Community* 9(3): 256–73.

Wagmiller, Robert L. 2013. "Blacks' and Whites' Experiences of Neighborhood Racial and Ethnic Diversity Intercohort Variation in Neighborhood Diversity and Integration in Early and Early Middle Adulthood." *Urban Affairs Review* 49(1): 32–70.

Williams, David R., and Pamela Braboy Jackson. 2005. "Origins of Disparities: Social Sources of Racial Disparities in Health." *Health Affairs* 24(2): 325–34.

Wilson, William Julius. 1987. *The Truly Disadvantaged: The Inner-City, the Underclass, and Public Policy.* Chicago: University of Chicago Press.

Wilson, William Julius, and Richard P. Taub. 2006. *There Goes the Neighborhood: Racial, Ethnic, and Class Tensions in Four Chicago Neighborhoods and Their Meaning for America.* New York: Alfred A. Knopf.

Wright, Richard, Mark Ellis, Steven R. Holloway, and Sandy Wong. 2013. "Patterns of Racial Diversity and Segregation in the United States: 1990–2010." *The Professional Geographer* 65(1): 33–124.

Yinger, John. 1995. *Closed Doors, Opportunities Lost: The Continuing Costs of Housing Discrimination.* New York: Russell Sage Foundation.

= Chapter 3 =

Declining Significance of Race?

SALVATORE SAPORITO AND CAROLINE HANLEY

As we approach the fiftieth anniversary of the Civil Rights Act, race remains a powerful social category that shapes patterns of residence and educational opportunity in the United States. This volume examines the relationship between patterns of residential and educational choice, seeking to problematize the concept of choice by asking how it reproduces social inequalities by race and class. As Paul Jargowsky demonstrates in chapter 4 of this volume, residential segregation by race and by class are mutually reinforcing, with racial segregation playing a key role in shaping patterns of economic segregation. Jargowsky shows that black-white residential segregation declined between 1990 and 2000—thereby demonstrating that the most recent declines in black-white residential segregation are consistent with the steady decadal declines that scholars have observed between 1970 and 2010 (Iceland 2009; Logan and Stults 2011). Still, black-white residential segregation remains high in most metropolitan areas and their core cities, and residential segregation drives racial inequality in public schools.

This chapter approaches the relationship between residential and educational segregation by race from a different perspective by focusing on the relationship between community racial composition and white private school choice. Previous research shows that white families are more likely to leave public schools as the proportion of black children in their community increases (Saporito 2003, 2009). The correlation between community racial composition and the school choices of white children has been directly linked with racial segregation in public schools (Saporito and Sohoni 2007). Yet, no studies have examined these patterns historically, over the entire post–civil rights period, and across a nationally representative sample of places. Developing a historical perspective describing the relationship between community racial composition and school choice is important because it directs attention to the shifting social context that shapes the actions of individuals, including school choice. As Kimberly Goyette discusses in chapter 1 of this volume, changes in the legal framework supporting racial integration and in the control and financing of education are institutional factors that may inform both the decision to send one's children to a private school, and the consequences of that decision for those families and their wider communities.

We examine the changing relationship between community racial composition and private school enrolment among white families from 1970 to 2010 using decennial U.S. Census data to evaluate the relative magnitude of household- and community-level factors that are correlated with private school enrollment—and, critically, whether these factors have changed between 1970 and 2010. We find that race remains a relatively important factor in predicting private school enrollment compared with other predictors such as a community's poverty rate or the social and economic characteristics of a child's family. Thus, compared with other predictors of private school enrollment, race still remains a relatively important factor shaping white parents' decisions to enroll their children in private schools.

Residential and School Segregation

A large body of literature seeks to unpack the causes of black-white residential segregation and public school segregation, as well as the relationship between the two. As Goyette discusses in chapter 1, black-white residential segregation declined substantially between 1980 and 2000 but remains high in absolute terms. Black-white school segregation, meanwhile, declined in the 1970s and 1980s but increased dramatically in the 1990s. Although residential segregation is a key dynamic contributing to public school segregation, school segregation is both greater in magnitude and more persistent than residential segregation. Private schools and public school choice programs are alternative processes contributing to public school segregation.

As Maria Krysan, Kyle Crowder, and Michael Bader discuss in chapter 2 of this volume, multiple potential mechanisms may contribute to residential segregation and, by extension, public school segregation. Krysan, Crowder, and Bader outline the Big Three explanations—economics, discrimination, and preferences—as well as interactions among the Big Three, information asymmetries, and differences in community knowledge and life course experiences. Following a preponderance of the sociological evidence, we adopt a preferences-based perspective and, specifically, use the concept of *out-group aversion* to inform our analysis and derive expectations. This perspective holds that preferences perpetuate segregation as members of sociohistorically advantaged groups try to maintain those advantages by avoiding social spaces occupied by disadvantaged groups. In the U.S. context, white Americans maintain segregation by avoiding neighborhoods and schools occupied by black people, even as the choices of black people, as a group, are invariant with the racial composition of neighborhoods and schools (for example, Clark 1991). However, as Krysan, Crowder, and Bader discuss in chapter 2 of this volume, preferences may be informed by individual prejudice, negative stereotypes, or the institutional structures that create opportunities and rewards for avoiding social spaces associated with out-groups. In other words, race-based and race-associated reasons for white preferences are often conceptually and empirically indistinct.

The purpose of this chapter is not to adjudicate the relative importance of factors that lead to racial segregation. Rather, we offer a historical analysis of the changing association between community racial composition and white families' likelihood of private school choice in the post–civil rights era. The analysis is important because regardless of the direct or indirect causes of white preferences, in the aggregate these actions have consequences. Mary Pattillo (2008) demonstrates how racial and class segregation are maintained by individuals who seek to secure or preserve social resources by moving to white and middle-class neighborhoods and organizing politically to prevent the influx of people who are considered undesirable. Crucially, the process of securing or maintaining resources for one group "necessarily leads to resource deficits for another group or neighborhood" (Pattillo 2008, 264). The types of residential neighborhoods and schools that families choose create and maintain group-level patterns of inequality. As white individuals seek neighborhoods and schools with higher proportions of white and wealthy people, the cumulative consequences of these choices leads to group-level inequality in which members of racially and economically disadvantaged groups are isolated in poor and minority neighborhoods and schools. The cumulative consequences of individual choices thus contribute to group-level patterns of racial segregation in both neighborhoods and schools.

Just as others have applied the concept of out-group aversion to understanding residential choices, we apply this perspective to the choice to send one's children to a private school. Since the 1970s, changes in legal and educational institutions have produced shifting social contexts for enacting out-group aversion. As widespread enforcement of court-ordered school integration emerged in the mid- to late 1970s—discussed in more detail in chapter 1 of this volume—white families began to avoid the prospect of integration by enrolling their children in private schools, especially if moving to white neighborhoods became less effective as a strategy for avoiding integrated schools. In the 1990s, the options for families wishing to avoid their neighborhood public schools multiplied with the growth of private, magnet and charter schools, along with related changes in local education funding (see chapter 1, this volume). Private school choice among white families thus emerged as a mechanism by which whites enact out-group aversion. Yet we do not know how school choice patterns have changed historically.

Neighborhood Composition and School Choice

Recent studies confirm that the choice of private, charter, and magnet schools by white families is responsive to community racial composition, and this association is consistent with the model of out-group aversion. However, existing studies have failed to examine the historical trend in the relationship between neighborhood composition and the school choices of white families across a nationally representative sample of places and over the entire post–civil rights period. Existing studies have also largely ignored the relative importance of racial composition compared with other household- and community-level predictors of private and public school choice. In this section, we review the evidence linking white school choice and neighborhood racial composition, and derive expectations for their historical relationship that guide our empirical analysis.

Case studies of individual cities indicate that community racial composition is a significant predictor of white families' choice to send their children to private schools. Haifeng Zhang (2008) uses detailed evidence on private school enrollment in the Columbia, South Carolina, metropolitan area from 1987 to 2003 and finds that white private school enrollment is significantly correlated with both the proportion of minorities in neighborhood schools and neighborhood racial composition. Similarly, Salvatore Saporito (2003) examines magnet school choice in Philadelphia for the 1999–2000 school year and finds that white families are more likely to apply to a magnet school as shares of nonwhite children in their school attendance zones increase—even when a wide range of family, school and attendance zone characteristics are controlled.

Studies using nationally or regionally representative data for selected years are consistent with these cases. Nationally representative data from 1980 demonstrate that private school enrollment rates among white children increase as the minority share of their county's or metropolitan statistical area (MSA)'s school-age population increases (Li 2009). Analyses of national data from the 1997–1998 school year show that black-white segregation is higher in private schools than public schools and differences in white and minority private school enrollment contribute to overall patterns of school segregation (Reardon and Yun 2003a). Investigation of private school enrollment among white, black, Asian, and Hispanic students from 1990 to 2000 also supports the perspective of out-group aversion: unlike that of their counterparts from other racial groups, white families' choice of private schools is strongly influenced by the representation of black children in their communities (Saporito 2009). A comparison of racial segregation in public schools and their catchment areas in the twenty-one largest school districts in the United States in 2000 affirms that private school enrollment contributes to public school segregation (Saporito and Sohoni 2007). Finally, an analysis of southern counties shows that white flight to private schools increased between 1970 and 1980 and persisted for during the following decades—between 1980 and 2000 the proportions of white children who enrolled in private school remained highly responsive to the presence of black children in those areas (Reardon and Yun 2003b). Thus, studies indicate that school choice among white families—whether for private, charter, or magnet schools—is correlated with racial composition (even while holding constant a variety of individual and school-level characteristics). The pattern of out-group aversion exhibited in school choice is consistent with evidence generated by scholars who study residential choice.

This chapter builds on the existing literature by asking how the association between private school enrollment and community racial composition among white students varies across the entire post–civil rights period. Understanding the historical association between the school choice of white students and community racial composition is important for understanding how patterns of racial aversion have sustained racial segregation in both schools and residential areas. Although our chapter examines historical trends in private school enrollment only, ample evidence suggests that our narrow focus on private schools is consistent with the preferences and choices of white families across a variety of settings (that is, magnet schools, charters schools, school districts, school catchment areas, census tracts). Moreover, Stephanie Ewert (2013) finds that the proportion of K–12 students enrolled in private school has fluctuated between about 8 to 10 percent between 1970 and 2011. Indeed, our evidence shows that private school enrollment rates among white students have remained consistent between 1970 and 2010 (see table 3.1). Although no studies examine trends in racial segregation in private schools, Ewert's research finds that, as of 2011, a larger share of private school students are white (about 75 percent) than in the United States as a whole (about 63 percent). Finally, analyses of data from the Private School Survey indicate that private schools are at least as segregated as public schools (Reardon and Yun 2003a). While these findings suggest that private school enrollment patterns likely contribute as much to the overall levels of racial segregation now as in the past, our goal is to see whether the association between private school choice and community racial composition, which we view through the perspective of out-group avoidance, is as important today as yesterday.

Given that many school districts were not compelled to take aggressive steps to desegregate their schools until the 1970s, we theorize that it was

Table 3.1   Descriptive Statistics, Individual and Family Variables

	Six to Eleven					Twelve to Seventeen					All Ages
	1970	1980	1990	2000	2010	1970	1980	1990	2000	2010	Total
	x̄ (σ)	x̄ (σ)	x̄ (σ)	x̄ (σ)	x̄ (σ)	x̄ (σ)	x̄ (σ)	x̄ (σ)	x̄ (σ)	x̄ (σ)	x̄ (σ)
Private school	.13 (.34)	.13 (.34)	.12 (.32)	.14 (.35)	.15 (.35)	.11 (.32)	.11 (.31)	.09 (.29)	.11 (.31)	.13 (.33)	.13 (.33)
Male	.51 (.50)	.51 (.50)	.51 (.50)	.51 (.50)	.51 (.50)	.51 (.50)	.51 (.50)	.51 (.50)	.51 (.50)	.52 (.50)	.51 (.51)
Married couple	.91 (.29)	.87 (.34)	.85 (.36)	.81 (.39)	.81 (.39)	.89 (.31)	.85 (.35)	.83 (.38)	.79 (.41)	.78 (.41)	.84 (.37)
Number siblings	2.49 (1.59)	1.69 (1.18)	1.56 (1.11)	1.53 (1.13)	1.59 (1.18)	2.28 (1.68)	1.75 (1.27)	1.41 (1.15)	1.38 (1.15)	1.38 (1.18)	1.6 (1.23)
Family income (in 1,000s)	65.91 (41.37)	61.42 (37.45)	70.93 (57.35)	86.22 (86.02)	94.17 (90.88)	73.11 (46.01)	71.18 (41.48)	78.97 (61.68)	91.83 (86.01)	97.65 (90.66)	77.41 (65.97)
Rent home	.24 (.43)	.22 (.41)	.25 (.43)	.22 (.41)	.21 (.41)	.19 (.39)	.15 (.36)	.19 (.39)	.17 (.38)	.17 (.37)	.20 (.40)
Number rooms in house	6.1 (1.45)	6.39 (1.54)	6.46 (1.61)	6.58 (1.70)	7.41 (2.53)	6.25 (1.44)	6.62 (1.50)	6.65 (1.58)	6.75 (1.64)	7.54 (2.56)	6.59 (1.67)
Number units in structure	3.32 (1.15)	3.33 (1.34)	3.17 (1.25)	3.15 (1.30)	3.16 (1.15)	3.29 (1.08)	3.27 (1.20)	3.13 (1.12)	3.1 (1.15)	3.11 (1.06)	3.2 (1.22)

(Table continues on p. 70.)

Table 3.1   Continued

	Six to Eleven					Twelve to Seventeen					All Ages
	1970	1980	1990	2000	2010	1970	1980	1990	2000	2010	Total
	$\bar{x}$	$\bar{x}$	$\bar{x}$	$\bar{x}$	$\bar{x}$	$\bar{x}$	$\bar{x}$	$\bar{x}$	$\bar{x}$	$\bar{x}$	$\bar{x}$
	(σ)	(σ)	(σ)	(σ)	(σ)	(σ)	(σ)	(σ)	(σ)	(σ)	(σ)
High school education	.44	.41	.29	.32	.21	.42	.43	.31	.34	.24	.35
	(.50)	(.40)	(.45)	(.47)	(.41)	(.49)	(.49)	(.46)	(.47)	(.43)	(.47)
Some college	0.15	0.22	0.34	0.28	0.26	.15	.20	.34	.27	.28	0.26
	(.36)	(.41)	(.47)	(.45)	(.44)	(.36)	(.40)	(.47)	(.45)	(.45)	(.44)
College educated	.19	.25	.31	.36	.50	.18	.23	.29	.35	.45	.30
	(.39)	(.44)	(.46)	(.48)	(.50)	(.38)	(.42)	(.46)	(.48)	(.50)	(.46)
Semi-skilled	.18	.20	.23	.20	.18	.18	.19	.21	.19	.18	.20
	(.38)	(.40)	(.42)	(.40)	(.38)	(.38)	(.39)	(.41)	(.39)	(.38)	(.40)
White collar	.19	.19	.18	.18	.18	.19	.21	.20	.19	.19	.19
	(.39)	(.39)	(.38)	(.38)	(.38)	(.39)	(.40)	(.40)	(.39)	(.39)	(.39)
Professional	.21	.23	.26	.31	.40	.22	.23	.26	.31	.37	.27
	(.41)	(.42)	(.44)	(.46)	(.49)	(.42)	(.42)	(.44)	(.46)	(.48)	(.44)
N	184,790	731,528	714,533	745,438	126,807	178,605	802,020	658,405	743,731	136,311	5,022,168

Source: Authors' calculations.
Note: Standard deviations in parentheses.

not necessary for white families to enroll their children in private schools to avoid integration in public schools until after that time. However, by 1980 many districts were under court order to desegregate—or took voluntary steps to do so. We expect that the enactment of desegregation plans prompted white parents who harbored racial animosity, or who used racial composition as a proxy for the educational quality of their local public schools, to send their children to private schools (and, more recently, to charter schools) to avoid public schools that serve racially integrated residential areas. We therefore expect to find a weaker relationship between private school enrollment and the racial composition of communities in 1970 than in subsequent decades. But we expect these race-based (or race-associated) patterns of private school enrollment among white children to gradually wane after 1980 as Americans' tolerance for racial prejudice declines (Schuman et al. 2001) and support for equal opportunity increases (Farley 1997). Finally, we expect the relative importance of community racial composition as an explanation for private school choice to decrease over time, as class interacts with or supplants race in motivating out-group aversion (for example, Wilson 1978).

Data and Methods

To examine historical patterns in private school enrollment, we assemble data from Public Use Micro Data Sample (PUMS) and the American Community Survey (ACS) data for the entire United States. We do this for five points in time: 1970, 1980, 1990, 2000, and 2010. Data for 1970 to 2000 are from the decennial census and 2010 data are derived from the ACS. To ensure consistency in variables and their categories, we extracted PUMS and ACS data from the Integrated Public Use Micro Data Sample (IPUMS) (Ruggles et al. 2010). The IPUMS dataset harmonizes historical micro data and provides consistent variable names, coding schemes, and documentation across all samples, facilitating the analysis of long-term change. Our analyses include only variables that are available for all samples to ensure comparability of statistical analysis across the five periods.

The sample fraction of the micro data is 5 percent of all households in 1980, 1990, and 2000; the sample fraction is 1 percent in 1970 and 2010 (Minnesota Population Center 2011a). These sampling fractions result in five, reasonably large, nationally representative, cross-sectional samples that allow us to track trends in private school enrollment over five decades, as shown in table 3.1. The decadal samples include students who were enrolled in public or private school; enrolled in kindergarten through twelfth grade; ages six to seventeen; not living in group quarters such a group home or juvenile detention center; and were the biological, adopted, or stepchild of the householder.[1] We conduct separate analyses of students age six to eleven and twelve to seventeen to explore whether historical trends in private school enrollment rates among white students vary by age group.[2]

Our sample is confined to non-Hispanic white students (hereafter *white students*). Our focus on historical trends in private school enrollment rates among white students is based on previous literature that white students are more likely to be enrolled in private school as shares of African American children in their communities increases. By contrast, among students from other racial groups, there is little to no relationship between private school enrollment rates and the racial composition of communities. This is particularly true among African American students—as a group they do not exhibit any tendency to be enrolled in private school as the racial composition of their communities fluctuates (Ledwith 2009; Saporito 2009). Given that prior findings based on local and national datasets reach consistent conclusions with respect to students of color, we examine the historical relationship between private school enrollment rates among white students and the percentage of black children in census areas.

The PUMS data report whether respondents are enrolled in school and, if so, whether the school is public or private. This enables us to construct a binary dependent variable specifying whether a student is enrolled in private school (assigned a value of 1) or public school (equal to 0). We use this dependent variable to create separate estimates of private school enrollment for the five periods from 1970 to 2010. Creating separate models for each year of data simplifies the analyses by eliminating the need to create a large number of interaction terms between year, community racial composition, and the remaining independent variables included in the analyses. Table 3.1 shows that overall private school enrollment rates among non-Hispanic white children have fluctuated modestly from decade to decade. Specifically, the percentage of white students enrolled in private schools ranged from 12 to 15 percentage points among six- to eleven-year-olds and between 11 and 13 points among twelve- to seventeen-year-olds.

Student, Family, and Household Variables

Table 3.1 also contains descriptive statistics for student, family, and household characteristics by year and age group. These variables are incorporated as controls in statistical analyses throughout this chapter. Basic demographic variables include a student's gender (coded as a dummy variable where values of 1 represent male students) and whether a student lives in a married-couple household. We also include the number of siblings with whom a student resides (including half-siblings, step-siblings, and adopted siblings) to measure strain on household resources. We use several variables to capture the social and economic standing of students' families, including parental education, parental occupation, family income, and housing characteristics. To measure educational attainment of parents, we create a series of dummy variables to measure the highest degree earned by a student's mother or father. The four categories are whether the highest degree held by either parent is less than a high school, high school, some college, and at least college. We use less than high school as the reference category in our models. We also use four categorical variables to capture the highest occupational status of a student's parents. The categories are unskilled, blue collar; skilled, blue collar; nonmanagerial, white collar; and professional, manager, or owner (where unskilled, blue collar is the reference category). The variable for family income is measured in 2009 dollars; we adjusted for inflation using the Consumer Price Index Research Series (CPI-U-RS) using current methods (Stewart and Reed 1999). Finally, we measure housing characteristics, including whether a student's home is rented (where rented is equal to 1), the number of units in the structure, and the number of rooms in the housing unit.

Community-Level Measures

In addition to student and household characteristics, we also incorporate several characteristics of Public Use Micro Sample Areas (PUMAs) in which children live. These PUMAs are relatively large areas that contain roughly 100,000 people and are too large to be reasonably considered as proxies for neighborhoods. Although many urban school districts contain multiple PUMAs, it is also true that some PUMAs contain multiple school districts; thus, in rural areas, PUMAs encompass many school districts. These expansive areas are certainly larger than we would like—and do not map onto school attendance boundaries, school districts, or other geographies that are meaningful to the families who live within them. Ideally, we would like to have access to a national database of school catchment areas from 1970 to 2010 but researchers have only just begun to collect such information for the 2009–2010 school year. Even though many urban school districts contain multiple PUMAs, another adequate representation would be school districts—but no dataset exists that embeds individuals within school districts—and a nationwide geography of school districts does not exist before 1980. Moreover, large school districts (such as New York City, Los Angeles, Miami-Dade, Philadelphia) and even midsized ones (such as Richmond, Virginia) have multiple PUMAs per school district. Thus, neither school districts nor PUMAs are ideal indications of neighborhoods. Despite this limitation, to undertake a historical analysis, we resort to the only readily accessible historical data that describes individuals and families nested within communities.

Descriptive statistics for community-level variables are shown in table 3.2. To create community-level variables, we aggregate child and family characteristics to "consistent communities" in which each PUMA in the series covers the exact same geographical area between 1980 and 2010. (We also produce results based on the original PUMAs and show these in the appendix.) There are 543 consistent communities in the 1980

Table 3.2 Descriptive Statistics, Community Variables

	1970		1980		1990		2000		2010		All Years	
	$\bar{x}$	σ	$\bar{x}$	σ	$\bar{x}$	σ	$\bar{x}$	σ	$\bar{x}$	σ	$\bar{x}$	σ
Percent African American	12.0	14.3	12.3	15.2	12.3	15.6	14.0	16.7	13.9	15.5	12.9	15.5
Percent white, non-Hispanic	82.7	17.0	79.6	19.4	76.7	21.0	71.6	23.1	67.9	23.1	74.2	22.0
Black-white dissimilarity*	57.0	19.9	49.2	23.7	43.3	20.1	40.1	18.8	36.9	17.2	45	21
Median family income (in 1,000s)	49.8	10.7	51.3	10.9	56.7	15.7	61.3	16.3	61.3	17.0	54.4	15.3
Percent poor	18.1	10.7	15.8	7.7	18.0	9.1	16.8	8.3	19.5	8.8	17.6	9.0
Percent college educated	9.9	4.1	14.7	6.7	18.5	8.7	22.8	10.2	29.5	11.8	19.6	11.0
Percent blue collar	34.2	7.3	30.7	7.4	27.0	6.9	25.3	6.5	20.8	5.6	27.3	8.1
N	408		543		543		543		543		2,580	

Source: Authors' calculations.
Note: *Multiplied by 100.

to 2010 time series.[3] The 1970 PUMAs are not coincident with the 1980–2010 consistent PUMAs and number 408. Still, we include the 1970 areas in our analysis because their number and size closely reflect those for 1980 to 2010. To measure a community's racial composition, we calculate the percentage of non-Hispanic black children (ages six to seventeen) within them. We also calculate the percentage of students who are non-Hispanic white children and include this variable in the models to account for the presence of other racial groups.[4] We use complete-count census data from the Summary File 1 block-level data set to calculate the percentage of children of a particular racial group. Using complete-count data eliminates estimation error associated with sample data.

To capture the socioeconomic composition of an area, we measure the percentage of persons age twenty-five and older who have a college degree and the percentage of employed persons over twenty-five who are employed as blue-collar workers. Median household income measures average community economic conditions. We use constant 2009 dollars. We also include the percentage of poor students in a community. These variables are all derived from the sample-based PUMS or ACS sample data. Thus, some estimation error is associated with aggregating information describing individuals to PUMAs.[5]

Although PUMAs are far less than ideal as a measure of community, and not a measure of neighborhood, we make a modest attempt to address this issue by examining racial segregation across census tracts within PUMAs. Another concern with PUMAs is that using only the racial composition of PUMAs may mask internal segregation within them. If PUMAs become less internally segregated over time, then the average white family will encounter more black families, given a fixed racial composition, in this case, and the trend in the coefficients for race would be biased— because actual racial composition that families encounter may change differently than the racial composition of their PUMA. To address this issue, we used historical census tract geography and census data from the National Historical Geographic Information System (NHGIS) to measure dissimilarity between black and white people across NHGIS census tracts within PUMA areas (Minnesota Population Center 2011b). To do this, we downloaded census tract geography for 1970 to 2010. We then used GIS to execute a simple areal interpolation that created consistent geographies for all five decades. Specifically, we used an overlay technique in GIS that split off any portion of 1980 census tract located within a 1970 tract. We then consolidated the pieces of the 1980 census tracts to conform to the 1970 outlines. Next, we allocated counts of people by race from the original 1980 tracts to the outlines of the 1970 tracts using areal weighting (Goodchild and Lam 1980). Last, we used the consistent definitions of census tracts to calculate black-white segregation across tracts within PUMA areas using the index of dissimilarity.

Table 3.3   Correlation Coefficients, Community Variables

		(1)	(2)	(3)	(4)	(5)	(6)	(7)
Percent African American	(1)	1.00						
Percent white	(2)	−.68	1.00					
Black-white dissimilarity	(3)	.20	−.09	1.00				
Median family income	(4)	−.16	.05	.08	1.00			
Percent poor	(5)	.52	−.57	−.06	−.68	1.00		
Percent college educated	(6)	.43	−.20	−.06	.78	−.31	1.00	
Percent blue collar	(7)	−.05	.29	.01	−.57	.15	−.83	1.00

Source: Authors' calculations.
Note: All years pooled.

Table 3.3 shows the correlations among community-level variables. There are slight to modest correlations between the percentage of people who are black (column 1) and other community-level variables. For example, the correlation coefficient between percentage of black students and percentage of white students is −0.68 and it is 0.52 between percentage black students and percentage poor people. None of the community-level correlations are collinear.

Ideally, we would like to have included school quality data to assess the extent to which parents' choices for schools are driven by factors such as school test scores. However, census micro data do not allow us to integrate school-level information into our analysis because neither the boundaries of school catchment areas nor school districts correspond with PUMAs. Although we can determine the extent to which private school enrollment is correlated with a community's racial composition, we cannot determine whether such a correlation would diminish (or potentially disappear) if we could incorporate a complete set of factors that parents might consider when making school choices. We also wanted to include measures of community safety and the religious denomination of students' families. Here again the decennial census do not collect this information. For example, it would be helpful to control for the percentage of a community's population of a particular religious denomination but no historical data exist that could be used to estimate religious populations in census communities.

Despite the unavailability of data that limit our ability to make robust causal inferences regarding the association between private school enrollment and the racial composition of local communities, our data do allow us to explore how much patterns of private school enrollment are correlated with the racial composition of communities in which children live. As Eric Brunner, Jennifer Imazeki, and Stephen Ross (2006) note, correlations between student race and the racial composition of local communities provide the opportunity to explore whether private school enrollment patterns might contribute to racial segregation of local public schools above and beyond that due to residential patterns—even if such correlations do not represent strong evidence that the racial composition of communities per se influences white families to enroll their children in private schools. It is also important to emphasize that our research question explores whether correlations between area racial composition and private school enrollment rates among non-Hispanic white children have attenuated—thus providing small clues as to whether recent, steady declines in racial segregation across residential areas (and to a lesser extent in schools) might be related to increases in racial tolerance and concomitant decreases in white flight to private schools and white neighborhoods.

Statistical Modeling Procedures

Given that the dependent variable is binary (where enrollment in private school equals 1) and children are nested within communities, we use two-level random intercept logistic regression models to estimate the probability that a student is enrolled in private school. We use Stata's xtlogit command to fit random intercept models; this procedure uses numerical integration based on adaptive Gauss-Hermite quadrature. We use twelve quadrature points because a larger number has virtually no impact on the regression coefficients. The two-level models address the assumption that school enrollment among students in the same communities are independent by including community-specific random intercepts in the regression models. Because random intercept models correct for potential intracluster correlations of students' characteristics, it produces more efficient parameter estimates and reduces bias in the standard errors (Guo and Zhao 2000; Wong and Mason 1985).

If y_{ij} is a binary dependent variable for student i in community j, x_{ij} represents the values of independent variables, and u_j is a random intercept for each community, then the log odds that a student attends private school $p_{ij} = Pr(y_{ij} = 1)$ is are

$$\log \frac{p_{ij}}{1 - p_{ij}} = \beta_0 + \beta_1 x_{ij} + u_j$$

For ease of interpretation, we graph estimated probabilities of private school enrollment across communities that vary in the percentage of their population that is black. Because each model includes a random intercept for each community, producing marginal probabilities necessitates integrating out the random intercept (u_j):

$$Pr(y_{ij} = 1) = \int \frac{e(\beta_0 + \beta_1 x_{ij} + u_j)}{1 + e(\beta_0 + \beta_1 x_{ij} + u_j)}$$

The predicted probabilities shown in this study represent the effect of community racial composition after accounting for other community characteristics that may influence the probability that a child attends private school. The estimated probabilities depicted in the graphs shown throughout this paper hold constant all control variables at their means— as shown in the total columns of tables 3.1 and 3.2. Values for dummy variables are set at either 0 or 1.[6]

To avoid creating an unwieldy number of interaction terms, we create separate regression models by year and age group. That is, we specify models for 1970, 1980, 1990, 2000, and 2010 and, within each of these five time points, create two separate models for each age range. To examine change over time in the relative importance of community racial composition versus other community- and individual-level factors as predictors of private school enrollment, we use a recent statistical method developed by Scott Menard (2011) that allows us to construct a fully standardized regression coefficient—b_M^*—for logistic regression results. Menard demonstrates that the construction and interpretation of b_M^* directly parallels the standardized coefficients in linear regression, and correspondingly, it is possible to apply the same standards used to interpret standardized coefficients in linear regression to fully standardized coefficients in logistic regression. Values for b_M^* are produced using the following formula:

$$b_M^* = b(s_x)R/S_{logit(\hat{Y})}$$

where b is the unstandardized logistic regression coefficient for a given independent variable, s_x is the standard deviation of the independent variable X, and $S_{logit}(\hat{Y})$ is the standard deviation of logit($\hat{Y}$). To produce logit($\hat{Y}$), we use the "xb" option in Stata's xtlogit command—and then calculate descriptive statistics to derive the standard deviation of logit($\hat{Y}$). The value R is the correlation between the observed values of Y (either 0 or 1) and the predicted values of Y (predicted probabilities for each case). The predicted values of Y are created using the pu0 option in Stata.

Results

Before producing and interpreting multivariate regression models, we tabulate the percentage of non-Hispanic white students who are enrolled in private school by the percentage of students in a community who are black for each decade of data 1970 to 2010. We create graphs for students ages six to eleven and twelve to seventeen. Results are shown in figures 3.1 and 3.2.[7] The most basic finding—for all years except 1970—is that white students are substantially more likely to be enrolled in private school as the percentage of black children in their communities increases. For example, in 2010, 12 percent of white children age six to eleven are

Figure 3.1   Private School Enrollments of White Students
             by Community Racial Composition

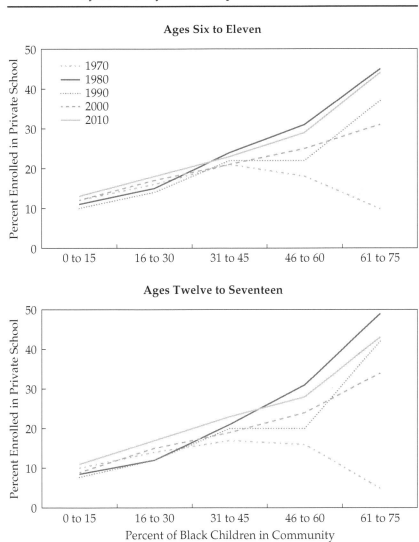

Figure 3.2   Estimated Percentage of White Students Enrolled
in Private School by Community Racial Composition

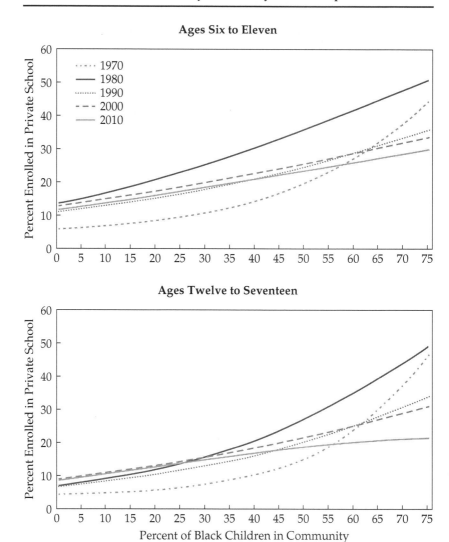

Source: Authors' calculations.
Note: Controlling for all covariates.

enrolled in private school if they live in a community in which 0 to 15 percent of the children are black, whereas 43 percent of white children are enrolled in private school if they live in a community in which between 61 to 75 percent of the children are black. This is a 31 point increase. The increases for 1980, 1990, and 2000 are 34, 27, and 19 percentage points respectively. Slightly stronger patterns exist among white students ages twelve to seventeen. The strength of the bivariate association between private school enrollment rates and community racial composition is almost as strong in 2010 as it was in 1980—indicating that over this duration at least some segregation in public schools is very likely due to the enrollment of white children in private schools.

One year—1970—is substantially different from the four most recent decades. In 1970, the strength of the relationships is weaker compared with all other years—indeed, there is little fluctuation in private school enrollment with changes in the racial composition of the community. Thus, at least for 1970, private school enrollment was not strongly correlated with race. This finding is consistent with our expectations: our literature review of school desegregation enforcement showed the school integration efforts accelerated after 1970, providing the impetus among white students to avoid local public schools by enrolling in private school from the mid-1970s onward. It appears that after 1970, the bivariate association between private school enrollment and community racial composition is as strong—if not stronger—in 2010 as it was in previous decades. Although the data available in this study do not allow us to determine the motivations that undergird apparent race-based associations observed since 1980, these correlations likely contribute to some of the persistent racial segregation observed in public schools. Indeed, other studies, using present-day data and with better units-of-analysis (for example, school catchment areas or census tracts) find that higher percentages of white children are enrolled in non-neighborhoods schools (that is, charter, magnet, and private schools) as the percentage of black children in their local area increases. The current study suggests that the current patterns are very similar to those of last several decades.

Does Race Persist When Controlling for Other Factors?

We extend the analyses with a series of regression models that include a variety of control variables. The first model in tables 3.4 and 3.5 provides a minimal specification that includes the percentage of children in a community who are black, its quadratic term, and the percentage of children in a community who are non-Hispanic white. The second set of models include community-level control variables including median family income, percentage of adults with a college degree, and percentage of adults with blue-collar employment. The third set of models incorporates

Table 3.4   Regression Coefficients, Students Ages Six to Eleven

	1970			1980		
	M1	M2	M3	M1	M2	M3
Percent black	.003	.017	.020	.022*	.028*	.031*
Percent black squared	.0002	.0003	.0002	−.00001	−.00003	−.0001
Percent white	.004	−.005	−.007	−.008	−.009	−.007
Percent poor		−.030	−.028		.000*	.005
Median family income		.051*	.044*		.039*	−.035*
Percent college degree		−.094*	−.093*		−.040*	−.046*
Percent blue collar		−.032*	−.026*		−.031*	−.024*
Male			−.036			−.033*
Married couple			.026			.103*
Number siblings			.164*			.077*
Family income[†]			.003*			.004*
Rent home			−.577*			−.356*
Number rooms in house			.046*			.048*
Number units in structure			.117*			.062*
High school			.427*			.440*
Some college			.486*			.675*
College			.410*			.736*
Semi-skilled			−.109*			−.035*
White collar			.149*			.195*
Professional			.167*			.250*
Constant	−2.81*	−2.17*	−3.565*	−1.81*	−2.236*	−3.940*
Log likelihood[†]	−65.8	−65.7	−63.7	−258.9	−258.9	−251.3
chi2	11	250	4,096	177	350	14,561
rho	.204	.133	.123	.158	.130	.033
sigma_u	.917	.710	.678	.786	.702	.711

Source: Authors' calculations.
Notes: Random-intercept logistic regressions.
[†]In thousands of dollars.
*p < .001.

all relevant control variables that are available in the IPUMS data for the period observed in this study.

Model 1 shows that white students are significantly more likely to be enrolled in private school as shares of black children in their communities increase—this is true for both age groups and in all years except 1970. Also, the quadratic terms for the percentage of black children in a community are not statistically significant and are substantively trivial. Contrary to common perceptions, no tipping point is observed in these basic specifications: regardless of age group or the period, there is no abrupt increase in private school enrollment rates among white children when they live in a neighborhood that has a particular racial composition. Finally, model 1 includes

1990			2000			2010		
M1	M2	M3	M1	M2	M3	M1	M2	M3
.024*	.011*	.008	.021*	.013*	.010*	.022*	.016*	.016*
.011*	.007	.003	.008*	.006*	.002	.008*	.007*	.004
	−.016	−.012		−.019*	−.015		−.006	−.005
	.015*	.013*		.008	.007		−.001	−.002
	−.005	−.001		.001	.005		.000	.003
	−.010	−.021*		.003	−.010		.027*	.014
	−.023*	−.016		−.011	−.005		.017	.017
	−.064*	−.065*		−.037*	−.038*		−.018	−.016
		−.018			−.043*			−.027
		.247*			.341*			.410*
		.059*			.094*			.196*
		.002*			.001*			.001*
		−.301*			−.331*			−.241*
		.042*			.050*			.026*
		.062*			.061*			.058*
		.235*			−.183*			−.603*
		.651*			.241*			−.339*
		.920*			.607*			.090
		−.047*			−.072*			−.083
		.222*			.204*			.202*
−2.24*	3.50*	2.03	−2.05*	.906	−.230	−2.03*	−1.53	−2.46*
−267.5	−267.4	−256.2	−307.8	−307.7	−291.6	−54.4	−54.4	−51.6
218	732	21,455	276	663	30,189	207	364	5,308
.102	.061	.063	.070	.047	.047	.065	.051	.048
.610	.463	.469	.497	.404	.402	.477	.422	.409

the percentage of white students in a community. This same-race variable does not render spurious the relationship between private school enrollment rates and the percentage of black children in the community, suggesting that the presence of white children in a community—or the lack of them—accounts for private school enrollment rates among white students.

Including additional control variables, as shown in models 2 and 3, is revealing in several ways. First, the percentage of black children in a community remains positive and statistically significant when available controls are included in the analysis. Regardless of decade, race remains a relevant predictor of private school enrollment among white children even when other family and contextual factors are controlled. Given that

Table 3.5   Regression Coefficients, Students Ages Twelve to Seventeen

	1970			1980		
	M1	M2	M3	M1	M2	M3
Percent black	−.012	.007	.009	.024*	.031*	.034*
Percent black squared	.001	.001	.001	.001	.001	.001
Percent white	.003	−.007	−.007	−.007	−.005	−.003
Percent poor		−.036*	−.032		.018	.023
Median family income		.062*	.056*		.052*	.048*
Percent college degree		−.111*	−.114*		−.043*	−.051*
Percent blue collar		−.037*	−.031*		−.037*	−.031*
Male			−.028			−.023
Married couple			−.021			.020
Number siblings			.139*			.079*
Family income[†]			.003*			.004*
Rent home			−.454*			−.361*
Number rooms/house			.061*			.066*
Number units/structure			.111*			.057*
High school			.312*			.342*
Some college			.377*			.543*
College			.388*			.705*
Semi-skilled			−.095*			−.036
White collar			.116*			.167*
Professional			.174*			.277*
Constant	−2.92*	−2.39*	−3.84*	−2.27*	−3.73*	−5.45*
Log likelihood[†]	−56.5	−56.4	−54.7	−246.3	−246.3	−238.0
chi2	8	287	3,503	194	401	16,286
rho	.250	.156	.149	.200	.161	.164
sigma_u	1.047	.780	.758	.907	.794	.802

Source: Authors' calculations.
Note: Random-intercept logistic coefficients.
[†]In thousands of dollars.
*p < .001

we cannot include every control variable that may influence private school choice (for example, school quality, levels of violence in the community, the religious denomination of the student), we cannot make a strong causal claim that race drives private school enrollment, ceteris paribus. Still, white students are more likely to enroll in private school as shares of black children in the surrounding area increase even when a range of family- and community-level covariates are included in the models (see also table 3.6).

A central issue—which we focus on in this study—is whether apparent racial antipathies have diminished over time. Are race-based (or race-associated) effects as strong now as they were decades ago? To answer this question, we present two graphs in figure 3.2 (one for each age group). The figures use coefficients from the third models in tables 3.4 and 3.5 to

	1990			2000			2010	
M1	M2	M3	M1	M2	M3	M1	M2	M3
.022*	.026*	.030*	.024*	.023*	.027*	.031*	.024*	.028*
.001	.001	.001	−.001	.001	−.001	−.001	−.001	−.001
−.012*	−.005	−.003	−.011*	−.007*	−.005	−.011*	−.007*	−.006*
	.019	.025		.013	.019		.009	.011
	.042*	.040*		.017*	.017*		.001	−.001
	−.039*	−.051*		−.003	−.015		.023*	.012
	−.040*	−.035*		−.022	−.017		−.002	−.001
		−.034*			−.021			−.054
		.130*			.212*			.290*
		.129*			.165*			.209*
		.003*			.002*			.002*
		−.351*			−.196*			−.238*
		.076*			.076*			.039*
		.044*			.026*			.029
		.132*			−.084			−.509*
		.431*			.213*			−.357*
		.686*			.548*			.058
		.004			−.007			−.024
		.242*			.191*			.131*
		.361*			.362*			.380*
−1.77*	−3.31*	−5.12*	−1.71*	−2.67*	−4.29*	−1.60*	−2.66*	−3.38*
−187.9	−187.8	−179.4	−243.6	−243.5	−231.9	−50.0	−50.0	−47.4
234	607	16,540	404	695	22,657	292	437	5,271
.161	.112	.120	.094	.072	.077	.084	.069	.071
.796	.645	.670	.584	.506	.522	.549	.495	.502

portray the predicated percentage of white children enrolled in private school (y-axes) against changes in the percentage of black children who live in communities (x-axes).[8] These predictions hold all control variables at their means (as shown in the total columns in tables 3.1 and 3.2). Each line of the graph represents an age group and each line within each graph represents a year of data.

Two clear and consistent patterns emerge. Between 1970 and 1980, the slope between private school enrollment and community racial composition rose precipitously. Clearly, the correlation between community racial composition and private school enrollment among white children was much stronger in 1980 than 1970. This is consistent with the bivariate results shown in figure 3.1. However, after 1980, the strength of the correlation between private school enrollment and

Table 3.6 Fully Standardized Logistic-Regression Coefficients, Dissimilarity

	Ages Six to Eleven					Ages Twelve to Seventeen				
	1970	1980	1990	2000	2010	1970	1980	1990	2000	2010
Percent black	.080	.152‡	.112	.128‡	.118‡	.106	.161‡	.125	.118‡	.097‡
Black-white dissimilarity	.000	.000	.000	.000	.000	.038	.061	.060	.048	.021
Percent white	.031	.047	.034	.044	.035	.025	.017	.024	.040	.033
Percent poor	.084	.013	.044	.013	.006	.081	.053	.065	.052	.031
Median family income	.134‡	.123	.147‡	.059	.041	.150‡	.144	.174‡	.079	.012
Percent college degree	.107	.099	.116	.056	.065	.119	.093	.114	.037	.052
Percent blue collar	.053	.057	.056	.019	.037	.058	.059	.055	.025	.002
Male	.005	.005	.009	.010	.008	.004	.004	.005	.004	.010
Married couple	.002	.011	.024	.045	.059	.002	.002	.016	.030	.043
Number siblings	.073	.030	.047	.061	.103	.066	.032	.047	.065	.089
Family income†	.030	.046	.042	.041	.048	.042	.057	.054	.050	.052
Rent home	.070	.048	.049	.051	.044	.050	.042	.044	.026	.031
Number rooms in house	.019	.024	.026	.034	.029	.025	.032	.038	.043	.036
Number units in structure	.038	.027	.027	.027	.023	.034	.022	.015	.010	.010
High school	.060	.057	.019	.045	.111	.043	.054	.019	.014	.079
Some college	.049	.090	.075	.023	.081	.038	.071	.064	.033	.057
College	.045	.105	.107	.081	.023	.041	.096	.100	.090	.057
Semi-skilled	.012	.005	.007	.009	.012	.010	.005	.000	.001	.004
White collar	.016	.025	.029	.028	.027	.013	.022	.031	.025	.018
Professional	.019	.034	.046	.059	.061	.020	.038	.050	.057	.065

Source: Authors' calculations.
†Indicates strongest Beta coefficient.

community racial composition diminishes somewhat. Although race remains a significant predictor of private school enrollment, its slope diminishes a little bit each decade since 1980. All else being equal, shares of black children were in 1980 a stronger predictor of private school enrollment than in any other decade. By 2010, the slope between private school enrollment and shares of black children in a community is flatter—especially among older children.

Relative Strength of Race-Based Factors and Other Variables

The primary question we explore in this chapter is whether correlations between community racial composition and private school enrollment have changed over time, all else being equal. The basic answer to that question is yes. The data at our disposal allow us to answer this question with some confidence. Given that we have a limited set of control variables, we are less sanguine about the prospects of attributing specific causes to the correlations that we see—particularly in the decades 1980 through 2010. Despite these caveats, we include enough covariates in our analysis to answer two related questions: First, what is the relative importance of community racial composition versus other community- and individual-level factors in predicting private school enrollment? Second, compared with other community characteristics, is race more or less important today than it was several decades ago?[9]

Fully standardized logistic regression coefficients show that two variables are consistently no less important—in relative terms—than others. These are the percentage of black children in a community and median family income in a community. This is an interesting and somewhat counterintuitive result. Race has diminished in absolute terms when controlling for other factors. Yet, in relative terms, community racial composition is consistently no less important than other variables included in the models. For example, in 2010, the percentage of black children in a community is as relatively important as median family income within a PUMA and is slightly stronger than individual-level factors such as family income and the education of a child's parents. Strikingly similar conclusions can be drawn for early decades. For 1980, 1990, and 2000, racial composition was no less important than other factors. Thus, even though community racial composition begins to gradually wane in strength in absolute terms, in relative terms it continues to play about as strong a role as other factors we are able to include in our models.

An examination of the models' pseudo-R-squared statistics (McKelvey and Zavoina 1975) sheds light on the apparent contradiction between declines in the absolute importance of community racial composition compared with the persistent, relative importance of community racial composition. The total, estimated explained variance in our models steadily declines between 1980 and 2010. For example, among students age twelve to seventeen, pseudo-R^2 in 1980 was 0.17. It dropped an average of 1.6 points per decade thereafter. Thus, though community racial composition wanes in substantive importance with each passing decade, it remains relatively important compared with other predictors—and the apparent contradiction is reconciled since the accuracy with which the model can predict the probability that a particular child is enrolled in private school diminishes each decade.

Discussion and Conclusion

Our examination of the relationship between community racial composition and white private school enrollment reveals three patterns. First, when we observe the bivariate relationship between the share of black children in a community and the probability that a white child is enrolled in private school, we find that this relationship is about as strong in 2010 as in 2000, 1990, and 1980. This is important because these patterns suggest that some racial segregation in public schools is likely due to private school enrollment patterns among white children—regardless of the factors that motivate these choices. This pattern is consistent during the last four decades—and is similar to studies that examine choices of neighborhoods and of magnet, charter, and private schools. Indeed, our results are strikingly similar to those of Sean Reardon and John Yun (2003b), who find that in southern states, where school districts are coincident with school districts, shares of white children enrolled in private school were modestly correlated with shares of black children in a county in 1970 but increased—and remained high—in the following decades. The conclusion that can be reached by examining our bivariate results—which are based on consistent PUMAs—largely corresponds with that earlier research: in 1970, there was virtually no correlation between the percentage of black children in a community and the probability that white children were enrolled in private school. As figure 3.1 shows, these numbers change in subsequent decades. White students were more likely to be enrolled in private schools as the proportion of black children in their PUMAs increased—and these slopes were fairly consistent across the last four decades. This again is consistent with Reardon and Yun's finding that "patterns of 'white flight' to private schools have persisted through 1980, 1990, and 2000. During this time, county-level white private school enrollment rates were tightly linked to the proportion of the county school-age population who were black" (2003b, 1563–564).

Although these bivariate associations are important, once other community- and family-level factors are included in the statistical models, the correlations between community racial composition and private school enrollment among white children seem to steadily erode with each passing decade. White families are apparently less and less sensitive to race than they were several decades ago and this sensitivity has apparently declined steadily with each passing decade, but changes in these unstandardized logistic regression coefficients should be treated with caution. After 1980 it became more difficult to predict which students are enrolled in private school. This is indicated by declines in pseudo R-squared values. Thus, most coefficients in the model decline in each subsequent decade (including, for example, the share of poor children in the community or median family income). The set of factors we can include in our models grows less effective in predicting private school enrollment—and it may be that other factors we are unable to include in our models (such as a student's religious denomination) have supplanted community racial composition and socioeconomic characteristics as relevant predictors.

The third and final result is that, compared with other factors that white families might consider in their decision to exit public schools, race remains a relatively important factor in predicting private school enrollment. Thus, while race has diminished in absolute importance over time (when other factors are held constant), it still remains a relatively important correlate of private school enrollment rates among white families.

Private school enrollment among white families in diverse communities is a sign of out-group aversion and thus an important yardstick of American race relations. Taking stock of trends in white private school enrollment since 1970 indicates that progress toward racial equality in the post–civil rights period is mixed. Decadal declines in black-white racial segregation in housing and schooling between 1970 and 2010 have been steady but slow. The picture that emerges of white private school choice is more complex: it more difficult to predict which white students are enrolled in private school, but compared with other factors that could explain private school enrollment, the central importance of race endures. This study continues in a tradition of understanding the sources of racial inequality in terms of whites' racially motivated attitudes and behaviors in choosing homes and schools and parsing the complex relationship between individual choice and social context.

Appendix

The reliance on Public Use Micro Data Areas as units to measure the social context in which individuals make choices is far less than ideal, for reasons discussed in the body of this paper. Our concern is amplified by the use of consistent PUMAs—areas that cover the same geographic area in each decade 1970 to 2010. Although we work with geographically consistent spatial units, using consistent PUMAs reduces the number of areas we would like to use.

One way we address this challenge—if only minimally—is to analyze data based on PUMAs that were created for each census. For example, there are 2,071 PUMAs in 2000 and 2010 (for details, see note 3). Arguably, using the most recent PUMAs is better than using school districts. In urban areas, multiple PUMAs are embedded in the largest school districts. For example, Miami-Dade County School District wholly contains twenty-four, Philadelphia eleven. At the same time, in rural areas, many 2000 and 2010 PUMAs encompass multiple school districts. Still, 2,071 PUMAs are at least as equally as valid as using urban school district boundaries, particularly given that researchers do not have ready access to information that describes individuals nested within school districts or counties.

Figures 3A.1 and 3A.2 are based on models that include the same independent variables as those in the chapter. The only difference is the definition of PUMAs. The results based on current definitions of PUMAs are remarkably consistent with those based on consistent PUMAs. We show this in two ways. First, the simple association between the percentage of white children who enrolled in private school and that of black children in PUMAs is much the same whether the 2,071 2000 or 2010 PUMAs or the 543 consistent PUMAs are used. This can be seen by comparing the results in figure 3.1 and in figure 3A.1. Thus, the results all indicate that some segregation in public schools is likely due to the enrollment of white children in private schools. Higher proportions of white children are enrolled in private school when they live in areas with higher shares of black children. This is true in 1980, 1990, 2000, and 2010—regardless of how PUMAs are defined. Thus, consistent with other findings (see, for example, Reardon and Yun 2003b), we find that it is likely the private school enrollment patterns among white students contribute to black-white segregation that has persisted in public schools since the 1980s.

Whether the bivariate associations between private school enrollment and area racial composition are driven by racial factors—or race-associated factors—is another question. We tentatively address this question in the chapter. We find that, in absolute terms, race appears to have diminished in importance between 1980 and 2010 when race-associated factors are controlled. For the purposes of this appendix, the issue is whether using different spatial units—that is, the 543 consistent PUMAs or the greater number of PUMAs that are available for more recent decades—leads us to different conclusions. It does not. We find that race appears to diminish in importance between 1980 and 1990 when other factors are controlled.

Figure 3A.1   Private School Enrollments of White Students by Community Racial Composition

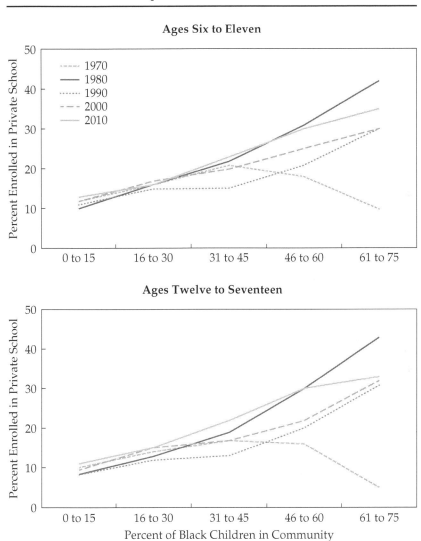

Source: Authors' calculations.
Note: No control variables; based on original PUMAs.

Figure 3A.2   Estimated Percentage of White Students Enrolled in Private School by Community Racial Composition

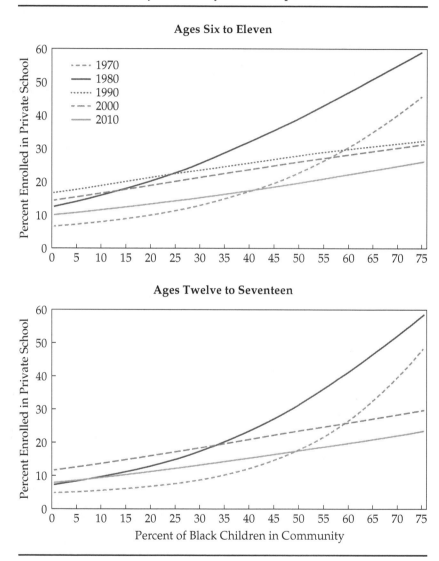

Source: Authors' calculations.
Note: Controlling for all covariates.

However, the slopes between areal racial composition and private school enrollment rates are slightly less decade by decade from 1990, 2000, and 2010. Thus, the use of consistent PUMAs—although far less than ideal— does not result in different conclusions than are reached when we use PUMAs that change by decade.

Notes

1. Fewer than 1 percent of students in the PUMS data are not the biological, adopted, or step-child of the householder. For these students, it is not clear whether the head of household is the primary decision maker in determining whether a child is enrolled in private school. More important, the PUMS data do not indicate how much economic support children in nonparent households receive from their householders, making it impossible to include adequate socioeconomic controls in statistical analyses of private school enrollment. We exclude these students from the analyses.

2. Although we would have preferred to use grade spans, student enrollment by grade is inconsistent across censuses. Moreover, as we explored the data, we ran separate models for students in a variety of age categories (for example, six to ten, eleven to fourteen, and fifteen to seventeen). Regardless of the age classifications we used, the results for the older and younger groups were strikingly similar and, to simplify the presentation of results, we consolidated the data into two age groups: ages six to eleven and twelve to seventeen.

3. The total number of communities for each year is as follows: 1,154 in 1980, 1,726 in 1990, and 2,071 in 2000 and 2010. As a benchmark, the United States has 3,144 counties in all. We believe that it is methodologically appropriate to hold each area geographically constant over time—even though this reduces some of the variation in our models—because more communities are added each decade. Nevertheless, the results based on consistent communities are substantively the same as results based on communities that change over time. We include the results for original PUMAs in the appendix.

4. We also created a variable to capture the percentage of Hispanic children. Substituting this variable into the models in lieu of non-Hispanic white children did not affect the substantive results reported in this book.

5. Because these aggregations are generated using sample information, an error term is associated with each variable for every community. Still, the errors are tolerable given that the typical number of observations used to compute any community-level characteristic is reasonably large—at least 244 observations per PUMA. Given this, the largest standard error for any of the community-level parameters is 3 percentage points.

6. The following categorical variables are set at these values: male=0; married=1; rent=1; the reference category for parental education is less than a high

school diploma and the reference category for parental occupation is unskilled, blue collar.

7. Because our main goal is to explore changes in the steepness of the slopes across years, we set the intercepts to the same values—in this case, the value for the intercept in 1970. Because most of the intercepts are within a few percentage points, interpretation of the results is not affected.

8. Comparing regression coefficients across models can be deceiving as these coefficients are expressed in log odds—and log odds are not linear. They represent the rate of change in the dependent variable with a one-unit change in the independent variable. Since the constants in each model are different and log-odds represent rate-of-change, it is not straightforward to compare, for example, the coefficients in model 1 with those in models 2 and 3 (or to compare coefficients across decades). It is easier and more accurate to rely on figure 3.2 than to decipher the unstandardized logistic regression coefficients.

9. It is not proper or useful to compare standardized regression coefficients across years; for example, the standardized coefficient for percentage black in 2010 cannot be compared with the 2000 coefficient for percentage black. A related concern is multicollinearity among the independent variables. In most decades, there are relatively high correlations among variables that measure the socioeconomic composition of people in a PUMS area. For example, median family income, poverty rates, and the percent of people who are college educated and percent of people who are employed in blue-collar occupations are highly intercorrelated. Across the five decades, the correlation coefficient between median family income and percent college educated ranges from 0.67 to 0.85. Other bivariate associations are similar (for example, r values ranged between -0.74 to -0.81 for median family income and poverty rates). This basic result can be seen in table 3.2. Given these correlations, we ran models in which we excluded three of the four variables to determine whether beta weights for percentage black and socioeconomic composition lead us to different conclusions that we observe in the fully specified model. They did not. Still, we urge the reader to interpret the results with some caution.

References

Brunner, Eric J., Jennifer Imazeki, and Stephen L. Ross. 2006. "Universal Vouchers and White Flight." *Economics Working Papers* no. 200601. New Haven: University of Connecticut. Available at: http://digitalcommons.uconn.edu/econ_wpapers/200601 (accessed July 12, 2012).

Clark, William A. V. 1991. "Residential Preferences and Neighborhood Racial Segregation: A Test of the Schelling Segregation Model." *Demography* 28(1): 1–19.
———. 1992. "Residential Preferences and Residential Choices in a Multiethnic Context." *Demography* 29(3): 451–66.

Ewert, Stephanie. 2013. "The Decline in Private School Enrollment." *SEHSD* working paper no. FY12-117. Washington: U.S. Census Bureau. Available at: https://www.census.gov/hhes/school/files/ewert_private_school_enrollment.pdf (accessed April 29, 2013).

Farley, Reynolds. 1997. "Racial Trends and Differences in the United States 30 Years After the Civil Rights Decade." *Social Science Research* 26(3): 235–62.

Goodchild, Michael, and Nina Lam. 1980. "Areal Interpolations: A Variant of the Traditional Spatial Problem." *Geoprocessing* 1:297–312.

Guo, Guang, and Hongxin Zhao. 2000. "Multilevel Modeling of Binary Data." *Annual Review of Sociology* 26:441–62.

Iceland, John. 2009. *Where We Live Now: Immigration and Race in the United States.* Berkeley: University of California Press.

Ledwith, Valerie. 2009. "Open Enrolment and Student Sorting in Public Schools: Evidence from Los Angeles County." *Environment and Planning* 41(5): 1109–128.

Li, Mingliang. 2009. "Is There 'White Flight' into Private Schools? New Evidence from High School and Beyond." *Economics of Education Review* 28(3): 382–92.

Logan, John, and Brian Stults. 2011. "The Persistence of Segregation in the Metropolis: New Findings from the 2010 Census." Census Brief prepared for Project US2010. Available at: http://www.s4.brown.edu/us2010 (accessed November 1, 2013).

McKelvey, Richard D., and William Zavoina. 1975. "A Statistical Model for the Analysis of Ordinal Level Dependent Variables." *Journal of Mathematical Sociology* 4(1): 103–20.

Menard, Scott. 2011. "Standards for Standardized Logistic Regression Coefficients." *Social Forces* 89(4): 1409–428.

Minnesota Population Center. 2011a. *Integrated Public Use Microdata Series, International: Version 6.1* [Machine-readable database]. Minneapolis: University of Minnesota.

———. 2011b. *National Historical Geographic Information System, Version 2.0.* Minneapolis: University of Minnesota. Available at: http://www.nhgis.org (accessed November 9, 2013).

Pattillo, Mary. 2008. "Race, Class, and Neighborhoods." In *Social Class: How Does It Work?* edited by Annette Lareau and Dalton Conley. New York: Russell Sage Foundation.

Reardon, Sean F., and John T. Yun. 2003a. "Private School Racial Enrollments and Segregation." In *Public School Choice vs. Private School Vouchers,* edited by R. D. Kahlenberg. New York: Century Foundation Press.

———. 2003b. "Integrating Neighborhoods, Segregating Schools: The Retreat from School Desegregation in the South, 1990–2000." *North Carolina Law Review* 81(4): 1563–596.

Ruggles, Steven, J. Trent Alexander, Katie Genadek, Ronald Goeken, Matthew B. Schroeder, and Matthew Sobek. 2010. *Integrated Public Use Microdata Series: Version 5.0* [Machine-readable database]. Minneapolis: University of Minnesota.

Saporito, Salvatore. 2003. "Private Choices, Public Consequences: Magnet School Choice and Segregation by Race and Poverty." *Social Problems* 50(2): 181–203.

———. 2009. "School Choice in Black and White: Private School Enrollment among Racial Groups, 1990–2000." *Peabody Journal of Education* 84(2): 172–90.

Saporito, Salvatore, and Deenesh Sohoni. 2007. "Mapping Educational Inequality: Concentrations of Poverty Among Poor and Minority Students in Public Schools." *Social Forces* 85(3): 1227–253.

Schuman, Howard, Charlotte Steeh, Lawrence Bobo, and Maria Krysan. 2001. *Racial Attitudes in America: Trends and Interpretations,* rev. ed. Cambridge, Mass.: Harvard University Press.

Stewart, Kenneth J., and Stephen B. Reed. 1999. "Consumer Price Index Research Series Using Current Methods, 1978–1998." *Monthly Labor Review* 122(June): 29–38.

Wilson, William Julius. 1978. *The Declining Significance of Race: Blacks and Changing American Institutions.* Chicago: University of Chicago Press.

Wong, George, and William Mason. 1985. "The Hierarchical Logistic Regression Model for Multilevel Analysis." *Journal of the American Statistical Association* 80(391): 513–24.

Zhang, Haifeng. 2008. "White Flight in the Context of Education: Evidence from South Carolina." *Journal of Geography* 107(6): 236–45.

═ Chapter 4 ═

Segregation, Neighborhoods, and Schools

PAUL A. JARGOWSKY

S ome degree of residential segregation is inevitable in urban settings. Perfect intermingling among disparate groups is statistically unlikely and runs contrary to human nature; people are frequently drawn to those with whom they have something in common. As Kimberly Goyette notes in the introduction to this volume, choices made by individuals, with or without racist intent, can contribute to segregation by race and class. Segregation does not stem from choice alone, however; evidence is ample of ongoing racial discrimination in the housing market (Turner 2005). Moreover, much segregation is driven by explicit policies with regard to zoning, transportation, and taxation that regulate urban and suburban development and shape the operation of the housing market (Bonastia 2006; Jargowsky 2002; Papke 2009; Squires 2002). Whatever the underlying causes, segregation by race and class has important implications for equality of educational opportunity. Most schools in the United States have explicit geographic attendance zones. Overlaying these catchment areas on a segregated housing map automatically produces segregated schools. Segregation within schools is further magnified through selection into private schools, magnet schools, and charter schools with themes that appeal to various racial and ethnic groups (Saporito 2003). For example, a charter school with an Afro-centric theme will likely draw from racial and ethnic groups differently than a classical magnet school.

Segregation by race and class is a perennial interest of sociologists and demographers. The focus on the spatial organization of demographic groups dates back to the Chicago School of Sociology, particularly the claim by Robert Park (1926) that spatial patterns arise from, and then help to shape social relations. More recently, the focus has been on the harm done by racial segregation (Massey, Condran, and Denton 1987) and economic segregation (Wilson 1987). Indeed, segregation of both types was decried by the Kerner Commission, appointed to investigate the race riots of the 1960s (National Advisory Commission on Civil Disorders 1968). This volume focuses on how residential patterns, regardless of whether they arise from individual choices, racial discrimination in housing, or public policies that regulate growth, act to restrict educational opportunities for those with lower incomes. By contributing to lower educational attainment of the children of low-income families, segregation by race and class helps to perpetuate poverty across generations and may contribute to growing income inequality given the importance of academic skills in the modern economy.

This chapter reviews recent trends in segregation by race and class, both of which contribute to educational isolation, and attempts to understand how they interrelate and reinforce one another. To briefly overview the results, the analyses presented below show that segregation between blacks and whites has declined slowly since about 1970, yet the level remains very high by any standard. In some large metropolitan areas, segregation of blacks and whites is still pervasive. In contrast, the segregation of Hispanics and Asians from whites, though lower than black-white segregation, is increasing. Segregation of the poor from the nonpoor is also increasing among whites, blacks, and Asians. The overall segregation of the poor from the nonpoor, however, is offset to a certain degree by the decline in black-white racial segregation. The segregation of poor households from affluent households is far greater within minority groups than for non-Hispanic whites. More important, all minority households—including affluent ones—are highly segregated from affluent whites. Finally, children enrolled in school, from pre-K through high school, are substantially more racially and economically segregated than people not enrolled in school.

Economic and racial segregation also contribute to one another (Massey and Denton 1993; Massey 1990; Quillian 2012). This chapter presents simulations that show how much of each type of segregation is a function of the other. This analysis reveals that racial segregation by itself contributes about a third of the total economic segregation, though the amount varies across metropolitan areas. In contrast, economic segregation contributes little, less than 10 percent in most cases, to racial segregation. Both forms of segregation operate largely independently, and both contribute to educational isolation and the resulting inequality of educational outcomes.

When minority groups with high-poverty rates are segregated from whites, and when those groups themselves are segregated by income, the result is neighborhoods of concentrated poverty. Nationwide, the number of people residing in high-poverty ghettos and barrios fell during the 1990s due to the strong economy. Since the 2000 census, however, the number of persons residing in neighborhoods where the poverty rate is 40 percent or more surged to 56 percent, rising from 7.2 million to 11.2 million. In the most recent data, 23.4 percent of the black poor and 15.8 percent of the Hispanic poor reside in high-poverty neighborhoods, compared to only 8 percent of the white poor.

These various forms of segregation combine to create neighborhood contexts that limit the educational opportunities available to low-income children, particularly low-income minority children. As Goyette notes in chapter 1, schools in wealthier, suburban communities have more resources, fewer behavioral problems, and higher educational expectations than schools in low-income neighborhoods. Segregation along race and class lines, whether driven by choices, markets, or public policy, contributes to vast inequality in the spatial distribution of high-quality educational opportunities. As noted in chapter 2 of this volume, these disparities in school quality may feed back into the process of housing choice, reinforcing the segregation dynamic.

The next section describes the data used in these analyses and outlines some of the methodological challenges in conducing segregation and concentration of poverty research.

Data and Methods

The results of segregation analyses can be affected by choices about the data, the racial categories used, and the geographic boundaries employed. Choices about data and methods explain some of the recent disagreements in the literature about the trend in segregation of blacks and whites (Glaeser and Vigdor 2012; Logan and Stults 2011; Vigdor 2013). It is important, therefore, to consider these issues carefully.

Geography

In segregation analyses, at least two levels of geography are needed. First is a primary unit for which segregation is being measured and reported, such as a city or metropolitan area. Second are smaller units that subdivide the primary unit, such as neighborhoods or blocks, and over which various demographic groups may be unevenly distributed. For this analysis, I use a consistent set of geographic boundaries for the primary geographic units for all time periods. The focus is primarily on metropolitan areas, defined as an urbanized area of fifty thousand or more people and the entire county in which the urbanized area is located, as well as contiguous counties that are closely related in terms of commuting patterns and other criteria. Metropolitan areas are often used in segregation studies because they approximate labor and housing markets (Berry, Goheen, and Goldstein 1969), although cities, counties, or states could also be used. Although the boundaries of cities and towns change frequently due to mergers, splits, and annexations, county boundaries rarely do. Thus, the state and county codes of the inventory of metropolitan areas can be retroactively applied to the census tract data of previous years or subsequent years.

As is common in segregation research, census tracts will serve as the smaller geographic unit, the proxy for neighborhoods. Tracts have an average population of around four thousand and are drawn to have a degree of socioeconomic homogeneity (White 1987). The actual physical size of census tracts varies enormously depending on population density, so that census tracts in New York City are much smaller in area than those in sprawling low-density metropolitan areas like Phoenix. Due to changes in population and housing over time, the correspondence between census tracts and neighborhoods as perceived by residents may be weak. Nevertheless, census tracts do provide a way of seeing who lives in close proximity to whom.

It should be noted that in response to population growth (or decline), the Census Bureau splits (or merges) census tracts in an attempt to keep the average tract population size constant. In this analysis, contemporaneous census tracts are used rather than data that have been normalized to tracts as they existed on a particular date. Segregation statistics are known to be sensitive the population size of the neighborhood units used to calculate them (Cortese, Falk, and Cohen 1976; Winship 1977; Wong 1997). Thus, the use of normalized tracts in the context of a growing population would introduce a systematic bias in the trend in segregation.

Data Sources

Given the more than seventy thousand census tracts, few data sources have a sufficient sample size to generalize about all of them. The data used in this analysis come from several sources. The first is the 1990 Census of Population and Housing, Summary File 3 (SF3) and the corresponding file for the 2000 Census. These data are based on the long form of the census that includes questions about income that are not part of the short form census filled out, in theory, by all households. These questions were asked of a sample of about one in seven households in the entire country and together constitute a snapshot of the nation at a particular point in time (April 15 of the census year).

The American Community Survey (ACS) is the replacement for the census long form, which was discontinued after the 2000 Census. Compared with the long-form program, the ACS surveys a much smaller number of households in any given year. However, unlike the census, new samples are conducted each month. The ACS releases data annually, but for small geographic areas like census tracts, the annual data release consists of the aggregation of sixty monthly samples over five calendar years to protect the confidentiality of survey respondents. The first ACS census tract estimates were released in December 2010, and consisted of the monthly survey responses from January 2005 to December 2009 (U.S. Census Bureau 2010). In 2011, the ACS released data based on samples from January 2006 to December 2010 (U.S. Census Bureau 2011). As of this writing, the most recent release was in December of 2012, aggregating monthly samples from 2007 through 2011 (U.S. Census Bureau 2012).

The benefit of the ACS approach to census tract data is that, after it has been operating for several years, researchers will have an annually updated time trend on census tracts. There is a downside, however. In general, the ACS numbers based on moving averages of sixty monthly samples are not strictly comparable to the point-in-time estimates from long-form census data. If the characteristics of a neighborhood are changing over the five-year window, the resulting data is an average value for the neighborhood over the period, rather than a snapshot. The sample size per census tract is smaller as well, introducing a greater degree of sampling error in the ACS data.[1]

Another difference between the ACS and the long-form census data is that respondents are interviewed every month, rather than just in April. Respondents are asked to report their income for the previous twelve months, regardless of which month they are being interviewed. In contrast, the census asked respondents in April to report their income for the previous calendar year. Given that April 15 is also the deadline for federal taxes, respondents to the census may have had a better sense of the their actual income for the previous calendar year than ACS respondents asked, for example, in July to report their income for the preceding twelve months. Caution should therefore be used in interpreting differences based on income or poverty estimates between ACS and census data.

Racial and Ethnic Groups

To measure the trends in segregation between groups, the groups must be defined as consistently as possible. Changes in the conceptualization and measurement of racial and ethnic groups, therefore, pose a challenge in segregation research. In 1990, the Census Bureau allowed respondents to identify only one race. Since 2000, respondents can identify as many racial groups as they desire.[2] In practice, about 2 percent of non-Hispanic respondents select more than one racial group. Given the inherent ambiguity in classifying those who choose more than one race, the category black in this analysis refers to people who indicated "Black or African-American" as their race in 1990, or who chose the category "Black or African-American" alone in the 2000 Census or ACS surveys. Asians are treated in the same way.

The census and ACS surveys also ask about Hispanic ethnicity. This is a separate question from the race question, meaning that Hispanics can be of any race. In the 2007–2011 ACS data (U.S. Census Bureau 2012, table B03002), thirty million of fifty million Hispanics self-identified their race as white and another fifteen million identified their race as other, perhaps reflecting an identification with Hispanic or Latino rather than one of the standard race categories. To avoid double-counting, the analyses in this chapter are based, to the extent possible, on mutually exclusive categories of Hispanic, on the one hand, and non-Hispanic whites, blacks, and Asians, on the other hand. In the 2000 Census and ACS surveys, it is possible to identify non-Hispanic whites by poverty status. In the 1990 data, I approximate non-Hispanic whites by poverty status by subtracting Hispanic and other race groups from the poor and nonpoor population figures.

Measurement of Segregation

There are many dimensions of residential segregation, including the evenness of the distribution of groups over an area, the clustering of segregated neighborhoods in certain parts of the area, and the tendency of a group to be centrally located or not (Massey and Denton 1988). Given that schools are often neighborhood based, the dimension of evenness is most relevant to understanding how children of different groups have or are denied access to educational opportunities.

The index of dissimilarity (D) is the most commonly used measure of segregation in the sense of the evenness of the distribution of groups across neighborhoods (Duncan and Duncan 1955). D is given by

$$D_{xy} = 0.5 * \sum_{i=1}^{n} \left| \frac{x_i}{X} - \frac{y_i}{Y} \right|,$$

where x_i and y_i are the population of two different groups, X and Y, in neighborhood i. X and Y represent the total population of the two groups, respectively, across all n neighborhoods in the primary geographic unit (normally metropolitan areas). While there are many other measures of segregation, those that measure evenness are highly correlated with D in practice (Denton and Massey 1988). D, which ranges from 0 to 1, also has an appealing interpretation. A value of D of 0.5 indicates that 50 percent of one group or the other would have to move to achieve perfect integration. A value of 1 indicates complete segregation and 0 indicates perfect integration.

The measurement of economic segregation is less well developed in the literature. In part, this reflects a greater degree of difficulty in measuring segregation along a continuous dimension, like income, relative to a categorical dimension like race. Many quite different measures of economic segregation have been proposed, including the neighborhood sorting index (Jargowsky 1996), the centile gap index (Watson 2009), the rank-order information theory index (Reardon and Bischoff 2011), and a spatial version of the Gini index (Kim and Jargowsky 2009). There are advantages and disadvantages of each measure. For the purposes of this chapter, I reduce the income variable to a set of categories. The simplest approach is to divide persons into two categories, poor and nonpoor, and calculate the Index of Dissimilarity between them. In another analysis, I divide households into four categories: low-income, working-class, middle-class, and affluent households. Then the index of dissimilarity can be applied to each pair of household income groups. While some information is lost in converting a continuous measure to a categorical one, D has the advantage of being easy to interpret. Moreover, I conduct an analysis showing how racial and economic segregation are related that requires categorical variables on both dimensions.

A person's poverty status is determined based on the income of all members of his or her family living in a particular housing unit. For that reason, those who live in group quarters, such as a jail, nursing home, or dormitory, are not classified as either poor or nonpoor. When calculating the segregation of the poor from the nonpoor, only those who have a poverty status can be included in the analysis, effectively excluding the 2.5 percent of the population that lives in group quarters. For consistency, I also exclude those who lack a poverty status from the racial segregation analysis as well to establish consistency in the population across the two analyses. Those in group quarters usually do not interact with neighbors in the same way that residents living in households do, so the exclusion of group quarters residents is sensible (Iceland and Scopilliti 2008).

Results

The following sections describe the basic trends in racial-ethnic and economic segregation.

Trends in Segregation by Race and Ethnicity

As shown in table 4.1, the change in the index of dissimilarity over time varies depending on which racial and ethnic groups are being examined. The values shown are population-weighted averages of the segregation levels in all 384 U.S. metropolitan areas. Because whites are the majority group, with greater control over resources and institutions, I focus on the segregation of minority groups from non-Hispanic whites rather than segregation of blacks from nonblacks. Continuing a trend that began in 1970, the segregation of blacks from whites fell from 0.644 in 1990 to 0.618 in 2000 and to 0.601 in the most recent ACS data, spanning the years from 2007 to 2011.[3] Little change is observed in the three ACS data releases, which is not surprising given that each sample's five-year window overlaps four-fifths of the previous sample.

Despite a slow trend toward integration, a segregation level of over 0.60 is still very high. Few groups in American history have ever experienced

Table 4.1   **Metropolitan Racial and Ethnic Segregation**

Whites from	Index of Dissimilarity		
	Blacks	Hispanics	Asians
1990 Census	0.644	0.447	0.421
2000 Census	0.618	0.474	0.441
2005–2009 ACS	0.601	0.480	0.462
2006–2010 ACS	0.606	0.484	0.479
2007–2011 ACS	0.601	0.481	0.480
Blacks from		Hispanics	Asians
1990 Census		0.561	0.637
2000 Census		0.502	0.593
2005–2009 ACS		0.500	0.606
2006–2010 ACS		0.503	0.613
2007–2011 ACS		0.496	0.610
Hispanics from			Asians
1990 Census			0.496
2000 Census			0.497
2005–2009 ACS			0.533
2006–2010 ACS			0.543
2007–2011 ACS			0.543

Source: Author's compilation of U.S. Census Summary File 3 data for 1990 and 2000 and American Community Survey data for 2005–2009, 2006–2010, and 2007–2011 (U.S. Census Bureau 1991, 2002, 2010, 2011, 2012).
Note: Figures are weighted averages of 384 metropolitan areas.

such high levels of segregation, let alone sustained them over decades (Massey 1990). Despite the Fair Housing Act of 1968, despite the emergence of a substantial black middle class, and despite black progress in many professions, the color line remains the primary division in America's neighborhoods. Indeed, at the pace of the decline in black-white segregation since 1990, it would take 150 years to achieve a low level of segregation (0.30 or less) of blacks from whites. John Logan and Brian Stults (2010), in their analysis of racial segregation, concluded that progress had come to a standstill.

Other researchers (Cutler, Glaeser, and Vigdor 1999; Glaeser and Vigdor 2012; Vigdor 2013) view the changes more positively. In part, their more favorable readings are based on examining the segregation of blacks from nonblacks, rather than from whites. The nonblack category of course includes other minority groups, such as Hispanics and the increasing number of Hispanic immigrants who compete with blacks for the same limited stock of affordable housing in the central city and older inner-ring suburbs. Blacks are indeed more likely to live near Hispanics;

as table 4.1 indicates, the segregation of blacks from Hispanics declined from 0.561 to 0.496 between 1990 and the 2007 to 2011 period, thus reducing the segregation of blacks from nonblacks. Yet segregation of blacks from non-Hispanic whites, the majority group that has the lion's share of resources and community amenities, is more relevant to the question of black children's access to quality education. The following analyses illustrate the extent to which current levels of racial segregation continue to hinder minority children's access to educational opportunities.

In contrast to the trend in black-white segregation, the segregation of other minority groups from whites is increasing. Hispanic-white segregation has increased modestly from 0.447 to around 0.481 between 1990 and the 2007 to 2011 period; this may be driven by immigration directly into barrio neighborhoods in gateway cities. White-Asian segregation has increased from 0.421 to 0.480 over the same period. Segregation of minority groups from each other is declining for the most part, resulting in more multiracial and multi-ethnic neighborhoods. The segregation of blacks from Hispanics has declined from 0.561 to 0.496, and the segregation from Asians has declined from 0.637 to 0.610. The exception is segregation of Hispanics from Asians, which increased from 0.496 to 0.543 between 1990 and the 2007 to 2011 period. The integration of minority groups with each other is an interesting development, but it does not address the question of access to the educational institutions and resources of non-Hispanic whites. Given the persistent achievement gaps between white and minority children, it is troubling that the nation has not been able to make more progress in reducing segregation of blacks from whites and that segregation of other groups from whites is increasing.

The story is more discouraging in larger metropolitan areas with substantial black populations. In a number of major cities, particularly in the Midwest and Northeast, segregation remains at historically high levels, as shown in table 4.2, listing U.S. metropolitan areas where black-white segregation exceeds 0.60. Four areas, including New York and Detroit, have black-white dissimilarity that exceeds 0.80. Another nine metropolitan areas, including Chicago and Philadelphia, exceed 0.70. In fact, all but two of the metropolitan areas with at least a half million black residents qualify for inclusion in this table because they exceed 0.60. The exceptions are Atlanta and Dallas, with 2007 to 2011 black-white dissimilarity scores of 0.596 and 0.583 respectively, barely below the table's threshold. As shown in figure 4.1, the level of black-white segregation increases steadily with the size of the black population.

Trends in Economic Segregation

Measures of economic segregation are numerous (Erbe 1975; Farley 1991; Jargowsky 1996; Reardon and Bischoff 2011; Watson 2009), but one of the most basic is the index of dissimilarity between the poor and the nonpoor

Table 4.2   Highly Segregated Metropolitan Areas

Metropolitan Area	White-Black Index of Dissimilarity			Black Population, 2007–2011
	1990	2000	2007–2011	
Milwaukee-Waukesha-West Allis, WI	0.835	0.843	0.819	249,887
Detroit-Livonia-Dearborn, MI	0.856	0.866	0.817	740,857
New York-White Plains-Wayne, NY-NJ	0.825	0.823	0.804	2,364,475
Newark-Union, NJ-PA	0.838	0.823	0.801	440,515
Chicago-Joliet-Naperville, IL	0.848	0.818	0.782	1,415,515
Philadelphia, PA	0.820	0.786	0.764	860,496
Cleveland-Elyria-Mentor, OH	0.833	0.792	0.757	404,029
Buffalo-Niagara Falls, NY	0.811	0.795	0.745	131,499
St. Louis, MO-IL	0.783	0.756	0.736	497,784
Nassau-Suffolk, NY	0.776	0.758	0.733	248,433
Boston-Quincy, MA	0.754	0.743	0.729	228,959
Miami-Miami Beach-Kendall, FL	0.721	0.723	0.721	455,001
Cincinnati-Middletown, OH-KY-IN	0.771	0.747	0.708	244,990
Los Angeles-Long Beach-Glendale, CA	0.717	0.698	0.687	819,952
Pittsburgh, PA	0.720	0.700	0.685	183,035
Birmingham-Hoover, AL	0.716	0.700	0.674	308,524
Indianapolis-Carmel, IN	0.758	0.735	0.674	248,895
Rochester, NY	0.693	0.708	0.670	115,744
Hartford-West Hartford-East Hartford, CT	0.716	0.686	0.667	119,084
Baltimore-Towson, MD	0.718	0.690	0.664	745,935
Washington-Arlington-Alexandria, DC-VA-MD-WV	0.685	0.670	0.658	1,215,383
Denver-Aurora-Broomfield, CO	0.652	0.650	0.651	135,881
New Orleans-Metairie-Kenner, LA	0.684	0.697	0.646	374,587
Memphis, TN-MS-AR	0.659	0.664	0.638	575,969
Columbus, OH	0.690	0.653	0.636	258,884
Kansas City, MO-KS	0.739	0.719	0.630	243,524
Warren-Troy-Farmington Hills, MI	0.780	0.711	0.622	225,201
Houston-Sugar Land-Baytown, TX	0.649	0.660	0.621	980,255
Oakland-Fremont-Hayward, CA	0.649	0.645	0.608	274,065
San Francisco-San Mateo-Redwood City, CA	0.600	0.643	0.605	72,705
Providence-New Bedford-Fall River, RI-MA	0.635	0.591	0.605	77,202

Source: Author's compilation based on U.S. Census Summary File 3 data for 1990 and 2000 and American Community Survey data for 2007–2011 (U.S. Census Bureau 1991, 2002, 2012).

Figure 4.1   Metropolitan Black-White Segregation by Number
of Black Residents

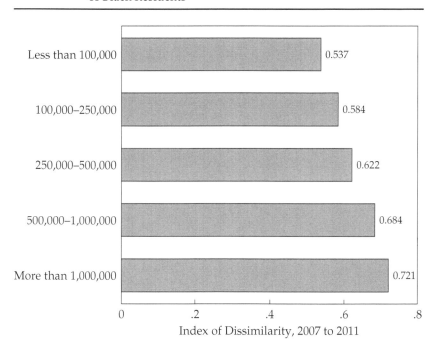

Source: Author's compilation of American Community Survey 2007 to 2011 data (U.S. Census Bureau 2012).

(Abramson, Tobin, and VanderGoot 1995; Abramson and Tobin 1994). The interpretation of the measure is analogous to the racial case; the index of dissimilarity of the poor from the nonpoor expresses the proportion of the poor that would have to move to achieve an even distribution of the poor across neighborhoods.

Table 4.3 shows economic segregation overall and within racial and ethnic groups. Economic segregation in the population overall has changed little since 1990. If anything, it has declined slightly, from 0.367 in 1990 to 0.354 in the 2007 to 2011 period, but that conceals increases in economic segregation within racial groups. The absolute level of poor-nonpoor segregation is quite a bit lower than the black-white segregation figure, but these figures cannot be compared directly. In part, the lower levels stem from the fact that income is continuous, so that someone just above the poverty line is hardly distinguishable from someone just below it. In contrast, race and ethnicity are categorical measures and reflect sharper and more visible distinctions between groups. Moreover, individual incomes fluctuate over time and so a person might be poor in one period and not

Table 4.3   Economic Segregation, Overall and Within Race/Ethnic Groups

Year	Total	White	Black	Hispanic	Asian
1990 census	0.367	0.310	0.373	0.456	0.612
2000 census	0.350	0.302	0.363	0.373	0.556
2005–2009 ACS	0.352	0.330	0.430	0.424	0.622
2006–2010 ACS	0.357	0.339	0.440	0.437	0.645
2007–2011 ACS	0.354	0.336	0.432	0.429	0.639

Source: Author's compilation of U.S. Census Summary File 3 data for 1990 and 2000 and American Community Survey data for 2005–2009, 2006–2010, and 2007–2011 (U.S. Census Bureau 1991, 2002, 2010, 2011, 2012).
Note: Figures are weighted averages of 384 metropolitan areas.

poor the next. For these reasons, the numerical values for the index of dissimilarity between the poor and nonpoor are not directly comparable to values for segregation of one racial group from another.

In contrast to the overall figures, a trend toward increasing poor-nonpoor segregation within racial and ethnic groups is evident. Economic segregation among whites increased from 0.310 in 1990 to 0.336 in the most recent data; among blacks, it increased more substantially, from 0.373 in 1990 to 0.432; and among Asians, who have the highest level of segregation of the poor from the nonpoor, it increased from 0.612 to 0.639. Hispanics were the only group to show a decrease in sorting based on poverty status, from 0.46 to 0.43. The increase in economic segregation within racial groups continues the trend from earlier decades. Using a different measure of economic segregation, Paul Jargowsky (1996) reported that economic segregation increased 24 percent for non-Hispanic whites, 41 percent for blacks, and 27 percent for Hispanics between 1970 and 1990. Sean Reardon and Kendra Bischoff (2011), also using a different measure, reported a 72 percent increase in economic segregation for blacks between 1970 and 2000, and a 26 percent increase for whites.[4] Apparently, the increase in economic segregation within the white and black populations was somewhat offset by the decrease in racial segregation between whites and blacks, resulting in the slight decline in economic segregation overall. This raises the issue of how racial and economic segregation interact, which is discussed later in the chapter.

To the extent that many of the poor may live in neighborhoods with others who are just above the poverty line and with few people who are truly affluent, the index of dissimilarity of the poor from the nonpoor may underestimate the full extent of economic segregation. To drill down deeper, I use data from the 2005–2009 ACS to explore the segregation of households by household income level. Households are divided into four groups based on total household income: less than $25,000; $25,000 to $49,999; $50,000 to $99,999; and more than $100,000. The boundaries between these categories are approximately the poverty line, twice the poverty line, and four times the poverty line, respectively, for a family of four. These groups contain 20.7 million, 34.2 million, 34.9 million, and 18.3 million households respectively, for a total of 108 million households. Thus, the low-income and the affluent groups here are roughly the bottom and the top quintiles of the household income distribution. For ease of presentation, I refer to the first group as poor households, though it should be understood that they may or may not officially be poor according to the federal poverty standard, depending on the size and composition of the household.[5] Similarly, I refer to the second group as working class, the third group as middle class, and the last group as affluent.[6]

As shown in table 4.4, the average segregation level across 384 U.S. metropolitan areas increases the further removed two groups are in the

Table 4.4   Segregation of Households by Income Level, U.S. Metropolitan Areas, 2005 to 2009*

	Within-Group Dissimilarity			Segregation from Affluent Whites
	Working	Middle	Affluent	
All groups				
Poor	0.20	0.32	0.46	0.50
Working class		0.19	0.35	0.40
Middle class			0.23	0.28
Affluent				0.09
Non-Hispanic white				
Poor	0.21	0.29	0.41	0.41
Working class		0.18	0.32	0.32
Middle class			0.22	0.22
Affluent				0.00
Black				
Poor	0.39	0.50	0.65	0.79
Working class		0.39	0.57	0.73
Middle class			0.49	0.68
Affluent				0.67
Hispanic				
Poor	0.44	0.52	0.67	0.73
Working class		0.42	0.61	0.66
Middle class			0.55	0.58
Affluent				0.57
Asian				
Poor	0.61	0.66	0.72	0.76
Working class		0.54	0.63	0.65
Middle class			0.53	0.57
Affluent				0.57

Source: Author's compilation based on American Community Survey 2005–2009 data (U.S. Census Bureau 2010).
*Weighted by total households. See text for description of income brackets.

income distribution. Low-income households are least segregated from working-class households and most segregated from affluent households, both overall and within racial and ethnic groups. Nevertheless, the figures for households overall and white households reveal modest to low levels of segregation by income even between the two extremes. The index of dissimilarity for poor households versus affluent households overall is 0.46, higher than the figure for poor persons versus nonpoor persons (0.35 for the corresponding years), but not dramatically so. Two issues need to be taken into account in assessing these figures. First, annual income fluctuates a great deal over the life cycle. In any given year, annual income is a limited proxy for a household's underlying economic position in society, what is sometimes called permanent income (Rothstein and Wozny 2011). For example, a household whose members had high incomes during their working years may have been able to purchase an expensive house in a suburban neighborhood. They may have substantial equity in the home and other assets that clearly establish them as affluent, but their current income may consist of pensions and appear modest. Unfortunately, the census does not have measures of wealth or permanent income. Second, even annual income is crudely measured in the American Community Survey, because respondents are asked to report their income over the previous twelve months. Respondents may over- or underestimate their income, or may deliberately misstate their income for a variety of reasons. Because income is measured with error, the levels of economic segregation may be understated by this analysis. Regardless, the differences in economic segregation between income and racial groups are still informative.

A third reason the overall segregation measures are low is that they are dominated by white households, among whom economic segregation is relatively low. Indeed, the differences in the levels of economic segregation across the racial and ethnic groups are quite striking. The lowest levels of segregation between black income classes (poor versus working class, 0.39) are almost as high as the most segregated white income group pairing (poor versus affluent, 0.41). Consistent with the results for poor-nonpoor segregation, economic segregation is higher in minority groups. Black poor households are highly segregated from affluent black households, with an index of dissimilarity of 0.65. Hispanics and Asians have even higher levels of economic segregation between poor and affluent households, 0.67 and 0.72 respectively. William Julius Wilson (1987) argues that middle- and higher-income families in a community constitute a social buffer that helps lower-income households weather economic downturns. These figures show that minority poor households are much less likely to benefit from the presence of wealthier households than their white counterparts. The economic isolation of minority poor households is particularly relevant in the educational context. Higher-income families, with higher than average social capital and more flexible employment hours, are more likely to take an active role in neighborhood schools—volunteering, raising funds, and participating in the parent-teacher association (Heymann and Earle 2000).

We can also examine the segregation of the various categories of minority households from affluent white households. Whites are 59 percent of all households in these data, but 72 percent of affluent households. Affluent white neighborhoods in the suburbs contain many of the best schools and educational resources. The rightmost column of table 4.4 examines the segregation of other race and ethnic groups of various income levels from this most advantaged group. Remarkably, all black, Hispanic, and Asian households, even affluent ones, are highly segregated from white affluent households. Segregation of black poor from affluent white households is nearly total, with an index of dissimilarity of 0.79. As high as this figure is, it is not driven primarily by the greater than four to one income difference between affluent and poor households. The segregation of black affluent households is 0.67, meaning that two-thirds of all affluent black households would have to move to achieve an even distribution with white affluent households. In fact, segregation of affluent blacks from affluent whites is 63 percent higher than that of poor white households from their affluent counterparts.[7] To the extent that better-off black families are integrating neighborhoods, they tend to move to inner-ring suburbs, not the neighborhoods of wealthier whites (Lacy 2007; Pattillo-McCoy 2000). The persistence and enduring strength of the color line cannot be denied when white households earning less than $25,000 can share neighborhoods with affluent white families far more easily than black families making over $100,000.

Hispanics and Asians, two groups that are less segregated from whites than are blacks in the aggregate figures, are nearly as segregated from affluent whites as blacks are. Segregation of these groups from affluent whites diminishes somewhat as their income level rises, but even affluent Hispanic and Asian households are still much less likely to live with affluent whites than poor whites are. This is indicated by dissimilarity scores of 0.57 for both affluent Hispanic and Asian households versus 0.41 for poor white households. To the extent that these groups are sharing neighborhoods with whites, they are not doing so with whites in households with incomes over $100,000, regardless of their own income level.

Segregation of Children Enrolled in School

So far, the analysis has focused on persons of all ages, or households that contain people of all ages. However, residential decisions of adults are affected by the presence and age of children in their families (Clark and Onaka 1983; Rossi 1955). To the extent that blacks and whites are colocated in central cities, bringing about the small reductions in racial segregation noted earlier, the whites may be disproportionately young childless adult professionals or, on the opposite end of the continuum, empty nesters drawn by urban amenities. Families with children, regardless of race, seek higher quality schools and safe environments, are less likely than childless families to locate in neighborhoods with higher poverty rates. As a result, whites who have children are less likely to be urban pioneers in integrated urban neighborhoods (Ellen, Horn, and O'Regan 2013).

As a natural consequence of this life-cycle selection, school-age children will be more segregated than persons overall, both racially and economically. The data bear this out. Figure 4.2 shows the segregation of children enrolled in different levels of education: kindergarten and pre-K, elementary school (grades 1 through 8), and high school (grades 9 through 12),

Figure 4.2   Residential Segregation, Students, 2007 to 2011

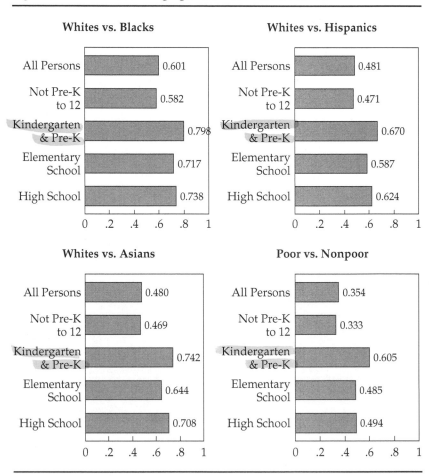

Source: Author's compilation of American Community Survey 2007 to 2011 data (U.S. Census Bureau 2012).

compared with persons not enrolled in school. The overall segreg figures for each racial, ethnic, and economic group, discussed p ously, are also shown for comparison purposes. The bars represen weighted average index of dissimilarity for the indicated groups across the 384 metropolitan areas. There is substantially more residential segregation of children enrolled in school than in the unenrolled populations. For example, the index of dissimilarity for whites and blacks not attending pre-K through twelfth grades is 0.582, whereas black and white children enrolled in elementary school have a 23 percent higher index of dissimilarity, 0.717. White and black high school students are even more segregated, with a segregation score of 0.738. The difference may be related to the finding, reported in chapter 7 of this volume, that highly educated middle-class parents worry more about the issues of academic quality and school safety at the high school level than at the elementary level.

Children are required to be enrolled in school during their elementary years and some or all of their high school years, depending on local laws. In contrast, attending kindergarten and prekindergarten is usually a choice. Children ages three to five may be kept at home with a stay-at-home parent, grandparent, or babysitter. Thus, the residential segregation of children enrolled in kindergarten and pre-K is influenced both by the segregation of families with children in that age range and by the choices families make about enrolling those children. Apparently, families exercise their choices in ways that further increase segregation: children enrolled in kindergarten and pre-K have the highest black-white segregation, measured at 0.798 (37 percent higher than those not enrolled). This extreme figure is the nationwide average of 384 metropolitan areas, not a select group of highly segregated cities.

Segregation of Hispanics and Asians from whites by school enrollment follows exactly the same pattern as black-white segregation, albeit starting from lower overall levels in the general population. Hispanic children enrolled in elementary school are 25 percent more segregated than Hispanics not enrolled in school, with segregation scores of 0.587 and 0.471 respectively. The index rises further to 0.624 for high school students and 0.670 for kindergarten and pre-K enrollees. On a percentage basis, the discrepancy between overall and school-age segregation from whites is largest for Asians, rising 37 percent from 0.469 for Asians not in school versus 0.644 for elementary school children. The index rises further for high school (0.708, 51 percent) and kindergarten and pre-K students (0.742, 58 percent). In terms of school-age children, Asians are more segregated from whites than blacks from whites overall.

Similarly, poor and nonpoor children enrolled in school are more segregated than the poor and nonpoor persons not in school, as is also shown in figure 4.2. Among children enrolled in prekindergarten, segregation of the poor from the nonpoor is 0.605, compared to 0.333 for poor and nonpoor persons not enrolled in school. Elementary and high school students also exhibit elevated segregation, with poor versus non-poor dissimilarity of 0.485 and 0.494 respectively. The ACS data do not have enough detail to examine the racial-ethnic segregation of students separately for poor and nonpoor students, but it seems clear that poor school-age minority students would be segregated on both dimensions from nonpoor white students.

Life-cycle choices of families with and without children about where to live, combined with racial steering and other institutional factors, magnify residential segregation for school-age children. Choices to enroll or not when schooling is optional apparently magnifies segregation further, leading kindergarten and prekindergarten to be the most segregated subset of each racial and economic group. Further, as reported in chapter 3 of this volume, whites are more likely to send their children to private school as the percentage minority in a neighborhood increases, further magnifying segregation as experienced by children.[8] When the concern is with the implications for education, generally reported segregation levels substantially underestimate effective level of residential segregation for the school-age population. Given the linkage between school composition and academic performance (Hanushek et al. 2003), the elevated levels of residential segregation among school-age children have important implications for equality of opportunity in education. As far as children enrolled in pre-K through twelfth grade are concerned, the United States has not come close to seeing the end of segregation.

Disentangling Race and Class Segregation

Given that racial and ethnic groups have different poverty rates, it is inevitable that residential sorting by race produces some economic segregation (Massey and Eggers 1990; Massey and Fischer 2000). Likewise, given that the poor and nonpoor populations have different racial compositions, residential sorting of the poor and nonpoor will also generate racial segregation (Massey 1990). For example, if some neighborhoods have affordable housing and others do not, even if the poor and nonpoor sort randomly into the units they can afford, some degree of racial segregation will be produced. The question is how much each form of segregation contributes to the other. Are we dealing with one underlying problem with two different manifestations, or with two independent processes?

To address this question, I conducted two simulations using the 2011 ACS five-year data, based on household surveys spanning 2007 to 2011. First, I simulated the contribution of racial segregation to economic segregation, followed by the contribution of economic segregation to racial segregation. This methodology is reminiscent of the racial and economic segregation matrices presented in Douglas Massey (1990) and Massey and Nancy Denton (1993) for hypothetical cities. Their analyses made the theoretical point that racial segregation of economically unequal groups would produce some economic segregation and that economic segregation in the presence of economic segregation could produce racial segregation. The analysis presented here goes further by empirically demonstrating how much of each form of segregation is a consequence of the other at the metropolitan level and describing local variations in the interdependence of racial and economic segregation across metropolitan areas.

Economic Segregation Due to Racial Segregation

To estimate the contribution of racial residential sorting to economic segregation, I conduct the following simulation. Within a given metropolitan area, I calculate the poverty rate for each racial and ethnic group. I then apply the metropolitan poverty rate to each groups' population at the tract level, creating a simulated number of poor and nonpoor persons for each group. The metropolitan totals of poor and nonpoor persons are preserved, but the poor and nonpoor persons from each group in the simulated data are spread evenly across the metropolitan area in proportion to their neighborhood population. By construction, the segregation of the poor from the nonpoor within racial groups is exactly zero in the simulated data. It follows that if all tracts had the same racial composition, they would also have equal poverty rates and there would be zero economic segregation. However, a tract with greater percentages of higher poverty groups will have a higher poverty rate than a tract of mainly lower poverty groups. Thus, any segregation of the poor from the nonpoor in this simulation is induced by unevenness in the distribution of racial-ethnic groups, that is, racial segregation. I then calculate the level of economic segregation using this simulated population and compare the results to the actual level of economic segregation calculated in the normal way. The difference between the two stems from the segregation by poverty status within minority groups. In effect, the simulation decomposes economic segregation into a part that is attributable to sorting by race and a part that is due to sorting by income within race.

The weighted average metropolitan-level index of dissimilarity of the poor from the nonpoor is 0.354, as reported earlier. After eliminating economic segregation within race, the index falls 63 percent to 0.130. Thus, about 37 percent of economic segregation, by this measure, is associated with segregation by race. The rest must be due to residential sorting of the poor and nonpoor within racial groups. It would be unwise to ascribe a causal interpretation to this decomposition, since economic and racial segregation are inherently endogenous. Nevertheless, the simulation sets an upper bound on the proportion of economic segregation that can be attributed to racial segregation.

Among the largest metropolitan areas, as shown in table 4.5, the percentage of economic segregation that is tied to racial segregation ranges

Table 4.5   Economic Segregation, Actual and Due to Race Segregation, 2007 to 2011

| Metropolitan Area | Population | Poor-Nonpoor Index of Dissimilarity | | |
		Actual	Simulated	%
New York-White Plains-Wayne, NY-NJ	11,322,061	0.375	0.149	39.7
Los Angeles-Long Beach-Glendale, CA	9,633,080	0.341	0.119	34.8
Chicago-Joliet-Naperville, IL	7,738,150	0.390	0.224	57.3
Houston-Sugar Land-Baytown, TX	5,758,463	0.363	0.152	42.0
Atlanta-Sandy Springs-Marietta, GA	5,125,448	0.333	0.147	44.0
Washington-Arlington-Alexandria, DC-VA-MD-WV	4,224,244	0.395	0.143	36.2
Dallas-Plano-Irving, TX	4,118,691	0.394	0.170	43.1
Riverside-San Bernardino-Ontario, CA	4,096,898	0.336	0.076	22.7
Phoenix-Mesa-Glendale, AZ	4,073,886	0.395	0.149	37.6
Philadelphia, PA	3,881,558	0.467	0.257	54.9
Minneapolis-St. Paul-Bloomington, MN-WI	3,205,108	0.391	0.159	40.7
San Diego-Carlsbad-San Marcos, CA	2,977,884	0.337	0.098	29.0
Santa Ana-Anaheim-Irvine, CA	2,952,214	0.324	0.128	39.5
Nassau-Suffolk, NY	2,773,928	0.332	0.139	41.8
St. Louis, MO-IL	2,768,371	0.371	0.195	52.7
Tampa-St. Petersburg-Clearwater, FL	2,727,371	0.318	0.100	31.5
Baltimore-Towson, MD	2,629,552	0.410	0.183	44.5
Seattle-Bellevue-Everett, WA	2,574,594	0.329	0.088	26.7
Oakland-Fremont-Hayward, CA	2,497,328	0.371	0.112	30.3
Denver-Aurora-Broomfield, CO	2,478,370	0.397	0.161	40.6
Warren-Troy-Farmington Hills, MI	2,454,209	0.336	0.081	24.0
Miami-Miami Beach-Kendall, FL	2,421,799	0.303	0.076	25.1
Pittsburgh, PA	2,299,910	0.353	0.119	33.7
Edison-New Brunswick, NJ	2,286,646	0.394	0.095	24.1
Portland-Vancouver-Hillsboro, OR-WA	2,170,298	0.296	0.070	23.7
Newark-Union, NJ-PA	2,098,931	0.438	0.259	59.3
Sacramento—Arden-Arcade—Roseville, CA	2,091,774	0.339	0.095	28.1
Orlando-Kissimmee-Sanford, FL	2,081,971	0.267	0.096	36.0
Cincinnati-Middletown, OH-KY-IN	2,074,782	0.395	0.152	38.5
Fort Worth-Arlington, TX	2,070,892	0.371	0.142	38.4
San Antonio-New Braunfels, TX	2,058,946	0.349	0.105	30.0
Cleveland-Elyria-Mentor, OH	2,040,595	0.435	0.242	55.5

Source: Author's decomposition based on American Community Survey 2007–2011 data (U.S. Census Bureau 2012).

Figure 4.3   Decomposition of Economic Segregation, 2007 to 2011

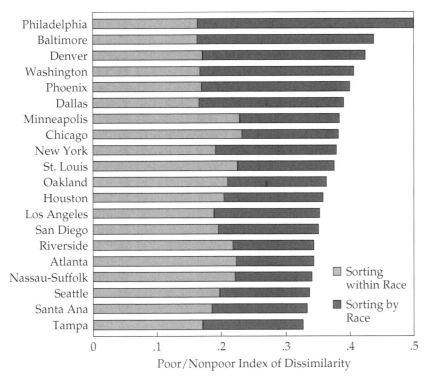

Source: Author's decomposition based on American Community Survey 2007 to 2011 data (U.S. Census Bureau 2012). See text for details of decomposition.

from 23 to 59 percent. It is not surprising that the contribution of racial segregation to economic segregation is highest in metropolitan areas with large black populations and high levels of black-white residential segregation. Although racial segregation clearly plays a role in generating economic segregation, the bulk of economic segregation—close to two-thirds, on average—is independent of racial sorting.

Figure 4.3 graphically depicts the decomposition of economic segregation into the part due to sorting by race and the part to sorting within race for the twenty largest metropolitan areas sorted by overall level of economic segregation. Interestingly, the portion due to sorting within race—depicted on the left—is relatively constant across these large metropolitan areas, reflecting that all racial groups show some degree of internal economic segregation. Some metropolitan areas, however, have a substantially higher contribution that stems from sorting by race—depicted on the right. Figure 4.4 shows a very strong positive

Figure 4.4   Economic Versus Black-White Segregation, 2007 to 2011

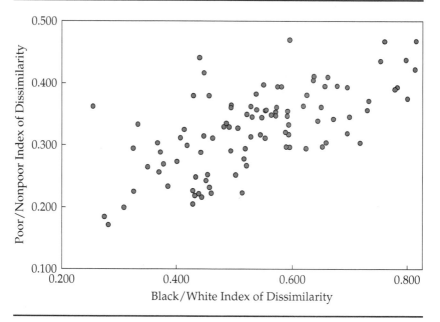

Source: Author's compilation based on American Community Survey 2007 to 2011 data (U.S. Census Bureau 2012).

correlation ($r = 0.65$, $p < 0.000$) between the overall economic segregation (poor versus nonpoor, all races) and black-white segregation for the 100 metropolitan areas with the highest percentage black.

Racial Segregation Due to Economic Segregation

Economic segregation may also contribute to racial segregation. To examine this possibility, I turn the previous simulation on its head. I eliminate race segregation within the poor and nonpoor populations, and then calculate how much racial segregation is generated just by the uneven distribution of the poor and nonpoor across neighborhoods. To do this, I first calculate the racial composition of the poor and nonpoor within each metropolitan area. These shares are applied to poor and nonpoor persons in each tract. The metropolitan number of poor and nonpoor persons as well as the total population in each tract is preserved. By construction, in this simulation the segregation by race within the poor population and within the nonpoor population is exactly zero. It follows that if all tracts had the same poverty rate, they would also have equal percentages of each racial group and therefore no racial segregation. However, a tract with a higher poverty rate will have a disproportionate share of racial groups overrepresented in the poor population. Thus, any segregation by race in this simulation is induced by unevenness in the distribution of the poor and nonpoor populations—in other words, economic segregation. I then calculate the level of racial segregation using this simulated population, which gives the amount of racial segregation that is associated with poor-nonpoor segregation, and compare the results with actual levels of racial segregation calculated in the normal way. The difference between the two stems from the segregation by race within the poor and nonpoor populations. In effect, the second simulation decomposes racial segregation into a part attributable to sorting by poverty status and a part due to sorting by race within poverty status.

Table 4.6 shows the results for metropolitan areas in the 2007 to 2011 period. Panel A shows the average actual index of dissimilarity of each racial and ethnic group with respect to the others. Panel B shows the racial segregation induced by poor-nonpoor segregation based on the simulated data. Panel C shows the proportion of racial segregation associated with economic segregation of the poor from the nonpoor: panel B divided by panel A. The results are striking. Virtually all racial segregation disappears in the simulation. The level of black-white segregation due to the residential sorting of poor and nonpoor persons is only 0.059, whereas the actual figure is 0.601. At the metropolitan level, therefore, less than 10 percent of

Table 4.6   Racial Segregation, Actual and Due to Economic Segregation, 2007 to 2011

	Black	Hispanic	Asian
Panel A.		Actual Racial-ethnic Segregation	
White	0.601	0.481	0.480
Black		0.496	0.610
Hispanic			0.543
Panel B.		Due to Economic Segregation	
White	0.059	0.054	0.016
Black		0.018	0.046
Hispanic			0.041
Panel C.		Proportion Due to Economic Segregation	
White	9.8%	11.2%	3.3%
Black		3.6%	7.5%
Hispanic			7.6%
N	384	384	384

Source: Author's decomposition based on American Community Survey 2007–2011 data (U.S. Census Bureau 2012).
See text for description of the decomposition.
Average of 384 metropolitan areas, weighted by population.

the measured level of black-white racial segregation comes from economic segregation. Only 11.2 percent of Hispanic-white segregation is contributed by economic segregation. Less than 4 percent of the index of dissimilarity between blacks and Hispanics is due to economic segregation. In part, this reflects that both groups have elevated poverty rates. The contribution of economic segregation to the racial segregation of Asians is less than 8 percent in all comparisons. In contrast to economic segregation, only a small fraction of sorting by race is a by-product of sorting by income.

Sorting on poverty status is associated with more than one-fifth of the total segregation between blacks and whites in only twenty-five metropolitan areas. These are listed in table 4.7. However, these metropolitan

Table 4.7   Metropolitan Areas in Which Economic Segregation Contributes More than One-Fifth of Racial Segregation, 2007 to 2011

	Population			B/W Dissimilarity		
	Total	White	Black	Actual	Simulated	%
Mankato-North Mankato, MN	90,492	82,934	1,941	0.431	0.179	41.6
Lewiston-Auburn, ME	104,390	96,855	1,624	0.605	0.204	33.7
Dubuque, IA	89,509	83,781	1,166	0.588	0.160	27.3
Lincoln, NE	284,417	244,026	8,935	0.464	0.119	25.7
Missoula, MT	107,005	97,619	454	0.561	0.143	25.5
Rockford, IL	343,653	252,290	36,619	0.597	0.149	24.9
Laredo, TX	242,438	8,438	879	0.762	0.188	24.6
Iowa City, IA	142,134	120,869	5,357	0.459	0.111	24.3
Lima, OH	101,989	84,525	11,706	0.552	0.134	24.2
Longview, WA	100,472	86,395	426	0.634	0.153	24.1
Danville, IL	79,992	64,793	10,049	0.692	0.164	23.7
Ithaca, NY	87,562	71,067	3,266	0.459	0.105	22.8
St. Cloud, MN	178,821	164,345	4,601	0.646	0.143	22.2
Janesville, WI	156,689	133,497	7,291	0.599	0.132	22.0
Fargo, ND-MN	196,793	179,058	3,615	0.446	0.096	21.5
Bloomington, IN	174,717	157,554	3,838	0.521	0.112	21.4
Altoona, PA	123,433	118,406	2,008	0.482	0.102	21.2
Madison, WI	547,464	461,855	22,958	0.556	0.117	21.1
Green Bay, WI	296,518	257,291	4,353	0.574	0.121	21.0
Fond du Lac, WI	97,959	90,646	660	0.451	0.094	20.8
Bloomington-Normal, IL	158,362	130,535	11,146	0.443	0.091	20.5
La Crosse, WI-MN	127,369	117,353	1,748	0.524	0.107	20.4
Spokane, WA	452,546	394,910	7,082	0.489	0.098	20.1
Appleton, WI	220,746	200,102	1,587	0.592	0.119	20.1
Corvallis, OR	79,717	67,033	867	0.571	0.114	20.0

Source: Author's decomposition based on American Community Survey 2007–2011 data (U.S. Census Bureau 2012).
See text for description of the decomposition.

areas are relatively small; only one—Madison, Wisconsin—exceeds a half million in total population and only a few have more than ten thousand black residents. In the largest metropolitan areas, as shown in table 4.8, the situation is quite different. Among metropolitan areas with two million or more persons, the black-white index of dissimilarity ranges from 0.47 to 0.80, but the index associated with the sorting of the poor and non-poor is less than 0.10 in all but two of thirty-two metropolitan areas. Thus, only in metropolitan areas with small black populations does sorting by income lead to a nontrivial proportion of sorting by race. In metropolitan areas with substantial black populations, racial segregation is largely independent of economic segregation.

In conclusion, economic segregation per se contributes very little to racial segregation except in smaller metropolitan areas with small black populations. In contrast, racial segregation seems to be a significant force in creating economic segregation, accounting for about one-third of such segregation in the typical metropolitan area. Moreover, the contribution of racial segregation to economic segregation is a main driver of the differences among metropolitan areas in the level of economic segregation. At the same time, two-thirds of economic segregation on average is not driven by racial segregation. They are related but independent spatial processes, and both contribute to the tendency of poor and minority children to live in racially and economically isolated communities. Because children most often attend schools near their homes, either because they are required to by geographic attendance zones or because of commuting time constraints, segregation by race and class has serious implications for equal access to educational opportunity. Scholars and policymakers concerned with reducing educational disparities in educational attainment need to address both racial and economic segregation, given that both contribute independently to the educational isolation of low-income children.

The Intersection: Concentration of Poverty

We have seen that racial and economic segregation contribute to each other but also that they are separate dimensions. At the intersection of segregation by race and class lies concentrated poverty (Quillian 2012). Poor blacks and Hispanics, for example, are highly segregated from the more affluent white population and increasingly segregated from middle-class members of their own groups. Many reside in high-poverty ghettos and barrios that are home to a wide range of social problems and a lack of access to resources that many members of society take for granted. The problems of poverty are exacerbated when poor people live in dysfunctional high-poverty neighborhoods, where they are exposed to high levels of crime and violence and have limited access to educational and economic opportunities (Wilson 1996). Growing up in such neighborhoods can affect children's educational achievement (Burdick-Will et al.

Table 4.8   Black-White Segregation, Actual and Simulated, 2007 to 2011

	Population			B-W Dissimilarity		
	Total	White	Black	Actual	Simulated	%
New York-White Plains-Wayne, NY-NJ	11,322,061	4,472,631	2,364,475	0.804	0.044	5.5
Los Angeles-Long Beach-Glendale, CA	9,633,080	2,695,527	819,952	0.687	0.041	6.0
Chicago-Joliet-Naperville, IL	7,738,150	4,102,356	1,415,515	0.782	0.080	10.3
Houston-Sugar Land-Baytown, TX	5,758,463	2,323,948	980,255	0.621	0.055	8.9
Atlanta-Sandy Springs-Marietta, GA	5,125,448	2,642,502	1,639,155	0.596	0.039	6.6
Washington-Arlington-Alexandria, DC-VA-MD-WV	4,224,244	1,989,060	1,215,383	0.658	0.033	5.0
Dallas-Plano-Irving, TX	4,118,691	1,968,400	648,215	0.583	0.062	10.6
Riverside-San Bernardino-Ontario, CA	4,096,898	1,525,677	298,311	0.469	0.037	7.9
Phoenix-Mesa-Glendale, AZ	4,073,886	2,418,343	192,769	0.496	0.057	11.5
Philadelphia, PA	3,881,558	2,485,327	860,496	0.764	0.096	12.6
Minneapolis-St. Paul-Bloomington, MN-WI	3,205,108	2,536,712	228,203	0.566	0.107	18.9
San Diego-Carlsbad-San Marcos, CA	2,977,884	1,458,898	145,661	0.558	0.033	5.9
Santa Ana-Anaheim-Irvine, CA	2,952,214	1,323,436	48,079	0.492	0.018	3.7
Nassau-Suffolk, NY	2,773,928	1,930,726	248,433	0.733	0.023	3.1
St. Louis, MO-IL	2,768,371	2,096,170	497,784	0.736	0.071	9.7
Tampa-St. Petersburg-Clearwater, FL	2,727,371	1,858,865	316,956	0.585	0.048	8.2

Baltimore-Towson, MD	2,629,552	1,595,924	745,935	0.664	0.052	7.9
Seattle-Bellevue-Everett, WA	2,574,594	1,755,548	128,735	0.549	0.062	11.3
Oakland-Fremont-Hayward, CA	2,497,328	1,007,925	274,065	0.608	0.051	8.4
Denver-Aurora-Broomfield, CO	2,478,370	1,643,347	135,881	0.651	0.075	11.5
Warren-Troy-Farmington Hills, MI	2,454,209	2,010,471	225,201	0.622	0.041	6.5
Miami-Miami Beach-Kendall, FL	2,421,799	375,176	455,001	0.721	0.052	7.3
Pittsburgh, PA	2,299,910	2,012,611	183,035	0.685	0.080	11.7
Edison-New Brunswick, NJ	2,286,646	1,564,581	157,698	0.577	0.030	5.2
Portland-Vancouver-Hillsboro, OR-WA	2,170,298	1,668,068	60,600	0.530	0.060	11.2
Newark-Union, NJ-PA	2,098,931	1,156,121	440,515	0.801	0.066	8.2
Sacramento—Arden-Arcade—Roseville, CA	2,091,774	1,181,828	146,792	0.575	0.054	9.4
Orlando-Kissimmee-Sanford, FL	2,081,971	1,120,021	323,794	0.522	0.035	6.6
Cincinnati-Middletown, OH-KY-IN	2,074,782	1,702,480	244,990	0.708	0.083	11.8
Fort Worth-Arlington, TX	2,070,892	1,177,206	260,944	0.589	0.055	9.3
San Antonio-New Braunfels, TX	2,058,946	748,234	128,600	0.530	0.050	9.5
Cleveland-Elyria-Mentor, OH	2,040,595	1,472,811	404,029	0.757	0.103	13.6

Source: Author's decomposition based on American Community Survey 2007–2011 data (U.S. Census Bureau 2012).
See text for description of the decomposition.

2011; Jargowsky and El Komi 2011; Ludwig et al. 2011). The burdens of poverty are, therefore, more intense for the minority poor, who are both racially and economically isolated, than for many of the white poor, who are low income but less likely to have the added burdens of living in very poor neighborhoods (Grady and Darden 2012).

The concentration of poverty quantifies the extent to which poor persons are likely to live in high-poverty neighborhoods and attend the schools that serve these severely disadvantage neighborhoods. Neighborhoods in which more than 40 percent of the population have incomes below the federal poverty line are characterized by high rates of single parenthood, low levels of educational attainment, and detachment from the labor force (Jargowsky 1997, chapter 4). Further, the lack of opportunities and role models in such neighborhoods contributes to a social milieu in which alcohol and drug abuse, gang membership, criminality and other self-defeating behaviors become more prevalent (Wilson 1987, 1996). Thus, a good measure of the concentration of the poverty is the percentage of the poor in a given area living in census tracts with poverty rates of 40 percent or more. By this measure, concentration of poverty rose dramatically during the 1970s and 1980s (Jargowsky and Bane 1991; Jargowsky 1997; Kasarda 1993). The increases were fastest in the Midwest and Northeast, areas that suffered from rapid deindustrialization and rising poverty. In fact, concentration of poverty is closely correlated with overall economic conditions at the metropolitan level. Concentration of poverty declined substantially during the 1990s, a decade of rapid economic growth and low unemployment (Jargowsky 2003; Kingsley and Pettit 2003).

Since 2000, the spatial concentration of poverty has surged again, particularly since the financial crisis and recession began in 2008. The number of census tracts with poverty rates of 40 percent or more fell from 3,417 to 2,510 between 1990 and 2000. Since 2000, it rose to 3,764 in the most recent ACS data, from 2007 to 2011.[9] In particular, as shown in table 4.9, the total population of all high-poverty census tracts in the United States was 9.6 million in 1990, but fell to 7.2 million by 2000 after the economic boom of the 1990s. Unfortunately, the year 2000 turned out to be something of an anomaly. In the 2005 to 2009 ACS data, the number of residents of high-poverty neighborhoods had returned to nearly the 1990 level. Note that most of the 2005 to 2009 sample was collected before the financial crisis struck in late 2008. As the recession took hold, the number living in high-poverty neighborhoods climbed steadily to more than eleven million persons in the 2007 to 2011 period. Given that 2007 and the beginning of 2008 preceded the recent downtown and consequent surge in poverty, a point in time estimate from 2010 or 2011 would likely be higher still.

The racial-ethnic composition of the population of high-poverty neighborhoods has changed due to different rates of growth in among demographic subgroups. For example, though the population in high-

Table 4.9   Population, High-Poverty Neighborhoods

	Census		American Community Survey		
	1990	2000	2005–2009	2006–2010	2007–2011
Population					
Total	9,592,333	7,198,892	9,506,534	10,309,844	11,224,438
White	2,632,075	1,439,889	2,551,695	2,713,180	2,932,517
Black	4,799,550	3,010,537	3,777,386	3,929,074	4,195,031
Hispanic	2,213,080	2,236,604	2,625,736	3,043,195	3,386,471
Asian	227,226	249,460	275,955	327,096	360,719
Demographic composition					
Total	364.4%	500.0%	372.6%	380.0%	382.8%
White	100.0%	100.0%	100.0%	100.0%	100.0%
Black	182.3%	209.1%	148.0%	144.8%	143.1%
Hispanic	84.1%	155.3%	102.9%	112.2%	115.5%
Asian	8.6%	17.3%	10.8%	12.1%	12.3%
Change over time		1990 to 2000		2000 to 2007–2011	
Total		−25.0%		55.9%	
White		−45.3%		103.7%	
Black		−37.3%		39.3%	
Hispanic		1.1%		51.4%	
Asian		9.8%		44.6%	

Source: Author's compilation of U.S. Census Summary File 3 data for 1990 and 2000 and American Community Survey data for 2005–2009, 2006–2010, and 2007–2011 (U.S. Census Bureau 1991, 2002, 2010, 2011, 2012).
Note: Residents of census tracts with poverty rates of 40 percent or more, all U.S. census tracts.

poverty groups has risen for all racial and ethnic groups, it has grown fastest among non-Hispanic whites; the count of whites in high-poverty areas more than doubled between 2000 and the most recent data. In comparison, the black and Hispanic population of those areas increased 39 and 51 percent, respectively. As a result, whites now make up more than 26 percent of the population of high-poverty tracts, versus 20 percent in 2000. The black population share has declined from 42 percent in 2000 to 37 percent in the 2007 to 2011 period. The Hispanic share has remained constant at approximately 30 percent.

Although the number of high-poverty neighborhoods has risen, it is also true that the number of poor persons has risen overall, both due to population growth and the general rise in the poverty rate since 2000. To ask whether poverty is more concentrated, we must examine the percentage of the poor living in high-poverty areas. In the average metropolitan area, this figure rose from 11.6 percent to 14.1 percent between 2000 and the 2007 to 2011 period, although the concentration of poverty is still lower than in 1990, when it was 16.8 percent. As shown in figure 4.5, it

Figure 4.5   Concentration of Poverty

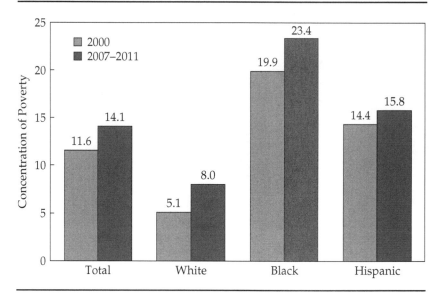

Source: Author's compilation of U.S. Census 2000 Summary File 3 data and American Community Survey 2007–2011 data (U.S. Census Bureau 2002, 2012).

rose for all groups, though the increase was fastest for whites—from 5.1 to 8.0. Despite the recent increase in whites living in high-poverty areas, concentration of poverty still affects minority groups differently. As shown in figure 4.5, the black poor are nearly three times more likely than the white poor to live in high-poverty neighborhoods, 23.4 percent versus 8.0 percent. The Hispanic poor are nearly twice as likely as the white poor to do so.

A number of metropolitan areas have much higher levels of concentrated poverty than the average figures reported earlier. Table 4.10 shows the ten metropolitan areas with the highest levels of concentrated poverty for blacks and Hispanics, respectively. For blacks, the list is dominated by metropolitan areas in the Midwest, such as Detroit, where 47 percent of the black poor live in high-poverty neighborhoods, followed by Milwaukee (46 percent), Gary (43 percent), and so on. A few southern metropolitan areas score high as well, such as Tallahassee (39 percent), Mobile (37 percent), and Memphis (36 percent).

Not surprisingly, southwestern and western metropolitan areas rank the highest in Hispanic concentration of poverty, exemplified by Laredo, Texas, where 55 percent of the Hispanic poor live in census tracts with poverty levels of 40 percent or more. One notable exception is Philadelphia, ranking third, where 50 percent of the Hispanic poor live in high-poverty neighborhoods. In these metropolitan areas, the children of poor minori-

Table 4.10   Metropolitan Areas, Highest Concentration of Poverty, 2007 to 2011

	Total	Poor All Census Tracts	High-Poverty Census Tracts	%
Black*				
Detroit-Livonia-Dearborn	740,857	255,604	119,241	46.7
Milwaukee-Waukesha-West Allis	249,887	90,790	41,651	45.9
Gary	128,695	40,938	17,718	43.3
Dayton	118,593	36,692	15,310	41.7
Louisville/Jefferson County	167,549	52,876	21,908	41.4
Cleveland-Elyria-Mentor	404,029	130,052	52,298	40.2
Rochester	115,744	39,323	15,601	39.7
Tallahassee	109,516	36,020	14,072	39.1
Mobile	139,119	43,854	16,309	37.2
Memphis	575,969	169,947	60,302	35.5
Hispanic**				
Laredo	231,791	72,530	39,647	54.7
McAllen-Edinburg-Mission	679,813	256,592	133,191	51.9
Philadelphia	279,249	88,077	43,686	49.6
Brownsville-Harlingen	347,338	132,341	64,363	48.6
Las Cruces	131,715	42,124	16,005	38.0
Camden	108,685	24,129	8,748	36.3
Fresno	450,052	137,048	46,013	33.6
Visalia-Porterville	257,929	79,081	26,371	33.3
El Paso	637,099	178,773	52,555	29.4
Milwaukee-Waukesha-West Allis	140,301	34,363	10,056	29.3
Bakersfield-Delano	385,415	108,451	31,434	29.0
Hartford-West Hartford-East Hartford	141,315	39,665	11,273	28.4
Tucson	325,318	82,134	19,290	23.5

Source: Author's compilation based on American Community Survey 2007–2011 data (U.S. Census Bureau 2012).
*Metropolitan areas with at least 100,000 blacks.
**Metropolitan areas with at least 100,000 Hispanics.

ties are likely to live in neighborhoods where schools are beset by a host of problems, including a high degree of student mobility, drug use and violence, low expectations, and high dropout rates.

These results show that concentration of poverty is still a major impediment to equality of opportunity. Although the white poor are increasingly found in high-poverty neighborhoods, African Americans and Hispanics still make up the majority of high-poverty neighborhood residents. Low-income persons of all major racial and ethnic groups experienced increases in the probability of living in high-poverty neighborhoods, but the risk is still much higher for blacks and Hispanics. In a number of major metropolitan areas, more than a third of the poor live in these socially and economically devastated neighborhoods. Poor children in these neighborhoods have to cope not only with the lack of resources in the home, but also with chaotic social environments and schools that are struggling, and often failing, to cope with the multiple social disadvantages of their students.

Implications for Educational Equity

The segregation of blacks from whites has declined somewhat, but is still very high, and segregation by income within racial and ethnic groups is increasing. Further, certain more subtle aspects of segregation have implications for the ability of low-income children, especially minority children, to access the high-quality, resource-rich schools that are most often found in affluent white neighborhoods. Poor black, Hispanic, and Asian households rarely share neighborhoods with affluent white households, with indices of dissimilarity of 0.79, 0.73, and 0.76, respectively. Even affluent households of these groups are highly segregated from affluent white households, showing segregation scores of 0.57 to 0.67. Segregation is more severe for children enrolled in school. The residential segregation of minority children from white children is 23 to 58 percent higher for children enrolled in pre-K through high school than for members of those groups not enrolled in school. This elevated level is before consideration of selection into private schools, charter schools, and home-schooling, and of the segregating effects of tracking within schools (Clotfelter 2004; Rivkin 1994; Saporito 2003).

Segregation by race and class for school-age children, therefore, is far more pervasive than for the adult population and exposes children to very unequal school contexts. Further, segregation by race and poverty interact to produce high-poverty neighborhoods, which have increased in number and population since 2000. Segregation of school-age children in racially and economically isolated neighborhoods may be more damaging than segregation in general. Adults have much greater scope and freedom to travel; they will often work outside their neighborhood, have more contacts outside it, and can decide to leave if they find the conditions unacceptable. School-age children will spend more time in the neighborhood and depend on their parents' choices about where to live. They will spend all day in school with other children from the same neighborhood. Their friends often will be drawn from other students in the same school or in a local church. Because children are more embedded in their neighborhoods than adults, they are more vulnerable to the neighborhood effects via pathways such as those Christopher Jencks and Susan Mayer describe

(1990): neighborhood institutional resource deficits, ineffective collective socialization, exposure to negative role models, competition over scarce resources, and perceptions of relative resource deprivation.

Segregation, in its many forms, has implications for educational outcomes because schools are creatures of neighborhoods (Levy 1995). In most cases, school attendance zone boundaries are strictly geographic. Despite the increase in charter and magnet schools, about 70 percent of children attend the local school based on the catchment zone in which they live (chapter 6, this volume). Indeed, the typical elementary school catchment area has about the same population as a census tract.[10] Even for schools that draw their students from larger and less precise areas, such as magnet and charter schools, commuting time and transportation costs often restrict attendance to those who live relatively nearby. As Annette Lareau observes, "because children [in this study] attended the local catchment school, once parents choose a residence, they chose a school" (chapter 6, this volume).

To the extent that the neighborhood has children from families that have problems with drugs, alcohol, and violence, these problems will come into the school and affect the school climate. Over time, the schools themselves become different. Schools in poorer neighborhoods have greater needs than schools with more advantaged children. Teachers and school administrators may develop lower academic expectations when they deal predominantly with poor children, many of whom do not have resources and support in the home (Farkas 1996). There is also a feedback effect, because school performance plays a role in parental decisions about where to live, and the effect is greatest for the parents who have the most resources to spend on housing and who place the greatest value on education. The neighborhood drags down the school, and the school drags down the neighborhood. Thus, as Amy Schwartz and Leanna Stiefel discuss in chapter 10 of this volume, children in high-poverty neighborhoods attend troubled schools and achieve less than similar students in more affluent neighborhoods.

Schools in segregated, economically isolated neighborhoods will be hard pressed to maintain high educational standards. Anyone who has been a teacher understands that learning is in part a group process. Students bring their own skills and abilities, but they learn from and with their fellow students (Manski 2000). Children, especially adolescents, want to fit in, so they may adopt the prevailing attitude toward the value of academic achievement. In some inner-city schools, working hard and getting good grades is derided as "acting white" (Fordham and Ogbu 1986). Even students who resist caving in to peer pressure may still be impeded in learning if enough classmates are disruptive and slow the pace of instruction (Figlio 2007; Lazear 2001). These so-called peer effects on students have been documented in a number of carefully controlled studies (Hanushek et al. 2003; Hoxby 2000; Summers and Wolfe 1977; Zimmer and Toma 2000).

Over and above peer effects, neighborhood conditions may have spillover effects on academic achievement (Crane 1991; Crowder and South 2003; Datcher 1982; Jargowsky and El Komi 2011). Neighborhoods develop cultures that in turn influence their members. Students may lack positive role models if few members of a community graduate from college or have steady employment in high-skilled occupations that require education. Students are more likely to drop out if they live in neighborhoods with few affluent neighbors (Brooks-Gunn et al. 1993). Parents are not immune to neighborhood influences either. It may be harder for parents to keep pressure on their children to achieve academically if other parents in the neighborhood do not demand the same effort from their children. These processes and feedback mechanisms translate the map of segregation into a map of school quality.

The vast differences in school quality are a cause for concern in and of themselves, but it is even worse if school inequality reinforces class differences and limits social mobility. Unfortunately, as Anna Rhodes and Stefanie DeLuca make abundantly clear in chapter 5 of this volume, low-income families often face many constraints and chaotic life situations that drive their place of residence. Their place of residence usually determines or at least influences the schools attended by their children and how often their children's education is disrupted by school moves. In contrast, middle-class and wealthy families often choose their residential location to facilitate their desired choice of schooling options. At the very least, real or perceived school quality is certainly a consideration in their choice. As a result, residential segregation by race and class, segregation of school children, and differences in actual and perceived school quality form a self-reinforcing vicious circle that leads to vast disparities in the availability of quality education (Kozol 1991). These disparities reduce social mobility and exacerbate inequality, and are therefore a major impediment to the possibility of equality of opportunity.

On the other end of the spectrum, middle- and upper-class parents have more opportunity to research schools. Yet, as Lareau notes in chapter 6 of this volume, many middle- and upper-class parents do little actual research on the schools in which they enroll their children. Instead, they find neighborhoods with attractive demographics, and enroll their children in the local schools. Those who are able to access housing in affluent suburban enclaves do not need to do in-depth research on good schools. The machinery of segregation did the work for them. Because they could choose neighborhoods that were segregated and that buffered them from the presence of working-class families, to say nothing of poor families, the elite parents did not need to activate some of the key resources in their formidable repertoire (chapter 6, this volume). In contrast, as discussed in chapters 8 and 9 of this volume, working-class parents and middle-class parents who, by choice or necessity, live in more economically and racially mixed areas, devote considerable effort to researching school quality. Yet they often are limited in their choices and they do not always know how to access information about school quality.

For all these reasons, the ideal of equal access to primary and secondary education that underlies American notions of equality of opportunity is inconsistent with racial and economic segregation. A serious commitment to increasing equality of educational opportunity must start with addressing the public policies that permit, and indeed require, economic segregation in the housing stock. We should continue to address racial discrimination in the housing market. The only real way to make school choice a reality is if neighborhood choice is a reality as well. Given the "converging evidence" that poor neighborhoods harm the academic performance of low-income children (Burdick-Will et al. 2011), it is imperative for scholars and policymakers to understand the choices, policies, and institutions that contribute to and help to maintain the segregated and overlapping maps of neighborhoods and schools.

I wish to thank Marie Chevrier, Helen Glenn Court, Kimberly Goyette, Annette Lareau, Lincoln Quillian, two anonymous reviewers, and the participants in the Choosing Homes, Choosing Schools conference at the Russell Sage Foundation, February 14–15, 2013 for helpful comments and suggestions.

Notes

1. The average unweighted sample count in Summary File 3 of the 2000 Census was 664 (from table P2) versus 387 from the 2007–2011 ACS data (table B00001).

2. The official categories are white, black or African American, American Indian and Alaska Native, Asian, Native Hawaiian and Other Pacific Islander, or some other race.

3. The numbers here are slightly different than those cited by Kimberly Goyette in chapter 1 of this volume, drawing on Logan and Stults (2011), due to differences in methodology between their study and the analysis presented in this chapter. The most important difference is that Logan and Stults used the 2010 Census, whereas the numbers in this chapter are based on the ACS. This analysis also excludes residents of group quarters and multiracial individuals, while Logan and Stults include them. Although the exact numbers reported here vary slightly from those reported by Logan and Stults due to these methodological differences, the basic trends we report do not.

4. My measure was the neighborhood sorting index, which reflects the variance in income between neighborhoods as a proportion of the total variance. Reardon and Bischoff's was the rank order information theory index. Neither study reported economic segregation figures for all race groups combined.

5. Poverty is determined on the basis of total family income, not household income; these will differ only when an unrelated individual lives with the family. These data have incomes expressed in 2009 dollars. The weighted average poverty threshold in 2009 was $21,954 for a family of four, $25,991 for family of five, and $29,405 for a family of six (http://www.census.gov/hhes/www/poverty/data/threshld/thresh09.html).

6. In another work (1996), I argued that breaking the income distribution into groups should not be used to study changes in economic segregation over time, because to do so could confound changes in the income distribution with changes in residential patterns. In this analysis, I examine a single point in time, so that is not a concern.

7. Similarly, using somewhat different definitions of poor and affluent households, Logan (2013) notes that the average neighborhood poverty rate for affluent blacks and Hispanics is actually higher than the average neighborhood poverty rate for poor whites. This is consequence of the fact that poor white families are able to access housing in affluent neighborhoods that minority families cannot.

8. On the positive side, Salvatore Saporito and Caroline Hanley note in chapter 3 of this volume that the effect of neighborhood percent black on the probability of white students enrolling in private school has declined since 1980. However, it remains a relatively strong determinant of white private school enrollment.

9. The total number of census tracts was also increasing over this period, from sixty thousand to seventy-two thousand as census tracts are split to accommodate population growth. Most of the new tracts are created on the suburban fringes, where very few tracts have high poverty rates, implying that the changes in the count of high-poverty tracts is not driven by the creation of new tracts.

10. An area with a population of four thousand would be expected to have about four hundred to six hundred persons attending kindergarten through eighth grade, depending the demography of the area.

References

Abramson, Alan J., and Mitchell S. Tobin. 1994. *The Changing Geography of Metropolitan Opportunity: The Segregation of the Poor in U.S. Metropolitan Areas, 1970 to 1990.* Washington, D.C.: Fannie Mae Office of Housing Policy Research.

Abramson, Alan J., Mitchell S. Tobin, and Matthew R. VanderGoot. 1995. "The Changing Geography of Metropolitan Opportunity: The Segregation of the Poor in U.S. Metropolitan Areas, 1970 to 1990." *Housing Policy Debate* 6(1): 45–72.

Berry, Brian Joe Lobley, Peter G. Goheen, and Harold Goldstein. 1969. *Metropolitan Area Definition: A Re-evaluation of Concept and Statistical Practice.* Washington: U.S. Census Bureau.

Bonastia, Christopher. 2006. *Knocking on the Door: the Federal Government's Attempt to Desegregate the Suburbs.* Princeton, N.J.: Princeton University Press.

Brooks-Gunn, Jeanne, Greg J. Duncan, Pamela Kato Klebanov, and Naomi Sealand. 1993. "Do Neighborhoods Influence Child and Adolescent Development?" *American Journal of Sociology* 99(2): 353–95.

Burdick-Will, Julia, Jens Ludwig, Stephen W. Raudenbush, Robert J. Sampson, Lisa Sanbonmatsu, and Patrick Sharkey. 2011. "Converging Evidence for Neighborhood Effects on Children's Test Scores: An Experimental, Quasi-experimental, and Observational Comparison." In *Whither Opportunity: Rising Inequality, Schools, and Children's Life Chances,* edited by Greg J. Duncan and Richard J. Murnane. New York: Russell Sage Foundation.

Clark, William A. V., and Jun L. Onaka. 1983. "Life Cycle and Housing Adjustment as Explanations of Residential Mobility." *Urban Studies* 20(1): 47–57.

Clotfelter, Charles T. 2004. *After Brown the Rise and Retreat of School Desegregation.* Princeton, N.J.: Princeton University Press. Available at: http://site.ebrary.com/id/10503248 (accessed October 1, 2013).

Cortese, Charles F., R. Frank Falk, and Jack K. Cohen. 1976. "Further Considerations on the Methodological Analysis of Segregation Indices." *American Sociological Review* 41(4): 630–37.

Crane, Jon. 1991. "Effects of Neighborhood on Dropping Out of School and Teenage Childbearing." In *The Urban Underclass,* edited by Christopher Jencks and Paul E. Peterson. Washington, D.C.: Brookings Institution Press.

Crowder, Kyle, and Scott J. South. 2003. "Neighborhood Distress and School Dropout: The Variable Significance of Community Context." *Social Science Research* 32(4): 659–98.

Cutler, David M., Edward L. Glaeser, and Jacob L. Vigdor. 1999. "The Rise and Decline of the American Ghetto." *Journal of Political Economy* 107(3): 455–506.

Datcher, Linda. 1982. "Effects of Community and Family Background on Achievement." *Review of Economics and Statistics* 64(1): 32–41.

Denton, Nancy A., and Douglas S. Massey. 1988. "Residential Segregation of Blacks, Hispanics, and Asians by Socioeconomic Status and Generation." *Social Science Quarterly* 69(4): 797–818.

Duncan, Otis Dudley, and Beverly Duncan. 1955. "A Methodological Analysis of Segregation Indexes." *American Sociological Review* 20(2): 210–17.

Ellen, Ingrid Gould, Keren Mertens Horn, and Katherine M. O'Regan. 2013. "Why Do Higher-income Households Choose Low-Income Neighbourhoods? Pioneering or Thrift?" *Urban Studies* 50(12): 2478–495.

Erbe, Brigitte Mach. 1975. "Race and Socioeconomic Segregation." *American Sociological Review* 40(6): 801–12.

Farkas, George. 1996. *Human Capital or Cultural Capital? Ethnicity and Poverty Groups in an Urban School District.* Hawthorn, N.Y.: Aldine de Gruyter.

Farley, Reynolds. 1991. "Residential Segregation of Social and Economic Groups Among Blacks, 1970 to 1980." In *The Urban Underclass,* edited by Christopher Jencks and Paul E. Peterson. Washington, D.C.: The Brookings Institution.

Figlio, David N. 2007. "Boys Named Sue: Disruptive Children and Their Peers." *Education Finance and Policy* 2(4): 376–94.

Fordham, Signithia, and John U. Ogbu. 1986. "Black Students' School Success: Coping with the Burden of 'Acting White.'" *The Urban Review* 18(3): 176–206.

Glaeser, Edward L., and Jacob L. Vigdor. 2012. "The End of the Segregated Century: Racial Separation in America's Neighborhoods, 1890–2010." Civic Report no. 66. New York: Manhattan Institute for Policy Research. Available at: http://www.manhattan-institute.org/html/cr_66.htm (accessed November 4, 2013).

Grady, Sue, and Joe Darden. 2012. "Spatial Methods to Study Local Racial Residential Segregation and Infant Health in Detroit, Michigan." *Annals of the Association of American Geographers* 102(5): 922–31.

Hanushek, Eric A., John F. Kain, Jacob M. Markman, and Steven G. Rivkin. 2003. "Does Peer Ability Affect Student Achievement?" *Journal of Applied Econometrics* 18(5): 527–44.

Heymann, S. Jody, and Alison Earle. 2000. "Low-Income Parents: How Do Working Conditions Affect Their Opportunity to Help School-Age Children at Risk?" *American Educational Research Journal* 37(4): 833–48.

Hoxby, Caroline. 2000. "Peer Effects in the Classroom: Learning from Gender and Race Variation." *NBER* working paper no. 7867. Cambridge, Mass.: National Bureau of Economic Research. Available at: http://www.nber.org/papers/w7867 (accessed May 18, 2013).

Iceland, John, and Melissa Scopilliti. 2008. "Immigrant Residential Segregation in U.S. Metropolitan Areas, 1990–2000." *Demography* 45(1): 79–94.

Jargowsky, Paul A. 1996. "Take the Money and Run: Economic Segregation in U.S. Metropolitan Areas." *American Sociological Review* 61(6): 984–98.

———. 1997. *Poverty and Place: Ghettos, Barrios, and the American City.* New York: Russell Sage Foundation.

———. 2002. "Sprawl, Concentration of Poverty, and Urban Inequality." In *Urban Sprawl: Causes, Consequences, and Policy Responses,* edited by Gregory Squires. Washington, D.C.: The Urban Institute.

———. 2003. "Stunning Progress, Hidden Problems: The Dramatic Decline of Concentrated Poverty in the 1990s." Washington, D.C.: Brookings Center on Urban and Metropolitan Policy.

Jargowsky, Paul A., and Mary Jo Bane. 1991. "Ghetto Poverty in the United States: 1970 to 1980." In *The Urban Underclass,* edited by Christopher Jencks and Paul E. Peterson. Washington, D.C.: Brookings Institution Press.

Jargowsky, Paul A., and Mohamed El Komi. 2011. "Before or after the Bell? School Context and Neighborhood Effects on Student Achievement." In *Neighborhood and Life Chances: How Place Matters in Modern America,* edited by Harriet B. Newburger, Eugenie L. Birch, and Susan M. Wachter. Philadelphia: University of Pennsylvania Press.

Jencks, Christopher, and Susan E. Mayer. 1990. "The Social Consequences of Growing up in a Poor Neighborhood." In *Inner-City Poverty in America,* edited by Laurence Lynn Jr. and Michael McGeary. Washington, D.C.: National Academy Press.

Kasarda, John D. 1993. "Inner-City Concentrated Poverty and Neighborhood Distress, 1970 to 1990." *Housing Policy Debate* 4(3): 253–302.

Kim, Jeongdai, and Paul A. Jargowsky. 2009. "The GINI Coefficient and Segregation on a Continuous Variable." *Research on Economic Inequality* 17(1): 57–70.

Kingsley, G. Thomas, and Kathryn L. S. Pettit. 2003. *Concentrated Poverty: A Change in Course.* Washington, D.C.: The Urban Institute.

Kozol, Jonathan. 1991. *Savage Inequalities: Children in America's Schools.* New York: Crown.

Lacy, Karyn. 2007. *Blue-Chip Black: Race, Class, and Status in the New Black Middle Class.* Berkeley: University of California Press.

Lazear, Edward P. 2001. "Educational Production." *The Quarterly Journal of Economics* 116(3): 777–803.

Levy, Frank. 1995. "The Future Path and Consequences of the U.S. Earnings/Education Gap." *Economic Policy Review* 1(1): 35–41.

Logan, John R. (2013). "The Persistence of Segregation in the 21st Century Metropolis." *City & Community* 12(2): 160–68.

Logan, John R., and Brian J. Stults. 2010. "Racial and Economic Separation in the Neighborhoods: Progress at a Standstill." Available at: http://www.s4.brown.edu/us2010/Data/Report/report1.pdf (accessed May 19, 2013).

Logan, John R., and Brian J. Stults. 2011. "The Persistence of Segregation in the Metropolis: New Findings from the 2010 Census." Available at: http://www.s4.brown.edu/us2010/Data/Report/report2.pdf (accessed September 14, 2013).

Ludwig, Jens, Lisa Sanbonmatsu, Lisa Gennetian, Emma Adam, Greg J. Duncan, Lawrence F. Katz, Ronald C. Kessler, Jeffrey R. Kling, Stacy Tessler Lindau, Robert C. Whitaker, and Thomas W. McDade. 2011. "Neighborhoods, Obesity, and Diabetes—A Randomized Social Experiment." *New England Journal of Medicine* 365(16): 1509–519.

Manski, Charles F. 2000. "Economic Analysis of Social Interactions." *Journal of Economic Perspectives* 14(3): 115–36.

Massey, Douglas S. 1990. "American Apartheid: Segregation and the Making of the Underclass." *American Journal of Sociology* 96(2): 329–57.

Massey, Douglas S., Gretchen S. Condran, and Nancy A. Denton. 1987. "The Effect of Residential Segregation on Black Social and Economic Well-being." *Social Forces* 66(1): 29–56.

Massey, Douglas S., and Nancy A. Denton. 1988. "The Dimensions of Racial Segregation." *Social Forces* 67(2): 281–315.

———. 1993. *American Apartheid: Segregation and the Making of the Underclass.* Cambridge, Mass.: Harvard University Press.

Massey, Douglas S., and Mitchell L. Eggers. 1990. "The Ecology of Inequality: Minorities and the Concentration of Poverty, 1970–1980." *American Journal of Sociology* 95(5): 1153–88.

Massey, Douglas S., and Mary J. Fischer. 2000. "How Segregation Concentrates Poverty." *Ethnic and Racial Studies* 23(4): 670–91.

National Advisory Commission on Civil Disorders. 1968. *Report of the National Advisory Commission on Civil Disorders* [The Kerner Report]. New York: Bantam Books.

Papke, David. 2009. *Keeping the Underclass in Its Place: Zoning, the Poor, and Residential Segregation.* Rochester, N.Y.: Social Science Research Network. Available at: http://papers.ssrn.com/abstract=1373537 (accessed May 20, 2013).

Park, Robert E. 1926. "The Urban Community as a Spatial Pattern and a Moral Order." In *The Urban Community.* Chicago: University of Chicago Press.

Pattillo-McCoy, Mary. 2000. *Black Picket Fences: Privilege and Peril Among the Black Middle Class.* Chicago: University of Chicago Press.

Quillian, Lincoln. 2012. "Segregation and Poverty Concentration: The Role of Three Segregations." *American Sociological Review* 77(3): 354–79.

Reardon, Sean F., and Kendra Bischoff. 2011. "Income Inequality and Income Segregation." *American Journal of Sociology* 116(4): 1092–153.

Rivkin, Steven G. 1994. "Residential Segregation and School Integration." *Sociology of Education* 67(4): 279–92.

Rossi, Peter H. 1955. *Why Families Move; a Study in the Social Psychology of Urban Residential Mobility.* Glencoe, Ill: Free Press.

Rothstein, Jesse, and Nathan Wozny. 2011. "Permanent Income and the Black-White Test Score Gap." *NBER* working paper no. 17610. Cambridge, Mass.: National Bureau of Economic Research. Available at: http://www.nber.org/papers/w17610 (accessed May 11, 2013).

Saporito, Salvatore. 2003. "Private Choices, Public Consequences: Magnet School Choice and Segregation by Race and Poverty." *Social Problems* 50(2): 181–203.

Squires, Gregory. 2002. *Urban Sprawl: Causes, Consequences & Policy Responses.* Washington, D.C.: The Urban Institute.

Summers, Anita A., and Barbara L. Wolfe. 1977. "Do Schools Make a Difference." *American Economic Review* 67(4): 639–52.

Turner, Margery Austin. 2005. "Housing Discrimination in Metropolitan America: Explaining Changes Between 1989 and 2000." *Social Problems* 52(2): 152–80.

U.S. Census Bureau. 1991. *1990 Census of Population and Housing Summary File 3 (Tape) Technical Documentation.* Washington: U.S. Census Bureau.

———. 2002. *Technical Documentation: Summary File 3.* Washington: U.S. Census Bureau.

———. 2010. *The 2005–2009 ACS 5-Year Summary File Technical Documentation.* Washington: U.S. Census Bureau.

———. 2011. *The 2006–2010 ACS 5-Year Summary File Technical Documentation.* Washington: U.S. Census Bureau.

———. 2012. *The 2007–2011 ACS 5-Year Summary File Technical Documentation.* Washington: U.S. Census Bureau.

Vigdor, Jacob L. 2013. "Weighing and Measuring the Decline in Residential Segregation." *City & Community* 12(2): 169–77.

Watson, Tara. 2009. "Inequality and the Measurement of Residential Segregation by Income in American Neighborhoods." *Review of Income and Wealth* 55(3): 820–44.

White, Michael J. 1987. *American Neighborhoods and Residential Differentiation.* New York: Russell Sage Foundation.

Wilson, William Julius. 1987. *The Truly Disadvantaged: The Inner-City, the Underclass, and Public Policy.* Chicago: University of Chicago Press.

———. 1996. *When Work Disappears: The World of the New Urban Poor.* New York: Alfred A. Knopf.

Winship, Christopher. 1977. "A Revaluation of Indexes of Residential Segregation." *Social Forces* 55(4): 1058–66.

Wong, David W. S. 1997. "Spatial Dependency of Segregation Indices." *Canadian Geographer* 41(2): 128–36.

Zimmer, Ron W., and Eugenia F. Toma. 2000. "Peer Effects in Private and Public Schools Across Countries." *Journal of Policy Analysis and Management* 19(1): 75–92.

= Chapter 5 =

Residential Mobility and School Choice Among Poor Families

ANNA RHODES AND STEFANIE DELUCA

T he number of school choice options for urban parents has exploded over the last two decades with the growth of intradistrict choice plans, school choice vouchers, magnet, and charter schools. However, despite expanding options for urban schooling, more than 70 percent of children in public school attend the one zoned for their neighborhood, making residential decisions consequential for children's development and educational attainment (U.S. Department of Education 2009). Given the strong link between residential location and school attendance, recent research has explored how school choices affect residential decisions, and finds that this connection factors strongly in the minds of middle-class parents. Many middle-class families move out of urban areas when their children are of school age, in anticipation of sending them to higher-quality schools outside of the city. Parents often purchase homes in neighborhoods because of the reputation of the local schools (Holme 2002). Annette Lareau (see chapter 6, this volume) finds that, among both working-class and middle- or upper-class families who moved to suburban neighborhoods, the reputation of neighborhood schools is a significant driver of their residential decisions.

This research demonstrates how residential and school decisions interact for some American households, but these samples do not include the poorest families, those for whom a calculated move to the suburbs is unaffordable. How do these school and housing choice processes operate for low-income families who face significant economic constraints? Do they connect their residential and school decisions in the same manner observed among higher income families? Which factors enter into the decisions about where to live and where to send their children to school?

Using longitudinal qualitative data from low-income African American families in Mobile, Alabama, we examine the interplay between residential trajectories and school choice, and describe the family circumstances, motivations, and structural factors that lead families to select, or in some cases end up in, their residential contexts and schools. In line with previous work, we find that the poor families in our study move frequently, and that their children change schools repeatedly (Hanushek, Kain, and Rivkin 2004). However, we find that because residential moves for low-income families often involve unplanned and distressed searches for hard-to-find housing, families try to meet basic needs such as safety, proximity to child care, and housing unit qualities rather than focusing on schools. In fact, we find that residential decisions are almost never driven by school considerations, standing in stark contrast to research that shows a clear connection between residential choice and school considerations for middle-class, white families (Holme 2002), and decades of research on residential mobility that assumes such amenities factor prominently in the housing choice process for all families (Rossi 1980; Speare, Goldstein, and Frey 1975; Clark, Deurloo, and Dieleman 2006; for further detail on residential mobility research, see chapters 1 and 2, this volume).

We find that poor families decouple their housing and school choices for several reasons. First, it seems that calculated school choices lose out in the highly constrained residential choice process. Second, the inability of these poor families to escape the disadvantaged neighborhoods of Mobile through their residential moves narrows their school experiences to a limited subset of highly segregated and lower performing schools. Although these families rely on their social networks for assistance in choosing schools, these friends and family members often possess information about the same schools, and do not expand the choice set of schools to be considered. This limited information is one reason that children are rarely enrolled in schools outside Mobile's poor and racially segregated residential areas. The lack of variation in information and experience with schools leads many parents to assume that all schools are quite similar, and this also diminishes the importance of schools as a driving factor in residential choices.

Although school considerations are not a major determinant of residential choices, just like middle-class parents, poor parents are eager to keep their children in safe and positive school environments where they can succeed. Because these families do not use residential mobility as a vehicle to exercise school choice, parents who want to change their child's school generally rely on the addresses of family and friends to enroll their child in a school zoned for a different neighborhood. These school decisions are often made based on considerations of school safety and the strictness of school leadership. However, factors unrelated to school quality also influence school choices because these decisions are embedded within the economic constraints, child-care demands, transportation issues, and housing needs that families must also address.

Over three years, our team spent hundreds of hours with a hundred low-income African American families in many of Mobile's poorest communities, talking to parents and children about their experiences in neighborhoods and schools. These rich life histories, which include residential and school moves, provide a unique opportunity to explore how housing constraints and neighborhood segregation shape school choices for low-income, African American families. In line with the national trend, the majority of the children in our sample attend their locally zoned school. This emphasizes the importance of understanding how residential and school choices connect for low-income families, and whether these processes differ from the patterns observed among middle-class families. These interviews help us understand the relationship between residential mobility and school trajectories, and the perpetuation of low-quality schooling environments for the children in these households, as well as the policies that might improve housing and school location among the poor.

Background Literature

Research shows that school choices, especially for middle-class and white families, are driven by school social status, racial composition, and wealth (Saporito and Lareau 1999; Holme 2002; chapter 6, this volume). Middle-class families learn about schools by relying heavily on information passed through social networks that help them locate, and access, highly reputable schools and neighborhoods (chapter 6, this volume; Holme 2002). Heather Johnson and Thomas Shapiro (2003) find that white parents choose their neighborhood for the school district, and that judgments about "good" schools and "good" neighborhoods are made with race serving as "a primary dimension of whites' choices" (176). Similarly, Salvatore Saporito and Annette Lareau (1999) found that white families tend to make decisions about where their children will attend school in a multistep process, first considering the school racial composition and avoiding the "black schools," and only then considering additional school specific qualities. Often these decisions are tied to residential—typically suburban—moves, and families move to school districts that come highly recommended and vetted by their social network (Holme 2002, Lareau 2012). Middle-class families, who exercise school choices in the absence of an interdistrict move, using choice programs or charter schools, also select schools with more white and affluent populations (Sikkink and Emerson 2008; Saporito 2003; Renzulli and Evans 2005; Kimelberg and Billingham 2012).

Research on the school choices of low-income families has typically focused on their choices among options within urban districts, such as charter schools, or the use of school vouchers (Neild 2005; Renzulli and

Evans 2005; Schneider et al. 1998). Like their middle-class counterparts, low-income families also rely heavily on information provided by their networks of family and friends, often considering schools that kin recommend (Neild 2005). However, if their family members do not live in a variety of school catchment areas that would allow them to provide information about a wide range of schools, low-income families will likely face significant barriers to knowledge about available school options (Neild 2005). Overall, the social networks of low-income families are less likely than middle-class networks to easily provide information about where better schools are located and how to exercise available options (Horvat, Weininger, and Lareau 2003; Schneider, Teske, and Marschall 2000; Neild 2005). Although the research on how low-income families learn about and engage with school choice options in urban spaces is important, we know far less about how these families connect their residential choices to school choices, which is consequential because more than 70 percent of children in public schools continue to attend their locally zoned school (U.S. Department of Education 2009). It is residential decisions, rather than school choice programs, that determine where most students attend school.

Theories of residential mobility, coming largely from economics, argue that if the benefits outweigh the costs, families will move to neighborhoods with more amenities, such as respectably ranked local schools and higher-quality homes, as their income increases (Cadwallader 1993; Clark and Flowerdew 1982). Empirical evidence shows that for white families, this explanation of residential mobility largely fits the observed residential data (Logan and Alba 1993; Charles 2003), because white families successfully translate increased income into higher-quality housing and more advantaged neighborhoods, typically in suburban areas. Research shows that school quality is often a significant factor in the residential calculus of white middle- and upper-class families (Bayoh, Irwin, and Haab 2006; Holme 2002).

For black families, however, residential mobility patterns do not clearly match the assumptions of most residential mobility research; rather, evidence demonstrates racially disparate patterns of residential mobility (see chapter 2, this volume). Black families frequently cycle through poor, segregated neighborhoods, even when income is held constant (Logan and Alba 1993; Sampson and Sharkey 2008; Gramlich, Laren, and Sealand 1992; Bruch and Mare 2006; Sharkey 2013), and black households are less able than white households to access low-poverty neighborhoods (Massey and Denton 1993; Hirsch 1983; Yinger 1995). For poor minority families, displacement through exogenous shocks (DeLuca, Wood, and Rosenblatt 2011), city investment, and even federal housing initiatives such as HOPE VI (Crowley 2003; Clampet-Lundquist 2004), have led to unplanned mobility over the last decade, leading poor black families to make residential decisions with less planning and fewer resources.

Some scholars estimate that these involuntary moves may happen more often than planned moves for poor families (Bartlett 1997, Schafft 2006; Crowley 2003).

Even black middle-class families are still more likely than their white counterparts to live in low-income neighborhoods (Pattillo-McCoy 2000). Those black families who do access housing in low-poverty census tracts are less likely to move to racially integrated neighborhoods (Sampson and Sharkey 2008) and are also more likely than their white neighbors to subsequently move back to high-poverty tracts, and even the highest income blacks are more likely to experience this kind of downward move than the lowest income white families (South, Crowder, and Chavez 2005). This research challenges the assumption that all families are equally able to leverage their resources to access more amenities in housing, schools, and neighborhoods (South and Crowder 1997).

Our sample provides a unique way to examine how poor families, those for whom a suburban move is financially difficult, navigate residential and school choices in an urban setting with only limited school choice options. Through our longitudinal, in-depth qualitative interviews and fieldwork, we explore how low-income African American families make their residential decisions, and how residential trajectories connect to school selection. The low-income black families in our sample engage in processes of school and residential choice that differ markedly from those of white middle-class families (Holme 2002), and these decisions have significant implications for the kinds of schools their children attend.

Methods

For three summers between 2009 and 2011, our research team conducted fieldwork in Mobile, Alabama, with low-income African American families who were selected from among those who had participated in a large neighborhood based panel study of youth. Starting in 1998, the Mobile Youth Survey (MYS) recruited children ages ten to eighteen in households from thirteen high-poverty neighborhoods and followed them over time (see Bolland 2003). Our study stratified the MYS sample by neighborhood, randomly selecting families from within these neighborhoods with at least one child under the age of eighteen living in the household at the time of our initial survey. This survey, designed to provide data on family characteristics, residential mobility trajectories, and school attendance was collected in 2009, resulting in the original sample described in table 5.1. In-depth interviews were conducted with most of these families again in 2010, and additional families were added from neighborhoods we had not been able to reach the first year. In 2011, we again visited these families—this time a subsample of our most residentially mobile families with children—to conduct more in-depth conversations about how

Table 5.1   Demographics

Average age	42
Average number of children	4
Female	89%
High school graduate	57%
Ever owned a home	19%
Receive income from wages-salary	38%
Receive food stamps	65%

Source: Authors' compilation based on 2009 survey data.
N=84

housing and moving affect children's school attendance. Over these years, one hundred African American families participated in our study, a significant portion doing so in multiple waves. Families were paid $50 for participating in the interview, and our response rate was over 80 percent for each wave of data collection.

As shown in table 5.1, the parents, who were head (or co-head) of their household, were mostly female, and were on average forty-two years old, and had an average of four children per household. These families are very disadvantaged: just under 60 percent of the household heads had a high school diploma; 38 percent reported income from wages or a salary; and 65 percent were receiving food stamps. As a result of our design, interviewing families across a range of low-income neighborhoods, our sample also includes families with a variety of housing arrangements, some renting in the low-income private market and others renting with housing subsidies including public housing, project-based assisted housing, and Section 8 (now Housing Choice) vouchers.

The interviews were semistructured, typically taking place in the family home, and lasted two to five hours each time. Our conversations began with a broad invitation to "tell us the story of your life," and as these stories unfolded, we probed with specific questions about the details of residential moves, double-ups with family, and children's schooling trajectories. Stories about family history, employment, neighborhoods, and landlords also often garnered additional details about housing and schooling trajectories. Through our repeated visits, we were able to build substantial trust and rapport, eliciting significant detail about the circumstances of family life in general, and residential mobility and school mobility specifically.[1] The longitudinal nature of the study allowed us to observe the moves families made in real time. We conducted most of our interviews in families' homes; we were able to see new housing units after they moved; and we heard about the residential search process from families actively moving while we were in Mobile. Some families also called with updates about particularly stressful relocations between our visits.

The first part of our chapter describes Mobile, Alabama, and the Mobile County School System. We use census data and data from the American Community Survey to characterize the study neighborhoods in Mobile, and data from the Alabama State Department of Education is used to describe the demographic composition and academic profile of the local schools in the metropolitan area. This sets the stage for understanding the contexts families live in and move between, as well as the school environments their children experience. This is followed by analyses of in-depth qualitative interviews to illustrate how families navigate residential opportunities, constraints, and choices, in which we pay particular attention to how school considerations shape residential decisions. Finally, we examine how families manage school choice for their children, describing the dynamics of family life and the school qualities that influence their decisions.

Neighborhood and School Context in Mobile

Through our interviews, we elicited the entire residential mobility history for each head of household, from their childhood through to the present. As children, and in their own households as independent adults, these residential trajectories are marked by frequent moves. However, despite the frequency of these moves, families end up relocating to poor and segregated neighborhoods, over and over again, rarely breaking out of the radius of the poor ghetto communities in the Mobile area. The housing stock in these communities looks bleak: public housing projects and the low-end private market neighborhoods alike are marked by boarded up homes, some practically falling down where they stand, and even many of the inhabited homes in these areas are visibly in need of repair. Many of the poorest and most segregated communities in Mobile are far off the beaten path for middle-class, white families and tourists, sequestered on most sides by swamps, docks, and highways. These neighborhoods suffer from drug activity, break-ins, and other crime that lead many parents to stay inside and keep their children from playing in the yard or on the street; two women separately described the active drug trade outside while we conducted their interviews, pointing out the sellers and users through the front window and from the front porch of their homes. Often, parents would describe their block as safe, but indicate that gunshots could be heard close by at night, describing that "down there" or "on that end of the street" things were "bad." These spaces stand in stark contrast to the brightly colored, regal row of southern coastal mansions on the tree-lined streets that mark the wealthier neighborhoods of the city.

The blockface differences visible when visiting the neighborhoods of metropolitan Mobile are also reflected in their demographic profiles. As shown in table 5.2, the families in our sample live in highly segregated

Table 5.2   Mobile Neighborhoods

Neighborhood	Census Tract Population	Percent African American	Poverty Rate (%)	Median Household Income
R. V. Taylor*	1712	96.09	81.10	6,559
Bessemer*	2471	96.40	60.00	13,444
Plateau	4127	78.68	59.00	15,000
Josephine Allen*	4127	78.68	59.00	15,000
Gulf Village*	1247	97.11	55.90	12,310
Toulminville	2912	98.08	52.30	15,605
Roger Williams*	2912	98.08	52.30	15,605
Oaklawn Homes*	3141	98.12	48.30	16,710
Alabama Village	2933	98.35	45.90	16,363
South Broad Street	6172	87.65	44.80	18,528
Whitley	2560	97.58	42.90	17,323
Maysville	2264	97.48	42.80	25,188
Orange Grove*	1565	96.99	42.25	14,444
Snug Harbor	1756	97.55	42.00	23,162
Martin Luther King	3609	98.62	41.75	20,734
West Prichard	4286	95.29	39.55	24,287
Trinity Gardens	2006	97.56	32.90	21,322
Upper Dauphin Island Pkwy	4914	96.78	31.75	22,777
Harlem	1169	93.07	29.70	18,789
South Chickasaw	3246	44.09	27.85	27,072
Morningside	4513	84.40	23.30	34,375
Whistler	2087	67.03	17.20	30,417
Wilson Avenue	2681	11.23	7.80	56,250

Source: Authors' calculation based on the 2010 census and 2011 5-year American Community Survey.
*Denotes public housing.

areas, African Americans making up over 90 percent of the population in the majority of these neighborhoods. These areas are also very poor. The Census Bureau defines poverty areas as census tracts with poverty rates over 20 percent (Bishaw 2011); strikingly, a third of the neighborhoods our families live in have poverty rates of over 50 percent, and over half have a poverty rate over 40 percent. The median household income is also low, below $20,000 per household in many of these neighborhoods. This is much lower than the median household income for the city of Mobile, $38,240, and for Mobile County, $42,187.

Similar patterns of segregation and poverty are also reflected in the Mobile County public school system as observed in table 5.3, which provides demographic information on Mobile County middle schools.[2] The schools marked with an asterisk are those regularly attended by most

Table 5.3   Middle School Descriptives

School	Percent African American	Percent Receiving Free or Reduced Lunch	School Test Score Percentile
Jackson Preparatory Middle	41.10	44.07	89
Prescot Magnet	50.99	60.26	77
Lassiter Middle	11.88	74.75	69
Rollins Middle	28.36	48.86	64
Hawkins Bay Middle	26.90	75.00	56
Gulf Middle	10.85	63.18	53
Beaumont Middle	17.88	79.89	53
Ryder Middle	16.86	64.58	51
Westminster Middle	50.75	72.24	47
Reade Smith Middle*	100	92.52	45
Frederick Douglass Training	38.55	65.92	43
Azalea Middle*	100	95.35	39
Martinswood	88.89	88.89	39
Fallsway Middle*	97.50	98.50	37
Tanner Williams Middle	85.28	90.97	37
Grelot Middle*	91.80	98.36	35
Shelton Middle*	96.67	97.33	34
McVay Training*	100	100	28
Hamilton Middle	92.19	92.19	26

Source: Authors' calculation based on data from the Alabama State Department of Education.
Notes: Seventh grade math, 2010–2011. Sorted by overall percentile score, which is the relative standing of the school compared to the nation (national average is 50). All school names in the table have been changed.
*Denotes schools that are frequently attended by children in our sample.

of the children in our sample. These schools are more than 90 percent African American and extremely poor, with more than 90 percent of students receiving free and reduced price lunch.[3] The demographics are similar for elementary schools but, due to the wider geographic catchment areas of the high school zones, some of the high schools have lower poverty rates, although the rate for most still remains over 75 percent.[4] The schools children in the sample do not attend, typically because neither they nor their family members live in the residential catchment area, have much smaller populations of African American and poor students. Hence, the schools children in our sample can access through their residential moves provide extremely limited variation in their racial and class composition. Residential churning through poor and segregated neighborhoods leads to similar patterns of attendance and mobility through poor and highly segregated schools.

These patterns of segregation by race and class also largely map on to differences in academic performance. Table 5.3 reports the Stanford

Achievement Test 10 (SAT10) percentiles for Mobile County middle schools and shows large variation in the academic outcomes of schools across Mobile County. Students at Jackson Preparatory and Prescot (both magnet schools) test over the 70th percentile.[5] However, the schools that children in our sample typically attend have overall test scores below the 50th percentile, and many children attend some of the poorest performing middle schools in Mobile County. Children also generally attend lower performing elementary and high schools, but a small number of elementary schools in the poorer neighborhoods, those newly renovated or reconstituted, do score in the higher test percentiles.

These patterns of highly segregated school attendance may be due in part to the institutional structure of school choice in Mobile. The Mobile public school system offers very limited school choice options for families beyond attending the school zoned for their residential address. School choices include magnet schools, mostly at the middle and high school level, which students can apply for and attend if selected.[6] The only additional school option is to apply for a transfer, which, if approved, allows families to send their children to a specific out-of-zone school. Although these provide options for families to exercise choice, they are not structured to allow significant mobility of children across the schools within the system. Given the lack of choice options in Mobile, residential moves are the primary way parents can access schools.

Decoupling Residential and School Choice

Much of the existing literature assumes that families make residential decisions based on weighing the costs and benefits of amenities such as housing size, neighborhood safety, and school quality, and that school quality is a significant factor—especially in the residential decisions of middle-class families (Bayoh, Irwin, and Haab 2006; Holme 2002; chapter 6, this volume). In our sample of low-income, African American families, considerations of safety, housing, and convenience were important when thinking about where to live, but their stories were notable because of what they did not talk about: schools. We found that families in Mobile often made residential decisions to leverage particular aspects of housing and neighborhoods conducive to child care, safety, and transportation, but not school characteristics. Families simply do not mention schools when telling us about their residential decisions. In other words, the low-income black families we talked to generally decouple residential choice from school choice (DeLuca and Rosenblatt 2010).

Like middle-class families, poor families value and emphasize education; however, accessing schools through residential mobility is difficult because of significant housing instability, and constraints on residential choice. Securing housing in relatively safe neighborhoods, with a minimal level of housing unit quality or necessary proximity to child care, trumps school location when families move, which often occurs under unpredictable and difficult conditions. We do not imply that families never think about school location because schools are not important to them; clearly, this is not the case. However, in hundreds of hours with families over three years, we almost never heard them mention moving somewhere because of the local schools.[7] Unlike middle-class families (see chapters 6 and 7, this volume), who explicitly connect their residential decisions to school considerations, our families prioritize nonschool factors in residential choices and decide on the school their children attend in a separate step. Parents can use the addresses of family or friends, or school transfers, to get their children into public schools outside their residential catchment area—but decent housing units are much harder to come by, and the constraints of housing programs, landlords, and rental costs are considerable hurdles to jump to avoid being homeless.

As a result of this decoupling, school and residential choices sometimes occur at separate times. However, because most children attend their zoned school, residential decisions often lead to school changes, even though these moves are not made to leverage access to a particular school. To demonstrate this decoupling, figure 5.1 presents the school and residential trajectories of Katrina, the thirteen-year-old daughter of Alicia, a mother of six who receives disability due to a heart condition. When Katrina started kindergarten, she attended her zoned school, Heritage Elementary. Alicia was pleased with the school for many years, but became unhappy when she felt an administrator was acting in a racist manner toward students and staff. This led her to move Katrina to an out-of-zone school, Harmon Elementary, during her fifth grade year. Alicia made this school choice by using the address of a family member to enroll Katrina, rather than moving to a neighborhood in the school catchment area.

While Katrina was attending Harmon Elementary, Alicia's boyfriend was shot and killed in their unit in the RV Taylor Homes. She told us, "somebody broke in my house, he was sleeping . . . and they shot him and left him." Alicia immediately moved her family out of the unit and stayed with her aunt for several months. Shortly after this move, Alicia again switched Katrina's school, this time to attend Carver Elementary, the school zoned for her aunt's home. Katrina thus makes two school changes during the course of her fifth grade year. Alicia's family eventually moved back to the RV Taylor Homes when a new unit became available, and again Katrina switched schools to attend Reade Smith Middle. This was both a promotional change, as she was starting sixth grade, and a change due to the residential move.

After a year in RV Taylor, Alicia received a Section 8 Voucher (now Housing Choice Voucher), after having been on the waiting list for

Figure 5.1   Katrina's Residential and School Trajectory

RV Taylor Homes					Aunt's House	RV Taylor Homes	Hillsdale
A					B	C D	E
K	1st	2nd	3rd	4th	5th	6th	7th

Source: Authors' compilation.
* A = Heritage Elementary, B = Harmon Elementary, C = Carver Elementary, D = Reade Smith Middle, E = Tanner Williams Middle.

eighteen years, and excitedly moved her family out of the projects and into a private rental market home in the Hillsdale neighborhood. This move also led Katrina to change schools to Tanner Williams Middle School. Alicia told us "Tanner Williams Middle School, that is not a good school to send your children to . . . the reason why I had to send them there . . . is because of my transportation . . . since I have moved here, my car was put in the shop." Alicia is very unhappy with Tanner Williams Middle, and describes the lack of school discipline saying, "they don't have any rules" compared to Reade Smith Middle, which "had rules. I mean, they were firm, Reade Smith is a very good school." Alicia believes that this school is negatively affecting her daughter's academic performance because "her grades were going down." This change to Tanner Williams demonstrates that the residential move to Hillsdale was made in pursuit of neighborhood and housing quality factors, as Alicia was able to move her family out of the projects with her Section 8 voucher. However, school considerations did not play a role in this decision, and ultimately left Alicia unhappy with Katrina's school environment.

Alicia's story demonstrates both the decoupling of school and residential choices, and the ways in which destabilized housing can destabilize schooling. Although Alicia was, in one instance, able to choose an out-of-zone school for Katrina, with subsequent residential moves Katrina attended the zoned school, mainly because of Alicia's transportation constraints. The separation of school considerations from residential moves, in particular during Alicia's move to Hillsdale, may have negative consequences for Katrina's education because Alicia believes the new school environment is leading to Katrina's poor academic performance. Thus, although the separation of residential moves from school considerations may ease the difficulty of residential decisions, the pattern of decoupling school and residential choices may have some significant consequences for children. This pattern is also notably different from the way residential and school choices are linked for middle-class (Holme 2002) and even working-class families (see chapter 6, this volume), who rely on information about schools from their social networks, to try and move into residential neighborhoods with schools their peers evaluate highly.

"Choosing" Homes

Given the context of neighborhood and school options across the Mobile metropolitan area, and the notable decoupling of residential choices from school considerations, we examined how families approach residential moves, the factors they consider when choosing where to live, as well as the constraints, opportunities, and trade-offs inherent in these choices. Among the low-income African American families in our sample, unplanned residential mobility occurs regularly for reasons outside their control, such as landlord conflicts or unit failure (see DeLuca, Wood, and Rosenblatt 2011). In addition to the stress of unplanned moves and the worry about going homeless, these residential trajectories often expose families to neighborhoods with high levels of crime and violence, such as break-ins, fighting, and shooting. Homes and apartments in these neighborhoods are also often poorly maintained, with issues such as water and fire damage, mold, sewage problems, and infestations of vermin and insects. Leasing up in one of these units often guarantees that before too long, families will need to move again as their homes literally crumble around them. Field notes from one of the homes we visited explain the dire conditions of some of these units: "the house . . . had some major problems. The outside was run down, and there was major water damage in the living room. The bedroom I conducted the interview in also had a damaged ceiling that had been taped up to keep things together."

Although an obvious factor, it is worth emphasizing that the overwhelming financial constraints faced by these families severely affect many of the decisions they make about where to live and how much to spend on rent. Many families struggled to find steady work, trying to get by on food stamps, and by living in public housing. Others tried to make ends meet on disability checks, and those who were able to find employment frequently worked in the fast food industry, as janitorial staff, or as nursing assistants, and their jobs were not secure. Most of these households earn less than $15,000 a year, making it difficult to cover rent even in the poorer areas of Mobile. Often, tight finances prompted families to stagger the bills they would pay from one month to another, choosing to pay the utilities instead of rent one month, or rent instead of a car payment the next.[8] Coot, a mother of two who lost her housekeeping job, puts it plainly.

Interviewer: Have you ever had a problem covering the bills during a month?
    Coot: Yeah, like now. I ain't got no money to pay them.
Interviewer: What, the rent?
    Coot: No, I can't even pay my light bill.

Coot told us that her light bill is usually around $176 a month, and that her rent, at $545 a month (still below the median rent for Mobile County at $796 in 2011),[9] was far outside her financial reach. Even among those families who have learned about higher-quality residential areas on the other side of the city, such as West Mobile neighborhoods they described as safer, more affluent, and closer to shopping centers, past and present financial difficulties put these areas out of reach.

These wealthier areas also have fewer rental options because many neighborhoods are not zoned for multifamily housing, and the rental apartments in these areas have more stringent leasing requirements, such as credit checks and security deposits, which act as additional barriers to low-income families. Veronica, a mother of six in her late thirties, is out of work because she lacks dependable transportation. She wanted to move to West Mobile, but old medical bills got in the way as she told us, "for fifty more dollars we could get a nice apartment in West Mobile, you can't get it, because your credit messed up for owing people that you can't pay for, hospital bills or whatever, on them that go on collection, that go on your credit, it's all messed up." Veronica said that she might be able to move to West Mobile if she could find a cosigner for a loan, but she has been unable to do so thus far. Landlords who will rent to her without a credit check are typically more willing to do so for their units in the poorest and most segregated neighborhoods (something we heard from several other mothers). Veronica's story suggests that not only does family income and experience shape neighborhood and school outcomes, but also institutional hurdles such as zoning, leasing requirements, and bank loan restrictions make it difficult for our families to break out of poor neighborhoods (Retsinas and Belsky 2008).

Beyond financial constraints, families also face unreliable living arrangements that destabilize their households and often leave them with few options and limited time. Denise, a mother of four, was unemployed during our last visit, after being laid off from a janitorial position. She was supplementing her income by serving as the "candy lady" in her apartment complex, selling candy she bought in bulk to the local children. Denise was unexpectedly forced to leave her first apartment in the Orange Grove public housing complex when lead paint was discovered in her unit. She told us that the RV Taylor Homes unit she subsequently moved to "was the only thing that was open at the time and in the little amount of time that we had [given by the Public Housing Authority] . . . we had to go right there." For Denise, like many parents, moving is time constrained, a parameter frequently imposed by the Housing Authority, and with limited time families often take units that are less desirable because they need to provide a home for their family (DeLuca, Garboden, and Rosenblatt 2013). Miss Jones, a mother of four boys who is not working because of an injury, has moved her boys fourteen times in ten years; one of her sons has changed schools nine times during this period. She talked about feeling "like refugees," saying, "I never lived in one place for a long period of time." Sara, a mother of three who works as a nursing assistant and has moved her family many times, put the feelings of many parents bluntly, saying, "I just want stability." The unplanned nature of moves, frequent time constraints, financial strain, and often limited information about housing options, leads families to make residential decisions within a bounded set of neighborhoods (compare DeLuca, Wood, and Rosenblatt 2011). Families also frequently rent units immediately when they find one that meets even their basic needs, and then they are hesitant to leave.

Under these circumstances, families seek particular qualities in their residential location, often to ease other family needs such as child care, transportation difficulty, and household space. Proximity to family members was discussed by many parents, both as a benefit of current housing arrangements and a consideration for decisions about where they move next.[10] Residential proximity to family can be important for the sense of community it provides, but also for practical reasons such as child care. Cool Mama, a fifty-six-year-old mother of three, employed as a case manager for a general educational development (GED) program, told us that she chose "a house that was . . . about three blocks down the street" from her mother when she moved into her first home as an adult because she "wanted to be close to [her] mom." Marilyn, a mother of two working as a grill cook at a local restaurant, describes transportation constraints and child-care needs that led her to try and move closer to family when her children were young. When she was considering where to move, Marilyn told us,

> I wanted to get out of public housing and we found that house, it was actually closer to the grandparents on James' side and I needed some help with the children . . . so I was trying to get closer, and I didn't have transportation, had to ride the bus back and forth to work and it was easier with them going to school close to their grandparents.

Choosing housing close to family helped Marilyn make sure her children would be looked after when they were not in school.

Safety is another major concern for the families we spoke with, and reluctant but necessary moves are made when families experience break-ins, witness violence on their doorstep, or fear too much "activity" (drugs, fighting, and shooting) in the area. Haley, a hairdresser and mother of three children, described leaving the Gulf Village housing project after being taken at gunpoint into her own home:

> I had went down to take out the garbage and to go get something to eat, and these three boys walked up on me and put a gun on me and walked me back up to the apartment, and it was like, kids were sitting there eating, at the table, eating pot pies . . . And they asked for my wallet and it was Christmas time and I had just made a little bit of money, and that was it.

Denise, the mother of four children who lost her janitorial job several months before our last visit, left the RV Taylor Homes because "it was too much shootin' and killin' out there." She described the particular incident that was the final straw, explaining "my kids, one day they was outside in the yard playing . . . and a guy from across the street just started shootin' at some dude that was runnin' that way and bullets just flyin' past their head and they runnin' in the house. It's time to go." Denise moved into a project-based Section 8 apartment complex where her sister and aunt were already living. She had put an application in to the apartment complex when violence began to escalate in the RV Taylor Homes, but after this shooting she contacted the landlord again and was able to quickly move into a unit in the new complex.

Alia, a mother of three who has worked at a local auto parts warehouse for the past three years, told us that several new families moved into her neighborhood and the number of burglaries increased. This led her to move because "the area got real bad . . . I ain't want my children in that environment cause I kind of seen the change in 'em, you know, the crowd, you know, the crowd they be around kind of makes a difference." When moves were motivated by concerns about robberies, shooting, fighting, and drug activity in their neighborhoods families emphasized seeking new neighborhoods that seemed like they had less crime and violence. Families moving for other reasons also typically sought to avoid neighborhoods known to have significant crime and violence.

Other families talked more directly about aspects of the housing unit as a reason they move from one place to the next. As noted in other research (compare Boyd et al. 2010; Rosenblatt and DeLuca 2012; DeLuca, Wood, and Rosenblatt 2011), housing unit failures frequently force families to move, such as when a unit rented with a voucher does not pass inspection, or issues with plumbing, flooring, or infestations make a unit uninhabitable. When families select new units, a desire for more storage space, more bedrooms, a backyard, or a place that was clean and in ostensibly good condition drove a number of the decisions about where to live (Wood 2012). Housing units, rather than neighborhood characteristics, were the focus of discussions about the trade-offs of different places to live for many families, especially when these aspects of the housing unit were associated with their strategies for parenting, such as enough bedrooms to reduce sibling conflict, and enough space to play indoors when it was unsafe outside (for detailed discussions of these trade-offs, compare Wood 2012; Rosenblatt and DeLuca 2012). Families frequently had to move because of unit failure or major household problems, thus it is unsurprising that qualities of the unit were important considerations when making a residential choice. Once they found a unit that satisfied some of these desires, they took it almost immediately (some sight unseen), for fear that another unit would not be available. However, some families, especially those renting with Housing Choice vouchers whose homes were required to pass inspections, also described trying to fix household issues rather than having to make a residential move that was unplanned or would be stressful and difficult (compare DeLuca, Garboden, and Rosenblatt 2013).

Exercising Out-of-Zone School Choice

In part, the decoupling of residential choice from school considerations is possible because families find ways to send their children to out-of-zone schools without moving. Although the majority of the children in our sample attend their zoned school, almost 50 percent of our families have an instance of out-of-zone school choice for at least one child. Most frequently, when families send children to out-of-zone schools they do so by using the addresses of family or friends; though less common, families also use transfer applications, send their children to parochial school (typically in the early elementary school years), or apply for magnet schools, as shown in table 5.4. These school decisions are embedded within the lives of these families, and choices are made not only on the basis of school qualities, but also in response to other family needs. Kin play a significant role, both providing information about schools, and often serving as child-care providers, with school changes made frequently to facilitate this kind of caregiving. These decisions are also made in light of severe economic constraints as well as unpredictable work schedules and transportation concerns. Families have found ways to navigate their residential and school choices given the circumstances they face, but they do so by managing these choices separately.

Table 5.4   Methods of Out-of-Zone School Attendance

Method	Numbers of Households
Address of family member or friend	19
Transfer	11
Parochial-private school	10
Magnet school	9

Source: Authors' calculation.

Using the address of a family member is a common method for enrolling children in an out-of-zone school. Red, a mother of four who works at a dry cleaners, described sending her children to the schools zoned for her grandmother's house: "Well, I had to work and I had to have someone . . . to pick them up and they can walk to my grandmother's house till I get off work." Tiara, an unemployed mother of five, also describes making an out-of-zone school change using her cousin's address. When her son was getting ready to enter elementary school, Tiara asked family members for information about schools in Mobile. She ultimately made the decision to send her son to the school her cousin's children were attending, using her cousin's address. She describes this decision, saying, "I had a cousin live down there, her children were going there, and she was telling me that it's a good school . . . so I put him in there, and he came out pretty good."

One of the few actual choice options for families in the Mobile public school system is to apply for a school transfer. Ashley, an unemployed mother of five children, discovered Carver Elementary School because her youngest cousin was attending the school. She did not want her children to attend her zoned school because she "wanted better" for her children, and the zoned school was "rowdy" and "it's a drug area right there." She made this school switch using a transfer that she reapplies for each April. She described the process, saying, "they have to approve . . . you just go to the school board and put your application in and they'll send you a letter. Mostly all the time you mostly be approved unless the school is over packed or something."

Parochial and private school attendance is another method families use to opt out of their zoned schools. Typically, this occurs when children are in early elementary school, a time when tuition costs are the most manageable, but financial constraints still often keep families from continuing to send their children to these schools after the first few years. Crystal, a mother of five who is unemployed due to health problems, described sending her daughter to Abiding Savior Academy: "She started school there when she was three . . . she stayed there until she was in third grade." When asked why her daughter left, Crystal told us, "that was my biggest downfall. I didn't want to send them to public school, and I couldn't afford to keep them in private." The cost of sending three children to parochial school was too much for Crystal to absorb in light of other bills, and ultimately her children attended public schools.

The final option we see parents using to exercise out-of-zone school choice is applying to a local magnet school. Patricia, a mother of three daughters who works as a cashier at a large grocery store, told us she decided to send one daughter to Prescot Magnet School, "cuz I wanted to challenge her and I wanted to put her in a good school." Her zoned school had "been a low, failing [school]," and she told us that she "knew Prescot was the right school cuz my nephew went to Prescot and he just graduated." As in Patricia's case, across all types of school choice that families exercise, networks of family and friends play a significant role in providing information on school options and evaluations of school quality. Parents frequently choose schools they learn about through family members, especially if those schools are highly evaluated by their family.

Across these school choice options, magnet school applications and, in some instances, private or parochial school attendance, can allow children access to some higher performing schools. However, most out-of-zone school choices, especially those made by using others' addresses to enroll their children in the selected school, still result in school changes that simply move children through segregated, poor, and lower performing schools. This limited subset of schools in the Mobile County school system (see middle schools marked with an asterisk in table 5.3) does not reflect the true heterogeneity of schools in both demographics and academic quality, as measured by test scores. Thus, the bounded set of neighborhoods these families (and their networks) have access to, and churn between, may prevent experience with schools of significantly different demographic composition and typically higher academic quality. This repeated experience with lower-quality schools may temper the motivation to consider schools when parents are making residential choices. Schools simply may not appear variable enough, in their experiences, to be a driving factor of residential choice when families can exercise school choice separately. This entrenched pattern of decoupling may, however, keep families from engaging in a different type of residential search that leverages residential moves for gains in school quality.

Choosing Schools

Although parents do not make their residential decisions based on considerations about schools, these families clearly want their children in positive school environments and to have them succeed in school. The majority of children in our sample attend their local schools for most of their education, but strikingly, almost 50 percent of the families in our sample have sought to send at least one child in the family to an out-of-zone school (see table 5.4). These school selections are often driven by the desire to send their child to a "good school," typically defined by qualities such as the strictness of school leaders and the relative safety of the school. In other instances, however, school selections are driven by family needs such as proximity to work or child care. Notably missing from discussions about school choice and what makes a "good school" are policy-focused measures of academic school quality;

families rarely talk about test scores, teacher qualifications, or classroom size. This is true for parents evaluating the zoned school—the most common arrangement for children in our sample—and for parents who have exercised some form of school choice, sending their child to an out-of-zone school.

An appreciation of discipline and strictness by school personnel comes through during many of our visits with parents in Mobile, and it is often connected to a perception of how safe the school is for their children. Mona, a mother of two and grandmother to eight, approves of Heritage, the local elementary school that four of her grandchildren attend, because the school's principal "was in the military, and they keep 'em in order [there]. They can't get out of line, they gotta come with the shoes on, there's a whole lot of different things. That's a good school." Alicia told us that she did not want to send her children to the zoned high school, and preferred that they attend Dauphin Island High School, because she likes the school leadership. She attended Dauphin Island when it was not strict, but says that the new principal is "on top . . . they don't play, and they mean business."

Parents are interested not only in the strictness of the school leadership, but also in the safety of the school, and these issues are often interconnected. Ms. Blue, a mother of nine who works as a housekeeper, told us that all of her children attended Dauphin Island High School because it was their zoned school. She also told us that her granddaughter is pursuing a transfer to Dauphin Island High School because Moffett, her zoned school, is "a bad school. Guns. They fight a lot. They have knives. It is a bad school to me. I don't like it." She animatedly discussed these issues, indicating that she felt strongly her granddaughter should not attend Moffett because it is not a safe school environment, compared to Dauphin Island, which she approves of because it "is a strict school. They don't get away with nothing over there." Shawn, a mother of two who recently received her associate's degree, chose not to send her daughter to elementary school in their Trinity Gardens neighborhood because "them fightin' and shootin' and stuff." Instead, she opted for a school in nearby Toulminville, "a good school. They have their problems but it's not as bad as some of the other ones."

Shawn's story demonstrates both concerns about school safety, but also a leveling of expectations that we observe for many of our parents regarding schools. She simply wants to send her child to a school that is "not as bad." She sought out a school with a baseline acceptable level of safety for her children. Leveled school expectations and discussions about all schools facing issues of fighting and violence seem to be the precursor to a belief that "all schools are the same." Red, a mother of two who works at a dry cleaner, told us that "all the schools are the same, you know, they have guns at their school, they have found drugs at their school, you know, all of 'em the same. Kids still fightin'." This view reflects the result of continued exposure to poor and segregated neighborhoods with low-quality schools, and although not all families express this view, it is a common one, also seen in other work in Baltimore (compare DeLuca and Rosenblatt 2010).

Beyond qualities of the school, such as strict leadership or safe classrooms, parents also make school choices based on other aspects of their lives. Proximity to home or work is a factor that loomed large for many parents, and those who send their children to the local school often positively evaluate the school precisely because it is close to home, or close to a child-care provider (not unlike considering where to live).

A number of parents work irregular job schedules and their places of employment change often. For some, work conflicts with their ability to drop their children off, or pick them up from school, and so they select an out-of-zone school close to their child-care provider, who is often a family member. Alia, the mother of three who works in the auto parts warehouse, switched her son to Holcombe Elementary School, which is closer to her godmother's house, so that "he could just walk from . . . here to up the street to Holcombe, so it was just a little closer and more convenient." Her work schedule kept her from being able to pick him up from school, but by sending her son to Holcombe her godmother could watch him before and after school. She describes this as a trade-off between Holcombe, the more "convenient school," and Magnolia, "a real good school, good teachers, good principal, good school." As noted earlier, families rely heavily on extended kin for child-care needs, and in part, this is why they frequently use the address of the family member caring for their children to enroll them in school, making it easy for the children to walk to and from school or have bus transportation provided. Alia's child-care options are likely limited to family members because of the cost of private after-school care, making this school change about child care, but driven by the underlying lack of financial resources.

Transportation needs also create proximity preferences; many families do not have access to a vehicle or family members who can easily assist them with transportation needs. Mr. Brown, a father of three receiving disability due to kidney failure, told us that his son Thomas received an offer to attend Southern Christian, a private school, with a football scholarship. He explained that the school was unfortunately not a real option for them because "I really don't know how I'm going to get him way out there. By me having to go to dialysis, and my wife have to go to work, so I really don't know how he's going to make it out there." Mr. Brown was frustrated that they could not make this work because he thought highly of Southern Christian, saying it "was no comparison" to Harmon, the local school, but that their circumstances and transportation constraints made it impossible for his son to attend Southern Christian.

Veronica, who described wanting to move to West Mobile, had two daughters switch from Owens High School to Moffett High when they were expelled from Owens for a year after fighting on school grounds. When they switched, both daughters improved significantly in their behavior and academics. The older daughter, Jackie, graduated from Moffett, but the younger daughter, Vanessa, had to switch back to Owens because Veronica did not have a dependable car. She explained her transportation issues, saying, "at Moffett, she was just being kind of late, because we was way across town, trying to bring her back and forth every day, to go to school. So, I said, 'Vanessa, I said you know this car don't run half the time, it's best for you to see that they let you back into Owens the following year.' They went on and took her back into Owens." In Veronica's case transportation constraints made it necessary to leave the out-of-zone school where Vanessa had "started doing good."

These examples suggest that many of the factors that lead poor minority families to choose specific schools are not explicitly connected with academic qualities of the school, such as teacher training and certifications, class sizes, or test scores. This finding prompted a thorough examination of the data, seeking atypical cases that do mention academic concerns. The result is a handful of parents who mention appreciating the academic qualities of the schools their children already attend, most frequently test scores. Even among these parents, however, academic qualities are always paired with some additional considerations reflecting those expressed by the broader sample, such as strict principals or lower levels of fighting, and no specific discussion of the significance of school-level test scores for their child's performance in school.

Alicia described her children's elementary school, saying, "the faculty . . . [are] all new. I don't know what schools they came from, but I thank God they're there. And the principal, she's strict, and she is on top of it, their test scores went from 0 to 100, you know, it's a very good school now." Although she mentions improved test scores, Alicia's focus on the school improvement centers around the principal. Miss Barbara, a mother of four working part-time at a dry cleaner, discussed her children's schools, saying that other people describe them as bad schools. When asked why, she said, "the test scores, the fighting," but Miss Barbara indicated that not all the students at her local school were bad, but "it's . . . the gangs, the younger crowd" that have a negative influence on the school. She told us that what makes a good school is "the students, working together not fighting together." So, although she mentions test scores as a factor used by some to evaluate schools, she emphasizes the students, and whether or not they create a safe and positive environment, as her primary metric of school quality.

Academic measures of school quality are not a significant component of the evaluation of schools, or school choices among our sample. This was true across all levels of schooling, elementary through high school, in contrast to the findings in chapter 7 of this volume, that middle-class families who remain in the city and send their children to public schools are often focused more on social and environmental school factors for elementary school but increasingly emphasize that academic considerations will be more important when their children are in middle and high school.

Discussion

Despite the increasing number of school districts implementing choice programs, most children attend schools zoned for their neighborhoods. In other words, where families live likely determines where their children attend school. As a result, considerations of school quality often loom large in the calculus about where middle-class families choose to move (chapter 6, this volume; Holme 2002; Bayoh, Irwin, and Haab 2006). However, even though low-income and minority families make more frequent moves than their middle-class counterparts, we find among our sample of poor African American families that their residential moves rarely land them in better neighborhoods or their children in schools of higher academic quality. Families churn through the highly segregated and poor neighborhoods of Mobile that have similarly segregated and lower performing schools. Our analyses suggest that families' economic struggles and repeated exposure to poor and highly segregated neighborhoods and schools condition how families approach residential and school decisions.

Many of the adults in our sample have spent their entire lives in poor, racially segregated neighborhoods with poor performing schools, and this experience appears to influence their decision making in several significant ways. In contrast to middle- and working-class families, who have been shown to link their residential and school decisions (Holme 2002; Bayoh, Irwin, and Haab 2006; chapter 6, this volume), poor families decouple their residential and school choices. Poor families do not make residential decisions based on school considerations; rather, they emphasize factors such as safety concerns, proximity needs for child care or transportation, and housing amenities. Decoupling school choice from residential moves is possible because families exercise out-of-zone school choice using others' addresses, transfers, and magnet schools. Thus, school and residential choices do not have to be connected for families to get their children into the schools they desire. Families also decouple these decisions, in part, because housing instability is such a significant part of their lives, given frequent unplanned moves that are difficult for these families, and often highly constrained by time, finances, and information. As a result, attaching school selection to residential choice may be both risky (in case an unplanned move forces the family to leave the neighborhood) and may make the move itself more difficult by adding another dimension to consider on top of an already bounded set of residential options.

In addition to housing instability and the difficulty of moving, families also articulate a perception that variation between schools is limited. Looking at the schools their children typically attend (marked with an asterisk in table 5.3), this perception seems largely supported by the aggregate picture of student composition and test scores. However, these families do not have experience with, or residential access to, schools that are significantly different in their student composition and test score profile. Their social networks are also limited in their access to these neighborhoods and schools, making it impossible to enroll a child in these schools even through out-of-zone school choice that uses another person's address or that relies heavily on family for information about schools. Thus, the choice to preclude school considerations from residential decisions is also based in part on constrained experience and information leading to a perception of limited, if any, variation between schools.

Although school and residential choices are decoupled, our families still place a high value on education, and almost half of them have pursued an out-of-zone school choice for at least one child. School evaluation and choice, however, occur without significant focus on academic qualities; families instead emphasize issues related to the school environment, such as the strictness of school leadership, the safety of the school, and student behavior. Families live in environments with high levels of violence, crime, and drug activity; as a result, parents seek safety in both residential and school environments (compare Rosenblatt and DeLuca 2012). Families also make their school choices in light of a host of other family needs and constraints that stand apart from the internal qualities of the school as a social or academic institution. School decisions often coincide with the location of child-care providers, or transportation availability, and parents sometimes appraise schools on the basis of their proximity over and above other qualities.

We have described patterns in the school and residential choice process for low-income African American families in Mobile, and this affects the conclusions and policy suggestions we can draw. The racial and ethnic composition of our sample keeps us from being able to generalize our findings to low-income white or Latino families, or to middle- and upper-class African American families. Although Mobile is similar to other Rust Belt cities in terms of white-black segregation patterns, it also has a unique housing market and school district characteristics that do not generalize to other cities. In particular, the lack of charter schools and other school choice options in Mobile sets it apart from many cities that have implemented school choice programs. It is important to explore the extent to which the patterns of school and residential choice differ across other class and race based subgroups, and how these processes interact with specific geographic contexts, as these findings may also have significant implications for school choice and housing policy.

Policy Implications

Many choice-based policies make assumptions about how parents will respond to maximize benefits for their children; they rarely take into consideration the many other challenges low-income families face, or how their experiences and survival strategies shape their view of the costs and benefits of various residential and school options. Therefore, the school and housing policy implications of our findings from low-income parents' experiences and decision-making processes are significant. School choice policies assume that families will capitalize on the opportunity to match their child to the educational environment best equipped to help the child learn. In practice, however, many of these programs show that minority parents do not always sign up for school choice options, and many drop out of private school voucher programs; research on why is thin, suggesting the need to better understand the school decision-making process for poor and minority families (see Howell et al. 2002; Lauen 2007). Our findings show that constrained experiences and lack of transportation and child-care options may lead to the emphasis of concerns other than academics, and, in fact, that academic concerns may not be part of the decision-making process at all for many families (compare Condliffe, Boyd, and DeLuca forthcoming). Parents emphasize the social context of schools, and the quality of daily school interactions, on the basis of factors such as safety, student behavior, and the strictness of school leaders. This alternative metric for school assessment may lead families to select schools that, though serving some important needs, have poorer academic qualities, defying the typical policy logic of school choice. Accounting for the reality of families' lives, the factors they value most highly, and the constraints that influence their available opportunities may lead to significantly different policy needs for certain communities and families.

Our findings also provide some insight for housing policy, especially programs such as Housing Choice Vouchers, which, unlike traditional public housing projects, allow low-income families to rent housing in the larger metropolitan area. In theory, this kind of program should also open the educational landscape for poor families. However, our findings and other recent research suggest that, even with vouchers, families struggle to find housing in neighborhoods with higher performing schools (Boyd et al. 2010; Ellen and Horn 2012; DeLuca and Rosenblatt 2010). Even the families in our sample who receive housing choice vouchers rarely ventured out of the poorest and most segregated parts of Mobile. This suggests that families might need housing counseling assistance to learn about the educational benefits of moving to low-poverty communities, and may also need support to engage schools in communities with which they are not familiar. Recent research suggests that some housing mobility programs have been successful in helping poor minority families access school zones with more middle-class peers, higher test scores, and more qualified teachers, and the experiences of living in these higher opportunity environments actually changes the way parents view the schooling implications of their residential experiences (DeLuca and Rosenblatt 2011; Darrah and DeLuca forthcoming). This is important because these changes in school and neighborhood quality can have significant effects on children's achievement gains over time (Schwartz 2010).

The authors are grateful to the William T. Grant Foundation for their generous support of the second author through a Faculty Scholars Award, which made the fieldwork, analysis and writing possible. A fellowship from the Institute of Education Sciences supported writing time for the first author. We would like to thank fellow fieldworkers Laura Bartos, Barbara Condliffe, Trevor Hummel, Tanya Lukasik, Holly Wood, Kate Nygaard, Peter Rosenblatt and Siri Warkentien for data collection in Mobile. We are deeply indebted to John Bolland, who created the Mobile Youth Survey; his long-standing commitment to this survey and these communities not only made this work possible, but it was a continuous inspiration for us. Kathryn Edin and Michael Oakes provided valuable guidance during the data collection and conceptualization of this project. We would especially like to thank the families in Mobile, Alabama, for generously sharing their homes and stories with us.

Notes

1. Our interview team was white and our respondents were African American, which may have affected the way families responded to us. However, we are confident that our continued visits helped families feel more comfortable with us, and over the years they increasingly revealed more private details. Although we cannot be sure that the racial differences did not shape or limit what families were willing to share with us, we were encouraged by the many interactions that signaled to us that we were being "let in" to the more intimate details of families' lives. These included phone calls throughout the year to let us know about major changes in their lives, such as bouts of homelessness, new homes, and reoccurring battles with cancer; one family even sent photographs after a house fire. Several parents also invited us to family gatherings, fundraisers and church services.

2. Data come from the Alabama State Department of Education. Available at: http://www.alsde.edu/accountability/accountability.asp (accessed November 4, 2013).

3. Our data do not include school visits or observations, limiting our description of school environments to those gained through the State Department of Education website and our interviews with families.

4. Tables on elementary and high school data reflect similar patterns to those observed in the middle school data. These tables are available on request but were omitted due to space constraints.

5. All respondent and school names have been changed.

6. Magnet school enrollment in Mobile County public schools involves an application and subsequent lottery enrollment process with preference for siblings. Students must pass to the next grade from their current school without having to attend summer school, and have been suspended fewer than twice in the previous school year to be eligible.

7. We undertook a thorough examination of our interviews, reviewing coded sections on residential and school choice to confirm this finding.

8. As Stefanie DeLuca, Phillip Garboden, and Peter Rosenblatt (2013) note, this strategy also places families at risk of conflicts with their landlords and possible eviction.

9. "Median Monthly Housing Costs," table B25105, *American FactFinder,* available at: http://factfinder2.census.gov/faces/tableservices/jsf/pages/productview.xhtml?pid=ACS_11_1YR_B25105&prodType=table (accessed November 6, 2013).

10. Although kin networks were often a critical source of support for these families, there was not a universal desire to move close to other family members. A few of the women we spoke with also mentioned the benefits of getting away from family members, wanting their own space, or getting away from conflict.

References

Bartlett, Sheridan. 1997. "The Significance of Relocation for Chronically Poor Families in the USA." *Environment and Urbanization* 9(1): 121–32.

Bayoh, Isaac, Elena G. Irwin, and Timothy Haab. 2006. "Determinants of Residential Location Choice: How Important Are Local Public Goods in Attracting Homeowners to Central City Locations?" *Journal of Regional Science* 41(1): 97–120.

Bishaw, Alemayehu. 2011. "Areas with Concentrated Poverty: 2006–2011." Washington: U.S. Census Bureau. Available at: http://www.census.gov/prod/2011pubs/acsbr10–17.pdf (accessed May 11, 2013).

Bolland, John M. 2003. "Hopelessness and Risk Behavior Among Adolescents Living in High Poverty Inner-City Neighborhoods." *Journal of Adolescence* 26(2): 145–58.

Boyd, Melody L., Kathryn Edin, Susan Clampet-Lundquist, and Greg J. Duncan. 2010. The durability of gains from the Gautraux Two residential mobility programs: A qualitative analysis of who stays and who moves from low-poverty neighborhoods. *Housing Policy Debate* 20, 119–46.

Bruch, Elizabeth E., and Robert D. Mare. 2006. "Neighborhood Choice and Neighborhood Change." *American Journal of Sociology* 112(3): 667–709.

Cadwallader, Martin. 1993. *Residential Mobility and Migration: Macro and Micro Approaches.* Madison: University of Wisconsin Press.

Charles, Camille Zubrinsky. 2003. "The Dynamics of Racial Residential Segregation." *Annual Review of Sociology* 29:167–207.

Clampet-Lundquist, Susan. 2004. "HOPE VI Relocation: Moving to New Neighborhoods and Building New Ties." *Housing Policy Debate* 15(2): 415–47.

Clark, William A. V., Marinus C. Deurloo, and Frans M. Dieleman. 2006. "Residential Mobility and Neighbourhood Outcomes." *Housing Studies* 21(3): 323–42.

Clark, William A. V., and Robin Flowerdew. 1982. "A Review of Search Models and Their Application to Search in the Housing Market." In *Modelling Housing Market Search,* edited by William A. V. Clark. New York: St. Martin's Press.

Condliffe, Barbara, Melody Boyd, and Stefanie DeLuca. Forthcoming. "Stuck in School: How School Choice Policies Interact with Social Context to Shape Inner City Students' Educational Careers." *Teachers College Record.*

Crowley, Sheila. 2003. "The Affordable Housing Crisis: Residential Mobility of Poor Families and School Mobility of Poor Children." *Journal of Negro Education* 72(1): 22–38.

Darrah, Jennifer, and Stefanie DeLuca. Forthcoming. " 'It Changed My Whole Perspective': How Escaping Inner City Poverty Shapes Neighborhood and Housing Choice." *Journal of Public Policy Analysis and Management.*

DeLuca, Stefanie, Philip Garboden, and Peter Rosenblatt. 2013. "Segregating Shelter: How Housing Policies Shape the Residential Locations of Low-Income Minority Families." *The Annals of the American Academy of Political and Social Science* 647(1): 268–99.

DeLuca, Stefanie, and Peter Rosenblatt. 2010. "Does Moving to Better Neighborhoods Lead to Better School Opportunities? Parental School Choice in an Experimental Voucher Program." *Teachers College Record* 112(5): 1441–489.

———. 2011. "Increasing Access to High Performing Schools in an Assisted Housing Voucher Program." In *Finding Common Ground: Coordinating Housing and Education Policy to Support Racial and Economic Integration,* edited by Philip Tegeler. Washington, D.C.: Poverty & Race Research Action Council. Available at: http://www.prrac.org/pdf/HousingEducationReport-October2011.pdf (accessed November 4, 2013).

DeLuca, Stefanie, Holly Wood, and Peter Rosenblatt. 2011. "Why Poor People Move (and Where They Go): Residential Mobility, Selection, and Stratification." Paper presented at the Annual Meeting of the American Sociological Association. Las Vegas, Nevada (August 22, 2011).

Ellen, Ingrid Gould, and Keren Mertens Horn. 2012. "Do Federally Assisted Households Have Access to High Performing Public Schools? Civic Rights Research." Washington, D.C.: Poverty & Race Research Action Council. Available at: http://www.prrac.org/pdf/PRRACHousingLocation&Schools.pdf (accessed November 4, 2013).

Gramlich, Edward, Deborah Laren, and Naomi Sealand. 1992. "Moving Into and Out of Poor Urban Areas." *Journal of Policy Analysis and Management* 11(2): 273–87.

Hanushek, Eric A., John F. Kain, and Steven G. Rivkin. 2004. "Disruption Versus Tiebout Improvement: The Costs and Benefits of Switching Schools." *Journal of Public Economics* 88(9): 1721–746.

Hirsch, Arnold R. 1983. *Making the Second Ghetto: Race and Housing in Chicago 1940–1960.* Chicago: University of Chicago Press.

Holme, Jennifer J. 2002. "Buying Homes, Buying Schools: School Choice and the Social Construction of School Quality." *Harvard Educational Review* 72(2): 177–206.

Horvat, Erin McNamara, Elliot B. Weininger, and Annette Lareau. 2003. "From Social Ties to Social Capital: Class Differences in the Relations Between Schools and Parent Networks." *American Educational Research Journal* 40(4): 319–51.

Howell, William G., Patrick J. Wolf, David E. Campbell, and Paul E. Peterson. 2002. "School Vouchers and Academic Performance: Results from Three Randomized Field Trials." *Journal of Policy Analysis and Management* 21(2): 191–217.

Johnson, Heather Beth, and Thomas M. Shapiro. 2003. "Good Neighborhoods, Good Schools: Race and the Good Choices." In *White Out: The Continuing Significance of Racism,* edited by Ashley W. Doane and Eduardo Bonilla-Silva. New York: Routledge.

Kimelberg, Shelley McDonough, and Chase M. Billingham. 2012. "Attitudes Toward Diversity and the School Choice Process: Middle-Class Parents in a Segregated Urban Public School District." *Urban Education* 48(2): 198–231.

Lareau, Annette. 2012. "'Non-Decision Decisions': Unpacking the Process Whereby Parents Decide Where to Live." Paper presented at "Storied Lives: Culture, Structure, and Narrative," the 82nd Annual Meeting of the Eastern Sociological Society. New York (February 23–26, 2012).

Lauen, Lee Lauen. 2007. "Contextual Explanations of School Choice." *Sociology of Education* 80(3): 179–209.

Logan, John R., and Richard D. Alba. 1993. "Locational Returns to Human Capital: Minority Access to Suburban Community Resources." *Demography* 30(2): 243–68.

Massey, Douglas S., and Nancy A. Denton. 1993. *American Apartheid.* Cambridge, Mass.: Harvard University Press.

Neild, Ruth Curran. 2005. "Parent Management of School Choice in a Large Urban District." *Urban Education* 40(3): 270–97.

Pattillo-McCoy, Mary. 2000. *Black Picket Fences: Privilege and Peril in the Black Middle Class Neighborhood.* Chicago: University of Chicago Press.

Renzulli, Linda A., and Lorraine Evans. 2005. "School Choice, Charter Schools, and White Flight." *Social Problems* 52(3): 398–418.

Retsinas, Nicolas Paul, and Eric S. Belsky, eds. 2008. *Revisiting Rental Housing: Policies, Programs, and Priorities.* Washington, D.C.: Brookings Institution Press.

Rosenblatt, Peter, and Stefanie DeLuca. 2012. " 'We Don't Live Outside, We Live in Here': Residential Mobility Decisions of Low-Income Families." *City & Community* 11(3): 254–84.

Rossi, Peter. 1980. *Why Families Move: A Study in the Social Psychology of Urban Residential Mobility,* 2nd ed. Los Angeles, Calif.: Sage Publications.

Sampson, Robert J., and Patrick Sharkey. 2008. "Neighborhood Selection and the Social Reproduction of Concentrated Racial Inequality." *Demography* 45(1): 1–29.

Saporito, Salvatore. 2003. "Private Choices, Public Consequences: Magnet School Choice and Segregation by Race and Poverty." *Social Problems* 50(2): 181–203.

Saporito, Salvatore, and Annette Lareau. 1999. "School Selection as a Process: The Multiple Dimensions of Race in Framing Educational Choice." *Social Problems* 46(3): 418–39.

Schafft, Kai A. 2006. "Poverty, Residential Mobility, and Student Transiency Within a Rural New York School District." *Rural Sociology* 71(2): 212–31.

Schneider, Mark, Paul Teske, and Melissa Marschall. 2000. *Choosing Schools: Consumer Choice and the Quality of American Schools.* Princeton, N.J.: Princeton University Press.

Schneider, Mark, Paul Teske, Melissa Marschall, and Christine Roch. 1998. "Shopping for Schools: In the Land of the Blind, the One-Eyed Parent May Be Enough." *American Journal of Political Science* 42(3): 769–93.

Schwartz, Heather. 2010. *Housing Policy Is School Policy: Economically Integrative Housing Promotes Academic Success in Montgomery County, Maryland.* New York: Century Foundation.

Sharkey, Patrick. 2013. *Stuck in Place: Urban Neighborhoods and the End of Progress Toward Racial Equality.* Chicago: University of Chicago Press.

Sikkink, David, and Michael O. Emerson. 2008. "School Choices and Racial Segregation in U.S. Schools: The Role of Parents' Education." *Ethnic and Racial Studies* 31(2): 267–93.

South, Scott, and Kyle Crowder. 1997. "Escaping Distressed Neighborhoods: Individual, Community, and Metropolitan Influences." *American Journal of Sociology* 102(4): 1040–84.

South, Scott, Kyle Crowder, and Erick Chavez. 2005. "Exiting and Entering High-Poverty Neighborhoods: Latinos, Blacks, and Anglos Compared." *Social Forces* 84(2): 873–900.

Speare, Alden, Sidney Goldstein, and William H. Frey. 1975. *Residential Mobility, Migration, and Metropolitan Change.* Cambridge, Mass.: Ballinger Publishing.

U.S. Department of Education. 2009. *The Condition of Education 2009.* Washington, D.C.: National Center for Education Statistics.

Wood, Holly. 2012. "When Only a House Makes a Home: How Home Selection Matters in the Residential Mobility Decisions of Low-Income, Inner-City Households." Unpublished manuscript.

Yinger, John. 1995. *Closed Doors, Opportunities Lost: The Continuing Costs of Housing Discrimination.* New York: Russell Sage Foundation.

= Part II =

Choosing Schools in a Residential Context

═ Chapter 6 ═

Schools, Housing, and the Reproduction of Inequality

ANNETTE LAREAU

Scholarly and popular conversations about inequality often focus on the experience of people living in cities. Yet, suburban communities also vary in the relative affluence of their neighborhoods and school districts. Indeed, recent decades have seen a growth of economic segregation across suburban neighborhoods (Reardon and Bischoff 2011). Suburban school districts today also vary in their budgets, teacher qualifications, and test scores.[1] Research also suggests that children's life chances can be influenced by the character of the schools and neighborhoods in which they live (for neighborhood effects, see Sampson 2012; Sharkey 2013; for the influence of schools and family background on life chances, see Duncan and Murnane 2011).[2]

One problem, however, is that most research on the influence of neighborhoods and schools begins after families have settled into these different communities (but see Holmes 2002).[3] The mechanisms through which parents of different social classes come to live in different suburban neighborhoods are not well understood. Yet any serious effort to reduce inequality would need to try to reduce the segregation of children into different spaces.

The key goal of this study is to understand how parents of young children went about selecting a home in a number of suburban areas comprised of multiple school districts. As with 73 percent of American children, the families in this study sent their children to the neighborhood catchment school (U.S. Department of Education 2009).[4] Because children attended the local catchment school, once parents chose a residence, they chose a school. Furthermore, the region was characterized by significant levels of inequality in economic development, housing values, parks, libraries, schools, crime, and public services. In general, children of middle-class and upper-middle-class families were concentrated in schools (and the neighborhoods) that were considered the most desirable. Because some schools were widely seen as being better than others, it is important to understand how parents gained access to these high-quality schools. In this study, I look at a key moment in the reproduction of inequality: how parents of young children go about selecting a house and a school for their children.

Literature Review

I consider three alternatives for how parents come to select their homes and hence schools: economic factors, a cultural logic of child rearing, and social networks.

One important debate in the study of inequality centers on the degree to which economic factors alone are guiding residential decisions. Some studies focus particularly on the connection between housing values and school decisions, implicitly suggesting that it is the economic value of the home that is key (Dougherty et al. 2009; Bayer and McMillan 2011). Nonetheless, a number of studies (chapter 5, this volume; Rosenblatt and Deluca 2012; Sharkey 2013) suggest that even with payment vouchers for housing, low-income families often settle in high-poverty neighborhoods rather than low-poverty neighborhoods.[5] We have less information, however, on the residential decisions of working-class and middle-class families.[6] There are also signs that economic factors are far from the only factor driving residential decisions. Because most moves, for example, are short distances, residents seem to have a preference for staying in their current neighborhood rather than looking for the best economic value in the entire region. Also, as Robert Sampson shows (2012), when moving, people disproportionately locate in a place where their former neighbors have taken up residence, suggesting the influence of neighbors in shaping preferences.

Second, research on social class and parenting suggests that there are class differences in a cultural logic of child rearing (Lareau 2011; see also Calarco 2011). In *Unequal Childhoods*, I argued that middle-class parents engaged in concerted cultivation in which they used organized activities, language development, and interventions in institutions to foster the development of children's talents and skills. By contrast, working-class parents, who saw looming hardship in adulthood, tried to protect their children by allowing them free time to watch television or play with kin, clarifying their obligations with directives, and trusting professionals to provide appropriate services in institutions (a pattern termed *the accomplishment of natural growth*). Because the choice of a school is widely seen as a very important moment in child rearing, it is possible that the search process would differ by social class. One might expect middle-class parents to vigorously search for data, visit countless schools, interrogate members of their networks about the strengths and weaknesses of the various options, and otherwise engage in a sustained process of concerted cultivation in school choice. By contrast, one might expect working-class parents to put equal trust in all educators to provide a high-quality education for their children, and therefore put less time and energy into researching school quality (Lareau 2000; chapter 9, this volume).

Third, research has pointed to the pivotal role of social networks in many aspects of life (see McPherson, Smith-Lovin, and Cook 2001) including schools (Holmes 2002; Neild 2005). Although studies of residential segregation have certainly discussed networks in the housing search, the role of networks has not been sufficiently elaborated in terms of the formation of preferences (chapter 2, this volume).[7] Nor has there been attention to how in the residential housing search social networks can intersect with members' cultural tastes, habits, and status preferences. Yet, as Bill Bishop (2008) points out in *The Big Sort,* there are signs that residents are drawn to live with like-minded individuals who have similar political and cultural tastes. Hence, networks may be rooted in geographical areas with different arrays of cultural amenities.[8]

In sum, the literature has identified key influences on the selection process, but the mechanisms through which these factors shape housing decisions remains somewhat unclear. Researchers have often suggested that economic factors play a crucial role in guiding the search for housing, but the ways in which economic factors guide shopping has not been fully developed. The residential segregation literature has also presumed the significance of housing preferences, but has paid less attention to the ways in which preferences are created. Here, using qualitative data, I look at three competing explanations for how parents formed preferences: economic resources, parents' child-rearing approaches, and social networks.

Overview of the Argument

This chapter draws on a qualitative study of parents' accounts of their search for housing; along with doctoral students, I interviewed primarily parents living in three suburban school districts. With few exceptions, economic issues could only partially explain how parents selected a place to live. To be sure, economic factors limited parents' options, but they did not appear to guide parents' selection practices. Although class differences in child rearing were readily apparent, social class did not affect how parents went about selecting a school or residence for their children. Instead, in deciding on a school district in which to settle, I found virtually all parents seemed to be guided by a central tenet: "trust what you know and who you know." Although economic factors and parents' tastes certainly entered the process, virtually all of the families in our study depended on informal social networks to narrow their focus and then to select a community. In a few cases, the parents supplemented that knowledge with information gathered on blogs or magazines, but even then informal networks seemed crucial. Hence, in this chapter I show how across social class, informal networks were crucial, though middle-class and working-class parents tended to glean information about different school districts from their respective networks.

The parents I interviewed relied on networks that were not only relatively homogeneous but concentrated in relatively few geographical areas. Parents sought to live with "people like them" or—put differently—status cultures. Strikingly, they tended to know only the names of districts where their friends and relatives lived, or that had a similar social class position to their current neighborhood. Parents did not tend to know names or details about suburban neighborhoods associated with a different social class. Middle-class families were particularly uninformed about low-status neighborhoods. Working-class parents had only the vaguest of information about schools in high-status neighborhoods. People seemed to be drawn to living with people like them. Parents generally made these residential decisions with little apprehension or consideration of other suburban districts.[9] Because the status cultures had a geographical character, and were associated with different areas (which differed in economic development, transportation, shopping, safety, housing values, and other factors), I have termed these micro-climates. These different micro-climates seemed to be crucial in determining the array of choices parents considered.

Although the processes where parents were guided to schools seemed very similar by social class, where they ended up was very different. The school districts were not uniform. They had different tax bases, per-pupil expenditures, educational programs, and test scores. Schools attended by middle-class and upper-middle-class children were ranked higher by the school district. No evidence, however, indicated that the middle-class and upper-middle-class parents ended up in better schools through their own diligence and hard work. Instead, these parents benefited from the relatively class-segregated nature of social networks that contributes to a social structure of inequality across neighborhoods.

In sum, residential preferences seem to result from a set of strikingly taken-for-granted happenings in parents' lives. Trusted friends or relatives identified good places to live. Often parents had visited these neighborhoods before. "Everybody" knew that they were attractive places to be. Although parents often systematically compared housing within neighborhoods, parents rarely systematically compared options across neighborhoods. Hence, by limiting the array of neighborhoods under consideration, the stratified nature of parents' social worlds facilitated a rapid and seamless reproduction of inequality.

Figure 6.1   School Districts

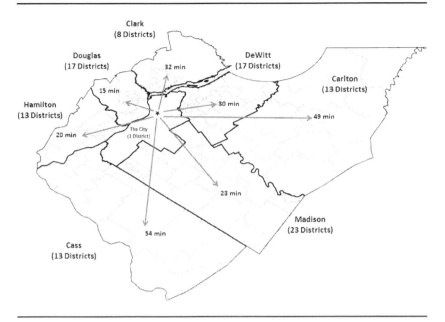

Source: Author's and research team's calculations using U.S. Census Bureau data, 2010. Slight adjustments have been made to protect the confidentiality of the research site.

Research Methodology

This chapter is based on in-depth, face-to-face interviews with parents of young children in the suburbs of a large northeastern city. Figure 6.1 describes the core study of upper-middle-class, middle-class, and working-class white and African American native-born parents in forty-six families.[10] It also describes the family structure arrangements of the families. The study focused on three suburban school districts with very different characteristics. Within each district, we selected parents of young children.

Qualitative work is emergent; as the study unfolded, we made adjustments to reflect our new knowledge. We initially selected one elementary school in each district, sending letters home to kindergarten parents and visiting during school events to recruit parents.[11] In interviewing these parents about how they came to live in their neighborhood, we found that many had bought their houses two or three years earlier, and were able to offer only vague answers to our central questions. Thus, hoping to improve the quality of the description by getting closer to the time of choice, we broadened the sample to include families with children in daycare. To recruit parents, we visited daycares located near the three focal elementary schools. Face-to-face meetings and recommendations from daycare directors provided some contacts, and snowball sampling helped to target families who had made very recent residential decisions. Although the majority of the families in the study had an eldest child who was three to six years old, some referred to us had children slightly older (that is, an eldest child six to ten years old). The snowball sample generally yielded parents in the three target districts, but in a few cases we interviewed parents in nearby suburbs. In addition, to fill out our different groups, a few parents, particularly two upper-middle-class African American parents, were found by activating the social networks of the researchers.[12] At the end of the study, we also returned to the elementary school at Kingsley and recruited parents at the visiting day for new students; we gained additional parents through this method.[13]

In the interviews, we asked general questions about how parents came to live in this residence, the factors they had considered in choosing the residence, and their knowledge of the local schools. In an effort to make the interviews more concrete, following Maria Krysan and Michael Bader (2009) we also developed maps of the region, which we showed to respondents to discuss where they looked and, especially, where they were unwilling to live and send their children to school. Most of the interviews were carried out in 2012, but some were done earlier. The author carried out thirty of the forty-six core parent interviews; the remaining interviews were conducted by a racially diverse research team of doctoral students and a postdoctoral fellow. Families received an honorarium of $50 for the interview. In addition, as a friendly gesture, researchers brought a pie or other dessert to the interview. The data set also includes interviews with all of the superintendents in the districts, including the previous and current superintendent in two districts; five real estate agents; and twenty-five recreation officials, librarians, township officials, and community leaders, such as school board members, church leaders, and parents active in educational organizations (for a discussion of the experience of urban middle-class and working-class parents in this data set, see chapter 9, this volume).

Given that previous work has demonstrated that middle-class parents play active roles in monitoring schooling, I was particularly keen to assess how middle-class parents sought to make residential decisions. Due to rising inequality, I distinguished between upper-middle-class and middle-class parents in the recruitment of parents in the sample (table 6.1). There were not, however, large differences in how upper-middle-class and middle-class parents approach the process of home selection. In a few instances, middle-class parents were economically strained; they could not afford to purchase a house in the most elite neighborhoods. These families are noted in the next section. Aside from those instances noted, however, I use the term *middle-class* to capture both upper-middle-class and middle-class families.

All of the interviews were transcribed verbatim. After looking for themes in the interviews, a coding scheme was devised by the author and a col-

Table 6.1   Sample of Suburban Parents

	White	African American	Interracial	Total
Upper-middle-class families Advanced degree (for example, JD, PhD, MD) and highly complex, educationally certified (postbaccalaureate) skills with substantial autonomy (freedom from direct supervision) in the course of his or her work	11	5		16
Middle-class families BA and a job that requires relatively complex, educationally certified skills (bachelor's degree or above); however, the job need not entail high levels of autonomy	9	4	2	15
Working-class families Usually high school grad but may include some college; skilled or unskilled job; usually with close supervision; includes those on disability or public assistance	5	9	1	15
Total	25	18	3	46

Source: Author's compilation.

league. The interviews from the core sample were then coded by research assistants using Atlas.ti. In this process, we sought to look for common themes as well as disconfirming evidence for the emerging argument.[14]

The Institutional and Social Context

Social structures are crucial in shaping the conditions under which parents make school and residential choices. The metropolitan area in which we did the study has around three million residents. In the city, slightly less than one-half of residents are African American, approximately 40 percent are white (non-Hispanic), and the remainder of residents are Asian, Hispanic, and of other racial and ethnic groups. By contrast, the suburbs are predominantly white, although some of the inner-ring, older suburbs have become overwhelmingly minority in recent years. In this instance, the sheer number of school districts was shaped by structural forces. Unlike many other regions in the country, such as Los Angeles, this particular region has significant social

Figure 6.2   Travel Time from City Hall

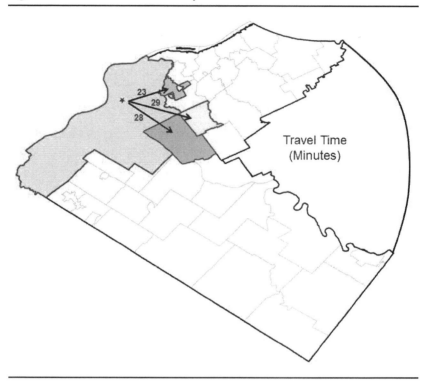

Source: Author's and research team's calculations using Google Maps, 2012. Slight adjustments have been made to protect the confidentiality of the research site.

diversity in a compact geographic space. As figure 6.2 shows, more than a hundred school districts lie within an hour's drive of the city hall in the central city; most are considerably closer. Most of these districts are small, for example, one high school, two middle schools, and six elementary schools. This structure influenced the array of choices parents faced.

Federal monetary policies and housing policies also were critical in influencing key aspects of the housing search. These policies have far-ranging influences. Housing interest rates were, for example, as high as 15 percent to 17 percent around 1980.[15] Since then, in part due to government fiscal policies, interest rates have dropped substantially. Generally interest rates were around 5 percent at the time that most of the parents purchased their homes, but some were higher or lower. In addition, some of the families had bought their houses at the height of the market around 2006; houses were selling very quickly. Some stayed on the market only a few days; they would have full-price offers. In the subsequent housing collapse, fueled in part by the Great Recession of the fall of 2008, real estate slowed, houses stayed on the market longer, and values fell. Yet, in this northeastern suburban area, housing did not rise as much as in other parts of the country nor fall as much as other areas.[16] Still, at the time of the study, some of the families had homes that had lost 10 to 15 percent of their value compared to when they had purchased them.

Other public policies have had an impact on the formation and the character of the neighborhoods parents considered. For example, federal policy and local politics developed highways through some neighborhoods and not others; regional systems provide buses and other local transportation. As noted, Peter Rosenblatt and Stefanie DeLuca (2012) show that low-income families with housing vouchers generally did not move into low-poverty communities unless a bus transportation system was in place. In the region in which our study takes place, the local transit system supported an unusually developed network of public transportation of local trains and buses into the suburbs of Kingsley, Gibbon, and Warren. Although the trains received limited government subsidy and were costly (often $4.00 each way), it is possible to take a train from many suburban communities into the downtown area. The trains run two or three times per hour at rush hour; they run hourly during non-peak hours during the week and on Saturdays (and every two hours on Sundays). Still, the routes are restrictive; many houses were not well-serviced by public transportation. Many parents based a housing decision on proximity to the train or the bus.

The surrounding suburbs vary significantly in their racial and class composition. We focused on three key suburban school districts. *Kingsley* is often referred to as the Garden Area and has a reputation as being particularly affluent. (It is comparable to the area around Chevy Chase, Maryland, the North Shore of Chicago, or Palo Alto, California.) Housing in Kingsley varies from small, brick row homes to massive mansions with broad expanses of gardens, hills, and carefully trimmed yards. Many single-family homes are expansive. Parents are often doctors, lawyers, college professors, scientists, architects, or other professionals. As figures 6.3 and 6.4 reveal, the median housing values and income of households in this area are among the highest in the region. Kingsley is predominantly white, but historically has also contained a small African American neighborhood with much smaller homes. There are five large grocery stores within a few miles. There is a well-known upscale mall that has many high-end chain clothing stores stocked with the latest fashions, small stationery boutiques selling wedding invitations, and special cards, and shops with crystal, Lenox china, and other wedding gift items. People from the region, including surrounding school districts, drive to the mall to shop. Specialty restaurants, coffee shops, sports clothing stores, fitness gyms, and other shops dot the main street of the garden area.

Gibbon shares a border with Kingsley. It is widely described as a more middle-class area (figures 6.3 and 6.4) that is heavily Catholic. Police officers, fire fighters, bank workers, and white-collar workers are many of the inhabitants. It is also mostly white (95 percent), but there are pockets that are more racially diverse (figure 6.5). Housing often consists of modest

Figure 6.3   Median Home Value

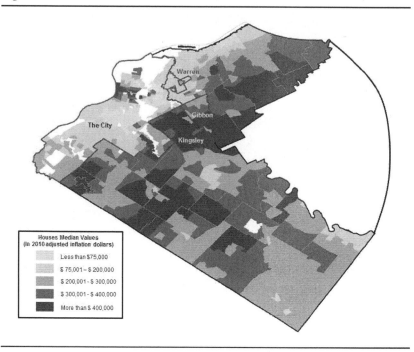

Source: Author's and research team's calculations using U.S. Census Bureau data, 2006–2010, and American Community Survey. Slight adjustments made for confidentiality of research site.

Figure 6.4   Median Household Income

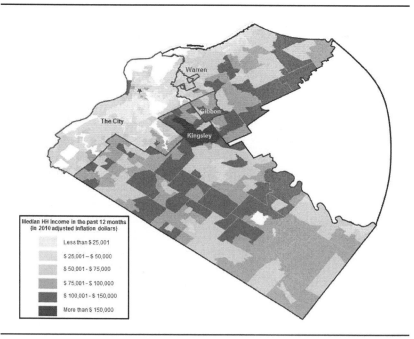

Source: Author's and research team's calculations using U.S. Census Bureau data, 2006–2010, and American Community Survey. Slight adjustments made for confidentiality of research site.

Figure 6.5   Percentage Black and Hispanic

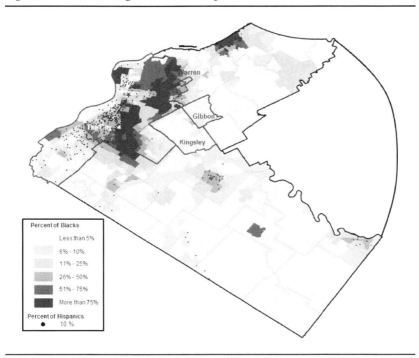

Source: Author's and research team's calculations using U.S. Census Bureau data, 2012. Slight adjustments have been made to protect the confidentiality of the research site.

ranch-style homes (around two thousand square feet) with neat, trimmed small yards in front of the home. There are some row houses. Shopping in Gibbons is less developed than in Kingsley. Shops are primarily located in strip malls. One such mall near the Gibbon elementary school has a donut shop, a dry cleaner, a convenience store, and an insurance company. An older downtown area has small shops, chain restaurants, older clothing stores, and a few bars.

Warren is a larger school district; it is also more heterogeneous (figures 6.3 and 6.4). Some areas of the district are suburban, single-family homes filled with white, middle-class families. Particularly in the areas of the district close to Gibbon, streets are tree-lined with expansive boulevards and single-family homes with carefully trimmed yards. A few small shopping districts offer diners, insurance shops, and a convenience store. (Realtors report that the families in these areas presume that they will send their children to private school when they purchase the home.) Other areas of the district, however, are more urban looking. For example a trolley car passes from the city into the Warren School District. On this thoroughfare,

Table 6.2   **Family Structure Within Sample**

	White Suburban		African American Suburban		Interracial Suburban		
	Intact, Two Parents	Single Parent	Intact, Two Parents	Single Parent	Intact, Two Parents	Single Parent	Total
Upper middle class	9	2	4	1			16
Middle class	7	2	3	2	2		16
Working class	4	1	0	8	1		14
Total	23	5	7	11	3		46

Source: Author's compilation.

numerous small shops line the streets, including corner stores, discount retail stores, check cashing entities, and other small shops. One large grocery store is located on the trolley line. The parents who attended the public school in Warren were overwhelmingly low income. A number were on government assistance; others worked in jobs such as a nurse's aid, waitress, or convenience store clerk. Some parts of Warren are similar to Gibbon, but others are very similar to, indeed indistinguishable from, poor neighborhoods in the central city.

Figures 6.6 and 6.7 and table 6.3 also provide details on the schools in each of the focal districts. Although the median price of a home in the Kingsley district is over $450,000, there are (small) homes for sale for $250,000 in Kingsley.[17] A significant number of apartment units are also available. As a result, parents who are less prosperous are able to find housing in districts with reputations for high-quality schools. Property taxes, however, are slightly lower in Kingsley than Gibbons School District (due to the benefit of the economic development such as the shopping mall in Kingsley). Although the property taxes are around $6,000 annually for a house worth $350,000 in Gibbons (and slightly less in Kingsley), they are almost 30 percent higher in Warren School District. Moreover, Kingsley was widely reported by middle-class parents to be "the best" school district in the area. Gibbons did not have this reputation among most of the middle-class families in the study, although the test scores at the elementary school are very close to the scores in Kingsley. Still, in interviews, realtors reported that they were prevented (by law) from discussing details about schools with clients. They told parents where they could collect this information,

Figure 6.6   Per Pupil Expenditure

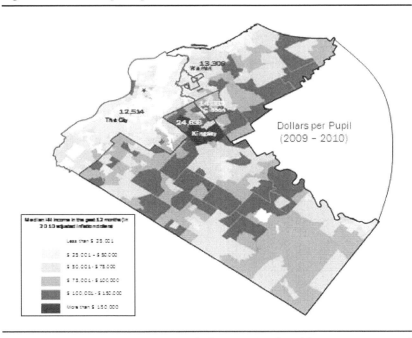

Source: Author's and research team's calculations using http://www.openpagov.org/education_revenue_and_expenses.asp. Figures adjusted slightly to protect confidentiality.

Figure 6.7   SAT Scores in Selected School Districts

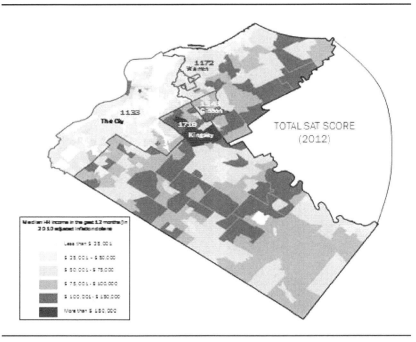

Source: Author's and research team's calculations using state government data, 2012.

Table 6.3   Characteristics of the School District

Elementary Schools	Grade 3, Percent Proficient Math	Grade 3, Percent Proficient Reading	Great Schools Rating	Percent Free or Reduced Lunch	Percent Black	Percent White
City School District	39	37	3	86	99	2
Warren School District	52	47	2	80	96	4
Gibbons School District	97	95	9	7	8	90
Kingsley School District	91	90	9	7	13	70

Source: Author compiled from websites of the school districts, zillow.com, greatschools.org (minor adjustments to protect confidentiality of the schools). Data are from 2009 and 2010.

but insisted that they did not discuss schools with parents. Realtors did, however, work in a small geographical area; they could show parents a home the parents found on the Internet, but normally they showed homes in only a few neighborhoods. Hence, by the time a family has chosen a realtor, they have generally chosen a place to live.

Trust What and Who You Know

As parents go about selecting a neighborhood and school district for their home, most had a plethora of school data at their disposal. Part of the goal of No Child Left Behind (NCLB) was to provide parents with detailed information about schools so that parents could make informed decisions.[18] Federal law requires schools to be assessed as to whether they are making adequate yearly progress (AYP). In the state in which the research was conducted, school districts are also mandated to annually disclose children's proficiency in reading and math, high school graduation rates, and data about teachers' qualifications. All of this information is widely available on school district websites, magazines, newspapers, and Internet sources. As numerous studies show (Reardon and Bischoff 2011; Spivak, Bass, and St. John 2011; also chapters 2 and 4, this volume), there is significant economic segregation in residential selection. Affluent families do not tend to live in the same block as low-income families. As we might expect, the middle-class and upper middle-class families in our study lived in the Kingsley or Gibbon school districts and the working-class families generally lived in the Warren school district. As a result,

I discuss them in separate sections. My evidence suggests, though, that parents of different class positions followed a similar process.

Middle-Class Families

The middle-class parents in our study had busy lives. Their children were involved in numerous organized activities, the parents played a prominent role in schooling, and there were signs that parents also engaged in long, detailed conversations with the children about their interests and preferences. But these child rearing patterns, surprisingly, did not lead suburban parents to systematically interrogate schooling options, visit numerous possible kindergartens, or pore over test scores.[19]

Rather than conduct careful research, suburban middle-class and upper-middle-class parents in this study selected a neighborhood and school district by drawing on either personal experience or information gleaned from trusted members of their social networks. Most of the parents in our sample had grown up in the community in which they were currently living, had been raised in a nearby community, or were married to someone who was from the area. Even those families who had come to the neighborhoods "cold" from other parts of the country usually for employment (that is, six of thirty-one middle-class families in the study) tended not to rely on formal research to guide their choice process. Rather, they relied on informal knowledge from their new coworkers.[20]

A number of parents were insistent that having "good schools" was a key criterion in selecting an area in which to live. The information through which parents assessed the viability of a school district came not from the empirical data available on the websites of school districts but from the word-of-mouth information vouched for by friends. Parents generally relied exclusively on this information in making decisions about where to look for housing. In a few cases, parents looked at test scores posted on Internet websites. Still, most parents never looked at websites. Instead, they had implicit faith in the information provided to them.

For example, the Peterson family moving to the east from the Midwest relied on word-of-mouth as well as their previous visits to the homes of relatives in their decision to settle on Kingsley. The Petersons lived in a large, one-story, modern home with an expansive sweep of floor-to-ceiling windows in the living room and dining room along with a fireplace constructed of small, round, silver rocks placed in an artistic pattern. In 2012, the house was worth around $400,000. Both of the parents, who are white, are scientists with doctorates; their family income is around $200,000. Ms. Peterson who, in her early forties is an older mother of a kindergartner, is a quiet, serious mother who greets me on a Saturday morning with her blond hair meticulously brushed in a bob, and wearing casual pants and an older sweater. The house is completely quiet.

The Peterson family sought energetically to give their son advantages in life. Ms. Peterson carefully monitored his kindergarten progress and did not hesitate to contact educators with her questions. Her mother (her son's grandmother) watched her son after school, and the grandmother volunteered in the elementary school library twice each week. Although Ms. Peterson (who is a prolific scientist) "was on the lecture circuit" for work, had traveled to Asia the previous week to give a lecture, and traveled overnight once a month, she made a point of volunteering with the PTA (Parent-Teacher Association). Yet, Ms. Peterson did not activate her considerable research skills in the selection of a neighborhood and a school:

> We wanted to be somewhere where there were good public schools, and we wanted some space, and we wanted to minimize our commute. And so that gave us a radius. And we looked, very half-heartedly in [a nearby state] and it wasn't anything about schools there, we didn't get that far, in logic we didn't want to have a bridge between us and work, [laughs], so, um, so that brought us to this general area, and we needed to be near a train line, because we wanted to have a one-car family, so that narrowed it down for us. So none of this had anything to do [with] school, and one of the things that school didn't come into it quite that early is my sense, partially from talking to other people was that most of the schools here, public schools here were very acceptable. So we looked.

Although they wanted to "be somewhere where there were good public schools," the Peterson family did not gather detailed information about the schools:

> And, and if the school, and I know you're not asking me that at this point, but if the schools came into it, it may have been sort of Madison County, Dewitt County, but even then when I look back, I don't think my information [that the Madison County schools were better than the Dewitt County schools] was particularly solid. You know, I'm a scientist, I know how to check things out, and the fact is I really didn't do it. But I do know that these were, were all pretty much considered to be very good schools.

In saying, "I'm a scientist" who knows how to "check things out," Ms. Peterson is acknowledging her occupationally based skill set that she did not activate in this instance. Yet, rather than actively search for verifiable information, the Petersons instead relied on recommendations from those whom they knew in the area.

Other parents repeated this succinct summary of how they settled on the school district. All of the parents insisted that the school decision was an important one. In addition, as the parents sought to develop their children's talents and skills in many areas of life, they engaged in "concerted cultivation" (Lareau 2011). Thus, the relative lack of research and systematic investigation of school districts in parents' decision about where to live in the suburbs appeared to be unusual given the parents' close scrutiny and management of almost every aspect of their young children's lives.

Take, for instance, Ms. Wauters and her husband, who both have doctorates in the social sciences from University of Nebraska. She works as a psychologist and enjoyed taking yoga classes as well as being in a mothers' group. She and her husband, who are white, earn between $125,000 and $150,000; they have two sons, six and three years old. With the help of an inheritance, they bought their house nine years earlier with a down payment of $100,000; it is currently worth about $320,000. Ms. Wauters engaged in concerted cultivation in the sense that she actively sought to develop her sons' talents and skills. She had play dates with her son, volunteered in PTA, had her older son in soccer, was planning to enroll him in Cub Scouts the following year, and generally monitored his development very closely. For example, although during the summer she had him in fun activities, she planned to help him with his writing because "the one area I feel he needs some more practice is fine motor skills." She and her husband did not hesitate to activate cultural capital to gain advantages; they worked to acquire even small advantages for their children. For example, for her younger son, she requested that the day-care center "move him into a slightly more advanced group" so that "instead of being the oldest kid in the group, we wanted him to be more among the youngest, because we felt like this is our younger son who is pretty developmentally advanced."[21] Thus, in the context of parenting it is striking that the selection of the school district was more casual and of a different ilk than other aspects of her child rearing.

For example, rather than having specific, detailed knowledge about the schools, Ms. Wauters's knowledge was vague and general:

> We just felt like the public schools are very good here.
>
> Q: How did you know the schools were good in this neighborhood?
>
> I mean, I feel like it's talked about and it's in the newspapers. We didn't really look up any test scores or anything like that before we moved here, but just by reputation, word of mouth. . . . I just feel like it's just so much that I'm maybe assuming about the schools. Some of my decisions are not like I've carefully researched.

Ms. Wauters reported that she liked the old houses in the area along with the trees and grass. By her own admission, Ms. Wauters volunteers that "some of my decisions are not like I've carefully researched."

In a similar vein, Keith Quigley, a musician and teacher, had grown up in the area. He had been away from Kingsley, however, for almost two decades. After his wife left him, he and his seven-year-old daughter moved in with his parents; his daughter was going to first grade in Kingsley. Mr. Quigley is African American; his father is a minister and his mother an educator. They live in the African American section of the Kingsley district. Although he recounts that, in the past, he has had "issues" with the district, he was convinced that Kingsley was an outstanding school district:

> The school system is one of the best. . . . A lot of things I like about it and some things that I don't like. But for the most part it gets respect around the country and I realized that once I actually left and went to [college] and realized that even like my freshman year they were doing things I had done in ninth grade.

He felt that children educated in Kingsley were "light years" ahead of children being educated in the city.

Mr. Quigley was a very involved father. In his interactions with his daughter, he patiently answered each of her questions with long answers; he encouraged her verbal development. His daughter had swimming lessons; he closely monitored and evaluated her art. In short, Mr. Quigley engaged in child rearing that could be termed concerted cultivation. Although he was a school teacher, Mr. Quigley did not feel the need to look at test scores; nor, when he lived in another state, did he look at the test scores of the school where he was considering sending his daughter. Rather, along with other parents in our study, through their informal networks, Mr. Quigley and other white and African American parents gained information about the reputation of the school districts in their area through trusted members of their social networks or their own childhood experiences. Although they saw the choice of the school to be of the utmost importance, middle-class and upper-middle-class parents appeared to scrutinize information about other aspects of their children's daily lives more closely than information about the school.

Few parents used the Internet to focus their residential search. Even in the few instances when they did, the informal knowledge they learned from other parents in their network was crucial. For example, a quiet brunette in her late thirties, Tonia Cantor moved to Kingsley with her educator husband and three-year-old daughter and dog after she was transferred there for her job in managing real estate for Old Navy stores. She did not have any other family in the area. She was busy at work and wanted to be close to her workplace. To orient herself to the area, she did searches. She also drove around during a visit. But, after becoming oriented to Kingsley, a crucial factor was the opinion of a friend:

> And I have a really good friend that lives in [Farington, another region]. So I had also talked to him and he said, "You know, the one thing you don't want to do is move." He goes, "I know your daughter's young, she's not in school yet," but he's like "The one thing you don't want to do is move and then have to put her in private school and pay ten to twenty thousand for school." So when I told him I was looking at the Kingsley area he was like,

"That's a good, that's a good spot to be." He was like, "I think you'll be just fine with that." And I trust him, you know, 'cause he's lived here and raised his kids. . . . He's like, "It'll be, and you'll be fine." And so that really, it just solidified everything.

Not all parents, even parents who were married and planned to have a family, considered the issue of schools when selecting a residence (see Bader, Lareau, and Evans 2013). A number of families indicated that although they had children, or planned to have children, the question of schools simply did not come up. Some were, in retrospect, self-critical of their earlier decisions. For example, Nate Vilmer, a divorced father (with 50 percent custody) had grown up in Kingsley. He had a doctorate and worked in the health industry. Looking back, he was incredulous that he and his then-wife had not considered schools when they were house-hunting. In 2001, though it was five years before the birth of their daughter, they planned to have a family and ultimately bought a house near Gibbon:

I'm embarrassed to say it was like we didn't even think about schools. We just didn't in our, you know, our mindset at all. You know, had we taken into account schools, we would not have bought a house there. We would have bought somewhere in Kingsley, although the problem was, at the time, that's where that housing bubble was still a bubble, it was not burst, and the housing prices were crazy. . . . And, you know, when we looked around Kingsley we couldn't afford anything. [We thought,] "This is crazy." We did not take school into account at all. . . . When we found the, the house, I was just in love with it and I loved the area. But we did not take schools into account at all and that was just a bad move. Ignoring the fact that we ended up getting divorced. . . . I wish in retrospect . . . we [had] bought somewhere in Kingsley, taken into account schools. . . . I wish I had the thoughtfulness that I have now.

After the divorce, Mr. Vilmer moved to an apartment in Kingsley. He considered only Kingsley, and did so specifically for the schools. Yet, rather than systematically compare school districts, he drew on his own experiences as a student there: "I always knew my school district was a phenomenal school district."[22]

A number of the suburban parents had a bedrock assumption that they simply could not raise their children in the city. In these cases, the parent began the discussion by asserting, "I didn't want to live in the city." One white couple who lived in Gibbon School District passed up the opportunity to move into the husband's childhood home, as the wife, who is a school teacher, recounts:

My husband's dad passed away and, my mother-in-law, because we were, you know, looking for houses and we didn't really have that much money to go on, she was considering giving us her house in the south part of the city.

While the mother liked the idea of "a house for free," she rejected the idea of raising her son in the city, where she was also raised:

> But, then I thought too about would I want to live there, would I want my son in the city school district? No. Would I want him to play on the streets that maybe weren't as safe? No. Garbage and trash everywhere, disgusting, graffiti. I don't like that kind of stuff. I grew up with that. I wanted to get away from that.

Other people loved the city, but they felt that they had to move to the suburbs for their children. For example, Antonio Columbo was divorced and shared residential custody with his wife, had grown up in the Italian part of the city. He was the first in his family to go to college. After attending a local state college, he became a social worker who worked as a case manager for a suburban county. Although he would have preferred staying downtown, he moved to the suburbs for his four-year-old daughter:

> Previously I lived in downtown, which I, which I really do love, it's convenient. But I think if you're going to have a kid over, I think it's better to be in the suburbs. . . . I came here because everyone knows that the Kingsley area is renowned for the school district. I think it's possibly the top public school district in the state. If not, very close to it. And a friend of a friend of a friend, I was looking to rent an apartment and I, I got a good price, so here I am. It's two bedrooms. My daughter visits on the weekend, so why not, it was good for her. . . . It's such a beautiful safe area and people of even moderate intelligence know that it has a reputation for the best school district. It has always been, kind of like Beverly Hills, it also had that classic reputation as the top area.

In short, most of our respondents described the reputation of the districts as the crucial factor in shaping their decisions of how they settled on a neighborhood. Many of the parents appeared to see it as a "no-brainer." Furthermore, given how obvious the decision seemed in retrospect, they had trouble recalling the details of when they first learned about the neighborhood or made a decision to move there. As Mr. Columbo said, "Even people with moderate intelligence know it has a reputation for the best school district." As far as he and other parents were concerned, the case was settled. Parents talked to people they knew; these people lived in a relatively limited number of areas.

Working-Class Families

Virtually all of the working-class families in the study had grown up in the community in which they lived or in a nearby community. A few people had moved several hours away for a few years, but they had returned. Hence, the working-class parents tended to live close to their extended families. Because they had grown up in the area, parents drew on their knowledge of the community in making decisions about where they would live and send their children to school. As with the middle-class and upper-middle-class families, the process was seamless. The working-class parents, however, considered different geographical areas. For example, Mona Edgerton, an African American single mother who had worked as a medical assistant but was currently unemployed, was raised in the Warren area and was surrounded by her extended family. I interviewed her in her two-bedroom apartment, which is on the second floor of a brick building. The television was on in the background; her two and one-half year old niece toddled around the living room while we talked. Ms. Edgerton is a Muslim; she had a maroon head scarf tied back to cover her hair. She generally had a quiet, subdued manner, but she became excited and smiled broadly as she quickly named all of her relatives in the immediate vicinity:

> My uncle lives right over this bridge. He has a duplex. My cousin lives downstairs from him. And around here up on Presidio I have another cousin. That's a five people household, two children, an older cousin, and then a couple. On River Street, my aunt has a store right next to the Sunoco. My uncle owns that building right next door so I have cousin family in that complex. It is just literally every other block; we have family all around [laugh]. My uncle is actually the constable of the town. That's my uncle. So we're pretty much ground all around here. No choice. I actually had my daughter in Denver, but I still came back. I came back. We came back when she was six-month old. Went back to the area. Went to school in this area and everything. You could try to go away, but it's just so close in it. Literally everybody knows, from the crossing guards to the police officer. You know everyone. It's safe. It's a lot better. In a bigger town, you don't know who're around. It's always like someone watching. Definitely. I love it. I definitely do.

Ms. Edgerton's six-year-old daughter went to the same Warren elementary school that she had attended as a young girl:

> I like Warren. Like I said I went there. It's so funny. I have a child at one and I went there. And the teachers are still there that I had. Her gym teacher was my gym teacher. It was just crazy. But umm I like Warren. It's . . . small. You know, even with that, you get to know the teacher, you get to know the students. Like I knew all the students, almost every student's name. You know, it was around the corner. I loved that. I would be there. I'm always there. They are real nice. I like the staff.

Other working-class parents had similar reports. They sent their children to the schools that they had attended. In some instances, parents moved to the nearby community guided by reputations of the schools. Sara Kennedy, an older white mother, had grown up in Gibbon, but she was adamant about raising her son in Kingsley. Although she and her husband (who was African American) were two months behind in their mortgage as she struggled to find work as a caterer, she refused to consider the option of moving into her mother's large house in Gibbon, saying, "Mom, it's Gibbon." Based on the reputation of the districts, she had enrolled her son in Kingsley. She drew on her experience in the Gibbon school system (including a very negative experience at Gibbon High School) in determining that she wanted her son to attend Kingsley schools.

In rare instances, we found families who did not rely on networks in the selection of a home. Ray and Lorna Lodoiska and their seven-year-old daughter, for example, moved to an expensive area a few miles from Kingsley High School because Ray took a job as an apartment manager (for 240 units). The job paid $16 per hour (the same as his previous position) but, unlike his prior job, the position included a free apartment (worth around $1,500 per month in rent). The young couple had their apartment in an expansive grassy apartment complex. Before the move, they had grown up in a city neighborhood that had shootings and frequent robberies. Although it was only a twenty-five-minute drive from their childhood homes, the Lodoiskas had not heard of the area before Ray interviewed for the job. Mr. Lodoiska immediately fell for it:

> It's a lot nicer neighborhood. I mean, it's really nicely landscaped, you know. It's, neighbors are pretty quiet, keep to themselves, there's no gunshots or nothing like that.

His wife did some confirmatory research when her husband moved up to the area ahead of her:

A: But I basically went online, did my research, found out, you know, about the schools and how many children are in each class. . . .
Q: So tell me the research you did.
A: I went on a couple Web sites regarding the schools, and then I went and found out where the police district was . . . and basically where the parks were. And when he brought up, because I, I didn't come up here right away. He moved up here before I did. And basically he knew where the parks were and stuff like that but I went online, found out where the parks were.

In this instance, all of the Lodoiskas' relatives and friends were in the city; none of them were familiar with the area. Ms. Lodoiska, however, was collecting information only after they had decided to move there; she was not looking at the information to make a decision.

The lack of focus by working-class parents on test scores or other Internet resources could not be attributed to lack of Internet access. Virtually all of the parents in the study had some Internet access. Ms. Elyse Harrington was an African American single mother, worked as a home health aide. A tall, friendly, and talkative woman, she was casually dressed in sweats as she relaxed on the loveseat in the living room. Ms. Harrington had excellent things to say about her five-year-old daughter's school in Warren. Although Ms. Harrington did not have a computer at home, her parents had a working computer she regularly used when she visited them two to three times per week; she had never, however, looked at the website for the school district. Thus, there were parallels in how the working-class, middle-class, and upper-middle-class parents in the study gather information before deciding to send their children to the local public school. They usually relied on the knowledge they gained from networks or from their personal experience, rather than on information gleaned from research.

The working-class families also seemed to be embedded in micro-climates, but the type of micro-climates were different. The working-class parents tended to live only a few miles from where they had grown up and typically had many relatives nearby. Most of the mothers spoke to their mothers on the telephone on a daily basis. Unlike the middle-class and upper-middle respondents, the working-class parents were likely to report that they had relatives or neighbors in other parts of the city, including parts of the city with very high poverty rates. Still, these suburban parents did not consider the city or areas other than their current neighborhood to be viable options. For example, Mona Edgerton, the unemployed African American single parent described earlier, firmly rejected it:

> It is too fast. Period. It's the city. . . . I would never put my child to city school district. . . . They are raising themselves in the city. I mean, they are just so fast. Fast, fresh fast, grown fast. . . . I don't like this city at all. Nope. Not at all. No, thank you. That would probably destroy my baby. . . . They are supposed to wear uniforms every day. They wear what they want because half the teachers are scared of the kids. Kids are big, you know. I mean if the parents aren't dealing with it. I wouldn't want to deal with it either. It's probably safer to say nothing than to say something. So it was like . . . what was it like last year that teacher got beat up? That's craziness. I'm sorry. You go to school to learn. You know, it should be simple like that. It's just so wild today. It's so wild. The city? Never.

A number of working-class parents in Warren expressed contentment that they were not raising their children in the city. Because their families and friends lived in the city or in the Warren school district, the adults considered those areas when they were moving.

Drawn to Where They Felt Comfortable: Status Cultures

In previous studies of residential segregation, researchers have pointed to the importance of preferences in guiding residential decisions. In this study, however, not only did we find respondents heavily guided by people in their networks in terms of framing a choice set of options for housing, but there were also signs that members of their network were not far-flung across a wide array of neighborhoods. Instead, it appeared that interviewees had family and friends in a concentrated area. This finding is consistent with other research (chapter 5, this volume) that movers of low-income families considered only a few neighborhoods, usually where they had friends or family, as well as research suggesting that most residential moves are short distance (chapter 2, this volume).

Thus, there were signs that families were embedded in relatively constricted social worlds. Working-class parents considered different neighborhoods more than middle-class and upper-middle-class families did. Many had heard of Kingsley in only a vague way; they also did not know people who lived there. Kingsley parents lived only a few miles from Gibbon, but many of the Kingsley parents did not know the name of district that bordered Kingsley. This lack of information is all the more striking given that the test scores for Gibbon at the elementary school level were very similar to those for Kingsley. The high school test scores for Gibbon, however, were lower than those for Kingsley. Gibbon simply did not have the same reputation that Kingsley held. Parents seemed to be embedded in different social worlds in terms of the information they had learned. Rather than considering a wide swath of space, parents considered homes only in small areas I have termed micro-climates.

We drew blank stares from the respondents when we asked parents in Kingsley about Warren (and vice versa). Although Kingsley was geographically contiguous to Gibbon, a number of Kingsley parents had never heard of Gibbon. Few Kingsley or Gibbon parents recognized the name of the Warren school district though it was only twenty minutes away by car. By contrast, all of the parents in Gibbon knew of the higher-status Kingsley school district.[23] As noted earlier, the region had dozens of school districts; it would have been difficult for parents to be informed about most of them.

As we showed parents maps of the region, their knowledge was not uniform, nor was their knowledge tied to the distance from home. As Kingsley parents narrowed their pool of choices, however, they tended to have information about a socially homogeneous set of school districts that were similar in profile to Kingsley (for a lucid review of the literature in behavioral economics, see Lehrer 2010).[24] As a result, more privileged parents did not even consider school districts that overwhelmingly enrolled children below the poverty line. Nor did these parents tend to know the names and location of districts that enrolled children of different social positions. Put differently, parents tended to function within micro-climates where they were informed about a narrow range of school districts similar to the one in which they were living. The interviews with parents revealed that many parents had looked for a home only in the area in which they bought. Although the geographical region was much more compact than many other urban centers, parents' knowledge of other geographical areas tended to be limited to school districts that were very similar in terms of the class and race composition of the students.

None of the schools in our study were very far from each other; they all could be reached from city hall in the central city (as well as traveling back and forth to one another) within a twenty-five to thirty-minute drive. In addition, the city paper annually published a "state of the schools" issue where the reporters provided extremely detailed information on all of the districts in the region. The local magazine did something similar. Despite these factors, however, we found that parents generally had very detailed knowledge of schools only in their *immediate* neighborhood. Parents appeared to be in different "micro-climates" for schools.[25] Indeed, few parents seriously considered a school more than a fifteen-minute drive from home.

Furthermore, in many interviews, parents alluded to a feeling of comfort they had about the area in which they live. They were often vague in their descriptions. Many said simply, "We liked the area." Normally articulate highly educated parents seemed stumped as they sought to explain why they liked the area in which they lived. Some described the closeness to work; others mentioned the convenience to their children's child care. Many enjoyed the closeness of the city and the availability of the train. But beyond these concrete amenities, there was also a feeling of a comfort with the area that surfaced in the interviews. Although often difficult for the respondents to put into words, the feeling was palpable. Parents seemed to suggest that they belonged in the area; it was comfortable for them.

In some cases, parents simply could not afford to be where they wanted to live. These parents saw a direct trade-off in the size and quality of the house and the quality of the school district. For middle-class parents who moved down the status hierarchy (such as from Kingsley to Gibbon), the change could be agonizing. For example, Noelle Conrad, a thin, poised, and quiet young mother of a five-year-old boy, and her husband live in Gibbon in a rental house with pink petunias and other annuals flourishing next to the small, immaculately kept lawn in the front yard. They moved to Kingsley from a city three hours away for a variety of reasons: Mr. Conrad wanted to start a new business, housing prices were lower in Kingsley than where they were living, her parents and his parents were in the region, and they had other relatives farther north. They selected Kingsley on the basis of her extensive time on blogs and listservs (which frequently mentioned Kingsley) and her husband's knowledge of the area when he lived there as a child. Although as a firm "city person" (with a degree in urban planning), Ms. Conrad very much wanted to live downtown, she felt that Kingsley was a good compromise for a one-car family; it was "close to the train" and "walking distance" to stores. Because they could not afford to buy, they rented a house in Kingsley. A researcher by training, Ms. Conrad did extensive research. Even eighteen months later she could rattle off the per-pupil expenditure, class size, test scores, and other features of Kingsley and Gibbon. They selected Kingsley. Their world was rocked, however, when the owner unexpectedly sold the house and gave them one month to move. Although apartments were plentiful, homes for rent were not. Ms. Conrad was preoccupied by the decision, tearful about it, and in agony. She worried:

> [Should we have] just decided to suck it up and just get a rental that was kind of stinky and crummy, um, based on the price range that we wanted, uh, just suck it up for the kids' sake and so that they could go to school there. Should we have done that instead of, you know, settling on what we felt was a nicer place but in a lesser district? . . . If you had the opportunity to give your kid the best, why wouldn't you take that opportunity, you know, why would you choose second best. It was on my mind. It was on my mind a lot. I mean, I was thinking about it a lot.

In the end, thinking of her own less-than-ideal education (as well as her husband's schooling), they moved to neighboring Gibbon for the bigger house and lovely street:

> I went to what would of, can be considered a completely failing, school growing up and I knew I had some catching up to do when I got to college. [At the time] I just was like [thinking to myself], "Hm, people know that? I should know that?" But you just kind of figure it out. And my husband too, you know, he didn't go to a, you know, a great school.

Thus, this mother downplayed the significance of the school choice in a life trajectory.

In addition to Ms. Conrad, I encountered a few families who systematically collected extensive and independent school information by touring schools, interviewing the principal, visiting websites to gather systematic information, and otherwise engaging in a sustained, systematic, and direct effort to create an independent assessment of the character of the school options. For example, Gayle Bailey is a slender, elegantly dressed African American upper-middle-class mother with a doctorate who works in the health field. She and her husband (a college graduate who works in transportation) live in Kingsley with their two children. She reported that she did not think about schools when they bought the house, but when her son was getting ready to attend kindergarten, she was deeply concerned about the options. She began to do research; she had a list that guided her conversation with the principal:

> I wanted to know how large the class size was. I wanted to know the demographics of the faculty as well as the student body. And I wanted to know

the level of training of the teachers . . . I wanted to know . . . what approach they took to teaching children with different level of capability because I knew that my children had been exposed to a lot at the Montessori School and . . . I expected the class to be full of children along a spectrum. And I wanted to make sure that they were able to attend to the needs of every child. . . . And then also how welcoming they were of parental involvement, not that I had a lot of time to be there, and then what else, I was looking at, uh, the facility overall. . . . And so I was pleased.

Ms. Bailey thus carefully scrutinized her children's school options in the same ways that she had monitored her son's child-care setting and his organized activities. Put differently, Ms. Bailey engaged in concerted cultivation in the process of selecting a public school (although not at the time of the home purchase). In this sample, however, Ms. Bailey was rare. The few parents who adopted this approach were middle class or upper middle class.[26]

Much more common was for parents to use the word *research* in their discussion of the search for the home. Yet, though mothers could rapidly recall numbers in other areas of their lives (such as interest rate on the mortgage, price of the house, and even their own SAT scores), they could not report the test scores of the schools, per-pupil expenditure, class size, or other details of the schools they had chosen for their children. Instead, their knowledge was vague. In other words, parents' assessment of websites was cursory; it appeared to be largely confirmatory and took place after parents had settled on this neighborhood.

Some people reported that they had done research but were surprised to learn that their children would attend a different elementary school than the one they had expected. For example, the Hart parents are an architect and a graphic artist. When they moved to Kingsley, they described themselves as being very attuned to research, as Ms. Hart stated:

> Well [city newspaper] does a school report every year. And *City Magazine* does a report card every year. Not a report card, they do more of a general survey of who are the best public schools and private schools in the area, and Kingsley [is] always there, you know. Because we're in the Garden Area . . . this is what we are.

The Harts were particularly concerned about the price of the home. The median home price differed substantially across the districts; as in other districts, the homes across the line from Gibbon and Kingsley jumped in value over $50,000 for the same type of home (see Dougherty et al. 2009). Some families saw themselves as making a direct trade-off in the size of their home and the character of the school district. Mr. Hart noted that the feel of the communities differed: "Kingsley is very white collar. Gibbons, Dewitt County is very blue collar." He and his wife reported that they made a direct trade-off between the size of the house and the school district as they chose Kingsley:

> [What] it came down for us is, "Okay, you haven't got a bigger house but we want our kids to have a good school district, so we will sacrifice having a smaller house so our kids can have a better school district." And again, just like [my mother-in-law] will tell you all the time, the parents have got to be involved with your students at school in order to benefit from the school. So you can have the best school in the world, but if you don't do anything and the kids just coast along, it doesn't mean anything. And that's why we, that's why we're involved.

Although the Harts insisted that they had done extensive research, read magazines, looked at houses in two districts, and chose their house because of the school district, clear limits to their knowledge were evident. For example, they had an incorrect understanding of the elementary school their child would attend:

> Ms. Hart: And when we thought, we moved here, we were going to Rochester, the school over there.
> Mr. Hart: We're actually closer to Rochester than we are to Oak Park . . . [demonstrating on a map] Rochester's here and Oak Park's all the way over here. And we are—I think we're here. So this is really closer. The roads are all crazy around here. But we could be to Rochester in probably five minutes and Oak Park, it's more like ten, fifteen. . . . I think we found out right about the time we moved in, because like I said, we started to know the neighbors. And there's a lot of, and there's a lot of kids on this street, so as soon as we started to meet people and kids started to play, you start to get to know them, you find, you know, we're like, "Oh, your kids go to Rochester?" And they're like, "No, we go to Oak Park."

The parents reported that their key concern was the district, not the elementary school:

> Ms. Hart: We really didn't care. Because again, we're in, Kingsley. It's still in the Kingsley School District. I mean, you most . . . You really didn't hear much about one elementary school versus another. Out here it was more the Kingsley High School versus the Gibbon High School.

Even parents who did extensive research had scant information on crucial issues.[27] Overall, parents were quite pleased with the quality of the schools their children attended. There did, however, appear to be a pattern in which parents ranked their children's schools favorably. Indeed, every year, the *Phi Delta Kappan* magazine does an annual survey of the schools.

They repeatedly find that parents rank their children's school more highly than they rate schools in other regions. For example, only 19 percent of parents give schools nationwide in general a grade of A or B, but 77 percent give these grades to the school their eldest child attends (Phi Delta Kappan/Gallup 2012). Thus it was not surprising that we found parents to be overwhelmingly positive about the quality of their children's school.

Ending Up in Different Spaces

Finally, although the steps parents took were similar, their children ended up in different kinds of schools. The schools had strikingly different funding levels; Kingsley paid over $26,000 per pupil, Gibbon slightly over $16,000; Warren's funding of $14,000 was almost $1,000 more per year than the funding in the city school district. Kingsley also offered foreign language, artist-in-residence, music, and other special classes not provided in Gibbon or Warren. The number of students proficient in math and reading differed strikingly across the districts; just under one-half of the Warren students were proficient in reading in third grade while the comparable figures in Gibbon was 95 percent and Kingsley was 90 percent. SAT scores were much higher in Kingsley (1754) than Gibbon (1577), Warren (1196), or the city (1156). The Greatschools.org rankings and other systems place Kingsley among the best schools in the nation; Warren was widely seen as having failing schools. The buildings and grounds also differed. Kingsley was a glistening one-story building with an elaborate mural done by the students as part of the artist-in-residence program; the grassy fields were expansive. They were also lush. Gibbon's one-story red brick building also had an artist-in-residence mural, but it was much smaller and less elaborate. The grounds were large, but the fields not as well maintained. The school had a mid-century feel to it; the ceilings were low; some rooms needed fresh paint. Warren school was brightly painted; the large hallways were also immaculate. The two-story cement building seemed plain, although efforts had been made to decorate it with cheerful posters or students' artwork. The asphalt playground was surrounded by a chain-link fence; there was no grass.

The websites for the districts also varied. Kingsley's district boasted the national merit scholars, large numbers of students graduating from the international baccalaureate program, and almost all of the students going to college. The word *excellence* is prominently featured across the website. The Gibbon site is far less developed, but boasts of high levels of school performance. By contrast, the Warren site discusses the importance of offering students a safe and nurturing context and of students making positive choices. The choices students make after high school are emphasized, but college-going rates are not mentioned. The word *excellence* never appears.

Discussion

In his book *The Big Sort: Why the Clustering of Like-Minded America Is Tearing Us Apart,* Bishop (2008) describes how he and his wife chose a neighborhood when they were moving to Austin, Texas:

> We didn't have a list of necessities—granite countertops or schools with killer SATs—as much as we had a mental image of the place we belonged. . . . When a place felt comfortable, seemed right, my wife . . . drew a smiley face on the map. We didn't intend to move into a community filled with Democrats, but that's what we did—effortlessly and without a trace of understanding of what we were doing.[28]

The families in the study also described an effortless process through which they ended up in places where, as Bishop put it, they felt that they *belonged.* Because families cared so much about the quality of the schools that their children attended, and because middle-class parents with young children were going through a very different process in the city (chapter 9, this volume), the "effortlessness" of the process for suburban parents is striking. In this chapter, I have sought to show that parents gathered informal information from the social networks in which they were embedded; this information guided them, relatively seamlessly, to different areas. To be sure, parents had different economic resources. These economic resources set limits on options. Yet the school districts had more economic heterogeneity than the parents' actions suggested. More to the point, almost no parents in our open-ended interviews discussed comparing houses of different values across school districts. Most parents didn't compare at all. Instead, they relied on trusted networks and their own knowledge to zero in on a neighborhood.

In addition, the middle-class parents appeared to be micro-managing most aspects of their children's lives. They fretted if their children were not in the most challenging group in day care. They volunteered in the library at school. They enrolled their children in organized activities. They sought to develop their children's talents and skills. In short, they engaged in what I have termed concerted cultivation (Lareau 2011). Yet, on one of the most economically and socially consequential decisions of their lives, they did not engage in similar behaviors. For example, middle-class parents did not follow the patterns in other aspects of their parenting by visiting every kindergarten classroom in the district or area they were considering, reading extensively on the elements of a good school, creating spreadsheets with test scores, comparing different options, or otherwise engaging in the kinds of activities middle-class parents take on in a college search for their adolescents. Rather, they felt comfortable with the knowledge presented to them through their routines of social life.

It is not completely clear why middle-class parents' patterns of parenting (that is, concerted cultivation) did not spill over into the selection of the school district. In in-depth interviews, it is difficult to ask people why they did not do something. Signs are ample, though, that the suburban landscape is highly stratified. Unlike in the city, middle-class parents moving into an elite school district can be confident that their children's peers will be restricted to a relatively narrow bandwidth of the social stratification system. Residential areas are often economically segregated, and these patterns are only increasing over time (Fry and Taylor 2012; Reardon and Bischoff 2011). In this way, parents depend on the economic residential segregation patterns to do the sorting process. Middle-class parents can afford to be nonchalant.

Hence, parents' efforts had only a limited role in choosing the school their children ultimately attended. Instead, as "Birds of a Feather" (McPherson, Smith-Lovin, and Cook 2001), networks consist of people of similar characteristics rather than of highly variable social characteristics (such as social class, race, occupation, religion, and so forth; see also DiPrete, Gelman, McCormick, Teitler, and Zheng 2011). These networks matter in that they are a conduit for valuable information. In this study, I found these networks shaped the creation of choice sets (Bell 2006), which in turn shape the kinds of schools that families and youth consider. Moreover, above and beyond the people that the parents in the study trusted to guide them were signs that these family and friends were embedded in a particular geographical area. These geographical areas had a different feel to them and parents reported that they felt comfortable. I have termed these micro-climates. Of course, the three suburban districts in this study may be unusually stratified and distinctive, but signs indicate that other areas around the country, such as what the Bishops found in Texas, have a different feel. Although the role of cultural amenities has been extensively discussed in the gentrification literature, few attempts have been made to integrate the cultural sensibility of neighborhoods with parents' school choices (Zukin 1987). Future research might fruitfully focus more directly on how different communities draw parents toward them and make families feel comfortable in particular geographic spaces. Because these cultural sensibilities in the micro-climates often are linked to schools with different levels of funding and performance, these decisions can be significant for children's educational futures. As I have noted, despite the lack of evidence that middle-class parents worked any harder than working-class parents, the middle-class parents ended up in schools that were seen as better. Their social worlds helped to pave the way, so that the choices seemed obvious.

Social policies and social institutions played a crucial role in setting up the conditions for these effortless decisions. Through multiple policies, federal, state, and local governments have supported the development of residential areas that are socially stratified by economic position and race rather than economically and racially integrated. Taxation policies facilitate highly unequal school districts with varying per-pupil expenditures. Highways are often routed through neighborhoods of low-income residents. Placement of grocery stores and shopping malls are also socially stratified (Deener 2013). Although the degree to which we have a strong state or weak state is subject to debate (see Prasad 2013), the lack of governmental policies to facilitate economic integration in suburban areas is undeniable.

Numerous policymakers and social scientists decry economic segregation in housing neighborhoods and schools. They argue that economic integration offers important benefits. For example, educational studies have suggested that low-income children traditionally are lower achievers than middle-class children; moreover, studies have also documented that low achievers often increase their levels of performance when they are placed in classrooms with high-achieving students. Political scientists also assert benefits to having diverse rather than segregated communities (Hall and Lindholm 1999; Bishop 2008). Despite these benefits, economic segregation in American society is growing (Reardon and Bischoff 2011). The results of this study are disquieting because the mechanisms of reproduction are social networks and micro-climates, mechanisms that do not provide clear policy interventions. But as chapter 10 in this volume shows, certain policy steps could readily strengthen the connection between housing policy and education. Only by problematizing the search for the school, and highlighting the ways in which class networks help parents settle on a desirable area, can we further unpack the mechanisms in the reproduction of inequality. This chapter is one small step in that process.

The author gratefully acknowledges the support of the Russell Sage Foundation for a writing fellowship (2012–2013) as well as for support for the conference. She is also grateful to the Spencer Foundation as well as the College of Arts and Sciences of the University of Pennsylvania for support of data collection. Michael Bader, Shani Evans, Rita Harvey, Leigh McCormack, and April Yee provided valuable assistance with interviewing; Mary Herring, Heather Curl, and Shani Evans carefully carried out the data analysis. Alejandro Falchattore and Claire Gabriel provided important research help. Elliot Weininger, Maia Cucchiara, Judith Levine, Vanessa Munoz, Jessica Calarco, Michael Bader, Amy Steinbugler, and Kimberly Goyette provided valuable comments on this project at numerous points. In addition, audiences at Columbia University, McMaster, New York University, the Southern Sociological Society, and the Eastern Sociological Society gave critical helpful feedback on an earlier version of this work. All errors, of course, are the responsibility of the author.

Notes

1. Paul Jargowsky (chapter 4, this volume) and Kimberly Goyette (chapter 1) show a growth in economic segregation across neighborhoods. Sean Reardon (2011) and Reardon and Bischoff (2011) show that the economic gap is highly consequential in influencing test scores; the class gap now outstrips the black-white test score gap.

2. Of course, as countless studies have shown, family background also influences children's life chances.

3. Much of the research on how people select homes has been conceptualized as part of the work on residential segregation (for a lucid review of this field, see chapter 2, this volume). With the notable exception of Jennifer Holmes's classic piece, the choice of school has generally been focused within urban districts (for an overview of school selection, see chapter 1, this volume). Given the presence of these two thoughtful pieces in the volume, and due to a desire not to repeat this information, the literature review here is scant.

4. The Digest of Educational Statistics 2011 reveals that 70.6 percent of children age five through seventeen are in assigned public schools, 15 percent are in a magnet, charter, or "chosen" public schools, 11.4 percent are in private schools, and 2.9 percent are in home-schooling. Whites are twice as likely as blacks to be in private school; blacks are twice as likely as whites to be in chosen public schools. See *Digest of Educational Statistics 2011,* available at: http://nces.ed.gov/programs/digest/d11/tables/dt11_041.asp (accessed November 9, 2013).

5. Patrick Sharkey (2013) uses the term *cognitive constraints* to characterize this process where families are constrained to consider options only in their current social worlds.

6. As chapters 1 and 2 in this volume show, residential segregation by race is attenuating over time, but it remains moderately high. In addition, a number of studies have shown that social class segregation is an important factor in creating racial segregation (on this point, see chapters 1, 2, and 4 of this volume). Yet, questions remain about the mechanisms through which this inequality is sustained. See also Sampson (2012).

7. Although an older literature, much of the literature on why people move has focused on the importance of key life events such as marriage, birth of a child, job change, or retirement. Yet, some signs indicate that neighborhood conditions may shape the formation of preferences (see Bader, Lareau, and Evans 2013; Rossi 1955; and Sampson 2012).

8. Studies of gentrification have focused on the role of cultural amenities, or lack thereof, as well as neighborhood transformation brought on by gentrification (for a review, see Zukin 1987; see also chapter 7, this volume).

9. Other work has highlighted the anxiety parents express in key aspects of parenting (Nelson 2010); in this context, the lack of anxiety parents displayed in these interviews was striking. Parents were confident they had ended up in a good area.

10. Three of the families are interracial; all are white women and African American men. Most of the interviews are with mothers, but four of the interviews are with fathers and in an additional four families the mother and the father were interviewed together. Three fathers are divorced; two of the fathers share residential custody; the third father is a single parent.

11. We also told parents we were interested in how they ended up sending their children to this school. As working parents with small children, many parents had trouble finding ninety minutes to two hours for an interview. They were simply too busy. We found that many parents suggested that we email them; they did not respond, however, to the email. As a result, we found that the best way to recruit was face-to-face or by having someone ask another parent if they were willing to be contacted by us; if the parents agreed to consider the request, we asked for their email and telephone number. Because many parents were suggested to us that we did not interview, it is difficult to calculate a response rate. Almost all of the interviews took place in the home of the parent. We found that parents frequently suggested meeting in a coffee shop. Because of the need to protect the sound quality in the tape recording, however, we sought to have the interviews be in the home or, rarely, in an office or other private setting.

12. We recruited parents who were acquaintances of our acquaintances so that we did not interview anyone we knew or would cross paths with in our work, church, or social life. In one case, a prospective graduate student came to meet me who taught in the city schools; I asked her if she knew anyone. She sent out an email to her colleagues, which yielded one interview. In the other case, an acquaintance in another department introduced me to a college friend.

13. At this point, we drew the conclusion that the age of the child was not influencing the vividness of the interviews.

14. In the quotations, to improve clarity, I have eliminated stutters, false starts, repetitions of words, "like," "you know," "um" and other utterances when they do not shift the meaning. In a few instances, I have altered the order of sentences to improve readability.

15. For historical variation in interest rates, see Mortgage News Daily, available at: http://www.mortgagenewsdaily.com/mortgage_rates/charts.asp (accessed November 9, 2013).

16. Citation withheld to protect confidentiality.

17. The figure is from census data, but the exact citation is suppressed to protect confidentiality. The median home price for Gibbon School District is around $315,000, Warren is around $145,000, and the city is $125,000.

18. See PL 107-100 No Child Left Behind Act of 2001 http://www2.ed.gov/policy/elsec/leg/esea02/index.html.

19. By contrast, the urban parents in this data set did engage in many of these activities (see chapter 9 this volume; Lareau, Evans, and Yee 2013).

20. Recruiting only elementary and preschool parents who had recently bought houses would have forced us to include more neighborhoods in our sample. Doing so would have made it difficult to understand how specific school and

neighborhood characteristics influence the choice process. Thus, we asked parents to provide retrospective accounts of the process of choosing a neighborhood. Because home-buying is a major life event, parents were able to recall key aspects of the decision process, including which houses they visited, home prices, and interest rates. Although the more fundamental decision of why they settled on a particular neighborhood was harder for parents to articulate, we concluded that this problem was not due to an issue with parents' memory, but rather the taken-for-granted nature of this aspect of the decision process.

21. This request did not immediately yield a move. "They group the kids in six-month periods, so . . . it's kind of subtle. It's not like, you know, he's with four-year-olds instead of three-year-olds, it was that he had a January birthday and so we were just hoping—and this year they did move him into a slightly more advanced group but last year they didn't."

22. He was, however, one of the few parents to look at the curriculum on the district website, compare elementary schools, and meet teachers before he decided where to live. I discuss parents who engaged in this kind of research later in the chapter.

23. Michael Sauder (2006) shows that in law school rankings, people had more knowledge about the most highly ranked law schools rather than law schools with lower standing (for a discussion of social-psychological literature on social class, see Fiske and Markus 2012). Experimental research, for example, shows that lower-status people are more attentive to the behavior of higher-status people than vice versa. Hence, it is consistent with this literature that Gibbon parents knew about Kingsley, but Kingsley parents were relatively unaware of Gibbon. Still, interviews in this study show that Warren parents were deeply aware of the problems of city neighborhoods; they were proud and pleased to be in the suburbs.

24. Lehrer also discusses home buying decisions which he sees as problematic where buyers choose a larger house rather than a smaller house with a shorter commute; since the buyers spend so much more time commuting, they don't have time to enjoy the additional room in the house.

25. This pattern hampered interviewing; we were unable to collect parents' assessment of other districts.

26. As other research has found, the African American parents in this study had friends and relatives living in all-black areas of the region (Krysan and Bader 2009). It was not surprising that white families did not have friends or relatives living in these areas. Thus, African American parents appeared to have a wider range of neighborhoods to consider than did white families. In particular, if African American families could not afford a house in Kingsley, they considered all-black economic heterogeneous neighborhoods in the city or inner-ring suburbs. These neighborhoods were never considered by white families (for a discussion of "blind spots" and parents' knowledge, see Krysan and Bader 2009; chapter 2 this volume; for a discussion of the black middle-class, and the ways in which black middle-class families face more challenges than white middle-class families, see Pattillo 2013; for the influence of race on housing decisions see, among others, Farley 1996; Clark 1992; and Sharkey 2013). For

a discussion of race and school choice see Goyette, Farrie, and Freely 2012; Orfield, Bachmeier, James, and Eitle 2006, and Saporito and Lareau 1999.

27. The study also asked parents about their conception of a good school. There were not striking class differences on this front. To be sure, middle-class and upper-middle-class parents offered more details in their portrait of what they meant by a good school. They tended to use professional jargon. They also clearly conceived of themselves as partners or evaluators of teachers, and working-class parents were far more respectful of the professional expertise of educators (Lareau 2000). Yet, in terms of what they wanted for their children, working-class parents tended to focus on the same general topics raised by more affluent parents. They focused particularly on teachers' knowledge of their children, teachers' willingness to communicate any concerns with parents, and their children's comfort and ease in the school setting. Many discussed the physical plant of the school. Working-class parents were more likely to raise the issue of safety, but a number of middle-class parents raised this issue as well. Strikingly, few parents, including middle-class and upper-middle-class parents, raised the issue of school leadership. Nor did they focus on collegial relations among teachers. Yet, some studies of effective schools have pointed to the critical role of school leadership and teacher collegiality in fostering school success (see Bryk et al. 2010). See also Goldring and Hausman 1999, Hamilton and Guin 2005; Henig 1990; Johnson and Shapiro 2003, Johnson 2006; Johnsson and Lindgren 2010; Schneider, Marschall, Teske, and Roch 1998 and Theobald 2005.

28. Bishop does not discuss the role of social networks in his decision. Instead, he reports that he and his wife got a map of the area and drove around. Hence, his experience suggests he was able to identity a micro-climate where he expected to feel comfortable. He is particularly concerned about the negative political implications from the "balkanization" of residences where Americans are less and less likely to encounter others with whom they disagree politically (Bishop 2008).

References

Bader, Michael, Annette Lareau, and Shani Evans. 2013. "The Social and Geographic Context of Residential Moves." Unpublished manuscript, American University.

Bayer, Patrick, and Robert McMillan 2011. "Tieabout Sorting and Neighborhood Stratification." *NBER* working paper no. 17364. Cambridge, Mass.: National Bureau of Economic Research.

Bishop, Bill. 2008. *The Big Sort: Why the Clustering of Like-Minded America Is Tearing Us Apart*. New York: Mariner.

Bryk, Anthony S., Penny Bender Sebring, Elaine Allensworth, Stuart Luppescu, and John Q. Easton 2010. *Organizing Schools for Improvement: Lessons from Chicago*. Chicago: University of Chicago Press.

Calarco, Jessica. 2011. "I Need Help! Social Class and Children's Help-Seeking in Elementary School." *American Sociological Review* 76(6): 862–82.

Clark, William A. V. 1992. "Residential Preferences and Residential Choices in a Multiethnic Context." *Demography* 29(3): 451–66.

Deener, Andrew. 2013. "Feeding Philadelphia". Draft manuscript under review.

DiPrete, Thomas A., Andrew Gelman, Tyler McCormick, Julien Teitler, and Tian Zheng. 2011. "Segregation in Social Networks Based on Acquaintanceship and Trust." *American Journal of Sociology* 116(4): 1234–283.

Dougherty, Jack, Jeffrey Harrelson, Laura Maloney, Drew Murphy, Russell Smith, Michael Snow, and Diane Zannoni. 2009. "School Choice in Suburbia: Test Scores, Race, and Housing Markets." *American Journal of Education* 115(4): 523–48.

Duncan, Greg J., and Richard J. Murnane, eds. 2011. *Whither Opportunity? Rising Inequality, Schools, and Children's Life Chances.* New York: Russell Sage Foundation.

Farley, Reynolds 1996. "Racial Differences in the Search For Housing: Do Whites and Blacks Use the Same Techniques to Find Housing?" *Housing Policy Debate* 7(2): 367–85.

Fiske, Susan T., and Hazel Rose Markus, eds. 2012. *Facing Social Class: How Societal Rank Influences Interaction.* New York: Russell Sage Foundation.

Fry, Richard, and Paul Taylor. 2012. "The Rise of Residential Segregation by Income." *Social & Demographic Trends* report. Washington, D.C.: Pew Research Center. Available at: http://www.pewsocialtrends.org/2012/08/01/the-rise-of-residential-segregation-by-income/1/ (accessed August 7, 2013).

Goldring, Ellen B., and Charles S. Hausman. 1999. "Reasons for Parental Choice of Urban Schools." *Journal of Education Policy* 14(5): 469–90.

Goyette, Kimberly A., Danielle Farrie, and Joshua Freely. 2012. "This School's Gone Downhill: Racial Change and Perceived School Quality Among Whites." *Social Problems* 59(2): 155–76.

Hall, John A., and Charles Lindholm. 1999. *Is America Breaking Apart?* Princeton, N.J.: Princeton University Press.

Hamilton, Laura, and Kacey Guin. 2005. "Understanding How Families Choose Schools." In *Getting Choice Right: Ensuring Equity and Efficiency in Education Policy,* edited by Julian R. Betts and Tom Loveless. Washington, D.C.: Brookings Institution Press.

Henig, Jeffrey R. 1990. "Choice in Public Schools: An Analysis of Transfer Requests Among Magnet Schools." *Social Science Quarterly* 71(1): 69–82.

Holmes, Jennifer Jellison. 2002. "Buying Homes, Buying Schools: School Choice and the Social Construction of School Quality." *Harvard Educational Review* 72 (2): 177–206.

Johnson, Heather Beth. 2006. *The American Dream and the Power of Wealth: Choosing Schools and Inheriting Inequality in the Land of Opportunity.* New York: Routledge.

Johnsson, Mattias, and Joakim Lindgren. 2010. "'Great Location, Beautiful Surroundings!' Making Sense of Information Materials Intended as Guidance for School Choice." *Scandinavian Journal of Educational Research* 54(2): 173–87.

Krysan, Maria, and Michael Bader. 2009. "Racial Blind Spots: Black-White-Latino Differences in Community Knowledge." *Social Problems* 56(4): 677–701.

Lareau, Annette. 2000. *Home Advantage: Social Class and Parental Intervention in Elementary Education.* Lanham, Md.: Rowman and Littlefield.

———. 2011. *Unequal Childhoods: Class, Race, and Family Life,* 2nd ed. Berkeley: University of California Press.

Lareau, Annette, Shani Evans, and April Yee. 2013. "The Importance of Field in Creating Capital: White Middle-Class Parents' School Choice in an Urban

Setting." Paper presented at the American Sociological Society. Washington, D.C. (January 24, 2013).

McPherson, Miller, Lynn Smith-Lovin, and James M. Cook. 2001. "Birds of a Feather: Homophily in Social Networks." *Annual Review of Sociology* 27: 415–44

Neild, Ruth C. 2005. "Parent Management of School Choice in a Large Urban District." *Urban Education* 40(3): 270–97.

Nelson, Margaret. 2010. *Parenting Out of Control: Anxious Parents in Uncertain Times.* New York: New York University Press.

Orfield, G., Mark D. Bachmeier, David R. James, and Tamela Eitle. 2006. "Deepening Segregation in American Public Schools: A Special Report from the Harvard Project on School Desegregation." *Equity and Excellence in Education* 30(2): 5–24.

Phi Delta Kappan/Gallup. 2012. "What Americans Said About the Public Schools." *Phi Delta Kappan* 94(1): 8–25. Available at: http://pdkintl.org/wp-content/blogs.dir/5/files/2012-Gallup-poll-full-report.pdf (accessed November 7, 2013).

Reardon, Sean. 2011. "The Widening Academic Achievement Gap Between the Rich and the Poor: New Evidence and Possible Explanations." In *Whither Opportunity? Rising Inequality, Schools, and Children's Life Chances,* edited by Greg J. Duncan and Richard J. Murnane. New York: Russell Sage Foundation.

Reardon, Sean, and Kendra Bischoff. 2011. "Income Inequality and Income Segregation." *American Journal of Sociology* 116(4): 1092–153.

Rosenblatt, Peter, and Stefanie DeLuca. 2012. "'We Don't Live Outside, We Live in Here': Neighborhoods and Residential Mobility Decisions Among Low-Income Families." *City and Community* 11(3): 254–84.

Rossi, Peter H. 1955. *Why Families Move: A Study in the Social Psychology of Urban Residential Mobility.* Glencoe, Ill: Free Press.

Sampson, Robert. 2012. *Great American City: Chicago and the Enduring Neighborhood Effect.* Chicago: University of Chicago Press.

Saporito, Salvatore, and Annette Lareau. 1999. "School Selection as a Process: The Multiple Dimensions of Race in Framing Educational Choice." *Social Problems* 46(3): 418–39.

Sauder, Michael. 2006. "Third Parties and Status Position: How the Characteristics of Status Systems Matter." *Theory and Society* 35(3): 299–321.

Sharkey, Patrick. 2013. *Stuck in Place.* Chicago: University of Chicago.

Spivak, Andrew, Loretta Bass, and Craig St. John. 2011. "Reconsidering Race, Class, and Residential Segregation in American Cities." *Urban Geography* 32(4): 531–67.

Theobald, Rebecca. 2005. "School Choice in Colorado Springs: The Relationship Between Parental Decisions, Location, and Neighbourhood Characteristics." *International Research in Geographical and Environmental Education* 14(2): 92–111.

Zukin, Sharon. 1987. "Gentrification: Culture and Capital in the Urban Core." *Annual Review of Sociology* 13(1): 129–47.

Chapter 7

Middle-Class Parents, Risk, and Urban Public Schools

SHELLEY MCDONOUGH KIMELBERG

Despite the substantial attention paid to the topic of school choice in academic and policy circles, it is still the case that roughly seven in ten children in the United States attend schools assigned to them by their district, rather than chosen by their parents (U.S. Department of Education 2009). Most of the scholarly work on those parents who do actively select a school examines the various choice mechanisms and institutional alternatives—including voucher programs, charter schools, pilot schools, and magnet schools—that have proliferated in recent decades, especially in large urban areas that serve predominantly disadvantaged student bodies (see chapter 1, this volume). Comparatively less research focuses on one of the primary means by which parents regularly exercise school choice: the residential market. As the educational policy scholar Jennifer Holme (2002) points out, in the "unofficial" choice market, parents with the financial resources to do so deliberately purchase homes in the best school district they can afford.

This trend was so commonplace in the latter decades of the twentieth century that it is still largely taken as a given that middle- and upper-middle-class families reflexively move, typically to the suburbs, "for the schools" (Holme 2002). As gentrification has reshaped the landscape of many cities, however, attracting and retaining more young families in urban neighborhoods (Butler and Robson 2003; DeSena 2009; Karsten 2003, 2007; van den Berg 2013), the need to revisit the conventional wisdom concerning schooling choice and housing choice is clear. For example, a growing body of literature examines the decisions of some middle-class parents to remain in the city and send their children to local urban public schools, many of which are majority low-income and nonwhite (Billingham and Kimelberg 2013; Cucchiara 2008, 2013a;

Cucchiara and Horvat 2009; Kimelberg and Billingham 2013; Posey 2012; Reay, Crozier, and James 2011; Stillman 2012). Although much remains to be learned about the conditions under which such parents are likely to embrace urban public schools—and the consequences for children, schools, and neighborhoods when they do—the initial evidence complicates the familiar narrative that schooling choices necessarily drive the housing choices of advantaged families toward predictable and uniform outcomes.

The assumption that middle-class families will relocate for the schools has also affected the way in which we conceptualize and operationalize the school choice process. The notion that parents gain access to quality schools primarily through the real estate market—specifically, by purchasing a home in a community with a highly regarded school district—contributes to an understanding of school choice as a one-time event. Indeed, the discourse around middle-class families and school selection is often neatly summed up as a single decision—"Should we stay or should we go?"—that presents itself to young couples as soon as children enter the picture (Billingham and Kimelberg 2013; Petrilli 2012). If parents are drawn to the reputation of a school district as a whole, then the decision to move to a community where "everyone knows" that the schools are good (see chapter 6, this volume) may be an attempt to lock in the school choice and ensure access to acceptable schools throughout the primary and secondary school years. However, given that this issue has received little attention to date, the question of whether parents see the selection of a suburban district as a bundled choice of K–12 schools, or think about the school choice differently at distinct junctures in the educational trajectory, such as elementary school versus high school, remains open (Billingham and Kimelberg 2013; Kimelberg and Billingham 2013).

In the urban schooling environment, where parents often simply have more choices available, and a perception (whether accurate or not) of greater variability in quality among those choices (Billingham and Kimelberg 2013; Roda and Wells 2013), it seems particularly important to examine the school choice process as a series of decisions, rather than a one-time event. Indeed, the image of a school "marketplace" so pervasive in education policy circles in recent decades (Chubb and Moe 1990) suggests that parents will repeatedly shop for schools.

This emphasis on increased parental control over schooling decisions tends to stress individual agency and downplay the role that institutional factors play in shaping both the schooling options that are available to families, as well as parents' evaluations of those options. Yet parents do not make schooling choices in a vacuum. Local districts draw catchment areas that determine the universe of schools from which parents may choose, and adopt rules that dictate whether, how, and under what conditions families may select certain schools. Landmark court cases have, to varying degrees, served to expand, constrain, or fundamentally alter the schooling choice sets presented to families. Last, the property tax–based funding mechanisms by which schools in the United States have historically been financed (see chapter 1, this volume) contribute to the reification of school inequality within and across metropolitan areas. The extent to which parents can exercise school choice is thus not simply a function of their individual capital (whether financial, social, or cultural), but also a product of their ability to deploy those resources within the boundaries of a specific social structure.

This chapter draws on qualitative data from a study of middle-class parents in Boston to explore attitudes toward school choice—and the choice of urban public schools in particular—in the context of two selections, an elementary school and a high school.[1]

Specifically, it considers the extent to which these parents' conceptualizations of the risks associated with urban public schools vary in meaning and importance, depending on which choice they are deliberating. In doing so, it builds on work by the sociologist Maia Cucchiara (2013b) examining the role of parental anxiety and uncertainty in the decisions of middle-class parents to select an urban public school for their children. Cucchiara's findings about how economically advantaged parents in one elementary school "struggle[d] with questions of risk, danger, and what is 'good enough' for their children" (2013b, 91) add nuance and balance to overly simplistic and unidimensional portraits of middle-class parents as resolutely determined to avoid any potential risk to their children (Nelson 2010).

Here, I expand the discussion of middle-class parents' perceptions of risk to consider how their evaluations of the risks associated with urban public schools may shift over time as their children age and encounter different types of institutions. Parents in this study articulated a range of factors they weighed when evaluating their local public schools, including the rigor and quality of the education provided, as well as the safety and appropriateness of the physical and social environment. As I demonstrate, these parents, nearly all of whom had young children, tended to downplay both sets of concerns when discussing the public elementary schools available to them in the city. When looking to the future, however, they anticipated worrying considerably more about both dimensions. These different views, in turn, are reflected in the number of schools deemed acceptable at each stage. Although generally open to several local elementary schools, these parents expected to be far less flexible in their choice of a high school, as evidenced in the deliberate, acute reduction in the number of secondary school options they would likely consider for their children.

Indeed, the perceived risks associated with urban public schooling at different stages of the educational trajectory represent not simply the latent worries or anxieties of these parents, but rather are explicitly tied to strategies of action. Many of the respondents who were comfortable "taking a chance" on an urban public elementary school explained that they would contemplate a switch to private schools or a move to the suburbs if they were unable to guarantee their child's access to the top public high school in Boston. By virtue of their resources, these parents were in a position both to decide which risks they could accept and manage, and to pursue different alternatives in the event that they grow unsatisfied with the urban school system. In this way, the data presented here highlight what I term the *privilege of risk* that advantaged families have at their disposal.[2] Aware that they had a safety net of financial, human, and cultural capital that they could activate to switch course if necessary, these middle-class parents were emboldened to consider a choice—urban public schooling—that enabled them to continue the urban lifestyle they had come to love.

This chapter contributes to the vast literature documenting how the behaviors and decisions of social actors in modern Western societies reflect a heightened awareness of risk in everyday life (Beck 1992; Giddens 1991, 1999; Luhmann 1993). Though much of the seminal work on the *risk society* focused on the environmental and health implications of scientific and technological change, the concepts of risk and risk management have since emerged in many strands of social science inquiry. For example, numerous studies explore how the practice of contemporary parenting in industrialized nations reveals a multitude of ways adults interpret and respond to uncertainties surrounding the physical care, protection, and cognitive development of children (Hoffman 2010; Jackson and Scott 1999; Jenkins 2006; Lee 2008; Lee, Macvarish and Bristow 2010; Murphy 2000; Nelson 2010; Scott, Jackson, and Backett-Milburn 1998). Related research examines how children themselves perceive and react to risks encountered daily in their social worlds of home, school, and play (Harden 2000; Harden et al. 2000; Leonard 2006; Little and Wyver 2010).

Of particular relevance to the present study are scholarly accounts documenting how middle-class parents define the choice of a school and related educational activities in terms of risk and anxiety (Ball 2003; Bialostok, Whitman, and Bradley 2012; Cucchiara 2013b; Roda and Wells 2013). Motivated in part by a desire to pass on to their children the advantages, status, and security that accompany their class position, middle-class parents frequently engage in what the sociologist Annette Lareau (2003) terms "concerted cultivation," deliberately nurturing their children's talents, and organizing family and school life to maximize opportunities for enrichment. Thus, concerns about protecting children from risk are oriented not only toward present-day threats to safety and well-being,[3] but also toward the future, as evidenced by efforts to avoid or minimize obstacles to long-term academic and professional success (Espino 2013).

At the same time, scholars have questioned the ubiquity and uniformity of middle-class parents' assessments of and responses to risks in the schooling environment. Cucchiara (2013b, 90), for example, underscores this point in her study of how advantaged parents in a large U.S. city approached the task of selecting a school for their children, and the meaning they attached to their decisions:

> descriptions of middle-class parents as overly (and unthinkingly) protective and risk averse are incomplete. The parents in this study were proactive and deliberate in their thinking about the costs and benefits of sending their children to an urban public school, and many were quite critical of what they saw as their peers' tendency to treat their children as if they were fragile or somehow more valuable than other people's children.

Furthermore, as the introduction to the edited volume *Education and the Risk Society* (Bialostok, Whitman, and Bradley 2012) suggests, although the notion of risk typically carries a negative connotation in education circles (as evidenced, for example, by the use of the term *at-risk students* or the title of the famous report on schooling in the United States, *A Nation at Risk*), risk and risk-taking may be framed in more ambiguous, or even positive, terms as well. An analysis of risk-taking among well-to-do young people venturing into the world of social entrepreneurship (Brice-Heath 2012) provides one clear illustration. Protected from the consequences of failure, these privileged youth see the pursuit of risky ventures as something to be embraced and rewarded rather than mitigated or avoided, in that it holds (at worst) the promise of personal growth and experiential learning, and (at best) the potential to effect change in broader society (Brice-Heath 2012).

Research Setting

After decades of white middle-class flight, Boston's population had fallen as the twentieth century neared a close to well below six hundred thousand from a mid-century peak of more than eight hundred thousand (Bluestone and Stevenson 2000). However, a recent influx of immigrants, coupled with the rapid gentrification of several formerly distressed neighborhoods, have led to a resurgence in the densely packed city's population, which stood at 636,479 in 2012. Despite its popular image as a collection of close-knit Irish and Italian enclaves, fewer than half of Boston's residents (47 percent) are non-Hispanic whites; African

Americans (24.4 percent), Hispanics (17.5 percent), and Asians (8.9 percent) now make up a significant proportion of the city's population base (U.S. Census Bureau 2010). Often referred to as a "city of neighborhoods," Boston is home to twenty-one officially recognized neighborhoods, each bearing a distinct reputation reflecting its demographic mix, degree and type of commercial activity, and housing stock.

In the 2012–2013 academic year, an estimated 77,200 school-age children lived in the city. Of these, approximately 74 percent (57,100) attended Boston Public Schools. At 40 percent of the student body, Hispanics have surpassed African Americans (36 percent) as the district's largest racial or ethnic group. Whites (13 percent) and Asians (9 percent) are represented in comparatively smaller numbers, though the presence of Asians, unlike that of whites, reflects its overall proportion in the city. The school district is predominantly low-income, with 75 percent of students qualifying for a reduced or free lunch. Nearly half of all students (47 percent) speak a language other than English as their first language (Boston Public Schools 2013a).

Desegregation Efforts and Consequences

Boston holds a place in the collective memory of many Americans as a symbol of the challenges associated with ameliorating racial segregation in urban public schools. In the case of Morgan v. Hennigan (1974), Judge W. Arthur Garrity concluded that the city of Boston maintained a dual system of schools—one for blacks, one for whites—and demanded that the inequity be rectified immediately. The plan drafted in response to the ruling resulted in the forced busing of large numbers of white students into schools in predominantly black neighborhoods, and the relocation of black students into schools embedded in the city's white ethnic communities. The anger, protests, and violence that greeted the court order reflected a heated mixture of racism, class hostility (the communities most affected by the busing were largely poor and low income), and territoriality (Bordas 2006; Formisano 1991; Lukas 1985). Notably, by not requiring nearby suburbs to participate in the desegregation plan, an approach effectively limited by the 1974 Supreme Court case Milliken vs. Bradley, Judge Garrity's ruling enabled discontented parents to avoid busing by exiting the Boston school system altogether.

By the time the Boston School Committee regained control over school assignment in 1989, the district had lost thousands of students, whites in particular.[4] Under orders not to allow its schools to resegregate, the city implemented a new policy of what it called "controlled choice," which divided the city into three large assignment zones designed to incorporate both predominantly white and predominantly black neighborhoods, and established "racial fairness guidelines" to ensure that each school's racial mix reflected that of the broader assignment zone in which it was located. Ten years later, however, the plan was challenged in court, and it was determined that race could no longer be used as a criterion in school assignment (Bordas 2006).

Current Enrollment Policies

Today, families may select any school in their assignment zone (North, East, West), as well as any school in their "walk zone"—a circular area defined by a radius of between one and two miles, depending on the child's age—even if that school falls outside the boundaries of a family's assignment zone. Each of Boston's high schools, as well as a few middle and K–8 schools, are open to all city students, although three of the high schools condition acceptance on an entrance exam. A series of assignment priorities determines which students get which slots. First priority is given to students with siblings already in the school. Next, 50 percent of the remaining seats are reserved for walk-zone students. Finally, random lottery numbers are given to nonsibling, non-walk-zone applicants. Boston is also home to several charter schools, in addition to numerous private and parochial schools in and around the city. Approximately three thousand city children, primarily black, participate in METCO (Metropolitan Council for Educational Opportunity), a program that enrolls students in high-performing suburban districts in the region (Boston Public Schools 2013a, 2013b).

In 2012, the city launched a major review of its school assignment policies. The Boston School Committee considered a range of proposals to expand the number of assignment zones, with the goal of increasing reliance on neighborhood schools and reducing the substantial transportation costs the city incurs to bus students across such large geographic spaces. In early 2013, the committee approved a "home-based school choice plan" to eliminate the three-zone model and replace it with a complex system designed to identify for each student a smaller, but more predictable, set of school choices based on a combined assessment of "quality, location, and capacity" (Boston Public Schools 2013c). The new plan is set to take effect in the 2014–2015 school year.

Data and Methods

The data presented here are drawn from thirty-two interviews conducted in 2009 and 2010 with middle-class parents residing in Boston. Subjects were recruited primarily through advertisements posted on several local online discussion forums dedicated to parenting.[5] Additional subjects were

Table 7.1   Sample Characteristics

Marital status	
Married	91%
Divorced	6%
Never married	3%
Race-ethnicity	
White	91%
Black	3%
Hispanic	3%
Other	3%
Education (highest degree attained)	
High school diploma	3%
Associate's degree	3%
Bachelor's degree	13%
Graduate degree	81%
Employment status	
Employed full-time	62%
Employed part-time or student	16%
Not in the labor force	22%
Homeownership status	
Owner	94%
Renter	6%
Median income (n = 25)	$150,000

Source: Author's compilation.
Note: N=32

referred by previous respondents. Potential participants were required to live within the city of Boston, have at least one child at or nearing school age, and have at least seriously considered enrolling their children in the Boston Public Schools (BPS) system. Each interview took place at a location of the respondent's preference, and was conducted by a member of the study's research team.[6] The interviews lasted between sixty and ninety minutes on average, and followed a semi-structured format. Questions focused on a range of topics, including the participants' schooling backgrounds, how they went about searching for, evaluating, and selecting schools for their children, and how their schooling decisions related to their residential decisions.

All of the volunteers were women.[7] This was not surprising, given that the discussion boards from which subjects were solicited are geared toward "moms," and that women typically bear primary responsibility for decisions concerning school choice and schooling more generally (Andre-Bechely 2005; DeSena 2006; Griffith and Smith 2005). As shown in table 7.1, respondents fit the profile of either the middle- or upper-middle-class.[8] All but two participants had completed at least a bachelor's degree,

Table 7.2 Age and School Status of Children

All children (n=57)	
Age range	<1–15 yrs
Median age	5 yrs
School-age children (n=38)	
Median age	7 yrs
Percent enrolled in Boston Public Schools	82%
Percent enrolled in private elementary school	16%
Percent enrolled in suburban public school	2%
Percent in grades K–6	89%
Percent in grades seven through twelve	11%

Source: Author's compilation.

and the majority had earned a graduate degree. Family incomes ranged from $33,000 to $350,000.[9] Among the women who worked, all held professional or managerial jobs. Roughly one-quarter of the women were currently staying home with their children full time, but nearly all of them had been employed in professional positions before leaving the paid workforce. With the exception of one Latina, one African American, and one Cape Verdean, all respondents were white. All but three were currently married.

As table 7.2 indicates, the women in the sample had a combined total of fifty-seven children, who ranged in age from three weeks to sixteen years (median age = five years). Nineteen of these children were not yet enrolled in school (some were cared for at home; others were enrolled in day care or preschool programs). The median age of the remaining thirty-eight children was seven years. Of these, thirty-one were enrolled in BPS, six were enrolled in private elementary schools, and one attended a public school in a district outside Boston.[10] The parents of the nineteen youngest children had either already decided to enroll them in BPS (typically in the same schools as their older siblings) or were still exploring schooling options.

All interviews were recorded with the permission of the respondent and transcribed. Each transcript was read multiple times by both members of the research team. The analysis involved an iterative process by which the research team inductively identified key categories and subcategories relating to the general theme of school choice, and then coded each transcript accordingly.

Findings

When evaluating their local public schools, respondents weighed a range of academic and social factors (for more on this, see Billingham and

Kimelberg 2013; Kimelberg forthcoming; Kimelberg and Billingham 2013). Their perceptions of which conditions posed an actual risk to their children, however, varied depending on the schooling decision in question. As I demonstrate, this has consequences for the number of schools that parents consider acceptable at different points in the educational trajectory.

"Until the Schools Fail Us": The Short-Term Plan

The middle-class parents in this study, like those in similar studies of advantaged parents and urban public schools (see, for example, Cucchiara 2013a; Stillman 2012) recognized that they had made (or were contemplating) a choice unlike that made by many, if not most, families in their position. In fact, the majority of respondents acknowledged that significant numbers of their peers—and in some cases, nearly all—had already left Boston for the suburbs. For example, when asked whether she knew any families like hers who had relocated, Allie,[11] a mother of two young girls, did not hesitate:

> Allie: Oh, like, twenty families, easy. Like, I wouldn't even have to work to come up with a list of ten and I could get to twenty if I thought for a minute.
> Researcher: And is it just about schools that they're leaving for?
> Allie: Yes. Absolutely. Like, have a baby, move to Brookline [a wealthy suburb that borders Boston]. Within a year. I can name three families that lived within two blocks of me that had a baby and moved to Brookline.

Yet the schooling decision made by most of the middle-class parents interviewed for this study was different not simply because it involved a less commonly selected option—an urban public school rather than a suburban school—but also because of its temporal nature. Specifically, all of the respondents described family and friends who had purchased a home in the suburbs "for the schools" or "for the good school district," suggesting that they intended for this to be a one-time or long-term decision (in other words, one that would carry their children through elementary school and beyond). In contrast, virtually none of the respondents characterized their decision to stay in Boston the same way. Rather, most were surprised to find themselves still living in the city with children (for more on this, see Billingham and Kimelberg 2013), and portrayed their school choice in much more tentative terms. As Josie recounted, for example, she and her husband had not fully committed themselves to Boston Public Schools, but were willing to start their preschool-age daughter there: "[We thought], let's try her in the public school. If it doesn't work out or she's not doing well or whatever, then we'll have to think about different options. But let's try that first and see if we can make that work."

This wait-and-see attitude was typical of the middle-class parents in this study, who largely saw themselves engaged in the task of selecting an elementary school, not a school district, for their children. Accompanying this belief, therefore, was the expectation that the choice of a kindergarten was merely the first of several decisions that they would ultimately need to make. After bemoaning the culture of "helicopter parenting"—a phenomenon from which she, like some of the parents in Cucchiara's (2013b) study, actively sought to distance herself—Colleen, a policy analyst who had attended an elite private high school herself, did not see the value in devoting too much time to weighing secondary school options for her young daughter, who had not yet entered elementary school: "Nope. No point in worrying about it now, because . . . the environment will probably be different in five or ten years. . . . Our plan right now is to stay here until the schools fail us."

Thus, for Colleen, the decision to stay in Boston reflected not a belief that BPS was the definitive right choice for their daughter, but rather a willingness to forgo drawing conclusions about its inappropriateness until proven otherwise.

Indeed, a common approach parents described in these interviews was to mentally break the daunting school decision into segments, with the intention of gathering experiential data and reevaluating options and priorities every year or couple of years. Eliza, a corporate banker who grew up in the suburbs of Boston, recalled how she had opted to send her young son to the local public school on a trial basis, not certain how it would turn out: "I was still thinking, like, one year. If it doesn't work out, we're out of here." Now with two children in BPS, and nothing but positive things to say about her experiences to date, Eliza still views her future schooling decisions in small increments: "worst case scenario, Kyle doesn't get into an exam school [for high school], but by then we've gotten through sixth, maybe eighth, grade. I'm still [on] a two year plan."

For some parents, merely thinking about the transition to middle school or high school caused significant consternation.[12] Donna, a single mother of two, dealt with her anxiety by consciously not thinking beyond the selection of an elementary school, a tactic that made her more comfortable with the decision to enroll her children in BPS:

> If they were to stay through the fifth grade [in BPS], I haven't quite started thinking about that. I mean, it's in the back of my mind, that I got to think about it. Middle school is a nightmare in BPS, so I feel a little anxious, so I kind of decided I don't really need to think about this right now. So I kind of don't.

Though Donna was perhaps unique in that she expressed a greater degree of unease with the prospect of Boston Public Schools than most of the other respondents in this study, her approach to the school selection process—to take it in stages—was quite common.

"You Could Screw Up Elementary School": Perceptions of Academic Risks

The willingness of the middle-class families in this study to try the local elementary school was aided, in part, by the belief that this experience, even if it went poorly, would not determine their children's future opportunities for success. All respondents were aware of the academic quality of candidate schools, and took it into account in the school search, but many downplayed the relative importance of formal schooling as a mechanism for educating children during the early years. As I explain elsewhere (Kimelberg forthcoming), these highly educated parents expressed a great deal of confidence in their ability to marshal cultural, human, and financial capital to provide early educational opportunities for their children inside and outside the home. As a consequence, most anticipated that their children would have an advantage over other students when they began kindergarten. This conviction allowed them a certain degree of flexibility in the school choice, enabling them to define and prioritize what was most important to them, and to minimize some of the perceived risks associated with attending a school that lacked the academic pedigree of its suburban or private counterparts.

For example, Hope, a sales executive with a daughter in elementary school and a son about to enter kindergarten, described how the opportunity to help shape the direction of the new pilot school in her district ultimately outweighed the risks associated with sending her child to an unproven school:

> A lot of choosing Boston Public Schools has a lot to do with people's comfort with risk [laughs]. . . . And I would not say that I'm comfortable with risk, but I think when I compare myself with other people now, I think I have to reassess that I have a higher tolerance for risk than other people do. . . . I knew a lot of parents who were very excited about PS 72, loved everything they were saying, but they couldn't cope with the risk, like "how could I send my kid to a completely untried school? They can say all the right things, but how do I know they can execute?" We were so excited about the school, and it was such a good fit for our daughter, that we decided we were gonna put it as our first choice, because that was a risk we could live with. And we felt like, yes, it's a new school, but then as parents, you're in on the ground floor with them, too, and, and, that your voice would probably fairly likely be heard if there was anything that wasn't going in a direction that you liked early on.

Hope's remark suggests an attitude expressed by many of the middle-class parents in this study, who searched for an elementary school that was "good enough" academically. As Meredith, a pediatrician and mother of two young teenagers, recalled, a first visit to the public elementary school that her daughter ultimately attended did not leave her with the sense that it was necessarily the most rigorous or inspiring option, but rather an acceptable one: "The teachers seemed fine to me. . . . It just looked like a normal public school like the one I went to. So I wasn't appalled or impressed by it."

Indeed, most respondents conveyed a willingness to risk a less than perfect elementary school, provided that their children were happy, engaged, and nurtured (for more on this, see Kimelberg forthcoming). Jody, a political consultant who was still undecided on a school for her young son, explained that her review of the public schools in her zone had uncovered more than one that she thought would work for her family:

> I think there's a couple of schools that, from what I know right now, I'd be totally comfortable with. Because I trust what I know about the teachers and the principals in those schools . . . that they really have a vision and are making decisions based on what they really think is best for kids. And . . . if they make some mistakes along the way, that is just life. But I think their hearts are really in the right place.

In sharp contrast, when discussing their thoughts about school choice after the elementary school years, nearly all of the middle-class parents in this study expected that they would be less laid back about issues of academic quality and rigor. Kitty and her husband John, both professionals at urban nonprofit organizations, described themselves as strong advocates for the local public schools. Nevertheless, they expressed uncertainty about their ability to secure a quality education for their young daughter once she enters the upper grade levels: "I think both of us . . . feel that the likelihood of finding a good elementary school in the public school system seems more likely. I start to get nervous when I think about the seven through twelve or six through twelve. That's when I start feeling a little bit more unsure."

On the most basic level, parents seem to believe that the choice of a high school is simply more consequential than the choice of an elementary school. In part, this appears to reflect a recognition that the home-based transfer of skills that provided them a sense of security when their children approached elementary school would not serve as an adequate substitute for formal classroom learning beyond the early grades (Kimelberg forthcoming). A heightened attention to the quality of the academic curriculum in secondary school, though, also reveals a concern with the acquisition of credentials deemed necessary for future academic and professional success (Brown 2001; Collins 1979; Stevens 2007). Reflecting on the tendency of middle-class families like hers to eschew the public high school that sits down the street from the elementary school that they had happily embraced, Cora, a psychologist with a son in first grade and another finishing preschool, drew a distinction between the stakes associated with each institution:

> Cora: I think that's probably part of the reason that something like Neighborhood High School doesn't get adopted in a way. Because you could screw up elementary school. You're not talking about college yet.
> Interviewer: There's just so much riding on it?
> Cora: Yeah. You feel like high school is important. They've got to do well.

Indeed, the parents in this study were generally far less willing to take a chance on high school than they were with elementary school; they needed reassurance that their child would attend an excellent secondary school that would serve as the platform for college and beyond. For nearly all respondents, only a handful of high schools—namely, the city's three schools requiring an entrance exam—would, they anticipated, meet this criteria. But for all practical purposes, only one of these three, the elite Boston Latin School, was universally seen as desirable. As the oldest and one of the most esteemed schools in the United States, Boston Latin held an undeniable appeal for these parents: its reputation rivals, if not exceeds, those of the many highly ranked suburban schools and prestigious private schools in the area.[13] Not surprisingly, then, the exam process—which students can undertake in sixth or eighth grade for admission in the subsequent years—is fraught with immense anxiety for both children and parents. As Kirsten, an accountant with two children in elementary school, described,

> When they get toward the end of fifth grade there's a built-in pressure for the whole exam school thing, for that certain subset of kids that are going to try to get into an exam school. . . . And as parents I think we try not to feed into it. I think we do feed into it. . . . And they put it on themselves. It's just going to happen and you're not going to avoid it. The best you can do is manage it.

"There's Nothing to Lose Because It's Free": Putting a Price on School

One clear manifestation of the relative importance that these middle-class parents ascribed to elementary school versus high school is the financial value that they associated with each. Indeed, several parents noted that because the local elementary school—unlike the private alternatives in the city—was free, it increased their willingness to take a chance on BPS, because they would suffer no real economic consequence for doing so. As Audrey, a stay-at-home mother with a background in child psychology, argued, "There's nothing to lose because it's free. . . . you're not going to lose your deposit or anything like that." Similarly, Colleen reasoned, "Look. It's free, for one thing. We don't lose anything by trying it." Nearly all of the parents in this study claimed that they could afford private school tuition (albeit, in some cases, with considerable sacrifice), but most questioned whether such a significant outlay of resources for elementary school was really worth it. Cora, for example, could not justify paying for her young son to go to a private kindergarten when he could be "perfectly happy" at their neighborhood school:

> I think the feeling I ended up having was that I wasn't sure what $20,000 was going to buy me in kindergarten that I wasn't going to get for free. So that was when I ended up feeling like this is a lot of money, and I think he might be perfectly happy for free in the public school right down the street. But I don't have that attitude about high school.

Other parents echoed this sentiment, explaining that if their child did not gain admission to Boston Latin School, that would be the juncture at which a financial investment—in either a private school or a move to the suburbs—would be warranted, and not before. This was the logic of Eliza, for example, who argued that if there would ever be a time she felt it necessary to spend money on her children's education, it would be during the secondary school years: "I'd much rather pay my private school money for high school [than for elementary school]."

Certainly, the expense of a private education in Boston, which can run between several thousand dollars a year per child at a local parochial school, and upward of $25,000 a year per child at one of the city's exclusive private elementary schools, would pose more of a hardship for some of the parents in this study than others. In fact, while most of the respondents had either actively considered private school at one point, or said they would do so if BPS did not work out, a few reported that the only economically viable alternative for their family was a move out of the city to a suburban public school district. Nevertheless, though it would be inaccurate to claim that all of the families in this study had access to the same set of unconstrained choices, it is important to emphasize that none of the respondents saw Boston Public Schools as their only choice for financial reasons.

"Honky-Tonk" Schools Versus Metal Detectors: Perceptions of Risk in the Physical and Social Environment

Although concerns about urban public schools often focus on the gap in academic quality and achievement—for better or worse, typically measured in terms of test scores—between city schools and their suburban counterparts, many of the middle-class parents in this study also reported fielding questions from worried family members and friends about the safety and condition of Boston Public Schools. None were particularly surprised by this; they, too, had considered the potential risks in the physical and social environment of disadvantaged urban schools when making the schooling decision. What is striking, however, is the degree to which the specific issues they focused on, and the way in which they framed and understood these issues, differed depending on whether they were discussing the elementary or high school decision.

Many of the parents reported being generally underwhelmed or even turned off by the facilities they found when first investigating prospective elementary schools for their children. Betsy, for example, a communications executive with two young sons, had visited the school that her young son now attends a few years earlier, in her role as a mentor in the Big Brothers, Big Sisters program:

> They don't have a cafeteria, so all the kids, they have to eat in their room. And they had these lunch monitors, who bellow like fishwives at the kids, and I thought, "Gosh, is this the kind of elementary school experience I had?" . . . And the girls' bathrooms . . . they didn't even want to go in there, so I would go in there with them. . . . I mean, I've used the bathroom in the Naples train station, so disgusting bathrooms don't do anything to me, but it's just, you know, like "Oh, really? This is it, huh?"

Despite this initial lackluster impression, Betsy did not see it as sufficient reason to cross the school off her list when it came time to decide on a kindergarten for her son. This is a choice she now celebrates, for though the bathrooms still "stink to high heaven," her son is thriving and loving school.

Similarly, Jessica, a management consultant who sent her two older daughters to the neighborhood public elementary school, recalled how before she started the school choice process she was not even aware of the school, despite its location around the corner from her house: "I swear to God, I never even noticed the place . . . I never even saw it. . . . And frankly, I mean, it's a beautiful school today, but it was not very nice looking . . . it just, you know, did not have the TLC that it has today."

As part of a group of self-proclaimed "pioneer" middle-class families who had embraced the local public school several years earlier, Jessica played a significant role in helping transform the physical landscape of the school, devoting time and money to improve the playground, classrooms, and interior and exterior of the buildings. This type of engagement, several scholars have noted, is quite common among middle-class parents who choose urban public schools (Billingham and Kimelberg 2013; Cucchiara and Horvat 2009; Posey 2012). Worn facilities, cramped buildings, or a lack of space and equipment for outdoor play and extracurricular activities, are often viewed not as reasons to reject the school, but rather as projects to be taken on. In this way, the attitudes and actions of the middle-class parents with regard to underinvested or distressed urban public schools echo those documented in the literature on neighborhood gentrification (Brown-Saracino 2010; Kennedy and Leonard 2001), where newcomers see potential advantages to be captured in renovating buildings in neglected or undercapitalized communities.

Other parents described an affinity or affection for elementary schools that were a little "rough around the edges." Nancy, a social worker with a six-year-old son, ultimately chose an elementary school that lacked an impressive physical space over one of the most established schools in the city: "It wasn't as much of a finished product as PS 11 was . . . I think PS 88 is getting there, but I don't feel it's quite as polished. . . . I love that about it, and I love that it's kind of, a little freer, a little more honky-tonk, a little—I don't know, I like that about it now."

Much like the gentrifiers in Japonica Brown-Saracino's (2009) work, several of the middle-class parents in this study expressed an apprecia-tion for urban spaces—including schools—that might be described as more "authentic," especially when compared to the gleaming private schools in the area, or what many decried as the stuffy or sterile environs of the suburbs (see Kimelberg and Billingham 2013 for more on this).

Interestingly, though most parents viewed less-than-perfect elemen-tary school spaces as something to tolerate, improve, or appreciate, descriptions of the high schools in the city were largely tinged with wari-ness. Kirsten, for example, cited the size of the high school in her neigh-borhood as a central reason she would not send her children there: "It's *huge*, it's just huge. There's, like, thousands of kids down there. It's just too big." It is worth noting that though it is one of the larger schools in the district, the high school in Betsy's neighborhood nevertheless has less than half the student body population of the much-desired Boston Latin School.[14]

Likewise, Audrey recounted being shaken after visiting one of the local public high schools on a work assignment: "It was frightening. I mean the idea of security guards and weapons and the size of the school. It was a scary experience." Again, although several respondents acknowledged that Boston Latin is an extremely large school—in fact, it ranks among the top thousand in the United States in terms of student population, and far exceeds the size of any other school in Boston—no one cited this as a substantial reason not to choose Boston Latin for their children. Rather, size emerged as an issue only in conversations about other (decidedly smaller) high schools in the city.

It is difficult to know what to make of these findings, but previous research in the sociological literature on neighborhoods highlights con-nections between the racial composition of an area and perceptions of safety or disorder (Quillian and Pager 2001; Sampson and Raudenbush 2004) that may be operating here. The student body at Boston Latin, for example, is among the whitest (at nearly 50 percent) in the city—and the most white among high school student bodies. As other studies have shown, concerns about stereotyping and social desirability bias may lead parents to use discourse about safety as a proxy for uneasiness with racial or class-based differences in social settings (Cucchiara 2013b; Martin 2008). Indeed, none of the middle-class parents interviewed here voiced explicit concerns about the racial or socioeconomic composition of the high schools in the city, though a few did acknowledge that Boston Latin was not representative of the school district as a whole. Some, however, did reveal worries about the types of issues or situations to which their children could be exposed in high school that would give them pause about continuing in an urban public school district. For example, Josie and her husband expected to send their young daughter to one of the local elementary schools, but anticipated moving her out of BPS once she reached her pre-teen or adolescent years:

> I think both of us are thinking until middle school-ish. Both of us would feel comfortable with her being in the Boston Public School system for elementary school until she's at the age where she's going to start experimenting with God knows what. And I'm just not sure that—I guess I'm thinking that being a girl in middle school, that's probably the age that we're going to want to have her be in a private school setting . . . to help manage the stuff that girls have to deal with in that age bracket, I guess.

In contrast, several respondents were quick to dismiss the concerns expressed by friends and family members about the safety or appropriateness of the racially and socioeconomically diverse elementary schools in Boston. Kirsten explained, "There will always be a certain segment of that class that's going to have challenges that your kid doesn't have. And you'd be surprised, because some people just don't want that. . . . 'It doesn't rub off on your kid,' is what I usually tell people. 'What rubs off on your kid is what you do with them.'"

As detailed elsewhere (see Kimelberg and Billingham 2013), many of the parents in this study celebrated the demographic diversity in the BPS elementary schools they considered for their children, and saw it as an attraction, rather than a risk to be managed or avoided. In fact, as shown in table 7.3, a survey of the elementary schools attended by the children of respondents reveals the range of racial and socioeconomic diversity contained in these institutions. It is not the case that all of the families in this study simply sent their children to the most white or the most affluent public schools in the city. Although the student bodies at some of the schools were less poor or more white than the district as a whole, others

Table 7.3 Demographics of Schools Attended by Respondents' Children

Institution	Number Students	Percent African American	Percent Asian	Percent Hispanic	Percent White	Percent Other/Multirace	Percent Low-Income
BPS—All	57,100	36	9	40	13	2	75
Elementary schools							
School #1	99	32.3	1.0	50.5	13.1	3.1	45.5
School #2	153	19.6	0.7	35.3	31.4	13.2	44.4
School #3	180	50.0	5.0	33.9	5.0	6.2	81.7
School #4	248	57.3	1.2	27.0	6.0	8.4	69.8
School #5	319	36.0	2.2	37.3	20.7	3.4	58.0
School #6	334	5.1	0.0	73.1	19.2	2.7	72.2
School #7	351	16.8	2.8	31.9	45.9	2.6	42.7
School #8	453	37.7	1.3	32.7	25.6	2.6	59.2
School #9	531	11.7	4.7	24.5	55.9	3.0	49.9
School #10	822	19.0	2.8	57.8	16.9	2.4	68.5
High schools							
School #1	2,353	10.3	29.2	9.7	47.5	3.2	30.4

Source: Author's compilation.

reflected the district averages, and still others were more poor or less white than the student population of BPS as a whole.

In addition, the minimization or outright rejection of their peers' concerns also reflects, in part, the privilege that middle-class parents have to define what constitutes risk in the school setting. By comparing the types of situations her daughter confronts in her urban public school to those more commonly found in the advantaged schools her friends' children attend, Allie illustrated the degree to which risk can be a subjective and relative concept:

> There are days when she comes home and tells me something, and I'm like, "Oh my gosh . . . you did not need to be exposed to that, you are not ready for that, and that's troubling." But on balance, I feel like, okay, so she could be exposed to a kid commenting on violence or using inappropriate language or whatever, or she could be in a school where people are pressuring her to, like, buy $100 sneakers. And [in] her school people don't do that . . . I mean, my kid is in second grade and she wears Sesame Street sneakers and nobody gives her a hard time. There just isn't the consumption and the focus on brands . . . It's just lovely, I have to say. You know, maybe she's just like the quirky white girl and people are like, "I don't understand anything about you. You wear basketball clothes to school" . . . like maybe she can get away with more because she's already so different that they're just like, "that must be what all white kids wear". . . . [S]he doesn't get flak about . . . doing all these other things that I know other kids in more affluent places, friends' kids, that they get peer pressured about. We felt like, it's gonna be a tradeoff.

Several parents echoed Allie's point that although they may be different in kind from the risks typically attributed to urban public schools, there are very real risks associated with expensive private schools and suburban schools where the majority of the student body is wealthy. A few also made impassioned arguments about the unfairness of equating disadvantaged students with danger or trouble. Again, Allie explained:

> People get very, like, "what kind of kids is she playing with?" I'm like, for God's sake, they're seven, six, five. Like, can we not decide which are the bad kids and which are the good kids when they're seven? Like, if there's a kid who's a bad kid in second grade, that is, like, a product of the environment. This kid is not evil in his core.

By highlighting the perils associated with different types of schools, these respondents demonstrate not only the fluidity of the concept of risk, but also how, given sufficient resources, risk can be framed as a choice. Nearly all of the middle-class families in this study described themselves as city people and sought an opportunity to remain in the city after they had children (Kimelberg and Billingham 2013). Although the common trend among many, if not most, in their position is to pursue the best schooling options they can afford in an effort to reduce any potential risk to their children's educational or social development, these parents chose to define and evaluate risk in ways that enabled them to maintain their urban lifestyle—at least for the time being. Indeed, in the short term, these parents determined that the benefits of sending their children to an urban public elementary school largely outweighed the costs. This was a decision they expected to revisit continually throughout their children's schooling, however. As they looked ahead to the high school years, these parents expected that they would assign more weight to the academic and safety issues they had downplayed in the earlier grades. If they could not successfully manage those risks in the city (by securing access to a "proven" school), they were prepared to activate their resources to take advantage of other schooling options.

Discussion

In this chapter, I sought to demonstrate two points about middle-class parents and the evaluation of urban public schools. First, for most of the respondents in this study, the school choice decision was a multistage process. It was common for parents to describe a willingness to try Boston Public Schools—fully intending to reevaluate that decision periodically to ensure that it still worked for their children—rather than an unwavering commitment to the district as a whole. This is important, in part, because some of the research on middle-class parents who embrace urban public schools suggests that the tendency to make a choice that others in their position routinely reject may be a function of these parents' core values, identities, or ideologies, such as a progressive or liberal philosophy (for more on this, see Reay, Crozier, and James 2011). This is quite likely true. But it is also plausible, as the current research shows, that certain parents may simply employ a different time horizon when thinking about educational decisions, one that enables them to test out schooling alternatives that may be appealing for a variety of reasons (including cost or the opportunity to remain in the city), but lack the reputation or pedigree to render them "sure bets."

Second, this chapter offers preliminary evidence to support the notion that middle-class parents conceptualize and rationalize the risks associated with urban public schools in different ways, depending on whether they are contemplating an elementary school or a high school. Respondents acknowledged a range of academic and personal risks they had considered when evaluating schools. In general, they tended to minimize the relevance or severity of these risks when exploring elementary schools for their children, and assign more weight to them when discussing secondary school options. Additional data would be required to fully explore the rationale behind these different perspectives. For example, it is possible that the disparate logics these parents applied when evaluating elementary schools and high schools are simply a reflection of their beliefs about the distinct developmental needs of each age group. However, as I discuss elsewhere (Kimelberg forthcoming), increased anxiety about high school appears to be largely a function of parents' desire to ensure that their children are adequately prepared for a successful transition to college. Despite prevailing stereotypes of urban public high schools as dangerous places, most respondents spoke in only general terms about the size and environment of various high schools. Few mentioned specific fears about widespread violence, crime, or gang activity.

It is unlikely that the parents in this study were unconcerned about such dangers; rather, the institutional structure of the BPS school system enables them to minimize the extent of their children's exposure to them. The recent move to K–8 schools, for example, has eliminated the need for many people to find an acceptable middle school for their young adolescent. Even more importantly, by offering three high schools that admit students only on the basis of a rigorous entrance exam, BPS provides a clear path for these parents to access a selective educational environment for their children. Heightened attention to academic quality in the high school years is thus likely to manifest itself in a sharp narrowing of the list of options deemed appropriate by middle-class parents when their children approach secondary school. Consequently, those schools that have gained notoriety for safety issues will simply not be on the radar screen.

Further study of the ways in which middle-class parents define and respond to the risks associated with different schooling environments is warranted for several reasons. First, given that the majority of the parents in this study had young children, few had actually selected a high school at the time of their interview. Thus, though parents spoke at length about how they anticipated making the high school decision, and what they believed would be most important to them in that process, it is impossible to infer from these data what they will actually do when the time arrives. Therefore, these findings should be considered speculative. A study that compares the decision-making processes of middle-class parents actively engaged in choosing an elementary school for their children with those of parents actively engaged in choosing a high school for their children would go a long way toward isolating the specific concerns and preferences that parents weigh in each case. Similarly, because some of the respondents had children who were already attending a Boston public elementary school, and others were still contemplating their choices, these findings raise questions about the potential gap between perceived risk and actual risk. In other words, the parents in this study had different degrees of "exposure to risk" in urban public schools. Some parents' views were likely informed by what they had actually experienced to date, and others reflected what they expected they might encounter. Additional research should therefore focus not only on parents who are considering different decisions (for example, elementary versus high school), but also on parents who are at the same point in each decision-making process (such as the year before kindergarten or the year before high school).

Second, it is important to recognize that this was not a representative sample of middle-class parents (it did not, for example, include any parents who had chosen to leave the city for suburban districts), or even of urban middle-class parents. Given the use of Internet discussion forums to recruit potential participants, it is likely that those who volunteered to be interviewed are an especially engaged and informed group of parents. In other words, this sample may include parents who have spent more time gathering information about urban public schools, deliberating the costs and benefits of various schools, or sharing their experiences with other parents. Thus, this study was not designed to address the question of which middle-class parents are willing to risk urban public schools, and which are not. Rather, it aimed to demonstrate how those who are open to trying urban public schools conceptualize and evaluate the risks associated with that choice—and, most important, how their understanding of those risks depends on the specific schooling decision in question.

Last, future studies should endeavor to examine the extent to which the dynamics uncovered here are evident in other cities, or are primarily a function of the ecological and institutional landscape of Boston. Even among urban public school districts, Boston is remarkable for both the degree of choice available to parents, as well as the complexity and unpredictability of the school choice process. Notably, in Boston, unlike in many other school districts, moving to a specific neighborhood does not guarantee a family access to a certain school, but rather only to a large set of potential options. On the face of it, the partial decoupling of residence and school assignment might be expected to dampen the effects of the growing income inequality in metropolitan areas (Reardon and Bischoff 2011) on school-level segregation. Even if Boston's neighborhoods remain segregated by class (and race), as long as the designated school catchment areas are not coterminous with them, but rather cut across neighborhoods, the possibility for "opportunity hoarding" (Tilly 1998) by members of advantaged groups may be, if not prevented altogether, at least circumscribed.

However, as this chapter suggests, although local policymakers can expand or reduce the number of school choices theoretically available to families, the ability of parents to make different choices is highly class dependent. By virtue of their resources, the middle-class parents in this study had the privilege to define what risk means in the schooling context, decide which risks are acceptable and which are not, and mitigate the consequences of an unsatisfactory experience in the urban public schools. Low-income families, by and large, do not have the luxury to selectively opt in or out of risky schooling situations. Even if they can, in the spirit of market-based school reform, reject substandard schools, the range of alternatives available to them are determined entirely by institutional forces (notably, the specific assignment policy or choice model in place in their community). In other words, they typically cannot deploy their individual resources to change the choice set available to them.

In contrast, the families in this study possessed a safety net of financial, human, and cultural capital that emboldened them to consider a choice—urban public schooling—that not only expanded their set of educational options, but also their residential options, enabling them to extend their stay in the city (even if temporarily). These findings, therefore, call into question the notion that choice in the schooling context works primarily to the advantage of lower-income families. Rather, we must be aware of the ways in which privileged families can bring to bear resources that allow them to identify, evaluate, and act on the risks associated with different schooling choices on their terms, effectively expanding the range of options available to them.

This study focused on the decision-making processes of a small sample of respondents, but the implications of the schooling choices of advantaged parents can extend beyond individual families. An increase in higher-income students may be a boon to urban public school districts, many of which suffer from inadequate resources and would welcome the various forms of capital that the families of such students could offer. In addition, a growing willingness on the part of privileged families to consider schools that many in their position have historically rejected holds the potential to facilitate socioeconomic and racial integration in urban school districts such as Boston, which have struggled to reduce stubbornly high levels of segregation.

Because nearly all of the work to date on middle-class families in urban public schools is based on qualitative research with individual parents or schools, we know little about the overall size or scope of this trend. However, the initial evidence stemming from this study suggests that the impact of the movement of privileged families into city schools may be felt most dramatically in individual schools, rather than across the district as a whole (for more on this, see Kimelberg and Billingham 2013). From 1998 through 2013, the proportion of BPS students who were classified as low income remained virtually unchanged, despite some minor year-to-year fluctuations. During that same period, however, some elementary schools, including a few attended by respondents' children, witnessed significant drops in their proportions of low-income students, in some cases by more than 30 percentage points (ESE n.d.). Furthermore, given that the middle-class parents in this study anticipated that they would consider far fewer schools when selecting a high school than they had or would when deciding on an elementary school—for many, there was only one high school that they deemed acceptable—increasing numbers of middle-class families in BPS could actually exacerbate, rather than reduce, class-based inequality in the district's secondary schools. Future research is thus needed to fully explore the nature and extent of the broader outcomes associated with the movement of middle-class families into urban public schools.

Notes

1. The institutional structure of the Boston Public School district is such that many students do not enter a separate middle school. In addition to those elementary schools that have expanded in recent years to include grades 6 through 8, the city's premier exam schools allow entry at grade 7, making it possible for some BPS students to attend only two schools—a K–8 and a high school—during their childhood years.

2. I am grateful to Amy Stuart Wells for insight on this idea.

3. As the sociologist Joel Best (1990) argued, the widespread use of rhetoric and statistics by child advocates, particularly in the mass media, has fueled popular images of children as increasingly threatened or at risk of victimization.

4. Although likely exacerbated by the desegregation efforts, white flight cannot be attributed solely to the busing mandate (Lee 2004). Indeed, before the ruling, Boston had already begun to shed large numbers of working-class whites, who headed to the suburbs in the wake of broad economic shifts that devastated the employment landscape in many major U.S. cities (Bluestone and Stevenson 2000).

5. One of these online sites has a very large, citywide membership; the other two are based in individual neighborhoods.

6. The research team consisted of the author (a white female faculty member at a local university), and a white male graduate student at the same university.

7. Two respondents invited their husbands to participate in the interview.

8. I use the term *middle class* throughout this paper, though a number of the families fit the portrait of the upper middle class. Given my interest in understanding the school selection process, the more relevant point, perhaps, is that nearly all of the participants had other schooling alternatives available to them by virtue of their financial resources.

9. The family at the low end of the scale had one parent enrolled in a doctoral program. Seven families did not provide their income; however, all seven owned homes in an expensive part of the city.

10. The parents of the children not enrolled in BPS all considered BPS, and in some cases went through the lottery process. Given the small number, it would be difficult to draw any conclusions from their decisions. However,

two things are worth noting. First, there were no common themes among the reasons these parents gave for selecting private school. Second, most of these parents either hoped to eventually send their children to Boston Latin for high school, or would consider doing so, something they shared in common with the rest of the sample.

11. The names of all respondents and schools are pseudonyms.

12. Many of the parents in this sample did not talk about middle school at all, but rather focused their attention only on the selection of an elementary school and a high school. This is largely due to two reasons. First, nearly all of the parents in the sample wanted their children to attend one of the city's exam schools, which allow students to enter in either the seventh grade or the ninth grade. Thus, if their children earned acceptance during the sixth grade year, they could transition right from an elementary school setting to the high school setting. Second, many of the elementary schools in Boston have in recent years expanded to include grades K–8, effectively reducing or eliminating the need to select a middle school. Among the ten elementary schools that respondents' children currently attended, six were K–8 schools.

13. As some critics have pointed out, however, it is not clear from the empirical evidence that elite exam schools such as Boston Latin necessarily deserve their reputation for delivering an education that is vastly superior to that of their nonselective school counterparts (Abdulkadiroglu, Angrist, and Pathak 2011).

14. Boston Latin is especially large, in part, because it houses students in grades 7 through 12. However, even if one only counts the size of the high school population (grades nine through twelve), the student body at Boston Latin is still nearly twice the size of that in Betsy's local high school.

References

Abdulkadiroglu, Atila, Joshua D. Angrist, and Parag A. Pathak. 2011. "The Elite Illusion: Achievement Effects at Boston and New York Exam Schools." *NBER* working paper no. 17264. Cambridge, Mass.: National Bureau of Economic Research.

Andre-Bechely, Lois. 2005. *Could It Be Otherwise? Parents and the Inequities of Public School Choice.* New York: Routledge.

Ball, Stephen. 2003. *Class Strategies and the Educational Marketplace: The Middle Classes and Social Advantage.* London: RoutledgeFalmer.

Beck, Ulrich. 1992. "From Industrial Society to the Risk Society: Questions of Survival, Social Structure, and the Ecological Enlightenment." *Theory, Culture, and Society* 9(1): 91–123.

Best, Joel. 1990. *Threatened Children: Rhetoric and Concern About Child-Victims.* Chicago: University of Chicago Press.

Bialostok, Steven, Robert L. Whitman, and William S. Bradley, eds. 2012. *Education and the Risk Society: Theories, Discourse, and Risk Identities in Educational Contexts.* Rotterdam: Sense Publishers.

Billingham, Chase M., and Shelley McDonough Kimelberg. 2013. "Middle-Class Parents, Urban Schooling, and the Shift from Consumption to Production of Urban Space." *Sociological Forum* 28(1): 85–108.

Bluestone, Barry, and Mary Huff Stevenson. 2000. *The Boston Renaissance: Race, Space, and Economic Change in an American Metropolis.* New York: Russell Sage Foundation.

Bordas, Hanna. 2006. "Desegregation Now. Segregation Tomorrow?" Harvard Graduate School of Education. Available at: http://www.gse.harvard.edu/news_events/ed/2006/summer/features/resegregation.html (accessed November 6, 2013).

Boston Public Schools. 2013a. "Boston Public Schools at a Glance 2012–2013." *BPS Facts* no. 19 (April). Available at: http://www.bostonpublicschools.org/files/bps_at_a_glance_13-0418.pdf (accessed November 6, 2013).

———. 2013b. "Introducing the Boston Public Schools." Available at: http://www.bostonpublicschools.org/files/introbps_13_english.pdf (accessed November 6, 2013).

———. 2013c. "School Committee Approves Neighborhood-based School Choice Plan." Press release, March 13. Boston, Mass.: BPS Communications Office. Available at: http://www.bostonpublicschools.org/news/school-committee-approves-neighborhood-based-school-choice-plan (accessed November 6, 2013).

Brice-Heath, Shirley. 2012. "The New Risktakers: Elective Biographies for Adolescents." In *Education and the Risk Society,* edited by Steven Bialostok, Robert L. Whitman, and William S. Bradley. Rotterdam: Sense Publishers.

Brown, David K. 2001. "The Social Sources of Educational Credentialism: Status Cultures, Labor Markets, and Organizations." *Sociology of Education* 74(Extra Issue): 19–34.

Brown-Saracino, Japonica. 2009. *A Neighborhood That Never Changes: Gentrification, Social Preservation, and the Search for Authenticity.* Chicago: The University of Chicago Press.

———, ed. 2010. *The Gentrification Debates.* New York: Routledge.

Butler, Tim, and Garry Robson. 2003. "Plotting the Middle Classes: Gentrification and Circuits of Education in London." *Housing Studies* 18(1): 5–28.

Chubb, John E., and Terry M. Moe. 1990. *Politics, Markets, and America's Schools.* Washington, D.C.: Brookings Institution Press.

Collins, Randall. 1979. *The Credential Society: An Historical Sociology of Education and Stratification.* New York: Academic Press.

Cucchiara, Maia Bloomfield. 2008. "Re-branding Urban Schools: Urban Revitalization, Social Status, and Marketing Public Schools to the Upper Middle Class." *Journal of Education Policy* 23(2): 165–79.

———. 2013a. *Marketing Schools, Marketing Cities: Who Wins and Who Loses When Schools Become Urban Amenities?* Chicago: University of Chicago Press.

———. 2013b. "'Are We Doing Damage?' Choosing an Urban Public School in an Era of Parental Anxiety." *Anthropology & Education Quarterly* 44(1): 75–93.

Cucchiara, Maia Bloomfield, and Erin McNamara Horvat. 2009. "Promises and Perils: Parent Involvement in Urban Schools." *American Educational Research Journal* 48(4): 974–1004.

DeSena, Judith. 2006. "'What's a Mother to Do?' Gentrification, School Selection, and the Consequences for Community Cohesion." *American Behavioral Scientist* 50(2): 241–57.

———. 2009. *Gentrification and Inequality in Brooklyn: The New Kids on the Block.* New York: Lexington Books.

Espino, Juan Miguel Gomez. 2013. "Two Sides of Intensive Parenting: Present and Future Dimensions in Contemporary Relations Between Parents and Children in Spain." *Childhood* 20(1): 22–36.

Formisano, Ronald P. 1991. *Boston Against Busing: Race, Class, and Ethnicity in the 1960s and 1970s.* Chapel Hill: University of North Carolina Press.

Giddens, Anthony. 1991. *Modernity and Self-Identity.* Palo Alto, Calif.: Stanford University Press.

———. 1999. *Runaway World: How Globalization Is Reshaping Our Lives.* London: Profile Books.

Griffith, Alison, and Dorothy Smith. 2005. *Mothering for Schooling.* RoutledgeFalmer.

Harden, Jeni. 2000. "There's No Place Like Home: The Public/Private Distinction in Children's Theorizing of Risk and Safety." *Childhood* 7(1): 43–59.

Harden, Jeni, Kathryn Backett-Milburn, Sue Scott, and Stevi Jackson. 2000. "Scary Faces, Scary Places: Children's Perceptions of Risk and Safety." *Health Education Journal* 59(1): 12–22.

Hoffman, Diane. 2010. "Risky Investments: Parenting and the Production of the 'Resilient Child.'" *Health, Risk & Society* 12(4): 385–94.

Holme, Jennifer Jellison. 2002. "Buying Homes, Buying Schools: School Choice and the Social Construction of School Quality." *Harvard Educational Review* 72(2): 177–205.

Jackson, Stevi, and Sue Scott. 1999. "Risk Anxiety and the Social Construction of Childhood." In *Risk and Sociocultural Theory: New Directions and Perspectives,* edited by Deborah Lupton. Cambridge: Cambridge University Press.

Jenkins, Nicholas. 2006. "'You Can't Wrap Them Up in Cotton Wool!' Constructing Risk in Young People's Access to Outdoor Play." *Health, Risk & Society* 8(4): 379–93.

Karsten, Lia. 2003. "Family Gentrifiers: Challenging the City as a Place Simultaneously to Build a Career and to Raise Children." *Urban Studies* 40(12): 2573–584.

———. 2007. "Housing as a Way of Life: Towards an Understanding of Middle Class Families' Preferences for an Urban Residential Location." *Housing Studies* 22(1): 83–98.

Kennedy, Maureen, and Paul Leonard. 2001. "Dealing with Neighborhood Change: A Primer on Gentrification and Policy Choices." Washington, D.C.: Brookings Institution Press.

Kimelberg, Shelley McDonough. Forthcoming. "Beyond Test Scores: Middle-Class Mothers, Cultural Capital, and the Evaluation of Urban Public Schools." *Sociological Perspectives.*

Kimelberg, Shelley McDonough, and Chase M. Billingham. 2013. "Attitudes Toward Diversity and the School Choice Process: Middle-Class Parents in a Segregated Urban Public School District." *Urban Education* 48(2): 198–231.

Lareau, Annette. 2003. *Unequal Childhoods: Class, Race, and Family Life.* Berkeley: University of California Press.

Lee, Chungmei. 2004. "Racial Segregation and Educational Outcomes in Metropolitan Boston." Cambridge, Mass.: Harvard University, The Civil Rights Project. Available at: http://civilrightsproject.ucla.edu/research/metro-and-regional-inequalities/metro-boston-equity-initiative-1/racial-segregation-and-educational-outcomes-in-metropolitan-boston/Lee-Segregation-Educational-Outcomes-2004.pdf (accessed November 6, 2013).

Lee, Ellie. 2008. "Living with Risk in the Age of 'Intensive Motherhood': Maternal Identity and Infant Feeding." *Health, Risk & Society* 10(5): 467–77.

Lee, Ellie, Jan Macvarish, and Jennie Bristow. 2010. "Risk, Health, and Parenting Culture." *Health, Risk & Society* 12(4): 293–300.

Leonard, Madeleine. 2006. "Segregated Schools in Segregated Societies: Issues of Safety and Risk." *Childhood* 13(4): 441–58.

Little, Helen, and Shirley Wyver. 2010. "Individual Differences in Children's Risk Perception and Appraisals in Outdoor Play Environments." *International Journal of Early Years Education* 18(4): 297–313.

Luhmann, Niklas. 1993. *Risk: A Sociological Theory.* New York: Aldine de Gruyter.

Lukas, J. Anthony. 1985. *Common Ground: A Turbulent Decade in the Lives of Three American Families.* New York: Alfred A. Knopf.

Martin, Leslie. 2008. "Boredom, Drugs, and Schools: Protecting Children in Gentrifying Communities." *City & Community* 7(4): 331–46.

Massachusetts Department of Elementary and Secondary Education (ESE). n.d. "School/District Profiles." Boston: Massachusetts Department of Elementary and Secondary Education. Available at: http://profiles.doe.mass.edu (accessed November 6, 2013).

Murphy, Elizabeth. 2000. "Risk, Responsibility, and Rhetoric in Infant Feeding." *Journal of Contemporary Ethnography* 29(3): 291–325.

Nelson, Margaret. 2010. *Parenting Out of Control: Anxious Parents in Uncertain Times.* New York: New York University Press.

Petrilli, Michael. 2012. *The Diverse Schools Dilemma: A Parent's Guide to Socioeconomically Mixed Public Schools.* Washington, D.C.: Thomas B. Fordham Institute.

Posey, Linn. 2012. "Middle- and Upper-Middle-Class Parent Action for Urban Public Schools: Promise or Paradox?" *Teachers College Record* 114(1): 122–64.

Quillian, Lincoln, and Devah Pager. 2001. "Black Neighbors, Higher Crime? The Role of Racial Stereotypes in Evaluations of Neighborhood Crime." *American Journal of Sociology* 107(3): 717–67.

Reardon, Sean F., and Kendra Bischoff. 2011. "Income Inequality and Income Segregation." *American Journal of Sociology* 116(4): 1092–153.

Reay, Diane, Gill Crozier, and David James. 2011. *White Middle-Class Identities and Urban Schooling.* London: Palgrave Macmillan.

Roda, Allison, and Amy Stuart Wells. 2013. "School Choice Policies and Racial Segregation: Where White Parents' Good Intentions, Anxiety, and Privilege Collide." *American Journal of Education* 119(2): 261–93.

Sampson, Robert, and Stephen Raudenbush. 2004. "Seeing Disorder: Neighborhood Stigma and the Social Construction of 'Broken Windows.'" *Social Psychology Quarterly* 67(4): 319–42.

Scott, Sue, Stevi Jackson, and Kathryn Backett-Milburn. 1998. "Swings and Roundabouts: Risk Anxiety and the Everyday Worlds of Children." *Sociology* 32(4): 689–705.

Stevens, Mitchell. 2007. *Creating a Class: College Admissions and the Education of Elites.* Cambridge, Mass.: Harvard University Press.

Stillman, Jennifer Burns. 2012. *Gentrification and Schools: The Process of Integration When Whites Reverse Flight.* New York: Palgrave Macmillan.

Tilly, Charles. 1998. *Durable Inequality.* Berkeley: University of California Press.

U.S. Census Bureau. 2010. "State and County QuickFacts." Available at: http://quickfacts.census.gov/qfd/states/25/2507000.html (accessed November 6, 2013).

U.S. Department of Education. 2009. *The Condition of Education, 2009.* NCES no. 2009–081. Washington, D.C.: National Center for Education Statistics. Available at: http://nces.ed.gov/pubs2009/2009081.pdf (accessed November 6, 2013).

van den Berg, Marguerite. 2013. "City Children and Genderfied Neighbourhoods: The New Generation as Urban Regeneration Strategy." *International Journal of Urban and Regional Research* 37(2): 523–36.

Chapter 8

High-Stakes Choosing

MARY PATTILLO, LORI DELALE-O'CONNOR,
AND FELICIA BUTTS

Much of contemporary school reform ideology is anchored in the ideas of accountability (Hanushek 1994) and choice (Chubb and Moe 1990; Schneider, Teske, and Marschall 2000). Even beyond schools, choice is the key word in health care, retirement and social security, housing policy, and most other arenas in which governments (federal, state, or local) are involved in the public welfare. Choice refers to the personal initiative of residents who must choose from the array of resources available from the state. The model has changed from one in which cities or other government entities "deliver" or "provide" public services like education, health care, and protection from crime, to one in which residents "shop for" these goods in a service landscape that includes more nongovernmental, private subcontractors (Brenner and Theodore 2002; Cucchiara 2013; Klinenberg 2002). In some cases, choice is required—as in the New York City Public Schools (Jennings 2010). In other cases, publicly administered options are scarce—as in post-Katrina New Orleans (Cowen Institute 2010). In all of these public-sector choice programs, the stakes are quite high because they deal with our ability to access and afford medications and doctors, our livelihoods in old age, and the care, socialization, and schooling of the next generation (Lipman 2004).

The rise of choice as an education reform strategy is the result of neo-liberal political-economic interventions more broadly. Although neo-liberalism is most precisely defined as the call for less governmental regulation and control of industries and markets (Prasad 2006), the ideological formations that motivate neoliberalism—for example, particular definitions of freedom, choice, and rationality—have permeated the public sector. For schools, this has meant the proliferation of "choice experiments," which "restrict government's traditional ability to assign children to a particular school, shifting this authority to parents. This transfer of power often is accompanied by efforts to diversify the types of schools made available to children" (Fuller, Elmore, and Orfield 1996, 2).

The empirical research on school choice is voluminous and politically contested (see chapter 1, this volume; Henig 2008). It is plentiful because school choice does not refer to any one particular policy, but instead may include vouchers, charters, busing, magnets, and many other local programs, each of which attracts attention from a range of scholarly disciplines with unique assumptions and research questions. The research is politically contested because the stakes are high for numerous constituencies—families, children, politicians, unions, teachers, foundations and philanthropists, bureaucrats, et cetera—and thus findings of all sorts are often read with an especially critical and skeptical eye.

The peer-reviewed scholarship on school choice is more measured than the research done by partisan organizations, and the consensus points to minimal or mixed positive effects of school choice on student achievement, usually defined as student test scores (see chapter 10, this volume; Center for Research on Educational Outcomes 2013; DeLuca and Dayton 2009; Cullen, Jacob, and Levitt 2006; Deming et al. 2011; Rouse and Barrow 2009). Phillip Gleason and his colleagues (2010) studied test scores and thirty-five other outcomes, such as student effort, behavior, and parental involvement for students who won and lost charter school lotteries across the country. They found some positive impacts, but the majority of the results showed no advantage for students who attended charter schools. The authors concluded, "Overall, our results suggest that [charter schools] are no more successful than nearby traditional public schools in boosting student achievement" (xxix). More specifically, they found that the range of results across charter schools was wide, such that some schools were very successful in raising student achievement and others significantly lowered it. Schools in large urban districts and with large populations of disadvantaged students were more likely to show positive results. One additional and intriguing finding was that parents of students in charter schools reported higher satisfaction than the parents of comparison children who did not attend charters. That is, making a choice made parents more satisfied, even if the quality of the education on some measures was no different. This may account for their growing popularity despite weak results, a point to which we return in our analysis.

Instead of adjudicating the academic evidence and political philosophies on school choice, this chapter turns to the words of ordinary people in Chicago who live in this era of choice, and are thus expected to choose schools for their children, and to choose well (for a similar approach, see Bell 2009; Cooper 2005; Neild 2005; Pedroni 2005). As the parent testimonies illustrate, the institutional environment of choice is key for what parents think is possible and how they approach the high school decision. Although Chicago does not have a voucher program, it does allow students to attend schools outside their designated attendance areas. With much controversy, Chicago Public Schools (CPS) has invested heavily in non-neighborhood schools since about the mid-1990s (Lipman and Haines 2007; Pattillo 2007). There is also significant variety in the types of schools available in CPS. For the 2012–2013 school year, school types and programs at the high school level included neighborhood, career, charter, contract, fine and performing arts, International Baccalaureate, magnet, military, selective enrollment, small, and special education. In any one school building, there might be multiple schools, and any one school may embody several school types, each with its own admissions process. For example, within Sullivan High School on Chicago's North Side, there was at one time a neighborhood school into which students in the attendance area were automatically admitted; a classical education program for which admission was through citywide applications; and two medical career academies for which admission was based on grades, test scores, an entrance exam, a writing sample, a letter of recommendation, and an interview. From the outside and from its name, Sullivan looked like one simple school in one big building, but on the inside were four coordinated but unique entities. Placing the panoply of options and the specificity of admissions criteria at Sullivan High School alone within the context of the approximately 145 high schools that CPS administered in 2013 illuminates the difficult task of choosing that parents and students face.[1]

CPS provides school statistics and information about school options on its website, in a hard-copy book that is available in public libraries and guidance counselors' offices, and through a fall high school fair. Other sources of information are available through local nonprofits, national school ratings websites like www.greatschools.org, and the U.S. Department of Education report cards (see, for example, chapter 9, this volume), but none of the parents we spoke to mentioned these external resources. As the testimonies show, the complexity and opacity of the institutional context was overwhelming and foreboding for many parents.

Interviewing Chicago Public School Parents

The data for this chapter come from surveys and interviews with seventy-seven parents, guardians, and parent-figures who had children entering two high schools in one Chicago neighborhood in the summer of 2007.[2] At the time of the interview, the children of these parents had completed eighth grade and the entire high school choice process, and were in the summer just before starting high school. Sixty-eight of the parents completed audio-recorded, in-depth interviews, which were transcribed, coded, and analyzed. The interviews ranged in length from thirty to ninety minutes. We asked parents to walk us through the process and timing of thinking about their child's transition to high school. We focused on what parents and students wanted in a high school, how and from whom they got their information, what they knew about the high school landscape, and their emotional experiences during the process (frustration, enjoyment, confusion, excitement, and so on).

The research was not designed to investigate how parents also chose their housing and where to live. Tellingly, however, parents did not spontaneously relate where they lived to their current set of school options. Had their residential choice been calculated to lead to certain school options, that should have surfaced in the interviews given that the transition to high school would have been prefigured in the housing choice. In agreement with the findings of Anna Rhodes and Stefanie DeLuca (see chapter 5, this volume), the low-income African American parents we interviewed did not follow a path of choosing their homes as the strategy for choosing their schools (also see DeLuca and Rosenblatt 2010; Sanbonmatsu et al. 2006; Keels 2013; Popkin, Harris, and Cunningham 2002).

To understand how parents faced school choice, we chose parents from one traditional public high school (Neighborhood High) and one charter public high school (Charter High), located in the same predominately African American neighborhood in Chicago. This framework allowed for the comparison of parents who had obviously participated in the choice process by entering their children into the citywide lottery for Charter High with parents who may or may not have exercised a choice to attend Neighborhood High. When we first began this research and asked parents to talk with us about how they "chose" Neighborhood High for their children, some parents responded like the following mother: "I was assigned to Neighborhood High. I didn't choose Neighborhood High." Hence, early in the research we modified our framing of the study and the survey and interview questions to capture this experience. In the end, we found that Neighborhood High parents were split nearly evenly between those who did in fact choose Neighborhood High and those who did not.

So as not to betray the identity of the two schools, we do not present precise statistics on the schools or the neighborhood in which both schools are located, but rather present sketches of each school based on publically available data from CPS. In general terms, then, when the interviews were conducted, the student body of Neighborhood High was predominantly African American and low-income as defined by qualifying for subsidized lunch. Only a small minority of Neighborhood High students met state benchmarks on standardized tests, fewer than half graduated, and at least one-third of the student body was chronically truant. Fewer than half of the students felt the school provided a "safe and respectful environment."

Table 8.1   Demographic Characteristics

	Neighborhood High	Charter High
N	28	49
Median age	40	42.5
Median education	12 years	13 years
Median income (midpoint of income ranges)	$5,000	$25,000
Percent unemployed	71	35
Percent married	14	31

Source: Authors' compilation.

Admission to Neighborhood High was automatic for students residing in the attendance area. Each student from the neighborhood's feeder public elementary schools was assigned to Neighborhood High unless another school claimed that student in the CPS central database. Hence, if parents in the attendance area did not enroll their children elsewhere, they had an automatic seat at Neighborhood.

Charter High's student body was also predominantly African American and low income. Charter High had more than double the proportion of students as Neighborhood High meeting or exceeding state testing standards, but still below 50 percent and below the citywide average. Charter High had significantly better attendance, graduation, and college attendance rates compared with Neighborhood High and the Chicago high school average. Also, a large majority of Charter High students felt the school was "safe and respectful." Hence, Charter High had generally better performance outcomes than Neighborhood High, but still struggled in the area of standardized test performance. Admission to Charter High, as with nearly all charter schools in Chicago, was done solely by random lottery. Any child in the city of Chicago was eligible to apply, and no grade or test score information was collected. Names were picked randomly from among all those who submitted their applications by the December deadline. Names were chosen until the freshman class was filled, and leftover names were picked to populate a waitlist. Charter High received roughly twice as many applications as it had open slots.

The demographic profiles of the two sample populations are presented in table 8.1. The Charter High parents we interviewed had higher incomes and more education, and were more likely to be employed and more likely to be married than Neighborhood High parents. Yet though relatively advantaged when compared with Neighborhood High parents, Charter High parents were clearly disadvantaged in an absolute sense, with just over a high school education on average, an unemployment rate over 30 percent and a low median family income.[3]

Table 8.2   School Decision and Satisfaction

	Neighborhood High	Charter High
Parent/student made decision	55%	98%
Other person made decision	3	2
Assigned to school	43	0
Satisfied	44	100
Ambivalent/resigned	37	0
Dissatisfied	19	0

Source: Authors' compilation.

Table 8.2 presents how parents characterized the high school choice process. All of the Charter High families made an active choice and, by definition of how charter school admissions work, none were assigned. Nearly half (43 percent) of Neighborhood High parents said that their children were assigned to the school, whereas 55 percent reported having chosen Neighborhood High. However, the interviews that followed the surveys shed light on the generous definition of choice that parents used. It often did not mean that they actively chose but rather that they knew that it was the neighborhood school and they were satisfied with, or resigned to, the assignment process as it existed. As we discuss later, many parents who chose Neighborhood High were unaware of the avenues they could have followed to enroll their children in a different school.

Table 8.2 also reports how satisfied parents were with their decision in the weeks before their children's freshman year. Reflecting the national findings in the Gleason and colleagues (2010) study, satisfaction was unanimous among Charter High parents. A minority of Neighborhood High parents were satisfied. Thirty-seven percent of Neighborhood High parents were resigned to or ambivalent about the fact that their child would attend Neighborhood High, and 19 percent were strongly dissatisfied.[4] These sentiments are illuminated in the testimonies.

Finally, table 8.3 characterizes the resource and information disparities between Charter High and Neighborhood High parents. Charter High parents were more likely to have access to the Internet, own a car, belong to a church, and have their children in outside activities. This amounted to considerable personal resources and social capital with which to facilitate their navigation of the school choice process.[5] Their greater likelihood to have considered private school suggests their confidence, however tentative, in marshaling the funds to pay tuition. Finally, they spent more time on learning about schools and making their decisions, and they put in more applications. However, on average Neighborhood High parents still put in more than two applications, which illustrates that they too were involved in the choice process.

Table 8.3   Resources for and Participation in Choice

	Neighborhood High	Charter High
Has Internet	43%	63%
Owns car	23%	65%
Attends church	57%	81%
Child in outside activity	57%	92%
Considered private school	18%	67%
Time spent on decision	2.4 hours	3.6 hours
Number of applications submitted	2.6	4.5

Source: Authors' compilation.

These data do not represent a random sample of the parent populations of the two schools, despite it being the initial intent of the research
design. Whereas the entering freshman class of Neighborhood High was
twice as large as that of Charter High, it took much more effort to get fewer
interviews of Neighborhood High parents. First, we sent letters to parents
explaining the study and offering a $20 incentive. At least 75 percent of the
letters to Neighborhood High parents were returned because of incorrect
or out-of-date addresses, and this was the information that the school itself
had provided us. A minority of Charter High letters came back. Then we
made phone calls and the pattern was repeated: disconnected and wrong
phone numbers for Neighborhood High parents versus greater availability,
including by email, of Charter High parents. In the end, we were able to
survey or interview twenty-nine Neighborhood High parents and forty-
eight Charter High parents. The differentiated experience in contacting
parents from these two schools illustrated the differences in their socioeconomic situation as much as, if not more than, the data in the tables.

What Parents Do

The transition from eighth grade to high school requires that parents
do something.[6] Even if a child is assigned to a high school, the parent
still has to register the child, provide contact information, supply health
records, and figure out new transportation routes and schedules. Like the
families in Elliot Weininger's research (see chapter 9, this volume), most
parents in our sample did more than this bare minimum, and they began
thinking about high school for their child months in advance. We characterize what parents do by introducing six verbs that unite parents from
Neighborhood and Charter High and that summarize their preferences,
priorities, and behaviors: We find that parents make sense of, educate,
protect, juggle, choose, and look forward. These verbs help guide the
reading of the parent testimonies that follow.

Parents Make Sense of

The first thing some parents might encounter when thinking about high schools for their child is the CPS website, which describes the process of enrolling one's child in a school as easy as 1, 2, 3: research, choose, register (Chicago Public Schools 2013a). Yet these are not the verbs we found to be most salient in parents' experiences of this process. Instead of researching, parents tried to make sense of the high school landscape and the particular schools within it. Their most dependable sources of information were their experiences with their older children. If they did not have older children, they depended on the advice of trusted family members, close friends, and sometimes neighbors (see also chapter 6, this volume). After personal networks came professionals at their child's elementary school—counselors, teachers, and principals. These people served as intermediaries between the distant bureaucracy of CPS and the high school decision, but their helpfulness varied widely across our sample. The other official information sources—the high school fair and the CPS High Schools book—were similarly difficult to navigate. Less important than direct people-to-people contact were the Internet, television, newspapers, and magazines. Given the sensationalism of news, the schools mentioned there were often characterized negatively for their violence or low performance; however, the increasing sophistication of the marketing apparatuses of charter and other schools increased the positive press for those schools (Cucchiara 2013).

Research suggests a floor of comprehension upon which intelligible data can be collected and evaluated in order to make decisions. *Making sense of*, on the other hand, better captures the greenness with which most parents approached this endeavor and the messiness of the information sources they encountered. One parent remarked, "To actually look for a school in one year was like, 'So how do you … ?' And then learning that there were the small schools inside of the big schools, and so I thought that was really interesting, but overwhelming at the same time." Many information sources conveyed the importance of test scores for opening and closing off possibilities for children and their families. This was the primary way in which the institutional context in Chicago shaped parents' decisions because the most prominent and high-performing schools all selected students based on achievement. Parents overwhelmingly used language about their child's test scores to make sense of where they could and could not attend, where they would fit and not fit in, even though most choice schools in Chicago do not select students based on their test scores.

Parents Educate

Before parents choose a high school (or opt not to choose), they identify what they see as most important. It is no surprise that in talking about schools parents foreground educational desires and preferences. The word Chicago parents used most to talk about their goal to educate was *academics,* often without any elaboration or specifics. "Okay, so what were your early thoughts about choosing a high school for Joseph?" we asked one mother. "Academics," was the response. "Like, what about it?" was the probing question. "Academics!" was the more emphatic response. We relentlessly asked again, "Like, what were you looking for as far as academics?" The interviewee, now thinking the interviewer was completely dense, responded, "In other words, his goal is to go to college." For this parent—and more common among Charter High parents—*academics* was synonymous with college. For other parents, often from Neighborhood High, it meant culinary classes or a curricular specialization in computers or a reading tutor or an individualized educational plan (IEP). Whatever the emphasis, both groups prioritized learning. Although parents generally expected to cede the role of educator to teachers, what they did in this critical moment of transition set the stage. They made clear that the job of parents to educate came prior to that of teachers and schools.

How do we define academics?

Parents Protect

Parents felt that they could not educate if they did not first protect. Safe schools are not a given in CPS and children's safety was of the utmost concern to parents. Charter High parents spoke about safety as a non-negotiable issue. As one mother commented, "Well the hard part in choosing a high school, first of all in the black community, was security, as far as a high school was concerned." Another parent stated even more plainly, "I'm looking for safety, security, the after school matters, keeping 'em, you know, occupied instead of being on the corners and, you know, doing drugs and all that old kinda stuff." In contrast, Neighborhood High parents discussed safety more as a desire and aspiration. One Neighborhood High parent told us, "They had quite a few fights up there this year. But I feel if he can go to school every day and just come straight home without hanging out, he'll make it. Because my other two sons made it, so he can make it too." The two groups often came to very different conclusions about what schools were truly safe and how best to ensure their children's safety, yet despite these differences they were clear that parents protect children by putting them in schools where they believe they will be safe.

Parents Juggle

In their quest to educate and protect, parents were faced with many obstacles, and thus juggled work schedules, their and others' illnesses, transportation hassles, other children and grandchildren, and exhaustion. Financial constraints were ubiquitous and perpetual. One parent had two eighth-graders, her daughter and her niece Marie. She was sending her daughter to a school outside of the neighborhood, but her niece would be attending Neighborhood High. Why send them to different schools, we asked. She answered, "Well you know, financially, I have [pauses] car fare, you know, like I said, you know, with me being on disability, I have financial money for [my daughter], but I don't have it for Marie because Marie's mother's not around. So, that's kind of hard. I have Marie's father's side helping here and there, but that's like reaching at air at times." Atop family and financial challenges, those who were working were working hard to keep their jobs; taking time off to visit Open Houses and meet with counselors was risky. Those who were not working were pinching pennies on every bus ride and school supply. Juggling all that needed to be done to keep the family afloat made it hard for both groups of parents we interviewed to put in the effort necessary to navigate the morass of school application requirements and deadlines.

Parents Choose

Many parents did choose. Other parents were assigned but were so cognizant of the choice framework that their responses were somewhat convoluted: "Well, like I said, basically, I come up with the decision that's what they selected for her." Or "With you being in the neighborhood, those kids get, you have to pick the neighborhood school." These statements—"that's what *they* selected for her," and "you *have to pick* the neighborhood school"—belie ambiguity and contradiction on the question of who is doing the choosing. The moment when parents chose was rarely based on expert knowledge, and was more often based on partial information or even things that were flat out wrong. When parents chose they were invariably filled with a mixture of hope, worry, confidence, and prayer.

From an institutional perspective, the action of choosing was not immediately followed by the verb *register*, as CPS's instructions suggest (Chicago Public Schools 2013a). For many parents it was as if their applications for schools disappeared into a bureaucratic abyss. The choice moment was characterized by too much information and too little communication. Hence, after they chose, parents were sometimes met with silence, resistance, rejection, or deception by the school district. Most important, somewhere between when parents chose and when they registered, they were informed of the more determinative selection process of the schools into which they were choosing. That is, schools were choosing students just as much as parents and children were choosing schools (Jennings 2010), and no amount of begging or yelling was going to make parents' choices win out over schools' choices, at least not for these disadvantaged parents.

Parents Look Forward

Finally, the reality set in and parents looked forward with emotions ranging from intense excitement about their children's high school futures—"I really feel great about it"; "We think it will be a good year"; "I just thank God that he got in"; "He's very hyped about it"—to utter despair—"I mean, the first day of school I don't know if she's gonna cry"; "But we gonna move anyway, so this is just temporary"; "That's frustrating, you know, because you have to see your child say she don't wanna go to school because of different things that's going on." For those who didn't choose, weren't chosen, or had second thoughts about their choice, there was also plenty of ambivalence, looking on the bright side, and making do with the reality.

Parent Testimonies

Parents were similar in that they all made sense of, educated, protected, juggled, chose, and looked forward, but their experiences were hardly uniform. The four extended first-person testimonies below elaborate on these themes as they contrast the two high school cases and offer details about parents' unique approaches and calculations, as well as the actions (or inactions) of the school system. Instead of using disconnected interview quotes to make the points we want to make, we made a conscious decision to present extended testimonies to keep intact the narrative arc of what parents described. Alongside the general themes already introduced and the interpretations after each testimony, we want to give readers access to the complex and whole logic that parents used, and to allow them to uncover themes that we may have missed. Although these are still excerpts and are still edited, our intent is to offer a fuller and representative sense of what parents confronted in this moment of transition. The excerpts may at times be confusing or inconsistent; this is a faithful illustration of both the character of the information that parents received and their attempts to process it.

Because the experiences of Neighborhood High parents showed more diversity than those of Charter High parents, we present three examples from the former and one from the latter. Given that the only way to gain entry into Charter High was to enter the lottery, all parents at Charter High made an active choice to apply there and then had to enroll in order to not be assigned to their neighborhood school. They all expressed satisfaction with the outcome as their children were poised to begin freshman year. For Neighborhood High parents, on the other hand, the experiences were more varied. We present a portrait of a parent who had actively chosen the school and was very satisfied, one of a parent who was assigned

`

to Neighborhood High and was ambivalent but hopeful about that assignment, and another of a parent who tried to choose another school, was angry about the assignment to Neighborhood High, and was still looking for a way to avoid enrolling her daughter there (for the distribution of these experiences, see table 8.2).[7]

Ms. Jarvis and Her Daughter Dee

Ms. Jarvis was a very proud parent. Even though the interview was about her daughter Dee, who was just starting at Neighborhood High, she talked energetically about her two older daughters, Annette and Ramona, both of whom had gone to and graduated from Neighborhood High ten years earlier. Ms. Jarvis did not mention what her older daughters were doing now, but she reminisced fondly about their time at Neighborhood High, and it was the primary reason she chose the school for Dee. Now, at sixty-four, retired, divorced, and with an annual income of less than $20,000, Ms. Jarvis was parenting two adopted foster daughters, Dee and Tarisha. Tarisha, the older of the two, was already in high school. Although Ms. Jarvis had wanted to send her to Neighborhood High, she ran into problems with the attendance boundaries. "Because with this new zoning, I don't know what's what," she commented. "They're forcing you to put the child where you don't want to go." As a result, Tarisha was sent to the new neighborhood high school, causing Ms. Jarvis financial strain because of additional transportation costs. "Ain't no way I can leave it because the kid gotta go to school, you know, so I had to take it. But people such as myself, I gotta pay like $60 a month car fare, that's another bill, see?" By the next year, the attendance boundaries had changed again and Neighborhood High was once again her neighborhood high school. Hence, it was easy for Ms. Jarvis to exercise her choice and send Dee to Neighborhood High.

Ms. Jarvis was serious but friendly in the interview. She wore a Florida T-shirt, glasses, and had her hair straightened with dark blonde highlights. She said that she would spend the $20 she received for the interview to pay for Tarisha's gym uniform. She talked at length about the extra costs of having two girls in two high schools. Ms. Jarvis's story represents parents who proactively chose Neighborhood High and were happy with that decision. She told us the following:

> It was settled from the beginning that she was going to Neighborhood. Neighborhood did a good job with one so why not give a chance to do it with the others? I wanted Dee to be in a school where she could get along well with others. That was my main concern, other than the education, that she could get along well with the others, the other children, you know, her peers. And since they were basically the neighborhood kids, they know each other and they would kind of like, you know, hit it off right away. I was

up there the second day. I was up there Wednesday, walking the halls, looking around, seeing what was going on, you know. Because I heard [about] a few troublemakers up there, you know. And, see, you go up to the schools and you kind of look around and see, so when your kid come home and telling you about things that happen to them, you remember seeing this kid back before when he was making trouble.

At one point, I felt like if Dee went to any other school that it would be a blind spot for her because she wasn't giving it her all. And I would think that she wouldn't be accepted. You know, if they tested her she wouldn't be accepted or they would set her back. But I just know that I know how to handle things better now. You know as each kid go you get experienced. Because when they start in high school we're starting too, you know. We're starting too because things are different. So we're learning too 'cause once you keep your ear open you find out what's what. And you know when your child is letting herself down.

Annette was the lead off of the team, you know, she was the lead off. Then it was just one child. So, you know, when you have one child you want the best. Even if it's not the best it be sounding like the best. But you don't really know what's the best until you [try it]. And it turned out real good. And I felt that Neighborhood was good for one child so it was the first high school that I had sent my kid to since my oldest child. And that was like ten years apart, so that was my first experience with today's high school. The fact that [Annette] came out with a scholarship for a southern school down in Jackson, Mississippi, and the fact that she got a lot of chances to travel, she went to college prep and that offers a lot—yeah, Neighborhood High offers a lot—that's what my decision was based on.

And because, like I said, they are steady improving. You know, they opened up a swimming pool and everything. And they've improved since my daughter Ramona left there, you know. So it was understood that Dee was going there. A good, solid, credited background of the school and to give Dee good, you know, a good education. Like, you know, some schools when you come out [that is, graduate] you automatically mention the name and you's credited, you know. With some schools it's not so much the high level. Well, I was looking into magnet schools and academies [for] my older daughter, the one that graduated. I looked into the magnet school for real good education. It really was the name that had me turned on about the schools, you know, putting my daughter in a magnet school or academy, that's what it was really about, you know. But then I found out that the public school, as stated before, they were just as good if the kid wants to learn. Like I said, it has to be Dee wanting to learn, you know. And I tell my girls, whatever school they're in, I tell them you get everything they got to offer you in there. And if you come out a failure it's no one's fault but your own. So that's that.

When I moved in this area [I asked my neighbors] just what type of school Neighborhood was. The only thing that I could get from the neighbors was that the school had a reputation for getting girls for pregnant. Not the school getting them pregnant, of course, but a lot of pregnant girls goes there. And comes out. And that was the only thing that I kind of like mulled it over.

But my thing is that whatever school they go to, if they gonna get pregnant they gonna get pregnant. It just didn't have to do with Neighborhood High. So that was the only thing I heard about Neighborhood. I had to really put my oldest daughter in there and find [out] for myself what type of school it was. And it worked out just fine because it's all in the kid. You know, it's all in the kid. Because I also looked around other schools like Walker, Greene [High Schools]. And everything kind of like weighed out. You know, if it wasn't pregnancy it was something else. So, you know, every school has its flaws, you know. And I'm pretty much happy with Neighborhood.

Ms. Jarvis's story highlights the broader themes previously introduced. It also offers additional specificity about how parents make sense of the school landscape. Three points merit additional emphasis: the importance of the experiences of older siblings, the powerful but subtle role of testing and test scores, and the combined philosophy that "every school has its flaws" and thus the child's effort is what is most important.

First, for most parents, the most common and trustworthy sources of information for making sense of the CPS landscape were their own personal experiences and those of family members, especially their older children. Parents had to gather, but also cut through, the overwhelming amount of information on schools in Chicago, which sometimes led to erroneous conclusions, as in Ms. Jarvis's distinction between magnet schools and public schools (magnet schools are public schools). Parents weighed, evaluated, and critiqued information and its sources, as Ms. Jarvis did with the news that Neighborhood High had a reputation for "getting girls pregnant." More important than reading CPS pamphlets or visiting websites or even visiting schools themselves, parents relied on what they knew from having raised older children. That is, they made sense of school reputations and quality with firsthand accounts.

A second important point in Ms. Jarvis's comments is perhaps too easily missed because it is almost common sense for her. One reason Ms. Jarvis did not apply to other schools for Dee was because she worried that Dee's test scores weren't good enough, or that she would be retained a grade because of low test scores. This assumption about the premier importance of test scores pervaded the interviews. Many parents assumed that their child's low test scores disqualified them from making any choices: "Basically his scores. I think that's the only school that he could attend right now until he bring up his scores," said one mother. Another parent had the following approach: "I said that he probably couldn't get into Clarion because of his scores. I knew Clarion was a high-rank school and you have to go through so much to get in there. Clarion might been best for him but he probably would have to catch up, you know." Yet another parent gave the following response to our question about if Chicago Public Schools did a good job letting parents know about school options: "Yes, I think they do a good job in preparing the parents and the students because they let the students know you can't go here because your reading is too low or you can't go here because your math is too low. Yeah, I think they do a excellent job in that." The last statement is particularly striking because it illustrates that the loudest message parents get about choice is not about the possibilities that exist, but rather about where their child cannot attend (or even apply) because of their test scores. The fact is that all of the selective enrollment schools and many of the magnet schools have test score requirements, but none of the charter schools do, and few of the small and other types of schools consider test scores. Nonetheless, the current climate of high-stakes testing makes parents think otherwise. Thus, both the local institutional context of CPS and the national emphasis on accountability shape parents' interpretation of choice to mean that it is the high scorers who have choices, and that other students have fewer, if any, options outside of their neighborhood schools.

A final theme is highlighted by Ms. Jarvis's conclusion that because all schools have some fault or faults the child's effort is really what determines his or her success or failure (see DeLuca and Rosenblatt 2010; also chapter 5, this volume). This sentiment was repeated in many interviews, especially among Neighborhood High parents. One father said, "I was looking for, basically a school that didn't have, I know every school has violence, but one that didn't have so much violence." Such comments illustrate the salience of parents' goals to protect their children. However, in making sense of the array of schools, violence is seen as omnipresent and thus unavoidable. Furthermore, this perception is coupled with the notion that a school's problems are surmountable with appropriate child effort. One father said,

> So you know it doesn't matter to me. I mean, if a child gonna get the education he gonna get the education because he want it, not because the school's supposed to be better. You hear things about the Catholic schools teach your kids better, or whatever it is. I don't believe that. You know what I'm saying? I believe it's in your child. So it's up to your child. You gotta stay on top of your child and, you know, get the understanding that your child understands that he could do better at whatever school he in: Catholic, public school, charter, whatever. It's not up to his school. It's up to your child and the child's parents.

This kind of strong belief in individualism and personal responsibility, to the exclusion of structural explanations of individual outcomes, is quintessentially American and widely shared by low-income African Americans (Hochschild 1995). Yet many parents expressed frustration with the dearth of good options. Ms. Jarvis was convinced by the positive things she had seen with her own eyes at Neighborhood High, but other parents were not so sanguine.

Ms. Carter and Her Daughter Jenice

The portrait of Ms. Carter and her foster daughter Jenice illustrates the group of families who were assigned to Neighborhood High, were disappointed by that outcome, but who then tried to make the best of the situation. Like Ms. Jarvis, Ms. Carter was also raising a second generation of foster children after her biological children had grown up and left the house. Ms. Carter was fifty-four years old, married, and worked full time in the health-care field. Together, she and her husband earned a lower-middle-class salary, but finances were tight because they had four foster children. While her sacrifice and commitment to raise foster children was admirable, she was clear that her generosity did not extend beyond her household, saying, "I have to see what's going on [in the schools] and get involved. But [in general] I don't feel like being bothered with these kids today. You can't tell them nothing and they be ready to beat you up. So let their parents deal with them and I'm just dealing with these back here. I'm just interested in mine." This is what she had to say about the process of getting one of her own into high school:

> Well, [I probably started looking for a high school] around Christmas, or the first of the year, January. I knew it was getting closer, you know, to her going to high school, so I started thinking. And they did send some different papers home to fill out for different schools. They did, but I guess she wasn't selected for none of those schools. Like Bonds [High School], and what else? She chose a few schools. I don't think she heard from those schools either because we didn't get letters or nothing. The only school that they chose for her was Neighborhood.
>   Well, I wanted her to go to a good school [like] Humphrey, you know. But, like I say, she didn't qualify for Humphrey. Bonds [High School], I think that was her choice. But we never heard anything from Bonds. [We wanted] someplace where, you know, safe for her, [where] she didn't have to really travel in a bad neighborhood. You know, technical schools. And then there was one, I can't think of the name of it, one charter school that had like a medical—what do you call that?—some medical training. Allied Health stuff, you know. And I'm looking in terms of introducing her to something where she can get a job, or can go further once she's been introduced to something in the Allied Health field. It was in the Chicago Public Schools book, but I can't think of the name of it. But, yeah, I wanted her to [go] where they had some technical stuff, Allied Health, any good training.
>   [I went to the counselor and I] was just asking her could she help me get Jenice in Humphrey and the other school we chose, and the charter schools. So she circled some stuff that was in the Chicago Public Schools book, and then I went home and called the charter schools. But they had did the lottery already, so it was too late for her to get in there. Then the counselor did tell

me that Humphrey, you had to have your scores up, you know, and hers weren't good. So, her chances weren't good to get in Humphrey.

After that I just was waiting for the letter of response of the schools that she [put down on her application]. You got to ask her what school she put down because her and my [older] daughter did that when I was at work. But I was just waiting for the letters, you know, to see if any other schools was going to write to say that she was accepted. But we didn't hear from anybody. Nobody but Neighborhood. And when my [older] daughter opened the letter up, [she] called me and she say "Guess what?" And I'm like, "What?" And she say, "Jenice [is] going to Neighborhood." And I was very disappointed. I was very disappointed. Because I had never heard any good stuff about Neighborhood, you know. And I didn't hear from Neighborhood until the last minute. I didn't know she was going to be sent to Neighborhood. Now who made that decision? And why we didn't hear from Clarion [High School]? And why we didn't we hear from the other schools that she put down? Because we were waiting for a decision to say that I accepted the child or I didn't accept the child, you know what I'm saying? Only thing we heard from was Neighborhood and we didn't choose that school. [Long pause].

So, what? They send black kids where they want to send them? Why did Neighborhood come up and we can't hear from any other schools? I didn't like the process. I didn't like it because, like I say, they didn't send information home or mail information to my house about the schools that she chose. And I don't like it because they sent Neighborhood and we didn't apply for it. I don't think I would've chose that school, just up and chose that school, no. Because, like I said, it was chosen.

She was afraid at first because Jenice haven't been around bad people. And she see how the kids function out here, you know, curse and do bad things. And she watched the news a lot too. So we see things on TV. So every time something happened at a school—like that boy [who] got shot on the bus—it kind of frightened her. So we talk about things that happen at school and I let her know what you have to do to stay safe in the schools: not mingle with too many people. You meet them there, you leave them there. So we talk about things like that and I let her know she got to finish school and go on and be able to get a job, you know.

I asked a question when I went to the [Neighborhood High] orientation: did she have to stay here or could we transfer? And they told me that if I find a school that would accept her that she can transfer. But after the orientation, like I say, I was impressed that they was strict with the kids. And I like that. Neighborhood High have different curriculums and she always wanted that culinary arts because she said she want to cook so, you know, she liked that about Neighborhood. And she did say she thinks she going to like Neighborhood, so we going to stay there. And then I look at the distance from the house. It wasn't too far. So I just said we'll just give it a try. And I said well at least she right at home. And then I stopped thinking about schools far out, you know, because if something happen then I can go right away. Like I said, I didn't choose Neighborhood but now that we're there we'll just make the best of it. That's all we can do.

If one thing echoes in Ms. Carter's words it is the fact that she did not choose Neighborhood High. It is in Ms. Carter's narrative that the lack of communication by CPS is most acute. It is impossible to know if Ms. Carter and her daughters did something wrong in the application process, if their application did not reach the intended schools, or if her acceptance or rejection letter got lost in the mail (as did many of our solicitations to Neighborhood High families). In any of these scenarios her experience with institutional actors was one of general disregard and dismissal. Ironically, however, Ms. Carter was well socialized in the language of choice. It was the logical vocabulary to use when she reported that "the only school that they chose for her was Neighborhood." But this idea of choice is not the one that CPS markets on its website. Schools are not to be "chosen for" parents but rather "chosen by" parents. Similarly, school choice is precisely the opposite of the passive voice, but that's what Ms. Carter used when she said, "Because, like I said, it was chosen."

From the outside, how Jenice ended up at Neighborhood High is clear: she lived within the school's attendance boundaries and she was not admitted to any other schools. Neighborhood High, however, wasn't even on Ms. Carter's or Jenice's initial list. She did not know that it would be what another similarly frustrated parent called "the automatic choice." All of these parents played the game of choice that CPS asked them to play, but then some found out that individual schools actually made the final choice. In Ms. Carter's case, the most frustrating thing for her was not getting any response about whether those other schools had chosen her daughter.

Still, Ms. Carter was an upbeat person. She was not happy with how the process unfolded, but she was ready to look forward and give Neighborhood High a try. No regrets. But other parents who were assigned to Neighborhood High expressed many regrets about their efforts and criticized their own level of engagement in the process. One mother said, "Yeah, I was told to go up to most of the schools and I didn't go and I should have went. They had another fair that I didn't attend because I thought the first fair was . . . ," her voice trailed off and she paused. She concluded with a tone of resignation, "You know, it's a lot of stuff on my part that I should have did and also on their part they should have did." Another mother of a daughter who had expressed strong interest in a charter school said, "I think I would've chosen that [charter] school faster for her because she wanted to choose it for herself knowing that it wasn't Neighborhood. I would've chose . . . ," and her voice trailed off as well. "Hmph," she continued, looking forward rather than backward, "I got one more coming outta grammar school and I'm gonna be on that." Finally, a father of five who along with his wife talked extensively about the work of juggling five school and activity schedules, blamed his

eighth-grade son, his job, his wife, and their caregiving responsibilities
for why his son would be going to Neighborhood High:

> If he would've filled the applications out maybe he would've had a better
> chance on picking a different school. You know what I'm saying? We didn't
> force him to go to Neighborhood or we didn't tell him he couldn't go to
> Meter [High School]. You know, it's just that he didn't apply himself and
> I wasn't there to help him apply because I was at work. So like [his mother]
> said, she should've, she could've stepped up and did a little bit more to
> make sure he filled out them papers. But like she stated, you know, we got
> a small child.

All parents had to look forward, but many briefly looked backward
and blamed themselves—or, more unfortunately, blamed their children—
for what they perceived as a bad outcome. CPS remained blameless even
though it structured the processes, procedures, and possibilities of school
choice that sometimes disempowered parents. Nonetheless, parents quickly
learned the rules of neoliberal public policy—citizens must be good and
active consumers of public goods. When they are not, in the words of one
mother, "we just got stuck with Neighborhood High."

Ms. Jarrett and Her Daughter Chantell

The most egregious example of the undermining of parental choice and the
acute disappointment that resulted from being assigned to Neighborhood
High came in the case of Ms. Jarrett. She seemed as if she had been waiting
for us to call her to do an interview about her experience. We had to rush
through the closed-ended survey questions because she was so eager to
tell her story. Ms. Jarrett was also a foster mother and was raising three
adopted girls. She listed this role as her full-time job, one from which she
reported earning $10,000 to 20,000 a year, an income below the poverty line
for her family of four. We did the interview in the local public library, and
all three of the girls checked out books before they departed. Chantell, the
daughter heading to high school, was a special education student with
visual and physical impairments. When Chicago Public Schools closed
the local elementary school a few years earlier, Chantell and one of her
sisters were sent to John Adams Elementary in a neighborhood several
miles away, but were provided free bus transportation. John Adams
Elementary fed into Adams High School, and Ms. Jarrett was sure that
she had finalized all the paperwork for Chantell to continue there. Then
she found out otherwise. This is Ms. Jarrett's story:

> The Board of Education closed Tubman Elementary School and they gave
> us a list to pick out five schools. They put her over there [at John Adams
> Elementary], I didn't. And I liked it, because where she was, well, I liked
> Tubman too. [And now] Tubman [is] back open as a charter school and they

ain't takin' no further than the fifth grade, fourth grade. That was a slap in the face, too. And I went, put my baby girl on the list. They said they was going to take the kids from the neighborhood first, but it hasn't happened. Tubman is a nice school. They renovated it. I saw 'em renovating it. It took two or three years. It's air-conditioned. She has asthma. I don't know what they doin'. But anyway, when they closed the school, they opened the school back up, from first through fourth grade. And then this year it's gonna go to fifth and next year it'll go to sixth. That's the way they doing the charter schools. So that slapped us in the face there.

I thought about John Adams [High School] because I knew that the [school] bus was going there and it'd been just good for us. 'Cause all I'd have to do is watch them to the corner and wait for the bus in the evening. And that was really good for me, with my age and everything. And safety. 'Cause I've been had Chantell ever since she was eighteen months old. And I've had to carry her back and forth. So, the last three years [with free school bus transportation] have been pretty easy on me.

Well, in December they had told me that in January they was going to sign Chantell up for John Adams [High School], which is right next door to the elementary. They have a lot more security there. I go over there a lot. Because if she get sick or somethin' I drive over there and I know that there is a lot more security there. So, they sent for me, and we set down and we picked out all the classes. Me and Miss Farkas decided what subjects she would take and put it on paper. Because she told me that the children out of eighth grade that were going to John Adams would be enrolled in January, so I went in January like she told me. And we did all the papers, had all the classes. And then she gave, after the graduation, they gave me the transfer into the Adams [High] School.

So, I got a transfer, so I could really take her over there.

But [then I find out that] she's in high school and I don't think they bus high school kids. But there's a bus coming to pick up the younger sister every morning, so she could have rode and came back with her. They payin' a lot of money for this bus so why can't she use this bus? And it's not a small bus, it's a large bus. Three children riding that bus over there everyday. Why Chantell couldn't have went on that bus and come back? She's special ed. [The Adams High School representative] told me she would let me know by the middle of August about the transportation, so I thought it was a done deal.

Then up pops this letter. On the 20th [of July], I got a letter that she had been sent over to Neighborhood High. So, I don't know who pulled that off. I thought it was a done deal. It burned me up. I think that the person that said they was going to send me that letter in August [about transportation to John Adams] is not going to send me that letter. They just took it upon theirselves to put me on over at Neighborhood after they gave me the transfer. And I got that transfer. Matter fact they didn't give me one transfer, they gave me two. They gave me two slips that said she would be transferred into [John Adams]. I felt good about [my decision] until they did what they did to me. And it made me very very [pause] . . . it hurt me. How they just can buck the system? See, 'cause, at that school . . . [pause] it was just . . .

[pause] my two little black girls and two more. I think they just did what they wanted to do. That's what it made me feel.

One reason I don't [pause] . . . We had a lot of trouble at Neighborhood. In this area, is high crime. My neighbor said—she's been in the neighborhood much longer than I have—and she said that she didn't think that Neighborhood would be a good school for Chantell 'cause it's such a rough school. And I do know there are some things that have happened at the school. I know a child that's got killed in a class at that school. And a little girl that got shot last year went to that school. And I know in the evening time the police have to come along 'cause they just crowd and fight so much. But I'm gonna take her and pick her up. But I don't know how close I'm gonna be able to get in 'cause the police surrounds it. So I'll probably have to walk on feet to get her back to the car. That's how it is. 'Cause a lot of evenings they, oh they fight terrible. And they be forty or fifty of them. And the police, they block it off every evening. So I seen that with my own eyes. This was one reason that I didn't want her to go 'round there. So that's why I was [pause] . . . and I thought it was a done deal. But somebody, looked like someone stabbed me in the back.

My next steps is to see why they did what they did and I got to talk to [the CPS] Transportation [Department]. I mean you see a lotta buses running back and forth and that just mean they could get our kids in a better school that's a little closer. And, now if Transportation don't let her ride that bus, then I have no choice [but Neighborhood High]. She got to go to school.

In the post-interview notes with Ms. Jarrett we wrote: "After the interview, I encouraged Ms. Jarrett not to give up on getting her daughter into Adams. It all sounded very shady." Ms. Jarrett's story was by far the most vexing. Even when she seemed to do all the right things, she still ended up with what she felt was a bad and inexplicable outcome.

Ms. Jarrett's case illustrates that when parents choose they are motivated as much by push factors from the neighborhood school as by pull factors to a different receiving school. Pulling her to Adams were good security—aligning with parents' desires to protect—and convenient transportation, which helped her juggle her three daughters' schedules and her own limited mobility. She also took academics seriously. She considered a selective enrollment school, but "Chantell's math score wasn't high enough" to get in. "I think the better the school the more she could excel," Ms. Jarrett commented with some disappointment because she felt that really good options were not available. Yet it was the push away from Neighborhood High—the protection role—that really motivated Ms. Jarrett. Because she did not have any countervailing positive experiences with Neighborhood High—as did Ms. Jarvis in the first portrait— push factors motivated her to such an extent that looking forward entailed figuring out how to avoid sending Chantell to Neighborhood High.

Ms. Jarrett's case provides a good bridge to the portrait of a Charter High parent because many Charter High parents had a similar "no way" stance toward Neighborhood High because of the violence. The portrait of a Charter High parent below illustrates these strong push factors, and adds to them pull factors of Charter High.

Ms. Webb and Her Son Aries

Diversity among the interviews with Neighborhood High parents was considerable, but the Charter High parent interviews quickly began to sound like a broken record. Overall, the families all started the process in the early fall of their child's eighth-grade year, and they all exhibited an aversion to neighborhood public schools, an attraction to selective enrollment schools, a strong consideration of Catholic schools but with serious financial barriers, and delight in finding Charter High as an attractive alternative.

The conversation with Ms. Webb about her son Aries exemplifies these threads. Ms. Webb was a single mother of five children who, with her petite stature, lip ring, and somewhat nervous demeanor, seemed young enough to be going to high school herself. Aries, the oldest, had inherited her small stature, which was something that Ms. Webb thought about when choosing a high school. She said, "Like me, he's kinda small for his age. I call him anorexic because he's so skinny. I tease him. But you know we just small people. But I don't want him to feel intimidated everyday when he going to school or something, you know. I just want him to be somewhere he feel comfortable." Ms. Webb worked full time in construction, earning between $30,000 to 40,000 a year. She lived only a few blocks from Charter High, but hadn't heard anything about it until a teacher at her son's elementary school gave her information. As she explains, this information was all she needed to make her decision.

> The year goes by so fast. Before you know, it's that time. So gotta start thinking about it [in eighth grade]. Well I probably should've been thinking about it in the 7th grade but . . . Well, at first I was kinda . . . what would I say? . . . not optimistic. Because I didn't know about Charter High at first. So I was just looking at the schools that I might wanna consider out of, you know, the lesser of the evils. Because I didn't like any of 'em. I didn't want him at none of those schools. I mean some of 'em was alright. But, like I said, the majority of the list either is in a terrible neighborhood where I risk my son getting shot or stabbed or something on a daily basis, which is unnecessary. Or he going somewhere to a zoo where it's a bunch of kids running everything and he's not gonna learn anything. I just couldn't have it. But I'm like, well outta these I have to pick something.
>
> I was just looking for a place where he can be safe, you know. Not have to worry about getting in altercations in the classroom or anywhere else in the school or even on the school grounds. Anywhere for that matter. And I want him to be somewhere that he can learn. You know, where the environment is controlled. Where the teachers are running the show and

not the students. You know, I go into his elementary school, those kids are ridiculous, you know. Everybody doing their own thing. The teacher's sitting there like, "Oh, I'm just waiting for 2:35 or whenever they go home and I just want my money," you know. They just there for a check, some of 'em. And that's not what I want. I want, you know, somebody that's gonna teach 'em something. And I want him to sit there and learn whatever it is they trying to teach him. And a lot of these schools, they're not doing that.

Like I say, I went to Eleanor Roosevelt [Selective Enrollment School], so I was trying to steer him that way. And he seemed to be alright with it until we found out about Charter High. And then I could see in his face that it was something that he really wanted. And after I heard more about it, it sounded like a good place for him to be. He wasn't really excited about any other school except Charter High. But, like I said, he wasn't resistant to the idea of going to Eleanor Roosevelt before we heard about Charter High. So had that not been an option I think I would've steered him that way. Or tried to anyway.

[The teacher] was the one who had mentioned Charter High. I didn't know anything about it. And he was telling me, "Well it's a new school, you know. It's gonna be up and coming and it's nice and I think it'd be a nice environment for your child." Like I said, the elementary school that he just came out of was like a zoo. [The teacher] was like, "Your child is not like the rest of these kids in here and he don't need to be around this. So, you know, we need to get him into somewhere where, you know, he can be productive and tune out all this madness and don't have to be bothered with it." So once he told me that, then that's when we started pursuing it.

What I wasn't expecting was the way Charter High operates. Because, like I said, you can't get their application to their school from the elementary school or whatever. A lot of the other schools he applied to, he came home with the application from the counselor. You can't get Charter High's application from your counselor; you have to go to one of their informational sessions to get an application. So I wasn't expecting that. But it didn't deter me either. I just got on over there and did what I had to do. And then, like I said, when they had the Open House and I went to that, then they reinforced everything [the teacher] said and more.

Because I think they do more screening as far as the children that they're letting in. And all of those children are like basically geared toward the same thing. You don't have, say, twenty-five out of thirty students that don't wanna learn nothing, don't wanna do nothing, and have five over here that's struggling to get some peace and quiet so they can hear the teacher and learn something, you know. So I think they are better than just the average regular Chicago Public School. So then I was really like, yeah, this is where he going. He gonna be right here, if they let him in. Because you know they got they students through the lottery. So I just had my fingers crossed that they would pull his name out so that he could be one of those 160.

It was exciting for me to see my son excited because I didn't think he would be, but he is. Because I got a couple of other kids. They're not that enthused about school at all. But I feel good about Charter High. I really do.

Looking at my son with his little uniform on going to school, yay! And he likes it. So he's happy. I'm happy.

Ms. Webb's story conveys a number of things that were shared across Charter High parents: in making sense of schools, nearly all had a negative appraisal of neighborhood Chicago Public Schools, especially as it related to their charge to protect their children. They were attracted to the structure of Charter High, which in their view facilitated educational goals rather than thwarting them. For example, few Neighborhood High parents voiced expectations (or aspirations) that their children would attend college, whereas references to a college preparatory curriculum and college as the end goal were very common among Charter High parents. One mother reported her son's excitement after an information session with a Charter High representative: "When Mark came home one day from school he was like, 'Mama, mama, this man, Mr. Jones, from Charter High, he cool. He cool just like my uncles. He say I can get in college. Man, they gonna prep me for college when I'm going to high school!'"

Finally, like Ms. Webb, each Charter High parent looked forward with optimism. They voiced very high satisfaction with their decision, and relief at having been chosen, frequently citing divine intervention, which Neighborhood High parents never did. For example, one parent said: "Charter High came out for recruitment and that opened the door for other options. Thank you, Jesus!" High rates of satisfaction among Charter High parents were partially the result of the strong push away from neighborhood schools, especially given that parents were already elated even though the school year had not yet begun. In other words, for these parents anything but the neighborhood public school would have made them more content. However, although parent satisfaction may be a goal of the school choice process, it should not be confused with an ultimate outcome. Clearly, the stated satisfaction of 44 percent of Neighborhood High parents does not absolve the school of the mandate to increase graduation rates or improve reading scores. School districts and other proponents tout school choice as a means to promote student growth, and on that measure the results are not uniformly positive.

On the whole, although both sets of parents went through similar motions, Charter High parents differed significantly from Neighborhood High parents, both on the demographic and resource characteristics represented in tables 8.1 and 8.3 and more qualitatively in their absolute rejection of traditional public schools on safety grounds and their emphasis on a college preparatory curriculum. This does not make Charter High parents better or more deserving of a good school for their children. Instead, it reflects different experiences and inputs that shape how Charter and Neighborhood High parents made sense of what was possible (see chapter 5, this volume), and their greater ability to play the choice game to ensure a positive outcome. But should access to a good and safe school depend on one's ability to choose well? We turn to this question and a summary of the findings in the following discussion and conclusion.

Discussion and Conclusion

In this chapter we have shown that despite a diversity of individual experiences and despite ending up in two quite different school settings, both sets of parents shared a similar set of actions in making a decision about high school for their children. As best they could, they made sense of the types and characteristics of high schools that existed in CPS and beyond; they prioritized their responsibilities to educate and protect their children; they considered schools while juggling the everyday tasks of life under significant financial and other resource constraints; they made a choice—whether actively, passively, or even against their will—to enroll their child in a high school; and then they looked forward to the next four years. Although our research focused on urban African American low-income parents within the public school system, this framework is one that could be used for comparing choice experiences across race, class, and place. Future research could extend our study by comparing parents' effectiveness and ease or difficulty in making sense of the school offerings, or by observing how much or little help parents have with juggling common family responsibilities and thus how much time and energy they can invest in evaluating schools. On juggling, Shelley Kimelberg (see chapter 7, this volume) writes about the "safety net of financial, human, and cultural capital" that the middle-class parents she interviewed could activate to help them make decisions or to change course in the event of a bad decision. Charter and Neighborhood High parents were not completely without such capacities or social support, but the uncertainties of work, income, transportation, safety, and poor health often turned everyday tasks into emergencies. Moreover, they had fewer backup options. Charter High mother Ms. Webb described her initial reading of the Chicago school landscape as choosing between the "lesser of evils." Given all the risks they juggled in the other arenas of their lives, the parents in our research were motivated to minimize risk in choosing a school.

The six action verbs help to generally characterize what parents did, but we also report specific findings about information and communication problems. We find compelling evidence that parents in CPS do not have clear information from the district about what high schools are available to their children. Although parents made considerable use of personal networks, CPS did not make official sources of information—mainly guidance counselors, the CPS website, the High Schools Book or the High School Fair—ubiquitous or accessible to the point that a majority of parents felt well informed. Also, information was sometimes dispersed. As

Ms. Webb reported, applications for Charter High were available only through the school itself, which was the case for several charter and non-charter choice schools. Finally, the high-stakes testing regime caused parents to fixate on their children's test scores as determinative for where they could go to school. "Well, I wanted her to go to a good school [like] Humphrey [High School]," Ms. Carter said about her plans for Jenice. "But, like I say, she didn't qualify for Humphrey." Both students and schools are labeled based on their test scores; students are tracked into advanced or remedial classes and schools are publicized as high-performing or denigrated for the opposite. When it is time to decide on a high school, parents have received so much information about the importance of test scores that they believe that good schools must accept only good (that is, high-testing) students. Although it is true that many CPS schools select students based on performance, charter schools and many magnet programs and small schools are open to students of all aptitudes.

Information is closely tied with communication. The CPS High Schools Book is an inch thick, but the presence of information does not ensure its successful communication. Lori Delale-O'Connor (2010) finds that the content is appropriate for readers at the level of a sophomore in college, quite above the educational attainment of the parents in our sample. As Elliot Weininger (chapter 9, this volume) shows, even upper-middle-class parents need spreadsheets and Web bookmarks and priority rankings to organize and process the available information about schools. Moreover, successful communication of the information often assumes access to the Internet or perhaps an automobile, which at least two-thirds of the parents we interviewed did not have. Overall, the problem for Charter High and especially Neighborhood High parents was a combination of too much information and too little communication. Too much information made it much more efficient for parents to depend on their experiences, as Ms. Jarvis did in putting her daughter Dee in Neighborhood High, and often meant that they needed help in processing the volume of information, as did Ms. Carter when she sought out the school guidance counselor. Too little communication resulted from an overextended, underfunded public school system, for which parents and children paid the price. As Ms. Jarrett recounted, after months of face-to-face communication, "up pops this letter" that undermined all of her efforts to participate in the school choice process that CPS promoted. Roughly one in seven parents reported getting no response from one or more of the schools to which they applied. Some of the failed communication could be because of high levels of residential mobility among families, but this is the reality to which CPS must respond with adequate systems and capacity. Even though all Charter High parents obviously heard back from that school, one mother echoed the frustration that many Neighborhood High parents expressed. She stated, "I'd send the application out and I wouldn't hear nothing. So it's like you would have to do all this follow up, calling around to five different schools." In the absence of a working system of communication, choice for many parents felt like they were yelling into the wind.

What are the possible educational policy responses to the challenges of information and communication that these parents raised as they struggled to make sense of, juggle, and navigate the school choice process? Of course there are several: Districts could create more and better school options from which parents and students could choose. Districts could improve parents' and students' access to information and better communicate content so that families have accurate details and feel more empowered to make good choices. Districts could—and must, if parents are increasingly charged with shopping for schools—be more responsive to inquiries, applications, and arrangements that parents make with schools and figure out how to stay in touch with families who move a lot or are homeless. In general, districts would need to invest significantly in improving what Richard Thaler and Cass Sunstein (2008, 6) call "choice architecture," which "alters people's behaviors in a predictable way without forbidding any options" and is essential for nudging people in the direction of good choices.

However, we must also consider alternatives to choice. We could scrap the idea of choice altogether as inappropriate in the arena of education—and "unlikely to provide the same quality choices as residential choice offers to middle- and upper-income families" (chapter 10, this volume)—and instead move from a choice to a "rights" paradigm (Perry et al. 2010). Whereas choice always depends entirely on the circumstances of individuals (knowledge, preferences, constraints, resources, and so on), rights are ideally granted without respect for individual circumstances. Hence, ensuring the quality of a right rests with the state and not with the citizen. In the case of schools, a rights paradigm would require uniformly good public schools. Of course the definition of a good school and the strategies to get there are debatable (Ladd and Loeb 2013); defining and evaluating school quality is complicated and contentious, even for experts (Favero and Meier 2013). Yet even if we have not created the precise formula to lift all students to proficiency, much less mastery, in basic academic skills, there are nonetheless many successful models that can be followed and best practices that can be executed (Payne 2008). Even proponents of choice like Thaler and Sunstein argue that "setting the best possible defaults" (2008, 35) is crucial for attaining desired social outcomes. If the default schools where children are assigned are excellent, then choice is gravy. The rights model creates an urgency to focus on and ensure the best defaults for all students in all schools, so that when parents are assigned to schools, as many Neighborhood High parents were, that assignment is a safe one in which their child will learn. No more high-stakes choosing, just high-quality schools.

Notes

1. It is telling that CPS itself uses the label "Approximate number of schools" in its listing of school types (see Chicago Public Schools 2013b). The lack of specificity and clarity at the organizational level engenders confusion among parents.

2. Twenty-five percent of the people we interviewed were not the mother or father of the student who would be entering high school. These guardians included grandparents, foster parents, aunts, and older siblings. We use *parent* throughout this chapter when referring in the abstract to all of the interviewees, but we identify the relationship of the interviewee to the student when using specific quotes.

3. Table 8.1 addresses the question, do choice programs skim the most advantaged students in the school district (Levin 1998)? Despite considerable research that choice schools serve similar or higher proportions of low-income and minority children as traditional public schools, evidence also indicates that the parents of children in choice schools have higher educational attainment than comparison parents (for a review, see Lacireno-Paquet et al. 2002; also see Martinez, Thomas, and Kemerer 1994), and higher levels of involvement (Bifulco, Ladd, and Ross 2009), but that parental differences are not so great so as to cause large effects on student achievement (Altonji, Huang, and Taber 2010; Walsh 2009).

4. It is not that all of the parents who were assigned to Neighborhood High were either ambivalent or dissatisfied, nor that all of the parents who chose Neighborhood High were satisfied. Instead, in a number of cases the assignment was welcome, especially after a pleasant visit to the school and conversation with the principal. In other instances, people had chosen Neighborhood High, but then had regrets and were thus ambivalent.

5. The interviews also revealed that Charter High parents were much more insiders to the public school bureaucracy. None of the Neighborhood High parents had family or friendship ties to employees in downtown CPS offices and in schools, but many Charter High parents reported such connections, which they used to help them maneuver the choice process. One Charter High grandmother got the help of her daughter (the student's aunt) who worked for CPS. She reported, "And my daughter works for the Board of Education. She's an administrative assistant. She was actually getting information from different teachers. She'd be reading some things [and would say], 'Ma, you might be interested, might be impressed with this. Read this.' And then when she got it, we all sat down and we read it."

6. This is not true in all cities but in Chicago the vast majority of schooling is organized into kindergarten through eighth grade "grammar schools" and ninth through twelfth grade "high schools." Middle schools, junior high schools, or combined middle and high schools are not common organizational forms in Chicago.

7. None of these portraits represents the roughly 38 percent of Neighborhood High parents who put forth little effort in the process, gathered little information and just assumed their child would go to Neighborhood High. They saw themselves as choosing Neighborhood High by not objecting to what would happen automatically anyway. In this sense, they were not active choosers, but passive choosers. This position is illustrated in the words of one mother who said, "Oh, I didn't think there was very much I had to do because I went through it with my other child. So I already knew what I had to do so I really kinda figured he was gonna go to Neighborhood High anyway. So it really wasn't much that I really had to do to do it." Some of these parents were satisfied with the outcome and so are generally reflected in the comments of the first parent testimony presented in this section.

References

Altonji, Joseph G., Ching-I Huang, and Christopher R. Taber. 2010. "Estimating the Cream Skimming Effect of School Choice." *NBER* working paper no. 16579. Cambridge, Mass.: National Bureau of Economic Research.

Bell, Courtney. 2009. "All Choices Created Equal? The Role of Choice Sets in the Selection of Schools." *Peabody Education Journal* 84(2): 191–208.

Bifulco, Robert, Helen Ladd, and Stephen Ross. 2009. "The Effects of Public School Choice on Those Left Behind: Evidence from Durham, North Carolina." *Peabody Journal of Education* 84(2): 130–49.

Brenner, Neil, and Nik Theodore. 2002. *Spaces of Neoliberalism.* Malden, Mass.: Blackwell.

Center for Research on Educational Outcomes. 2013. *National Charter School Study.* http://credo.stanford.edu/documents/NCSS_2013_Final_Draft.pdf (accessed Nov. 25, 2013).

Chubb, John, and Terry Moe. 1990. *Politics, Markets, and America's Schools.* Washington, D.C.: Brookings Institution Press.

Chicago Public Schools. 2013a. "Enroll in a School." Available at: http://www.cps.edu/Schools/Enroll_in_a_school/Pages/Enrollinaschool.aspx (accessed November 10, 2013).

———. 2013b. "High School Types." Available at: http://www.cps.edu/Schools/High_schools/Pages/Highschooltypes.aspx (accessed April 10, 2013).

Cooper, Camille Wilson. 2005. "School Choice and the Standpoint of African American Mothers: Considering the Power of Positionality." *Journal of Negro Education* 74(2): 174–89.

Cowan Institute. 2010. *The State of Public Education in New Orleans Five Years after Hurricane Katrina.* New Orleans, La.: Tulane University. Available at: http://www.coweninstitute.com/wp-content/uploads/2010/07/katrina-book.final_.CIpageSmaller.pdf (accessed September 9, 2013).

Cucchiara, Maia. 2013. *Marketing Schools, Marketing Cities: Who Wins and Who Loses When Schools Become Urban Amenities.* Chicago: University of Chicago Press.

Cullen, Julie, Brian Jacob, and Steven Levitt. 2006. "The Effect of School Choice on Student Outcomes: Evidence from Randomized Lotteries." *Econometrica* 74(5): 1191–230.

Delale-O'Connor, Lori. 2010. "Parents and Public School Choice: Information, Demand, and Social Stratification." Paper presented at the American Educational Research Association Annual Meeting. Denver, Colorado (May 1, 2010).

DeLuca, Stefanie, and Elizabeth Dayton. 2009. "Switching Social Contexts: The Effects of Housing Mobility and School Choice Programs on Youth Outcomes." *Annual Review of Sociology* 35:457–91.

DeLuca, Stefanie, and Peter Rosenblatt. 2010. "Does Moving to Better Neighborhoods Lead to Better Schooling Opportunities? Parental School Choice in an Experimental Housing Voucher Program." *Teachers College Record* 112(5): 1441–489.

Deming, David J., Justine S. Hastings, Thomas J. Kane, and Douglas O. Staiger. Forthcoming. "School Choice, School Quality, and Postsecondary Attainment." *American Economic Review.*

Favero, Nathan, and Kenneth J. Meier. 2013. "Evaluating Urban Public Schools: Parents, Teachers, and State Assessments." *Public Administration Review* 73(3): 401–12.

Fuller, Bruce, Richard Elmore, and Gary Orfield. 1996. "Policy-Making in the Dark: Illuminating the School Choice Debate." In *Who Chooses? Who Loses?: Culture, Institutions, and the Unequal Effects of School Choice,* edited by Bruce Fuller and Richard F. Elmore with Gary Orfield. New York: Teachers College Press.

Gleason, Phillip, Melissa Clark, Christina Tuttle, and Emily Dwoyer. 2010. *The Evaluation of Charter School Impacts. NCEE* no. 2010–4029. Washington: U.S. Department of Education.

Hanushek, Eric. 1994. *Making Schools Work: Improving Performance and Controlling Costs.* Washington, D.C.: Brookings Institution Press.

Henig, Jeffrey R. 2008. *Spin Cycle: How Research Is Used in Policy Debates: The Case of Charter Schools.* New York: Russell Sage Foundation.

Hochschild, Jennifer L. 1995. *Facing Up to the American Dream: Race, Class, and the Soul of the Nation.* Princeton, N.J.: Princeton University Press.

Jennings, Jennifer L. 2010. "School Choice or Schools' Choice? Managing in an Era of Accountability." *Sociology of Education* 83(3): 227–47.

Keels, Micere. 2013. "The Importance of Scaffolding the Transition: Unpacking the Null Effects of Relocating Poor Children into Nonpoor Neighborhoods." *American Educational Research Journal* 50(5): 991–1018. doi: 10.3102/0002831213497247.

Klinenberg, Eric. 2002. *Heatwave: A Social Autopsy of Disaster in Chicago.* Chicago: University of Chicago Press.

Lacireno-Paquet, Natalie, Thomas Holyoke, Michele Moser, and Jeffrey Henig. 2002. "Creaming Versus Cropping: Charter School Enrollment Practices in Response to Market Incentives." *Educational Evaluation and Policy Analysis* 24(2): 145–58.

Ladd, Helen, and Susanna Loeb. 2013. "The Challenges of Measuring School Quality: Implications for Educational Equity." In *Education, Justice, and Democracy,* edited by Danielle Allen and Rob Reich. Chicago: University of Chicago Press.

Levin, Henry. 1998. "Educational Vouchers: Effectiveness, Choice, and Costs." *Journal of Policy Analysis and Management* 17(3): 373–92.

Lipman, Pauline. 2004. *High Stakes Education: Inequality, Globalization, and Urban School Reform.* New York: RoutledgeFalmer.

Lipman, Pauline, and Nathan Haines. 2007. "From Accountability to Privatization and African American Exclusion Chicago's 'Renaissance 2010.'" *Educational Policy* 21(3): 471–502.

Martinez, Valerie, Kay Thomas, and Frank Kemerer. 1994. "Who Chooses and Why: A Look at Five School Choice Plans." *Phi Delta Kappan* 75(9): 307–11.

Neild, Ruth Curran. 2005. "Parental Management of School Choice in a Large Urban District." *Urban Education* 40(3): 270–97.

Pattillo, Mary. 2007. *Black on the Block: The Politics of Race and Class in the City.* Chicago: University of Chicago Press.

Payne, Charles M. 2008. *So Much Reform, So Little Change: The Persistence of Failure in Urban Schools.* Cambridge, Mass.: Harvard Education Press.

Pedroni, Thomas C. 2005. "Market Movements and the Dispossessed: Race, Identity, and Subaltern Agency Among Black Women Voucher Advocates." *Urban Review* 37(2): 83–105.

Perry, Theresa, Robert P. Moses, Joan T. Wynne, Ernesto Cortés Jr., and Lisa Delpit. 2010. *Quality Education as a Constitutional Right.* Boston, Mass.: Beacon Press.

Popkin, Susan J., Laura E. Harris, and Mary K. Cunningham. 2002. "Families in Transition: A Qualitative Analysis of the MTO Experience." Washington: U.S. Department of Housing and Urban Development.

Prasad, Monica. 2006. *The Politics of Free Markets: The Rise of Neoliberal Economic Policies in Britain, France, Germany, and the United States.* Chicago: University of Chicago Press.

Rouse, Cecilia, and Lisa Barrow. 2009. "School Vouchers and Student Achievement: Recent Evidence and Remaining Questions." *Annual Review of Economics* 1(1): 17–42.

Sanbonmatsu, Lisa, Jeffrey R. Kling, Greg J. Duncan, and Jeanne Brooks-Gunn. 2006. "Neighborhoods and Academic Achievement: Results from the Moving to Opportunity Experiment." *Journal of Human Resources* 41(4): 649–91.

Schneider, Mark, Paul Teske, and Melissa Marschall. 2000. *Choosing Schools: Consumer Choice and the Quality of American Schools.* Princeton, N.J.: Princeton University Press.

Thaler, Richard H., and Cass R. Sunstein. 2008. *Nudge: Improving Decisions About Health, Wealth, and Happiness.* New Haven, Conn.: Yale University Press.

Walsh, Patrick. 2009. "Effects of School Choice on the Margin: The Cream Is Already Skimmed." *Economics of Education Review* 28(2): 227–36.

═ Chapter 9 ═

School Choice in an Urban Setting

ELLIOT B. WEININGER

For the majority of families in the United States, residential location governs access to schools. Thus, within the broad parameters of federal and state law, the characteristics of the schools children attend are determined by the local jurisdiction in which they live—in other words, the choice of a particular home is simultaneously the choice of a particular set of schools. Of course, growing dissatisfaction on the part of many families with neighborhood public schools has led to the partial erosion of this system: in addition to the long-standing private school sector, we now have an increasing number of hybrid institutions, in the form of charter and magnet schools, as well as district-level policies permitting out-of-catchment attendance. These changes are notable precisely because they seek to uncouple attendance from residential location. Instead, children can attend only if their parents take the step of applying to a particular school.

Whether it takes place via the real estate market or via an application process, the key characteristic of the matching of children to schools is choice. Both from a policy perspective and a social scientific one, parents are viewed as having made an affirmative choice that results in their children attending particular schools.

Recent educational policy has codified the importance of choice by requiring not only that all public schools routinely undergo high-stakes assessments, but also that the results of these assessments be publicized. The assumption underlying this requirement is that well-informed parents will be able to make knowledgeable decisions about which schools their children should attend, and in doing so, function as a check on school quality. In other words, it is assumed that by using high-quality, objective information on school performance, parents will be able to make educational choices for their children in a way that effectively channels their demand for educational services. Thus, as chapter 8 richly documents, recent policy confronts parents with an imperative: research.

The emergence of the Internet has facilitated this policy shift. School districts now frequently publicize assessment results—broken out by school and by demographic groups within schools—directly on their Web pages. Moreover, a number of consumer-oriented websites (such as Greatschools.org and Schooldiggers.com) have emerged that aggregate school and district-level data on demographics, funding, and test performance, and present them in easy-to-digest form. Additionally, media publications that evaluate school quality on either a regional or national basis using test score data now make their results available online as well (most famously, the *U.S. News and World Report* ranking of high school quality). The confluence of a federal mandate to publicize assessment results with a medium for freely disseminating information implies that a "consumer" interested in "school shopping" now finds herself with easy access to large quantities of information on "school quality".

In this chapter, I investigate the various sources of information on school quality that parents actually draw on when choosing schools for their children, focusing, in particular, on publicly available performance data. I use a set of in-depth interviews with parents of young children who currently reside in a large city in the northeast. This city has numerous charter and private schools, as well as an extensive system of neighborhood schools. The interviews contain detailed information on how children in these families came to attend their current schools—whether via neighborhood assignment or some kind of choice process. Based on descriptions of this process, I examine the use of No Child Left Behind (NCLB) "report cards" and consumer-friendly rankings based on these data. I also consider the role of performance data in parents' decision making vis-à-vis other sources of information—primarily, word-of-mouth recommendations from trusted network members (see Holme 2002; Neild 2005), as well as school visits and online parent testimonials.

To preview my results, I find that concerns about schools are ubiquitous among this sample of urban parents, and that none report that they were indifferent. Parents of all backgrounds expressed a great deal of anxiety over the quality and safety of neighborhood schools. Moreover, parents of all backgrounds actively considered alternatives, including charter schools and out-of-catchment schools; and some—including some working-class parents—went so far as to change residences within the city to escape an undesirable school. In doing so, they often relied on informal networks to gather information that could be used to guide their decision making.

Nevertheless, the use of performance data was almost entirely restricted to middle-class and upper-middle-class parents. In my sample, it was only these parents who spent large amounts of time scouring district websites or Greatschools.org, assembling spreadsheets, and researching school quality. Indeed, though variation was substantial in the importance ascribed to test scores, no one in these groups was wholly oblivious. Furthermore, variation in the weight placed on performance data appeared to be inversely associated with reliance on network ties: parents who did not find their network ties to be a useful source of information on schools relied much more heavily on this type of data. This difference appeared to be associated with race, albeit loosely.

Among working-class respondents, by contrast, there was almost no discussion of performance data in the interviews, and information on school quality came almost exclusively through network contacts. Given that one of the explicit purposes of NCLB-mandated reporting was to enable these parents to become more effective school "shoppers," this finding raises a number of issues, which I take up in the conclusion.

Parents, Students, and Choice

The emphasis on local control in public education has a long and deep history in the United States. Nevertheless, the realization of this value through school systems built around residential matching of children to schools—especially when coupled with local funding—contains potential inequities that are easily recognized. Thus, since at least the 1950s, often-heated debates have centered on whether and how to break the system of residential assignment. These debates intensified during the 1980s and 1990s, with a number of influential arguments about school choice finding a receptive public audience.

While there is no need to recapitulate the history of these debates, a few key points are germane. Most choice arguments revolved around the idea that residential assignment created a kind of monopoly, with students and their families as the captive audience of local educational organizations. The antidote was thus asserted to be competition: permitting students and their families to vote with their feet by exiting neighborhood schools—and take their funding with them—would pressure schools to increase the quality of their services or face the prospect of losing their "clientele."

The construal of students and their families as quasi-consumers was, for some participants, a matter of assumption. For many others, however, it was an empirical hypothesis that warranted testing. Indeed, longstanding research on both market consumption and voting suggested that the tendency to systematically gather information on alternative options was both relatively rare and heavily conditioned by factors such as social class and educational attainment. Evidence quickly emerged suggesting that this might be the case with regard to schools, as well.

Thus, for example, influential work by Mark Schneider, Paul Teske, and Melissa Marschall (2000) reported that highly educated parents relied primarily on social networks—generally composed of other highly educated individuals—when searching for information about schools; their less educated counterparts, by contrast, relied on formal sources—such as media reports—to the extent that they sought to gather this type of information. The researchers found, further, that in general, parents of all backgrounds did not have very accurate information about the schools their children currently attended—even if they resided in a community that had a choice program in place. They thus concluded that "school districts . . . need to make a determined and sustained efforts to provide the opportunity for all parents to gather useful information. [W]ithout outreach efforts by school districts, relatively higher socioeconomic status and more involved parents may be the ones to find the information they need to make good choices (163)."

The school report cards mandated by NCLB are, of course, intended to remedy these kinds of issues, and may be viewed as part of a wider trend to enable market-like forces to affect the production or delivery of nonmarket goods (see Coe 2003). The accountability provisions of the law explicitly require that school-level data on student performance be made "widely available through public means, such as posting on the Internet, distribution to the media, and distribution through public agencies" (U.S. Department of Education 2001). In compliance with the law, all states now provide access to NCLB report cards over the Web; additionally, school districts—and sometimes individual schools—often make performance data available directly on their websites.

Nevertheless, as researchers have noted (Garcia 2011), NCLB report cards are highly complicated, in large part because the performance data they are based on is subject to various statistical adjustments. This potentially blunts their salience for parents. However, a variety of nongovernmental websites have recently emerged whose stated purpose is to help parents select schools for their children. Typically, these websites use NCLB test score data, sometimes in combination with demographic information, to construct simplified "quality ratings" that are then assigned to schools.

In the data I report on, the most commonly referenced of these websites is Greatschools.org. This site provides users with easy access to information on nearly all K–12 schools in the country. For public schools, the site includes a single rating (on a scale of one to ten) that is prominently displayed toward the top of each school's page in a large orange circle. (The ratings represent deciles of school-level proficiency rates on NCLB tests.) Also presented are test score results for various subgroups (for example, grade, subject area, and student group), information on student demographic characteristics, and ratings (on a scale of one to five stars) and testimonials from parents and students.

Research on the general question of whether and how parents react to publicized school performance data has been inconclusive. On the one hand, studies going back to at least Sandra Black (1999)—which predates NCLB—have shown that home prices exhibit substantial sensitivity to the test scores of the schools they are zoned to, suggesting that buyers and sellers have enough information to move prices (see also Figlio and Lucas 2004). Moreover, a study of lower income parents in Milwaukee and Washington, D.C.—both cities with long-established choice systems that include vouchers—by Paul Teske, Jody Fitzpatrick, and Gabriel Kaplan that uses survey data to assess information gathering practices reports that respondents are "remarkably satisfied, well-informed, and active information seekers" (2006, 979). Additionally, some research indicates that the publication of student performance data can have a significant effect on low-income parents' beliefs about the quality of their children's schools, triggering school exit in the case of institutions with weak records (Friesen et al. 2012). On the other hand, however, several studies have noted very low rates of uptake of the NCLB transfer provisions among eligible parents (Howell 2006; Mickelson and Southworth 2005). Furthermore, recent research by Anna Rhodes and Stefanie DeLuca (chapter 5 this volume; see also DeLuca and Rosenblatt 2010) establishes that insofar as schooling considerations enter into the residential decision-making calculus of low-income parents, it is often non-academic characteristics of schools that receive the most weight. And, researchers in England have concluded that choice programs tend to be inherently class-biased, since they presume cultural capacities that are closely class linked (Gewirtz, Ball, and Bowe 1995; see also Henig 1994; Reay and Ball 1997).

In this chapter, I seek to contribute to these discussions by examining parents' use of school performance data in the process of school choice. I consider whether the use of these data vary across lines of class and race, and investigate what the parents who report using this information actually do with it—that is, how it factors into their decision making. I also look at how performance data relates to the other main source of information parents draw on when choosing schools: that provided by trusted network contacts.

The Setting

Data were collected in a large city in the northeastern part of the country. As part of the institutional review board (IRB) process, we committed to refraining from revealing the identity of the city. Unfortunately, this obligates us to provide a slightly imprecise description of the location.

Demographically, African Americans and whites are the largest groups by substantial margins. The city also has a significant number of Hispanic residents. The poverty rate is high, at well over 20 percent, and the proportion of adults with bachelor's degrees (or higher) is well below the national average. Housing type is approximately split between rental and owner occupied. The city is informally divided into a large number of neighborhoods with relatively distinct identities. As in most large, eastern cities, these neighborhoods tend to be highly segregated by both race and class, though some include a few gentrified areas.

The metropolitan school district is characterized by a long-standing set of neighborhood schools with established attendance zones. Substantially more than half of the students attending public schools qualify for free or reduced-price lunch. Moreover, more than half of public schools in the city failed to make adequate yearly progress (AYP) in a recent year. As is the case in many cities, the district has created a number of magnet schools, and more recently, a robust system of charter schools has evolved. Additionally, the city has long had a significant number of private schools, both religiously affiliated and unaffiliated. In addition to these alternatives, the public system also provides families with some options for exiting neighborhood schools. Per NCLB mandates, a student whose school fails to make AYP for two consecutive years is granted the opportunity to transfer to one that has met this criterion; additionally, the law also creates a transfer option for students whose schools are deemed dangerous. The school district also gives parents the option to apply for a transfer to an out-of-catchment school; slots in highly "popular" schools are assigned on the basis of a lottery. More than 25 percent of children in public elementary schools do not attend their neighborhood school. Importantly, the district maintains a website that makes available standardized test proficiency rates (broken out by grade and student group) for every school.

Methods and Data

In this chapter, I analyze a set of in-depth interviews carried out with parents of young children living in this city. The interviews were part of a larger project that examined the role schooling considerations play in parents' residential decision making. As such, it also included a large number of parents located in suburban districts; these interviews form the basis of chapter 6 in this volume.

The sampling matrix for the urban subsample of the project contained six cells, defined by social class (upper middle class, middle class, and working class) and race (African American and white). Social class was defined in terms of the educational requirements of respondents' jobs and the amount of autonomy they experienced in them. The upper middle class includes families in which at least one adult has a full-time job that requires highly complex, educationally certified (that is, postbaccalaureate) skills and also entails substantial autonomy (that is, freedom from direct supervision) in the course of his or her work. The middle class includes families in which no adult meets these criteria, but at least one is employed in a full-time job that requires relatively complex, educationally certified skills (that is, a bachelor's degree or higher); this job need not entail high levels of autonomy, however. (Thus, our sample folds a small number of families in which one parent has a master's degree into the middle-class category, on the grounds that he or she is closely supervised. Their occupations include social worker and insurance claims evaluator.) Working-class families are those in which no adult has a job requiring complex, educationally certified skills. The sample was restricted to African Americans and whites because these are largest racial-ethnic groups in the city, and practical constraints would have made it difficult to expand the scope of the sampling matrix.

We originally intended to interview parents whose eldest child was in kindergarten. However, because this did not prove feasible, we broadened the criteria to include families whose eldest child was between the ages of three and ten. The initial research subjects were recruited via day cares in the city. We made contact with day-care providers in different parts of the city, eventually securing permission to recruit from three organizations. In some cases, with the director's assistance, we sent letters to parents soliciting their participation; in others, we recruited parents at the day-care site directly during morning drop-off or afternoon pickup, giving parents a brief explanation of our project and providing them with our contact information. Those who contacted us were then screened to ensure that they met our sampling criteria, and the interviews were scheduled. Every time we conducted an interview, we also asked our subjects if they would provide us with contact information for other city residents who met our criteria and who might be willing to participate in the study, enabling us to snowball the sample. Certain cells of the sample design proved impossible to fill completely using this method (in particular, upper-middle-class African Americans), however, and we therefore relied on personal networks to locate additional participants. Respondents were given an honorarium of $50 in return for their participation.

Interviews were conducted face-to-face, usually in the respondent's home, and typically lasted from 90 to 120 minutes. In the vast majority of cases, we spoke with the children's mothers, although in two instances we spoke with the father, and in two cases both parents participated. We looked for emergent themes over the course of the data collection and adjusted the questionnaire to gather greater detail on key issues as we progressed. The interviews were audio-recorded and verbatim transcriptions were made. As we collected more data, a coding system was

Table 9.1   Sample Counts by Social Class and Race

	White	African American	Total
Upper middle class	7	6*	13
Middle class	6	7	13
Working class	6	9	15
Total	19	22	41

Source: Author's compilation.
*Includes one interracial family in which the husband is African American and the wife is white.

developed and applied to the transcripts by research assistants using the Atlas.ti. Table 9.1 presents the distribution of families broken out by class and race.

Results

Among the urban parents we spoke with, schools were a concern—and frequently a burning concern—for parents of all class backgrounds, both black and white. Of course, the source of these concerns varied, often encompassing issues of safety as well as school quality. Nevertheless, whatever the exact nature of their discontent with their neighborhood schools, nearly all of the city parents reported considering—and the majority actively investigated—alternative options at some point.

For all families, the school choice process was inevitably constrained by various factors. The most essential of these was transportation. Indeed, the district would provide transportation to non-neighborhood schools only when required to by the provisions of NCLB. Because none of the parents in the data set were using this option, the school choice process necessarily entailed careful consideration of issues relating to transportation, and the way they intersected with employment responsibilities and other parenting obligations. Indeed, many of our respondents did not own a car (a few did not have a driver's license), and though the city had an extensive public transportation system, it was geographically large enough to make travel over longer distances very costly in terms of time.

Beyond this, the size of the city also meant that school choice was constrained by parents' experience. Simply put, a parent's awareness of the schools that might form part of his or her choice set became increasingly vague (and quickly faded to nonexistent) the farther these schools were located from parts of the city with which he or she was familiar. This, in turn, varied according to how long he or she had lived in the city and how many neighborhoods he or she had lived in. To be sure, there was a small set of elementary schools—numbering perhaps six to twelve in total (neighborhood, charter, and private)—that had significant name recognition throughout the city because of their positive reputations. Although awareness of these schools was not uniform throughout the sample, many respondents had heard of one or more of them, whether through media mentions or conversations with friends or family members. Nevertheless, these schools were rarely a realistic option, for reasons ranging from catchment rules to cost to a simple lack of seats. Thus, most parents had to undertake some kind of active information-gathering process to make a school choice.

A number of features of the choice process were similar across lines of social class. In particular, the reliance on information provided by trusted network contacts was common among parents from all backgrounds. In this regard, the urban parents described here are similar to their suburban counterparts, as described in chapter 6 of this volume. However, a notable difference emerged with regard to performance data. Use of this type of information was largely restricted to members of the middle-class and upper-middle-class groups. Indeed, this was the starkest finding of the analysis: within the upper-middle-class and middle-class groups, the collection of some kind of performance information was nearly ubiquitous, but it was rare among working-class respondents.

Because there were no clear differences between the upper-middle-class and middle-class groups in the extent to which or the way in which they made use of performance data, I examine them together in the analysis. Subsequently, I analyze the process of school choice among working-class respondents.

Upper-Middle-Class and Middle-Class Families

As noted, awareness of performance data was more or less ubiquitous among upper-middle- and middle-class parents in the sample. Nevertheless, the process of choosing a school was not one of simply maximizing test scores, to the exclusion of other considerations. To the contrary, parents inevitably used performance data in combination with other sources of information. For example, a number of parents—though by no means all—also made visits to potential schools to take a tour and meet with administrators, teachers, or parents. Moreover, nearly all parents relied to some degree on information provided by trusted network contacts: friends, neighbors, and relatives frequently offered reports on their experiences or explanations of their decision making that fed into parents' choice processes. This information channel was especially powerful in the case of parents who belonged to neighborhood associations of one sort or another, and who therefore had connections to large numbers of other (usually middle-class) parents.

Within the context of this elaborate process, significant variation was apparent in the way that parents made use of performance data. Scrutiny of test scores sometimes initiated the process of school choice, when parents used them to rule out or rule in the neighborhood school. And, frequently, performance data were employed as a means of validating information provided by a friend or relative concerning the quality or desirability of a school. Additionally, in some instances parents used performance data as grounds for including a school that they knew little or nothing about in their choice set. However, these practices usually worked both ways, and parents were often unwilling to seek a spot in a school with high scores until they had visited it in person, met with the principal, and spoken with parents of currently enrolled children.

Beyond the multiple uses of performance data, variability was also apparent in the weight placed on them. Some parents considered test scores a key criterion and consulted them at each step of the choice process. Others used scores to make sure that a school was OK—but otherwise took their cue from friends or neighbors. A few even explicitly rejected the validity of scores as indicators of school quality or decried the policy of standardized testing. In my data, this variation corresponds, at least weakly, to the respondents' race, with blacks placing greater emphasis on performance data than whites did. Underlying this association, however, would appear to be a more fundamental factor. To be useful, social network ties had to be local: the information provided by friends and relatives was only likely to be of practical value if it encompassed schools that were located in the same section of the city. And, within the confines of the sample, black respondents' local networks—especially as these encompassed other parents—were sparser than those of their white counterparts. Thus, the data suggest that blacks' relatively heavy reliance on performance data was, to some extent, a functional substitute for dense local networks. I examine these issues by first discussing the way in which the school choice process unfolded for a set of African American parents, and subsequently consider a set of whites.

Dolores Carlton, an African American woman, was a graduate student working in a PhD program at a prestigious university. Her husband held a master's degree and was employed in health-care administration. They lived in the Central City, in a neighborhood convenient to her school. They had purchased their home six years earlier for $120,000 and estimated that its value had increased by about 25 percent. Nevertheless, despite being fond of her neighbors, she did not like the area and said that she wished she "could take this house and just like lift it and put it somewhere else." Her main concern was crime and violence; she reported that she had heard gunshots from the living room.

The couple had a nine-year-old daughter and a two-year-old son. Ms. Carlton became heavily involved in the process of selecting a school for her daughter long before the child was ready to enter kindergarten. She was aware that the school issue would loom large when they bought their house, but "I kind of felt like we couldn't afford the areas that had good neighborhood schools, and in my mind there's only a handful of those." She quickly determined that her neighborhood school was not a viable option on the basis of its test scores, the results of a visit, and her judgment of other parents in the neighborhood:

> They didn't make AYP several years in a row. I went inside to look and I didn't like the way the facility looked, kind of dusty and dirty, and then I know that a lot of the parents from this area send their kids to the neighborhood school, and I don't feel like the parents—I'm not speaking about everybody—but for the most part I don't feel like the parents value education in the way that I do.

Ms. Carlton quickly mobilized a set of weak ties to acquire information about alternative options:

> Parents have this kind of anxiety starting from around daycare or even before. You have to really prepare in advance for your child's primary school education. You have to think about it. You have to plan. You have to kind of strategize, well in advance, so the conversations for me started around daycare when my daughter was about two. And, [I] just started asking parents, 'well what schools are you looking at?'—especially as we got to age three—the kind of preschool age—we knew that pretty soon if we didn't find an option that was really satisfactory, that we'd be forced to go to the neighborhood school.

At one point, Ms. Carlton stated that she felt "panic" at the prospect that her daughter would have to attend the neighborhood school.

When Ms. Carlton encountered other parents from her daughter's day care, the question of schools often dominated the conversation. In informal discussions at the day care or the playground, they would swap information and sound out each other's views of different strategies: "You always wanna see what the next parent's plan is because they might have considered something or found out about something you don't know yet." Ms. Carlton also undertook extensive research on the various alternatives that were open to her. Indeed, at one point she tried to take advantage of the NCLB transfer policy to get her daughter (not yet enrolled in kindergarten, and therefore ineligible) admitted to a highly desirable public school in another part of the city—an effort that was ultimately unsuccessful.

Although swapping information with other parents helped Ms. Carlton learn about her options, she spent a considerable amount of time gathering information online. Indeed, she selected a set of potential schools by combining information she acquired through her network with performance data:

> as you hear about a school that you hadn't heard of before, you check it out and if you continue hearing about it or if there's something on the website— I think I went to the state's website to check test scores—if there's something that really stands out to you as extraordinary about the school . . . I started organizing a formal list. . . . It emerged from this informal mental list.

Thus, for Ms. Carlton, performance data primarily functioned as a means of confirming what she heard from her network contacts. As her research progressed, she created a spreadsheet with extensive information on various schools:

> Oh, I had a lot of stuff! I had bookmarks in my Web browser. . . . There was a section for the school websites. There was a section for state resources, you know, places to find test scores and things about funding. I don't remember all the sections, but it was pretty organized. And then I had a spreadsheet where I listed all the schools that I planned to apply to and I prioritized them according to, what's my top choice? And then I had kind of different columns—like, had I submitted the application? what materials are they asking for? what's the due date?—so I can stay organized.

She also avidly read the parent testimonials on Greatschools.org that covered these schools.

Ms. Carlton focused her search on charter and magnet schools in the city. She visited five institutions, including one Catholic school. Her first choice was a charter school with a lottery system. She understood that her daughter's chances of being selected were roughly one in twenty. She decided to attend the lottery drawing in person: "You know, I had to be there to see, and I actually had to be there to kind of police the lottery. . . . I'm not the only desperate one." To her relief, her daughter was ultimately selected.

Not all of the black upper-middle-class and middle-class parents we spoke with had the kind of dense local network that Ms. Carlton was able to draw on. For these parents, school performance data often played an especially central role—although here, too, it was still interwoven with other sources of information, such as school visits. This is illustrated by Hope Smith, a black, middle-class mother we interviewed. Ms. Smith was fifty years old. She and her husband had married three years earlier; each was raising a child from a previous relationship. Her daughter, Tamika was nine years old, and her stepdaughter, Cheryl, was twelve. Ms. Smith's husband did not have a college degree. He worked for a telephone company for much of his career, "rising through the ranks" until he became a regional director, but decided to take early retirement during a round of layoffs. She had a bachelor's degree, and for many years worked providing specialized support to surgeons in the operating room, at one point earning $90,000 per year. The job required extensive cross-country travel, however, which made it difficult for her to spend time with her family, and she left to form a private company with two doctors that provided these services on a local basis. Nevertheless, even the new job was difficult to reconcile with her family life because the surgical procedures were of uncertain duration and the company did not have enough employees to offer scheduling flexibility. She therefore left, and began to teach on a part-time, adjunct basis in a nursing program at a local college as well as in her church's Sunday School.

Before her marriage, Ms. Smith had enrolled her daughter in a religious school, a decision motivated by her deep faith. However, at the time of the marriage, the family's financial situation was unsettled, and she and her husband decided that they could not afford to send both children to a private school. The process of searching for a public school was complicated by the fact that each partner owned a house in a different part of the city, giving them two neighborhood schools to consider.

Ms. Smith and her husband quickly decided that his house was a better choice for the family. Among the central factors leading to this decision were the size of the yard; the leafy, quiet neighborhood it was located in; and the quality of the school it was zoned to: "Their scores are pretty good," Ms. Smith reported. Nevertheless, Ms. Smith was unsure about this school and actively investigated alternatives. She would have liked to send the children to one of the city's high-reputation schools—her cousin teaches at one—but transportation logistics made this impossible even if the children were to be admitted. Indeed, although she has a number of educators in her extended family—and various cousins have small children—she does not have relatives or friends with young children in the neighborhood. She reports that the immediate neighborhood is mostly populated by retired people.

Ms. Smith began researching local schools: "My husband said, 'boy, when you get fixed on something.' [chuckles] 'You're searching and searching and searching.'" She was initially drawn to a nearby school called Browncroft: "We pulled up their [NCLB test scores] and [the percentiles] were in the eighties and nineties." Unfortunately, however, the family's house was zoned to a different elementary school, Winton: "We missed it by . . . I think we're a block too far." Because Winton's scores were in the fifties, Ms. Smith reported, she was "having a fit": "I was looking on Schooldiggers.com and the scores, the cited scores, were very, very low. I was like, 'Oh, look at these schools. They're awful! They're bad! I don't wanna send [my daughter] there.'"

Two subsequent events changed Ms. Smith's view of the situation. First, a visit to Browncroft left her unimpressed. The school struck her as disorderly: "I was going by the internet and not really going by being there. And then when we were there, we went to talk to the principal. I just said, 'This school looks a mess and why is this little boy running around?' And then [I] come to find out that they're not as great as I thought they were."

Around the same time, she became aware that Winton had recently gotten a new principal who was heavily focused on improving scores. She was able to engineer a quick turnaround: "Then they had a brand new, young, principal come in. The scores [were in the] fifties and now they're ninetieth percentile, and it's like oh. . . ." Among other measures, the new principal instituted a weekend "boot camp" for students: "They did reading, math, comprehension, all that stuff for preparation for the [standardized tests] and it made a big difference." Ms. Smith reported that the improvement in the school's test scores led to an award for the new principal.

Ms. Smith enrolled Tamika in Winton. Although in an ideal world she would have preferred that her daughter attend a religious school, her view of Winton remains positive. She uses the free time made available by her shift to part-time work to involve herself in the school. In addition to becoming an active member of the school's Home-School Association, she frequently volunteers there: "The days I'm not working, I'm at her school. I'm ver—, maybe too involved."

Although none of the parents we spoke with relied exclusively on performance data to select schools for their children, some placed considerable weight on test scores. Cassandra Clark and her husband James provide an example. Both were thirty-two-year-old African Americans. They had a son, eight years old, and a daughter, five years old. Ms. Clark was employed as an "intervention specialist" who worked with children with developmental disabilities. She said of her job, "Although I have my master's, it's not a master's level position." She began working on her master's degree at a local university, but quit when she became pregnant. She subsequently completed a degree through an online institution. Her husband has a bachelor's degree in restaurant management. He worked as a chef at a chain restaurant, but was in the process of switching over to a managerial position. Their combined income was between $55,000 and $65,000. They lived in a 1,400 foot, three-bedroom house they had purchased for $69,000 eight years earlier. They have made significant upgrades to the house, and Ms. Clark estimated that it would sell for about $130,000.

Ms. Clark was raised in a strict Seventh Day Adventist family; her father was a deacon in the church. At one point during her childhood, she attended a private school associated with the church of which she had very positive memories. Indeed, if she could have sent her children anywhere, it would have been to a private school where they would receive a "Christian education." However, the cost was prohibitive.

The family chose the neighborhood in which they live after making a series of visits: "I came here several times and did not notice a whole lot of riff-raff, guys hanging on the corner, you know, high drug areas. This is a block with a lot of older people." She has become a block captain in the local neighborhood watch association.

When it came time to consider schools for her children, Ms. Clark, undertook extensive research into her options. Despite liking the neighborhood, she quickly ruled out the school it was zoned to:

> Interviewer: And for Moreland, do you have any idea what the test scores are for that?
>
> Ms. Clark: Very poor. I don't want to give you numbers because I don't remember the accurate numbers, but their test scores, they don't meet AYP. . . . I was looking for AYP—do they meet AYP?—and that kind of thing.

She thus began an intensive search of other public schools in their part of the city.

Ms. Clark described herself as "very social person." However, there were few people in the neighborhood with whom she felt she could discuss schools. Although she had friends with kids of similar age, none of them lived in the area. Indeed, the only other parents she mentions having had conversations about schools with are some of the mothers at her daughter's ballet class. These discussions, however, did not appear to have been very important in her school choice process.

Instead of relying on network contacts, Ms. Clark gathered information mainly on the Internet: "You would think I'm online all day because I go right to the internet for everything." She relied mainly on the district's website, from which she culled information on school performance, and on Greatschools.org, where she also scrutinized parent testimonials. The criteria she used to select possible schools focused centrally on performance measures:

> Interviewer: And to you what are the elements of a good school?
>
> Ms. Clark: The test scores are my biggest thing.
>
> Interviewer: Yes.
>
> Ms. Clark: And how you teach [children on different levels] to learn these things are the bulk of what I'm looking at. The class size, classroom size.

Elsewhere Ms. Clark mentioned diversity as an important consideration, which she was also able to research online.

Ms. Clark was able to get her son admitted to a neighborhood school outside the family's catchment zone that she was comfortable with (although this required petitioning the principal informally). She was generally happy with the education he was receiving there. However, as her daughter approached kindergarten, Ms. Clark worried that she would not thrive in the school. She thus resolved to get both of them into a charter school. She therefore began a new round of research: "I went online and looked up the different charter schools in the city and went on the websites." She chose four charters that she liked and attended open houses at each. She also checked test scores and parental reviews at Greatschools.org. Although she found all of the charters on her list to be impressive, she settled on Blaine Academy because it had the most diverse student body. She made several visits to the school, meeting with teachers and with other parents. Her daughter was admitted via the lottery, and she intended to have her son transfer to Blaine by taking advantage of the school's sibling preference policy.

As noted, the weight placed on performance data varied considerably among upper-middle-class and middle-class black parents in the sample. Relatively few, however, expressed significant doubts about the relevance of test scores or dismissed them entirely. Among white parents in these class groups, by contrast, doubts and dismissals were frequent. Indeed, a substantial number of white parents in the sample decried the impact of standardized testing on the curriculum and on educational policy more generally. Others questioned the relevance of test score data as an indicator of school quality. White upper-middle-class and middle-class respondents also differed from their black counterparts with regard to their reliance on local networks. Many of the white respondents were able to take advantage of a dense web of weak ties, which they drew on heavily.

A white, upper-middle-class family, the Nelsons, provides a good example. Mandi and Sam both had bachelor's degrees in fine arts and advanced certificates from a specialized academy. Both were children of ministers. She worked in marketing at an engineering firm, where she also ran a managerial training program; she had previously been a first-grade teacher at a private school. He was an administrator at a large university. The couple had two sons, age four and two. They had purchased their house for less than $60,000 thirteen years before the interview. At the time, they reported, they were looking for a location that was safe, had amenities such as grocery stores, and was close to public transportation. They were only "thinking about having kids" then, and so schools were not a consideration.

Shortly after they purchased their home, the neighborhood unexpectedly became a destination: "After that . . . I think everyone began moving. We had friends within six months from moving down here, and the neighborhood changed. Restaurants started opening, bars, coffee shops, other things that you can do, things that you go to. The park got renovated."

The gentrification process brought younger, more affluent families to the neighborhood, and despite the recent turmoil in the market, the Nelson's house was assessed at $280,000. The neighborhood had also diversified, with a number of Latino families moving in.

Although many of their friends moved to the suburbs when their children approached kindergarten, the Nelsons said that they were "committed to living in the city." They devoted significant energy to the process of choosing a school for their children. When asked what school characteristics are important to her, Ms. Nelson said, "Classroom size is important to me. Test scores are important to me." She also "want[s] her kids to be able to walk to school." Elsewhere in the interview, she referred to the importance of a "multicultural" student body.

Parents in the Nelsons' neighborhood are connected through a dense network. There is a highly active neighborhood association, with an email list that includes two hundred members, which often sponsors family activities. Choosing a school is a frequent discussion topic among parents of young children: "I would say there's probably a conversation about schools every day when you go to the playground. You're going to run into somebody talking about schools, especially this time of year when school's starting." The dominant theme of these conversations was charter schools, which, according to Ms. Nelson, most parents in her local social circle strongly favor: "The conversation is, which charter school are you applying to? Have you heard [yet]? How do you get in? How long [have] you been on the waiting list?"

The Nelsons began researching schools when their elder child was three because "we were being told by other families whose kids were older, 'Well, if you're gonna get your kids into charter school, you can start applying now.'" They gave serious consideration to Artistic Charter, whose focus resonated with their background in the arts, and to Galileo Charter. They became aware of both through "neighborhood talk." To research these schools, the Nelsons reported, they looked at their websites and spoke with parents whose children were attending, but did not visit either school. They disliked "the hoops you had to jump through to get into the charter schools and then also the not knowing, not knowing for a long time."

While researching the charters, they also began looking into the neighborhood school, Smithfield. According to Ms. Nelson, "There's problems," but the school is now improving: "Before they had really low test scores, there was a lot of conflict between the teachers themselves. The school has some challenges 'cause, for a long time, it's been a very poor neighborhood; now it's better."

She was particularly impressed by a presentation that the principal made to the neighborhood association, exhorting parents to get involved in the school and to see it as a "resource." Ms. Nelson met with the principal individually, and was highly impressed with her. She and her husband therefore decided to send their sons to Smithfield, and Ms. Nelson joined the Home and School Association even though her children were not yet school age.

This decision brought a mixed reaction from their friends, with about half supportive and half critical. They accepted that Smithfield may not offer some of the educational opportunities that a charter—especially Artistic—would have. However, they saw it as part of their job to pick up where the school leaves off:

> It's our responsibility to make sure that they have a full experience. . . . If the school's terrible that's not great, but if it's so-so—we're going to be reading to the kids, we'll be doing things with them, so it's mostly if it's a safe environment where they can be with other kids and it's the cultural stuff. It's learning how to relate to other children in their own age range.

The Nelsons therefore resemble the gentrifying parents that Shelley Kimelberg describes in chapter 7 of this volume (see also Cucchiara and Horvat 2009). In particular, the decision not to maximize more conventional indicators of school quality rested on a more or less explicit assumption that they could use their own resources to offset any deficits the neighborhood school might have.

In a few instances, white upper-middle- and middle-class parents found themselves deeply conflicted: professing general skepticism about the validity of test scores as a relevant source of information, they nonetheless found it impossible to ignore the numbers of a neighborhood school or a nearby charter when confronted with them.

This conflict is apparent in the case of the Prices, a middle-class family. Ms. Price and her husband, Tim, both worked in museums—she in fundraising, he as a facilities supervisor. Ms. Price had a bachelor's degree in art history; her husband was a philosophy major, but never completed his degree ("Frank Zappa told me to drop out and educate myself before it was too late," he explained with a chuckle). Their combined annual income was between $90,000 and $99,999. The couple had two sons, age four and two years old.

The Prices had lived in their current home, which they owned, for five years. They had begun looking while they were still dating. Initially, they had hoped to purchase a home in the catchment area of Lab Public, one of the high-reputation schools in the city. They didn't have children at the time, and their motives were entirely financial: "I was thinking about the resale value of the house," Ms. Price explained. However, they quickly discovered that they didn't like any of the houses in the catchment area that were within their price range. They therefore purchased a three-bedroom home just outside the catchment boundary, at a cost of

$239,000. Mr. Price described the neighborhood as one in the process of gentrification. With the exception of the Prices and one other family, the block they live on was entirely African American.

Like many of the mothers we spoke with, Ms. Price reported that she became extremely anxious ("freaked out") when she first began thinking about schools. Despite her dislike of test scores, she quickly became disillusioned with Medford, the neighborhood school, when she began researching it:

> First and foremost, I went right to the [district's] website and started digging around, and I found the statistics, [with]—I hate to rely on them, but, you know—proficiency levels [indicating] how kids are doing at different schools, and while I don't believe in those tests—I really, I really, really don't—but the school had something really scary, like they were so far underneath the national average, because they had these charts with the lines. I was like, woo, that's red flag, red flag.

She also used Google's Alert function to inform her of media articles on city schools.

Although the Prices had relatively few friends in their immediate neighborhood, they had developed friendships with a large number of parents in their part of the city. This occurred mainly through a babysitting co-op they joined through a friend of a friend. Co-op members played a central role in helping the Prices navigate the school choice process. Indeed, Ms. Price reported that she relied mainly on word-of-mouth information acquired from co-op members. The co-op had an online discussion list, and members frequently forwarded media articles dealing with education. Advice from co-op members was useful precisely because many had recently been through the process the Prices faced: "some of these people have kids that are like twelve, thirteen, so they've been [here] for a while, and then others have kids just a little bit older than ours, so we have like these great perspectives."

Many of the co-op members had children attending the elite Lab Public, and some reported that the school had become overcrowded and "chaotic" in recent years. Ms. Price therefore focused her energy on finding a different school. Her values drove her away from considering private schools (which were also cost prohibitive) and charters (which she believed charge tuition). Co-op members pointed her toward three public schools in the area they considered desirable—including Springside and Brownside, both of which had highly positive citywide reputations—and gave her with tips on navigating the admission process. Because she "didn't believe in those standardized tests," she attended open houses at each. She was highly impressed by the principal at Springside, who she found to be young and dynamic (a "pretty hip guy"), as well as aspects of the curriculum, and made it her priority. Also important was that the school was located near her job, making transportation manageable. At the time of the interview, she had not yet heard whether her son had been admitted.

Working-Class Respondents

Among the working-class respondents in these data, we observed heavy reliance on word of mouth as a means of acquiring information on schools. As with their upper-middle-class and middle-class counterparts, suggestions and recommendations from trusted network contacts were a central factor in the process. However, we observed little concern for—or indeed awareness of—performance data among the working-class parents we spoke with. Very few of these parents sought out information on websites such as Greatschools.org or on the district's website. Moreover, we often found that working-class parents were not familiar with the jargon (for example, AYP) that suffuses mandated accountability reporting.

These findings are exemplified by Janine Mondi, a white mother of two children, five and four. Ms. Mondi's husband was Mexican and in the United States illegally; he worked as a cook in a restaurant. She was enrolled in nursing school and worked part-time in an ophthalmologist's office. Their annual income is between $30,000 and $40,000.

Ms. Mondi had been told a lot of "negative stuff" about the neighborhood school, explaining, "You hear, 'oh, the school's not safe, they're not going to get a good education.' " She therefore decided to pursue the charter option. While she had access to a computer, she relied primarily on information she received from friends and acquaintances:

> Interviewer: And so how did you go about learning about the schools?
> Ms. Mondi: Um, a lot of word of mouth at playgrounds and just through walking through the neighborhood and finding out where different public schools are, where different charter schools are. That's all I could do. I mean, sometimes you go online and download an application and that's about it.

Ms. Mondi applied to a single charter school, Oakdale, which she first heard about from relatives who had applied on behalf of their own children. She didn't attempt to gather information on Oakdale prior to submitting the application:

> Interviewer: And do you know the racial balance where she's going to be going?
> Ms. Mondi: I don't know much about the racial balance.
> Interviewer: And have you ever heard of something called AYP?
> Ms. Mondi: No.

Interviewer: Okay. And you don't know where that school is on test
scores or anything?
Ms. Mondi: No.

Ms. Mondi's older daughter was accepted to Oakdale before kindergarten, and because of the school's sibling policy, both children will
attend. This outcome brought her "lot of peace of mind."

Although the working-class parents in our sample all demonstrated a
concern for their children's schooling and nearly all were able to recount
concrete steps they took to evaluate their child's school before or at the
time of enrollment, there was very little interest in performance data.
This was evident in the case of Latifa Ingram. Ms. Ingram had two
daughters, one seven years old and the other two. The children had different fathers, and only the younger daughter had regular contact with
hers. Ms. Ingram had a high school degree despite having become pregnant with her first child when she was sixteen years old. She enrolled in
a vocational program to become a medical assistant after graduating,
but dropped out about halfway through due to financial concerns. At the
time of the interview, she worked part-time at a clothing store for $7.70
an hour with no benefits; she wanted more hours. Ms. Ingram received
a transportation allowance from the state, as well as food stamps. The
family lived in her mother's house, along with her twenty-four-year-old
brother.

Before moving back in with her mother, Ms. Ingram spent a year in an
apartment in another part of the city; her elder daughter attended kindergarten at the neighborhood elementary school. However, she quickly
came to loathe both the area and the school. As she described it,

> My daughter wasn't learning nothing at the schools. The teacher, she was a
> older lady, so it was just like the kids was just running over her. She couldn't
> keep up with the kids. She couldn't handle the kids. (Chuckles.) The area
> was just so bad. They had people outside drinking and fighting in front of
> the . . . I wouldn't even bring my kids out to play, ride their bikes. I was like,
> I gotta go, and then I came back here.

When asked whether she ever looked up information on this school on
the Internet, she responded negatively: "Hm—mm."

Ms. Ingram had a positive view of Catholic schools, having attended
one for a year herself as a young child; she mentioned strict discipline
when asked to explain why. Before moving in with her mother, she considered sending her elder daughter to a nearby Catholic school on the
basis of positive reports she received from a relative whose child was
enrolled. When asked to explain what she had heard about it, she said, "I
don't hear about people just trespassing the school. . . . Vandalizing the

school, I don't hear too much about that." However, before following up, she decided to move out of the neighborhood.

Faced with the need to find a school for her daughter, she considered a charter she had heard about from her "girlfriend down the street." However, she never seriously investigated it. Instead, she began looking into the neighborhood school—which she had attended as a child:

Interviewer: And when you were getting ready to enroll your oldest daughter . . . did you hear anything about the school—how things were going at that school these days?

Ms. Ingram: Yeah. I took a tour of the school, so I got in with the teachers, and it was fine. I liked it 'cause we grew up in this area so it was pretty cool. The teachers, . . . the teachers that I went—they were still there, so it was pretty cool.

Ms. Ingram was quite pleased with the school. Her daughter enjoyed the many activities that she participates in, and the teachers (some of whom remembered her) were nice. Ms. Ingram reported that her daughter "learns a lot." However, at no point did she attempt to examine the school's performance:

Interviewer: And do you have access to the Internet here?

Ms. Ingram: I think on my phone.

Although she had Internet access, she had never looked at the school district website. Indeed, she had no information on how the school has fared on it assessments:

Interviewer: [Do you] know anything about the test scores at the current school?

Ms. Ingram: No.

In addition to making little use of performance data, the working-class parents in our sample evinced little facility with the jargon that comes with it, nor with the intricacies of charter school lotteries and the like. As with Ms. Mondi and Ms. Ingram, this is evident in the responses of Ms. Norton, a working-class mother who lived in the city.

Interviewer: And you've never heard of AYP, have you? Most people haven't heard of it.

Ms. Norton: I have.

Interviewer: What have you heard?

Ms. Norton: No, the name sounds familiar but I don't like remember like—

Interviewer: Oh.

Ms. Norton: What does it stand for?

> Interviewer: AYP is adequate yearly progress. It's about if a school is passing—
>
> Ms. Norton: Oh, OK, OK, alright, yeah.
>
> Interviewer: And do you know how his school is doing in terms of test scores, about if the kids are—
>
> Ms. Norton: I'm not even sure. That's something to look into though. I'm not sure.

Among working-class respondents, the school search process overwhelmingly resembled that recounted by Ms. Mondi, Ms. Ingram, and Ms. Norton. We did, however, find one exception in our data in the case of Ms. Werner, a thirty-five-year-old African American woman. Ms. Werner had a son who was about to turn three. She was separated from his father but in regular contact with him; he saw his son about once a month. Ms. Werner attended a nonselective local college after finishing high school, but dropped out after two years. She subsequently spent a short time in a homeless shelter. However, she was able to find several positions doing temporary work, and eventually was offered a permanent job (with benefits) at a chemical company as an administrative assistant. The company offered to reimburse her tuition if she enrolled in a local community college, and she had recently received her associate degree, graduating with honors. At the time of the interview, she was applying to an online bachelor's degree program run by a local university, which her company would also pay for. She lived in a book-filled condo with her son, for which she paid $975 per month. Although their home life was difficult during their childhood, Ms. Werner's sister graduated from an elite university, and worked as a researcher at the time of the interview. Her brother, despite not completing any education beyond high school, had become a manager at a footwear store.

Ms. Werner was deeply concerned about finding a good school for her son. Her siblings and other relatives did not live in the immediate area, and she had not made friends with any parents in the neighborhood. She also reported that most of her colleagues at work had much older children and lived in the suburbs. Thus, she began avidly researching elementary schools online. Indeed, she had assembled a spreadsheet: "I've been doing some research, let me tell you. That's one thing I do is plan when it is in regards to him, so I have about six schools that I'm looking into." She relied heavily on Internet sources:

> Ms. Werner: I'm using a resource called Greatschools.org to investigate, [and] also the school district's website. I don't want him to go to an inner city school, like a public school, so he's gonna go to a charter. So now I'm just trying to figure out what charter it is.

Interviewer: How did you choose these charters?
Ms. Werner: Basically how they're rated on here, also by people's comments. Also, [I] looked them up on Google, see if people
comment.

At the time, she was just "seeing how everything looks on paper." As
her son grew older, she intended to "start going to schools and checking
them out personally." Among the working-class respondents in our sample, it needs to be stressed, Ms. Werner was unique.

Discussion

Without exception, the parents in our data set wanted their children to
thrive in school and to be academically successful. Nearly all had grave
concerns about aspects of their neighborhood public schools and actively
considered alternatives to them. For many, this meant conversations with
other parents at a playground or at their child's organized activities; in
some instances, it meant soliciting advice from kin with older children,
from friends and neighbors, or from members of a neighborhood association. Concern about neighborhood schools also motivated innumer-
able school visits and other forms of information gathering. Thus, it is
reasonable to suggest that something approximating a "culture of school
choice" has emerged in the city.

However, the form taken by this culture varies in several ways. Within
the middle-class and upper-middle-class groups, we find that multiple
sources of information tend to be interwoven. Advice and opinions
received through the network are often combined with standardized test
scores, local reputational knowledge, and firsthand experience of schools
(for example, at open houses and other visits) in a complex mesh that
parents draw on to make their choice. To be sure, the weight ascribed to
these different sources varies. In particular, some respondents appeared
to rely heavily on the network channel and others to make less use of
it, and inversely, some tended to discount the importance of test scores
and others ascribed substantial significance to them. In my sample, these
differences appear to map onto the respondent's race, although imper-
fectly. These results suggest the possibility that the heavier reliance on
test scores apparent among African American respondents is, at least to
some degree, attributable to relatively sparse local network ties.

I also found that working-class respondents, black and white, had little
awareness of publicized performance data and did not rely on it for purposes of school choice. Indeed, with the one exception of Ms. Werner, they
tended to have little or no familiarity with the jargon and procedures of
school choice, and instead relied on informal network contacts, reputation,

and school visits for information on schools. It needs to be stressed that this was not due to a lack of access to the Internet; all working-class respondents had access, if not through an Internet-linked computer, then through a phone or at a public library. Nor was it due to indifference: most working-class parents, as noted, took various steps to investigate possible schools for their children, and indeed, Ms. Ingram moved to escape her local school and neighborhood. Thus, it seems doubtful that, at least in the city where our data were collected, publicized performance data are playing the role that was intended for them—namely, enabling working-class and poor parents to engage in the same kind of school shopping that their more affluent counterparts regularly undertook. Rather than simplifying school choice for working-class families, performance data appears mainly to have fueled middle-class anxiety about social reproduction.

Interventions intended to facilitate the use of performance data in school choice have been rare. Justine Hastings and Jeffrey Weinstein (2008) describe an experiment in Charlotte-Mecklenburg in which simplified, district-level report cards containing test score information on all relevant public schools (given a child's grade level) were distributed to parents. The report cards were designed to facilitate easy comparison across institutions, and were provided to parents of children in randomly selected schools, with families at nonrecipient schools serving as a control. The majority of families in these schools were low to middle income. Weinstein and Hastings report that receipt of the simplified report cards triggered increased transfer requests into high-scoring schools, and among students who transferred, significant gains in academic performance. However, though these results are intriguing, the simplified report cards replaced an especially cumbersome information packet produced by the district. In light of the emergence of websites that present streamlined performance data—and that also strive to make comparison easy—it is not obvious that this strategy would have a large impact if pursued today.

The other main intervention of note is the emergence of community groups assisting working-class families navigating choice programs, such as SchoolHaven in New Haven, Connecticut, and Parent Power Project in Rochester, New York. At a broad level, these organizations aggregate information, help parents navigate application processes, connect parents with service providers, and present quantitative information on schools to them in a "narrativized" form. Although no formal assessments of these organizations have been carried out, they might be compared to the traditional role played by the guidance counselor in facilitating the matching of high school graduates with colleges (see Neild 2005). Indeed, as choice policies become more pervasive, it seems plausible that school districts themselves may eventually feel compelled to take over the function of actively assisting low-income and working-class families in managing choice. Whether this would, in fact, facilitate the goals of "educational competition" is, of course, an open question.

The author gratefully acknowledges the generous support of The Spencer Foundation as well as SUNY Brockport in facilitating the collection of the data reported in this paper. An earlier version of this chapter was presented at a conference at the Russell Sage Foundation, February 14 and 15, 2013, in New York City. I thank the conference participants and Mira C. Debs, Melody Boyd, and Jennifer L. Jennings for helpful suggestions. Any errors are the responsibility of the author and not the sponsoring agency.

References

Black, Sandra. 1999. "Do Better Schools Matter? Parental Valuation of Elementary Education." *The Quarterly Journal of Economics* 114(2): 577–99.

Coe, Charles K. 2003. "A Report Card on Report Cards." *Public Performance and Management Review* 27(2): 53–76.

Cucchiara, Maia B., and Erin M. Horvat. 2009. "Perils and Promises: Middle-Class Parental Involvement in Urban Schools." *American Educational Research Journal* 46(4): 974–1004.

DeLuca, Stefanie, and Peter Rosenblatt. 2010. "Does Moving to Better Neighborhoods Lead to Better Schooling Opportunities? Parental School Choice in and Experimental Housing Voucher Program." *Teachers College Record* 112(5): 1443–91.

Figlio, David N., and Maurice E. Lucas. 2004. "What's in a Grade? School Report Cards and the Housing Market." *American Economic Review* 94(3): 591–604.

Friesen, Jane, Moshen Javdani, Justin Smith, and Simon Woodcock. 2012. "How Do School 'Report Cards' Affect School Choice Decisions?" *Canadian Journal of Economics* 45(2): 784–807.

Garcia, David R. 2011. "The Achilles' Heel of School Choice Policies: The Obstacles to Reporting School Accountability Results to Parents." *Journal of School Choice* 5(1): 66–84.

Gewirtz, Sharon, Stephen J. Ball, and Richard Bowe. 1995. *Markets, Choice, and Equity in Education.* Buckingham, UK: Open University Press.

Hastings, Justine S., and Jeffrey M. Weinstein. 2008. "Information, School Choice, and Academic Achievement: Evidence from Two Experiments." *The Quarterly Journal of Economics* 123(4): 1373–414.

Henig, Jeffrey R. 1994. *Rethinking School Choice: Limits of the Market Metaphor.* Princeton, N.J.: Princeton University Press.

Holme, Jennifer Jellison. 2002. "Buying Homes, Buying Schools: School Choice and the Social Construction of School Quality." *Harvard Educational Review* 72(2): 177–206.

Howell, William. 2006. "Switching Schools? A Closer Look at Parents' Initial Interest in and Knowledge About the Choice Provisions of No Child Left Behind." *Peabody Journal of Education* 81(1): 140–79.

Mickelson, Roslyn Arlin, and Stephanie Southworth. 2005. "When Opting Out Is Not a Choice: Implications for NCLB's Transfer Option from Charlotte, North Carolina." *Equity and Excellence in Education* 38(1): 1–15.

Neild, Ruth Curran. 2005. "Parent Management of School Choice in a Large Urban District." *Urban Education* 40(3): 270–97.

Reay, Diane, and Stephen J. Ball. 1997. "'Spoilt for Choice': The Working Classes and Educational Markets." *Oxford Review of Education* 23(1): 89–101.

Schneider, Mark, Paul Teske, and Melissa Marschall. 2000. *Choosing Schools: Consumer Choice and the Quality of American Schools.* Princeton, N.J.: Princeton University Press.

Teske, Paul, Jody Fitzpatrick, and Gabriel Kaplan. 2006. "The Information Gap?" *Review of Policy Research* 23(5): 969–81.

U.S. Department of Education. 2001. "No Child Left Behind." http://www2.ed.gov/policy/elsec/leg/esea02/index.html. Accessed October 9, 2013.

Chapter 10

Linking Housing Policy and School Reform

AMY ELLEN SCHWARTZ AND LEANNA STIEFEL

A common mantra in the real estate world asserts the importance of "location location location." Much of the locational advantage of residential property has to do with the quality of local public schools. Parents consider the quality of the schools their children will be able to attend when choosing where to live, although choice sets vary greatly by class and race. Teachers also weigh locational factors, including salaries, cost of living, and working conditions at local schools when deciding where to apply for jobs and when to transfer between school districts. These decisions of parents and teachers result in close ties between housing policy and educational attainment of our elementary and secondary school students. Yet, despite these ties, local, state, and federal policies that recognize and coordinate the relationship between education and housing are relatively rare.

In this chapter, we first explore the mechanisms by which housing and education are related. Although the links between education and housing affect students across the income distribution, we focus particular attention on disadvantaged students in urban areas, as these students often face a unique set of challenges that set them apart from their more advantaged or nonurban counterparts. We begin with the *housing unit* itself, describing the ways in which a child's physical home environment might impact his educational outcome. Next, we explore the relationship between education and the institutions, individuals, and overall quality of a child's residential *neighborhood*. Finally, we consider the *political economy* of public schools and the ways in which the school district links housing and education decisions, policies and outcomes. We then turn to a discussion of the implications of these mechanisms for education and housing policy, focusing on the links between schools and housing.[1]

We address, in turn: policies that govern school choice within districts; policies that affect student mobility; policies that create neighborhood support for children in low-income housing; and policies regarding the siting of low-income housing. We highlight recent efforts to strengthen the ties between education and housing policy and discuss how the lessons learned from these efforts might be brought to bear as policymakers consider new education and housing initiatives.

Impact of Housing Unit on Children's Education

Adequate housing is critical to a child's ability to learn in myriad ways. Children are affected not only by the physical amenities and layout of their housing unit, but also by the stability that comes with secure and constant housing. What seems particularly critical today is the way in which housing instability leads to student mobility across schools, neighborhoods, and school districts. This mobility, particularly when it occurs frequently or within a school year, is more harmful to a child's education than is commonly understood. Although some mobility can improve academic performance if it is made strategically to provide a good match between student and school, and occurs at appropriate times, such strategic moves are often unavailable to low-income families, who often do not make joint decisions regarding residential and school mobility (see chapter 5, this volume). Mobility can, and often does, negatively affect a student's learning by rupturing the continuity of his curriculum and social relationships (Coleman 1988; Kerbow 1996). Mobility can also hurt teachers and the nonmovers in the student mover's new classroom if the new student arrives midyear and is unprepared for the curriculum of the new school.

A significant body of literature suggests that particularly high levels of mobility have a negative impact on student learning. Highly mobile students perform significantly worse in school, and are more likely to drop out, than less mobile students (Crowley 2003; Astone and McLanahan 1994; Rumberger 2003; Swanson and Schneider 1999). Children who switch schools four or more times before sixth grade are about one year behind those who have not changed schools (Kerbow 1996). Further, mobility varies by class and race. In our work at the Institute for Education and Social Policy, we find that poor students are approximately twice as likely as wealthier students to switch schools in the middle of a school year and that by eighth grade, black students have, on average, attended a greater number of schools than white students. Of students who switched schools, most blacks moved to new schools with lower test scores than their old schools, whereas most whites moved to new schools with higher test scores than their old schools (Schwartz, Stiefel, and Chalico 2007). Moreover, students who switch schools after the academic year begins are particularly likely to suffer academically and to harm fellow classmates (Schwartz and Stiefel 2013; Schwartz, Stiefel, and Whitesell 2013; Gibbons and Talej 2011; Raudenbush, Jean, and Art 2009). Similarly, Eric Hanushek, John Kain, and Steven Rivkin (2004) find that though student turnover has a negative impact on movers and their non-mover classmates, the impact is greatest for lower income and minority students because they typically attend higher turnover schools and move more frequently. Taken as a whole, these findings suggest policies aimed at ameliorating the impact of high family mobility due to housing instability on student outcomes.

In addition to questions of mobility and housing stability, the physical design of a child's housing unit and the configuration of the living space may have an important effect on student educational outcomes. For example, a student who has his or her own bedroom may have an easier time finding a quiet place to study within the housing unit than a student who shares a bedroom with other family members. For those children without their own bedroom, an important question then becomes whether there is another quiet place for studying within the housing unit. Health and safety concerns, though less directly related to academic achievement, may have an indirect effect on student outcomes—students who live in unhealthy or unsafe conditions may suffer from attendance problems as a result or find it more difficult to concentrate on schoolwork at home and in the classroom. Finally, a relationship between the household unit and the way it is used by its residents is likely. For example, the number of people in the housing unit, the household age distribution, and the density of space usage are all likely to be important. Students who are crowded into small housing units with numerous other residents may well face challenges, such as difficulty finding space and time to study and sleep, beyond those of other students.

Research on the relationship between the housing unit and student academic outcomes is, however, relatively thin. Researchers often take a broader approach, focusing on housing quality, which may include crowding and physical conditions, but also frequently includes neighborhood characteristics, access to amenities, home values, and issues related to housing tenure and home ownership (see the following section for a discussion of neighborhood characteristics). Most research on physical housing conditions as they relate to school performance focuses on the effect of crowding. Students who have less dedicated space for school work tend to perform less well in school (Gaux and Maurin 2005; Currie and Yelowitz 2000; Maxwell 2003). Notably, although public opinion surrounding the quality of public housing is often negative, Janet Currie and Aaron Yelowitz (2000) find that after controlling for the endogeneity of project participation, crowding, and the likelihood of being held back in school are less likely in public housing projects. Opposite-sex siblings who may have to share a bedroom in a private housing unit are more likely to have their own bedrooms in public housing because of housing unit assignment rules. Consequently, residents entitled to a larger housing unit based on family sex composition are 24 percent more likely to live in public housing (Currie and Yelowitz 2000).

A tangential body of research looks at the relationship between housing conditions and physical and mental health. A significant amount of this literature focuses on the relationship between housing conditions and asthma, the most common chronic condition among children. The studies consistently show that substandard housing conditions, particularly water intrusion and inadequate ventilation, contribute to increased occurrences of asthma and other chronic respiratory symptoms among children (for a review of literature on housing and health, see Krieger and Higgins 2002). Although the majority of these studies go beyond the scope of this paper, Lisa Harker (2007) notes that substandard housing units, such as those with mold and moisture, a lack of heat, or crowded conditions, have a negative impact a child health, thus affecting student absenteeism.

Finally, students with stable housing are less likely to experience the frequent moves between schools that can negatively impact the academic performance of their more mobile counterparts. Thus just as the layout and use of the housing unit is tied to a student's ability to study at home, simply having a permanent unit can affect academic performance and other school-related outcomes such as attendance, by the consequent attachment to one school over time. Next, we turn to a discussion of the mechanisms by which a child's neighborhood may impact his educational achievement.

Impact of Neighborhoods on Children

A family's housing choices extend beyond the selection of a particular housing unit. Each housing unit is situated within a neighborhood that brings with it a certain set of institutions, individuals and issues. In their 1997 review of the literature on neighborhood effects, Ingrid Ellen and Margery Turner identify "six mechanisms through which neighborhood conditions may influence individual outcomes: quality of local services, socialization by adults, peer influences, social networks, exposure to crime and violence, and physical isolation and distance" (836). Here we turn our attention to these and other mechanisms through which neighborhoods might specifically influence children's educational outcomes.

A considerable amount of research explores how a child's neighborhood shapes academic performance, and these studies consistently find that children growing up in more affluent neighborhoods outperform children from poorer neighborhoods (Ellen and Turner 1997). This relationship might not be causal—it has been difficult for researchers to demonstrate that neighborhoods have an effect, ceteris paribus—but we can still discuss why there might be a strong correlation. One plausible reason is that children in less affluent communities have less access to the kinds of local services and amenities that benefit children in wealthier areas. A child's housing situation places him within a set of neighborhood institutions that can influence his educational opportunities and achievement. Middle- and high-income neighborhoods regularly provide students with out-of-school supports that may contribute to their educational success. For example, these neighborhoods commonly have community centers that provide students with a safe place to congregate after school or participate in extracurricular enrichment activities. Similarly, students in more affluent neighborhoods may have greater access to after-school sports, tutoring, arts, dance and other neighborhood programs that support and complement the education they receive in school. Middle- and high-income neighborhoods are also more likely to have libraries with high-speed Internet connections, reference librarians, children's reading hours, and quiet space for homework or research. In a study of four Philadelphia-area neighborhoods, Susan Neuman and Donna Celano (2001) find that the quality and condition of public and school libraries improve with neighborhood income level. Additionally, they find that children's access to print reading materials varies widely by neighborhood income level; children in middle-income neighborhoods benefit from greater access to and a wider variety of print materials than their low-income counterparts.

Although local enrichment activities may provide academic benefits to student participants, these activities and services are also important because they provide students with an opportunity to interact with adults who can serve as role models and mentors. These figures can provide students with valuable advice and assistance as they progress through their academic careers. To the extent that students in lower-income neighborhoods have less access to local extracurricular opportunities and thus adult role models, they may find themselves at a disadvantage in the classroom.

Neighborhoods also influence the peer groups with whom students interact in and outside of school. Children are likely to form friendships with other children who live in their neighborhoods and school zoning regulations, which means that neighborhood peers are also likely to be school peers. Several studies find a link between a student's academic performance and the performance or behavior of his classmates (see Boozer and Cacciola 2001; Zimmer and Toma 2000; Hanushek et al. 2003). Therefore, students who live in neighborhood with a higher concentration of high-achieving, school-oriented peers may have a greater chance of academic success. This relationship is complicated by the fact that students are not randomly assigned to classrooms; thus, it may be the case that a lower-achieving student with high-achieving neighborhood peers may be placed in a different course track than the higher achievers, as occurred among students in public housing units sited in low-poverty neighborhoods in Montgomery County (Schwartz 2010). Nonetheless, students who live in neighborhoods with more academically oriented peers may find more academic support from peers in after-school hours, such as study groups, and less pressure to engage in other activities. This is supported by evidence from the literature, which finds a positive relationship between neighborhood socioeconomic status and school attainment such as high school graduation and college attendance, and stronger relationships among white than among black students (Brooks-Gunn et al. 1993; Duncan 1994; Halpern-Felsher et al. 1997; Wodtke, Harding, and Elwert 2011). Other research using data from the Moving to Opportunity (MTO) experiment has found positive effects on achievement for adolescent males who move from high- to low-poverty neighborhoods, which is partially explained by increased time spent on homework and school safety (Leventhal and Brooks-Gunn 2004).[2] Conversely, students who are surrounded by negative peer influences may face pressure to engage in activities, such as skipping school, that are detrimental to academic achievement. For example, Jonathan Crane (1991) finds evidence for an "epidemic" model of peer effects, whereby neighborhood social problems are contagious and spread through peer influence. Specifically, he finds sharp increases in the probability of dropout among white and black students who live in the poorest neighborhoods. Further evidence of the negative consequences of neighborhood disadvantage on student performance is demonstrated by Robert Sampson, Patrick Sharkey, and Stephen Raudenbush (2008), who find that among African American children in Chicago, living in severely disadvantaged neighborhoods leads to a 4-point reduction in verbal abilities—an effect equivalent to missing a year or more of school.

Children in certain neighborhoods must also cope with the stress and insecurity that comes from being surrounded by higher levels of crime and violence (Sharkey et al. 2013; Lacoe 2013). These problems are often exacerbated by a lack of local employment opportunities and corresponding high levels of unemployment. Parents and teenage students may have trouble finding employment and turn instead to alternative (and possibly illegal) means of earning income. These factors, though not directly linked to a child's education, are likely to make for a more difficult home life that may spill over into a student's educational performance.

In the end, because schools tend to draw students from the local neighborhood due to school zoning policies, they often reflect and even reinforce local socioeconomic patterns. Research continues to show that the price of housing is higher in neighborhoods and school districts with high-quality schools (Black 1999; Schwartz and Voicu 2007; Hayes and Taylor 1996). Sandra Black (1999) finds that parents are willing to pay 2 percent more for homes located in school zones that have test scores 5 percent higher than the mean test scores for that particular district. Additionally, neighborhood quality is often an important factor in a teacher's decision about where to work, making it more challenging for troubled neighborhoods to attract high-quality teachers. In the following section, we expand on the ways in which the existence of school districts, and more broadly, the political economy of public schools, may affect a child's education.

The Political Economy of Public Schools

The school district provides perhaps one of the most important links between housing, neighborhoods, and schools. Housing and education are jointly chosen and institutionally linked through a reliance on place-based assignment rules for local elementary schools, and in most districts, local middle and high schools; children are assigned to a local public school based on the school zone in which they reside. Thus, a family's decision to reside within a particular neighborhood is also a decision about the school district to which children will be assigned, and within that district, which zone school children will attend. These decisions also have important financial implications for families, school districts, and the local economy. Schools are funded through a combination of local, state, and some federal funds. Local school districts currently rely on a combination of local property taxes and state aid, with small amounts of federal funds; states, on average, fund over 50 percent of K–12 education and local property taxes account for the majority of local funding. A typical urban area is likely to include many school districts, differentiated by their size, quality, and spending. Given these relationships, how might the political economy of public schools affect a child's education?

School resources often reflect the economic circumstances of local residents and, despite equalizing state aid, on average a tie remains between school funding and local property values. Higher home values in more affluent neighborhoods often translate into increased funding and more educational opportunities in local schools. In turn, higher-quality schools in middle- and high-income neighborhoods attract residents who can afford high home prices and come with academically prepared students, creating a cycle that perpetuates school quality differences across districts. In addition, parents in these neighborhoods may place higher demand on their local schools to provide high-quality resources and educational opportunities for students. Families balance the quality of schools and cost of housing when choosing a place to live, and many families are willing to pay more to live near higher-performing schools (Black

1999; Hayes and Taylor 1996). Funding inequalities across districts have decreased in recent decades, in large part because of state-level efforts to use income and sales tax revenues to increase state shares and reduce the reliance on local property taxes (Corcoran, Romer, and Rosenthal 2008). David Card and Abigail Payne (2002) find that redistribution efforts lead to more equal spending across districts and a modest decrease in the test score gap among high school students from different family background groups. Local property taxes, however, continue to serve as the source of local school funding in most districts and policies that erode the property tax base may have the unintended consequence of reducing school spending overall in a state (on California, see Downes and Shah 2006).

The relationship between local property taxes and school funding is of particular importance as city officials decide where to site new subsidized housing. Ingrid Ellen and her colleagues (2007) examine the impact of the construction of new subsidized housing units in New York City on local school quality and find that the construction of subsidized rental housing is associated with significant school change, including an increase in attendance rates and teacher turnover and a modest decline in academic performance several years later. New subsidized housing units are also likely to increase the demands on local public schools by creating an influx of children, many of whom may need supplementary support services. The implication is that the cost of education will rise. If the district is not provided with adequate additional funds through state or federal aid, the strain on the local budget may have a secondary, pernicious effect as higher income families move out in response to the higher cost of education, ultimately reducing the property tax base and with it, school funding.

Unfortunately, further decoupling school spending and local finance, as has been done over the past three decades through increases in state aid, may not provide a fully satisfying solution for equity issues. State and federal efforts to delink local funding and school spending can lead some students to exit the public school system or decrease per-pupil spending for all students. For example, state education finance reforms in California led to an increase in the state's share of education funding from 46.25 percent in 1975 to 73.85 percent in 1985 (Downes and Shah 2006). Subsequently, this state has witnessed a decrease in per-pupil expenditures and a substantial increase in the number of students enrolled in private schools. In addition, efforts to loosen the ties between school funding and local property taxes may be constrained by a lack of political support from residents of more affluent neighborhoods, who fear that such measures will decrease the quality of their local schools.

Similarly, within-district segregation can lead to substantial differences in neighborhood resources, including the quality of local schools—due at least in part to inequality in social, economic, and political resources and perhaps to the difficulties of attracting high-quality teachers to challenging positions. Indeed, the low quality of public schools in poor neighborhoods is well documented, often in sharp contrast to high-quality schools elsewhere in the city or district (Kozol 2012). That said, some recent reforms have disproportionately benefited low-income neighborhoods with struggling schools, perhaps most visibly in the nationwide charter school movement (for example, in New Orleans where all public schools were turned over to charter management organizations after Katrina). As another example, the Gates-funded new small schools in New York City and Chicago are disproportionately sited in low-income neighborhoods (Schwartz et al. 2012). Due to the attention focused on low-quality schools in high-poverty neighborhoods, low-quality schools in middle- to high-income districts may be largely ignored.

Finally, even if financial resources are equalized, the family backgrounds and peers can remain differentiated across districts and schools, leading to disparate outcomes. For example, in a simulation exercise, Thomas Nechyba (2004) finds that as long as housing prices and family background characteristics are positively related, students from poor neighborhoods attend lower quality schools even under a scheme where all schools receive equal amounts of funding.

Implications for Policy

Our discussion thus far has focused on the mechanisms through which housing and education are related at the home, neighborhood, and school district levels. These relationships suggest that increased coordination of education and housing policies could benefit students and schools. In this section, we discuss some of the implications of these relationships for policymakers and highlight policies that have attempted to bridge the gap between housing and education policy.

Polices for Increasing School Choice

Giving students choices of schools outside their residentially zoned area has become a popular policy in urban districts, although few policies allow crossing of district boundaries.[3] The within-district choices take several forms. One is publicly financed charter schools that have freedoms beyond traditional public schools to choose their staff, mission, length of day and year, uniform and parental involvement policies, but are accountable to "chartering organizations"[4] for their students' performance. Another is voucher programs in which students are allowed to choose nonpublic schools and are given some funding to pay for the schools. A third is magnet schools that, through use of a theme such as science or math and admission criteria, try to integrate students by race or income. Last are high school or middle-school district-wide choice programs. Few district policies allow unconstrained school choice to students regardless of background, notably high school choice in New York City and Boston and the newly implemented voluntary transfer program in Philadelphia. Rather, in most districts, the majority of students will attend a zoned, comprehensive school, with a limited supply of seats in alternative "choice" schools that are allocated on a first-come basis or by either lottery or admissions criteria.

Research is considerable on the effects of these various choice programs for the students who use them. Overall, little evidence indicates that this choice harms student performance, but the evidence of a positive effect is mixed (on charters, see Davis and Raymond 2012; Bifulco and Ladd 2006; Sass 2006; on Milwaukee voucher choice, Witte 1998; on vouchers in New York City, Washington, D.C., and Dayton, Howell et al. 2002). However, because choice comes in many variations, some research finds positive effects for specific types. Part of the explanation for these mixed findings is that some types or choice appear to be more effective than others. For example, KIPP charter schools appear to result in improved performance for students (Angrist et al. 2010; Tuttle et al. 2010) and some unpublished evidence suggests that the early charters in New York City had positive performance effects (Hoxby and Murarka 2009). Therefore, there may be some evidence that offering choices (or at least certain types of choices) may help to decouple housing and education. On the other hand, because choices occur primarily within districts, and urban districts educate very high proportions of poor and minority students (71 percent of students in New York City public schools and 83 percent of students in Chicago public schools qualify for free or reduced-price lunch), it is often not possible for these programs to change peers of students significantly. For example, in a recent study on the New York City high school choice program, Sean Corcoran, Lori Nathanson, and Christine Baker-Smith (2013) find that vast majorities of students ultimately attend a school close to home, and that the first choice schools indicated by low-achieving students tend to have higher concentrations of low-achieving, minority, and low-income peers. Some researchers have hypothesized that school choice can work well only if parents and students are informed about the quality of the schools from which they choose. Studies have looked at the effects on choices made when additional information is provided and have found some changes in choices (Hastings and Weinstein 2008). But, again, these studies look at the effects for individual students and not for the system as a whole. Only if informed choice leads to a better quality of school supply (thus providing all students with better schools) would these policies improve district-wide performance. In an analysis of the small school reform strategy in New York City, whereby large failing schools were closed and small themed ones opened, we found evidence of system-wide improvement in performance (Schwartz et al. 2012), but such scaling effects have not often been found.

Although opportunities for school choice are increasing, reliance is still heavy on school attendance zones and few students attend schools outside their home district. School choice policies that do not result in large numbers of students crossing district boundaries to access "better schools" can affect large student performance gains only if the supply of the high-quality schools increases dramatically. Thus far, evidence that this is happening is scant, or at least not in the decade or more that the policies have been in effect. Thus without more residential choice (to move to good neighborhoods or good school districts), school choice is unlikely to provide the same quality choices as residential choice offers to middle- and upper-income families.

Strategies for Reducing Student Mobility and Its Impact on Schools

Strategies to reduce student mobility seem particularly important given the relationship between high levels of mobility and student outcomes. One way to reduce mobility is to allow students to remain in the same school even if their families switch housing. This can be done by loosening constraints of traditional catchment zones and allowing a student who moves to remain at his or her old neighborhood school. Some schools and districts—for example, most charter schools in New Orleans—have experimented with guarantees that students will be bused to their schools from anywhere in the city. In New York City and Charlotte-Mecklenburg, students who move within the city are entitled to remain in the school they were previously attending, even if they no longer live within that school's attendance zone, until they have completed the school's terminal grade. This appears to be a promising policy response, especially in urban areas, where student mobility occurs largely within the school district (Kerbow 1996; Family Housing Fund 1998). Providing students with transportation to their existing school from their new location, possibly in the form of public transit, is a critical component of this policy response (Kerbow 1996). The federal government has implicitly acknowledged the benefits of this approach in the McKinney-Vento Act, which guarantees homeless students the right to remain in their existing schools regardless of where they live currently (Lovell 2008).

Another possible response is to directly address the problem of student mobility through housing subsidies. Such a solution specifically targets those prospective movers for whom current housing costs are the main determinant of a move. For example, the Schools Families Housing Stabilization Program (SFHSP) in Portland, Oregon, provided $5,000 annual housing assistance and a year of case management services to 143 student families identified as high risk for moving during the school year. The money could be used for rent, mortgages, deposits, and move-in costs. SFHSP achieved measurable reductions in student mobility and improved academic performance among participants, with 76 percent of the program students improving their performance relative to their peers in math and reading. The program was funded by the City of Portland, which was able to recoup a significant part of its outlay by retaining about $5,000 in state education funds for those pupils who would have otherwise left the city school system (Ledezma 2008). Although these results are promising, the program has been in place only for a year, and aggregate data will give a better indication of how the program works in the long term.

The Genesee Scholars Program, a similar pilot initiative in Flint, Michigan, provided $100 monthly rent subsidies for two years to the families of selected classrooms of second graders. Participating classrooms also kept the same teachers for the two years of the program. Before the program began, the two participating schools had intrayear student mobility rates of 75.3 percent and 58.9 percent, respectively—meaning that the majority of students who started the year at each school left by the end of the school year. Classrooms in which the program was implemented consistently showed major reductions in student mobility and increases in student performance compared to nonparticipating classrooms during the program's first cycle of students (Cook 2006). The first cycle of the program isolated all the Genesee scholars in one classroom, but the second selected students throughout the various second-grade classrooms to counteract any effects one particular teacher may have had on performance. Subsequently, the results of the second cycle were more ambiguous, finding inconsistent changes in mobility and academic performance between Genesee scholars in the different schools.

At the federal level, subsidies are also being used to address housing instability. The Homelessness Prevention Program, part of the American Recovery and Reinvestment Act (ARRA) of 2009, provides assistance to currently housed individuals and families at risk of homelessness in the form of rental and utility assistance or support for relocating to a more affordable space. This $1.5 billion program is not focused on lessening student mobility, but will likely reduce residential mobility among many families with school-age children. This type of program presents an opportunity for housing and education officials to draw attention to the negative effects of school mobility as families are faced with the possibility of a housing transition.

In an effort to reduce mobility in a single school in St. Paul, Minnesota, the East Side Housing Opportunity Program (HOP) has used financial support, in the form of a revolving loan fund, and school-based staff to assist families with housing needs (Metropolitan Housing Coalition 2004). In 2008, this integrated approach resulted in more than two dozen families completing housing plans and finding placement in stabilized housing, more than fifty families in case management, and staff contact with seventy-three landlords (East Side Neighborhood Development Company 2009). The use of specialized staff within the schools to provide housing assistance for students' families, as well as identify students at risk of moving, is a well-regarded strategy for addressing mobility (Rumberger 2002).

Yet other ways to reduce the negative impacts of frequent mobility are to develop a common curriculum across schools serving highly mobile students, develop programs to help incoming students adjust to new schools and help schools assimilate new students, closely track and monitor educational progress of highly mobile students, and train teachers to better meet needs of highly mobile students.

Creating Neighborhood Support for Children in Low-Income Housing

Improving local support for children and their families in low-income housing is another way to address student mobility and potentially improve student academic outcomes. Research in Great Britain has reinforced this approach finding that the highest use of school resources by community members takes place in poorer areas where "the school effectively acted as a key public resource at the hub of the community" (PricewaterhouseCoopers 2003, 27). The resources most often used by the community included information technology, child-care facilities, auditoriums, and athletic facilities, which led the authors of the study to conclude that investment in these areas would provide the greatest community benefits. Efforts by the Gates Foundation to expand library and internet access to impoverished areas provide an example of such targeted community investment (Bill and Melinda Gates Foundation 2009). The 21st Century Community Learning Centers program, administered by the U.S. Department of Education, is also an example of an effort to bolster the support system in low-income neighborhoods. Specifically, centers are established in schools with high-poverty and low performance for academic enrichment during out-of-school time (U.S. Department of Education 2004).

Some low-income housing developers have used new housing development as an opportunity to create new schools and community centers, and to increase the capacity of existing neighborhood infrastructure more generally. When the firm McCormack Baron Salazar began to redevelop housing around the Washington University Medical Center in St. Louis, it also used innovative financing strategies to rehabilitate the historic Adams School in the neighborhood, which is now classified as a school of excellence within the public school system. McCormack went further, and created a new gymnasium, ball field, and a community center offering recreational programs for youth, adult education, and day care (Matthews 2004).

In Georgia, the East Lake Foundation redeveloped a public housing development to include mixed-income housing, a YMCA, a public golf course, and a charter school that has dramatically outperformed the prior local school (Markiewicz 2008). The New Columbia Development in Portland used an amalgamation of housing and education to redevelop a downtrodden community. Columbia Villa, a low-income housing development that was a center for gang activity, was redeveloped with the conscious goal of reattracting families and rejuvenating the area. To that end, the city set aside two blocks for a new public school, built a park and a community center, and gave out contracts to local businesses to encourage them to relocate to the area (Center for Cities and Schools 2007). Similar examples, often using HOPE VI money to redevelop public housing units, exist nationwide.[5]

Skeptics argue that no firm data shows that place-based social programs are especially effective at altering educational outcomes for children. For instance, a comprehensive effort to rehabilitate the blighted Sandtown-Winchester neighborhood in Baltimore with far-reaching social programs produced only mixed results. Although educational gains were made, high student mobility is cited as a limiting factor to further improvement (Olsen 2003). Nonetheless, the circumstances under which place-based social programs are more effective than individual-based programs remain an open question.

Siting Low-Income Housing and Supporting Local Schools

Low-income housing developments, which often include high-density housing and many school-age children, can also have a significant financial impact on local school districts. New developments can add many children to local school rolls very quickly. Further, low-income students may be more likely to require special education and other high-cost educational services. Finally, low-income developments often provide lower property tax revenues than market rate housing to fund the local share of schools. For these reasons, as mentioned, some developers have decided simply to build new schools. More generally, advocates have proposed subsidizing local school districts for the costs of educating new low-income students.

The federal government already provides some additional funding to schools with high percentages of low-income students through Title I of the Elementary and Secondary Education Act, and funds some special education services through the Individuals with Disabilities Education Act. Most states also provide additional funds for poor and disabled students. These programs could be expanded to more fully cover the marginal costs of poor or disabled students. In addition, funds could be more directly tied to new low-income housing in an effort to fully offset the effects of new developments. One such model could be the Impact Aid program, intended to subsidize the costs to local school districts of educating military children, who do not proportionately expand the tax base (Buddin, Gill, and Zimmer 2001). Using a complex funding formula, the Impact Aid program provides about $900 million annually to approximately 1,400 local education agencies nationwide.

Local land use regulations, which often set minimum lot sizes and many other requirements for new housing, can limit the socioeconomic and racial composition of a community. When local regulations and local opposition prevent the construction of new low-income housing in middle-income and wealthy communities, the poor and often minority children who might have lived there are denied access to what tend to be high-quality schools. But historically, when low-income housing is introduced, and those schools are forced to educate poorer students who provide fewer local tax receipts, some families have left for neighboring communities, or private schools, where they need not subsidize the education of low-income students. Research further suggests that when provided with school choice, the outflow of students from public schools tends to increase the racial and economic segregation of the remaining students (Lankford and Wyckoff 2001).

Massachusetts seeks to resolve this tension by providing low-income students more access to quality schools while offsetting their financial impact on local school systems, through its 40R and 40S statutes. Chapter 40R allows some Smart Growth developments (incorporating mixed land use, affordable housing, compact design, community aesthetics, the conservation of open space, transportation choices, and the rebuilding of communities) to bypass otherwise applicable local land use regulations. Simultaneously, the state passed Chapter 40S, creating a Smart Growth School Cost Reimbursement Fund. The fund provides reimbursement for any net new education costs that result from housing units built under 40R, where those costs are not already covered by the property and excise taxes paid by the new households (Rollins 2006). Although the programs do not currently have a reliable funding source, together 40R and 40S may provide a conceptual model for how to allow more poor children access to excellent schools while reducing incentives for incumbent families to abandon the public school system.

Further, it is not clear that such a tension need always exist. Montgomery County, Maryland, operates one of the oldest inclusionary zoning programs in the country. Introduced in the early 1970s, the policy mandates that 12 to 15 percent of all homes in subdivisions of thirty-five homes or greater be sold or rented at below-market prices. Further, the housing authority maintains the right to purchase up to one-third of these homes in any subdivisions. The result is that children in public housing in Montgomery County experience a range of neighborhood poverty levels (Schwartz 2010). It should be noted that Montgomery County may be a special case, however, as the overall poverty rates are below the national average so that concentration of children in public housing is relatively low.

Conclusions

In the previous section, we discussed education policies and housing interventions that recognize the relationship between education and housing and may serve to improve student outcomes. More ambitious, but politically and social difficult, would be to address directly the poverty of many of the nation's children and to economically and racially integrate America's communities.

We thank Vicki Been and Ingrid Gould Ellen for their guidance on this project and Jaclene Begley, Alan Biller, Abigail Conover Carlton, Sarah Cordes, Todd Ely, Andrea Halpern, and John Tye for their assistance.

Notes

1. In this chapter we do not discuss the large set of issues and policies related to improving schools (for an overview of school reform, see Darling-Hammond 2010).

2. The Moving to Opportunity demonstration provided 4,600 participating families living in public housing in Baltimore, Boston, Chicago, Los Angeles, and New York City with housing vouchers. These families were then randomly assigned to three conditions. In the experimental condition, families were assigned vouchers that could only be used to move to low-poverty neighborhoods, whereas in the two control conditions families were assigned unrestricted vouchers and no vouchers, respectively. Although neighborhood advocates hoped that MTO would provide strong evidence of the impact of neighborhoods on child and family outcomes—including children's educational outcomes—the results fell short. Impacts on educational outcomes were, overall, insignificant due, in part to both low compliance rates and the small sustained change in neighborhood and school environments actually realized by families in the experimental group (see Sanbonmatsu et al. 2006).

3. The Boston METCO program and busing program in Ann Arbor, Michigan, are two of the oldest and best known that allow students to cross district boundaries (when there are spaces open outside the urban area). There is some evidence that participants in METCO perform better than similar students who do not participate (see Angrist and Lang 2004) but because such programs are so few and the ones that exist are limited to so few students, we do not discuss them further.

4. Often the local school district, the state, a nonprofit such a university.

5. The HOPE VI program, active since 1992, is an effort to reshape and revitalize public housing projects administered by the Department of Housing and Urban Development.

References

Angrist, Joshua D., Susan M. Dynarski, Thomas J. Kane, Parag A. Pathak, and Christopher R. Walters. 2010. "Inputs and Impacts in Charter Schools: KIPP Lynn." *American Economic Review* 100(2): 239–43.

Angrist, Joshua D., and K. Lang. 2004. "Does School Integration Generate Peer Effects? Evidence from Boston's METCO Program." *The American Economic Review* 94(5): 1613–634.

Astone, Nan M., and Sara S. McLanahan. 1994. "Family Structure, Residential Mobility, and School Dropout: A Research Note." *Demography* 31(4): 575–84.

Bifulco, Robert, and Helen F. Ladd. 2006. "The Impacts of Charter Schools on Student Achievement: Evidence from North Carolina." *Education Finance and Policy* 1(1): 50–90.

Bill and Melinda Gates Foundation. 2009. "Libraries." Available at: http://www.gatesfoundation.org/topics/Pages/libraries.aspx# (accessed March 31, 2009).

Black, Sandra E. 1999. "Do Better Schools Matter? Parental Valuation of Elementary Education." *The Quarterly Journal of Economics* 114(2): 577–99.

Boozer, Michael, and Stephen E. Cacciola. 2001. "Inside the 'Black Box' of Project Star: Estimation of Peer Effects Using Experimental Data (June 2001)." Yale Economic Growth Center Discussion Paper No. 832.

Brooks-Gunn, Jeanne, Greg J. Duncan, Pamela Kato Klebanov, and Naomi Sealand. 1993. "Do Neighborhoods Influence Child and Adolescent Development?" *American Journal of Sociology* 99(2):353–95.

Buddin, Richard, Brian P. Gill, and Ron W. Zimmer. 2001. *Impact Aid and the Education of Military Children.* MR-1272-OSD. Santa Monica, Calif.: RAND National Defense Research Institute. Available at: http://www.rand.org/content/dam/rand/pubs/monograph_reports/2007/MR1272.pdf (accessed November 10, 2013).

Card, David, and A. Abigail Payne. 2002. "School Finance Reform, the Distribution of School Spending, and the Distribution of Student Test Scores." *Journal of Public Economics* 83(1): 49–82.

Center for Cities and Schools. 2007. "Planning for Families: The Housing and Education Nexus." Proceedings Summary. Berkeley: University of California. Available at: http://citiesandschools.berkeley.edu/reports/CCandS_2008_planning_for_families.pdf (accessed March 31, 2009).

Coleman, James S. 1988. "Social Capital in the Creation of Human Capital." *American Journal of Sociology* 94: Supplement S95–S210.

Cook, J. 2006. "Genesee Scholars make the grade with stable living arrangements." Department of Human Services, Flint, Michigan. http://www.michigan.gov/dhs/0,1607,7-124-5458_7691_7752-151915—,00.html (accessed June 2009).

Corcoran, Sean P., Lori Nathanson, and Christine Baker-Smith. 2013. "High School Choice in NYC: A Report on the School Choices and Placements of Low-Achieving Students." New York: The Research Alliance for New York City Schools and the Institute for Education and Social Policy.

Corcoran, Sean P., Thomas Romer, and Howard L. Rosenthal. 2008. "The Troubled Quest for Equality in School Finance." In *What Do We Owe Each Other? Rights and Obligations in Contemporary American Society,* edited by Howard L. Rosenthal and David J. Rothman. Piscataway, N.J.: Transaction Publishers.

Crane, Jonathan. 1991. "The Epidemic Theory of Ghettos and Neighborhood Effects on Dropping Out and Teenage Childbearing." *American Journal of Sociology* 96(5): 1226–259.

Crowley, Sheila. 2003. "The Affordable Housing Crisis: Residential Mobility of Poor Families and School Mobility of Poor Children." *Journal of Negro Education* 72(1): 22–38.

Currie, Janet, and Aaron Yelowitz. 2000. "Are Public Housing Projects Good for Kids?" *Journal of Public Economics* 75(1): 88–124.

Darling-Hammond, Linda. 2010. *The Flat World and Education: How America's Commitment to Equity Will Determine Our Future*. New York: Teachers College Press.

Davis, Devora H., and Margaret E. Raymond. 2012. "Choices for Studying Choice: Assessing Charter School Effectiveness Using Two Quasi-Experimental Methods." *Economics of Education Review* 31(2): 225–36.

Downes, Thomas A., and Mona P. Shah. 2006. "The Effect of School Finance Reforms on the Level and Growth of Per-Pupil Expenditures." *Peabody Journal of Education* 81(3): 1–38.

East Side Neighborhood Development Company. 2009. "East Side Housing Opportunity Program." Available at: http://www.esndc.org/EHOP.html#Anchor-Case-14210 (accessed March 31, 2009).

Ellen, Ingrid G., Amy E. Schwartz, Leanna Stiefel, and C. Chellman. 2007. "Does Subsidized Housing Affect Local Schools?" Chicago: MacArthur Foundation.

Ellen, Ingrid G., and Margery A. Turner. 1997. "Does Neighborhood Matter? Assessing Recent Evidence." *Housing Policy Debate* 8(4): 833–66.

Gaux, Dominique, and Eric Maurin. 2005. "The Effect of Overcrowded Housing on Children's Performance at School." *Journal of Public Economics* 89(6–5): 797–819.

Gibbons, Stephen, and Shqiponja Telhaj. 2011. "Pupil Mobility and School Disruption." *Journal of Public Economics* 95(9–10): 1156–167.

Hanushek, Eric A., John F. Kain, Jacob M. Markman, and Steven G. Rivkin. 2003. "Does Peer Ability Affect Student Achievement?" *Journal of Applied Econometrics* 18(5): 527–44.

Hanushek, Eric A., John F. Kain, and Steven G. Rivkin. 2004. "Disruption Versus Tiebout Improvement: The Costs and Benefits of Switching Schools." *Journal of Public Economics* 88(9–10): 1721–746.

Harker, Lisa. 2007. "The Impact of Housing on Children's Life Chances." *Journal of Children's Services* 2(3): 43–51.

Hastings, Justine S., and Jeffrey M. Weinstein. 2008. "Information, School Choice, and Academic Achievement: Evidence from Two Experiments." *Quarterly Journal of Economics* 123(4): 1373–414.

Hayes, Kathy J., and Lori L. Taylor. 1996. "Neighborhood School Characteristics: What Signals Quality to Homebuyers?" *Federal Reserve Bank of Dallas Economic Review*, 4th quarter: 2–9.

Howell, William G., Patrick J. Wolf, David E. Campbell, and Paul E. Peterson. 2002. "School Vouchers and Academic Performance: Results from Three Randomized Field Trials." *Journal of Policy Analysis and Management* 21(2): 191–217.

Hoxby, Caroline M., and Sonali Murarka. 2009. "Charter Schools in New York City: Who Enrolls and How They Affect Their Students' Achievement." *NBER* working paper no. 14852). Cambridge, Mass.: National Bureau of Economic Research.

Kerbow, David. 1996. "Patterns of Urban Student Mobility and Local School Reform." *Center for Research on the Education of Students Placed at Risk* report no. 5. Chicago: University of Chicago.

Kozol, Jonathan. 2012. *Savage Inequalities: Children in America's Schools.* New York: Broadway Paperbacks.

Krieger, James, and Donna L. Higgins. 2002. "Housing and Health: Time Again for Public Health Action." *American Journal of Public Health* 92(5): 758–68.

Lacoe, Johanna. 2013. "Too Scared to Learn? The Academic Consequences of Feeling Unsafe at School." *IESP* working paper no. 02–13. New York: Institute for Education and Social Policy.

Lankford, Hamilton, and James Wyckoff. 2001. "Who Would Be Left Behind by Enhanced Private School Choice?" *Journal of Urban Economics* 50(2): 288–312.

Ledezma, D. 2008. *School Families Housing Stabilization Program Year One Report.* Washington, D.C.: Bureau of Housing and Community Development.

Leventhal, Tama, and Jeanne Brooks-Gunn. 2004. "A Randomized Study of Neighborhood Effects on Low-Income Children's Educational Outcomes." *Developmental Psychology* 40(4): 488–507.

Markiewicz, David A. 2008. "Program Puts Students on Post-High School Path." *Atlanta Journal-Constitution,* June 26, 2008, p. 4JE.

Matthews, Sherrie V. 2004. "Building a Community, Not Just Housing." *Planning* 70(3): 10–13.

Maxwell, Lorraine E. 2003. "Home and School Density Effects of Elementary School Children: The Role of Spatial Density." *Environment and Behavior* 35(4): 566–78.

Metropolitan Housing Coalition. 2004. "Moving On: Student Mobility and Affordable Housing." Louisville, Ky.: MHC. Available at: http://www.metropolitanhousing.org/pdf/mhcdoc_32.pdf (accessed November 10, 2013).

Nechyba, Thomas J. 2004. "Prospects for Achieving Equity or Adequacy in Education: The Limits of State Aid in General Equilibrium." In *Helping Children Left Behind: State Aid and the Pursuit of Educational Equity,* edited by John Yinger. Cambridge, Mass.: MIT Press.

Neuman, Susan B., and Donna Celano. 2001. "Access to Print in Low-Income and Middle-Income Communities: An Ecological Study of Four Neighborhoods." *Reading Research Quarterly* 36(1): 8–26.

Olsen, J. 2003. "The Hundred-Million Dollar Question: Can Inner-City Neighborhoods Be Transformed?" *Next American City,* June.

PricewaterhouseCoopers. 2003. "Building Better Performance: An Empirical Assessment of the Learning and Other Impacts of Schools Capital Investment." Report no. RR407. Nottingham, UK: DfES Publications.

Raudenbush, Stephen, Marshall Jean, and Emily Art. 2009. "Year-by-Year and Cumulative Impacts of Attending a High-Mobility Elementary School on Children's Mathematics Achievement in Chicago 1995–2005." In *Whither Opportunity,* edited by Greg J. Duncan and Richard J. Murnane. New York and Chicago: Russell Sage Foundation and Spencer Foundation.

Rollins, D. 2006. "An Overview of Chapters 40R and 40S: Massachusetts' Newest Housing Policies." *New England Public Policy Center* policy brief no. 06–1. Boston, Mass.: Federal Reserve Bank of Boston.

Rumberger, Russell W. 2002. *Student Mobility and Academic Achievement.* ED466314. Champaign, Ill.: ERIC Clearinghouse on Elementary and Early Childhood Education.

———. 2003. "The Causes and Consequences of Student Mobility." *Journal of Negro Education* 72(1): 6–21.

Sampson, Robert J., Patrick Sharkey, and Stephen W. Raudenbush. 2008. "Durable Effects of Concentrated Disadvantage on Verbal Ability Among African American Children." *Proceedings of the National Academy of Sciences* 105(3): 845–52.

Sanbonmatsu, Lisa, Jeffrey R. Kling, Greg J. Duncan, and Jeanne Brooks-Gunn. 2006. "Neighborhoods and Academic Achievement Results From the Moving to Opportunity Experiment." *Journal of Human Resources* 41(4): 649–91.

Sass, Tim R. 2006. "Charter Schools and Student Achievement in Florida." *Education Finance and Policy* 1(1): 91–122.

Schwartz, Amy E., and Leanna Stiefel. 2013. *Mobility Matters.* Draft manuscript.

Schwartz, Amy E., Leanna Stiefel, and Luis Chalico. 2007. "The Multiple Dimensions of Student Mobility and Implications for Academic Performance: Evidence from New York City Elementary and Middle School Students." New York: Education Finance Research Consortium.

Schwartz, Amy E., Leanna Stiefel, and E. Ruble Whitesell. 2013. "The Impact of Mid-Year Movers on Stable Students." Paper presented at the Association for Education Finance and Policy 38th Annual Conference. New Orleans (March 14–16, 2013).

Schwartz, Amy E., and I. Voicu. 2007. "Which Schools Matter? Disentangling the Impact of Zones Schools and Unzoned Schools on House Prices in New York City." Unpublished paper.

Schwartz, Amy E., Matthew Wiswall, Leanna Stiefel, and Elizabeth Debraggio. 2012. "Does High School Reform Lift Urban Districts? Evidence from New York City." *Wagner* research paper no. 1996702. Prepared for National Center on Scaling Up Effective Schools (NCSU) Conference, Vanderbilt University (June 2012).

Schwartz, Heather. 2010. "Housing Policy Is School Policy: Economically Integrative Housing Promotes Academic Success in Montgomery County, MD." New York: The Century Foundation.

Sharkey, Patrick, Amy E. Schwartz, Ingrid G. Ellen, and Johanna Lacoe. 2013. "High Stakes in the Classroom, High Stakes on the Street: The Effects of Community Violence on Students' Standardized Test Performance." *IESP* working paper no. 03–13. New York: Institute for Education and Social Policy.

Swanson, Christopher B., and Barbara Schneider. 1999. "Students on the Move: Residential and Educational Mobility in America's Schools." *Sociology of Education* 72(1): 54–67.

U.S. Department of Education. 2004. *When Schools Stay Open Late: The National Evaluation of the 21st Century Community Learning Centers Program New Findings.* Washington, D.C.: Institute for Education and Social Policy.

Witte, John F. 1998. "The Milwaukee Voucher Experiment." *Educational Evaluation and Policy Analysis* 20(4): 229–51.

Wodtke, Geoffrey T., David J. Harding, and Felix Elwert. 2011. "Neighborhood Effects in Temporal Perspective." *American Sociological Review* 76(5): 713–36.

Zimmer, Ron W., and Eugenia F. Toma. 2000. "Peer Effects in Private and Public Schools Across Countries." *Journal of Policy Analysis and Management Volume* 19(1): 75–92.

═ Index ═

Boldface numbers refer to figures and tables.

absenteeism, 298
academic achievement: housing unit impacts, 296–98; Mobile public schools, 145–46; neighborhood effects, 129–30, 298–301; peer effects, 129–30, 200; and school choice policies, 238, 304; and school quality, xiii; segregation effects, 9–10. *See also* test scores
academic curriculum, 245, 260, 307
accountability, 237, 271
ACS (American Community Survey). *See* American Community Survey (ACS)
Adelman, Robert, 46
adequate yearly progress (AYP), 14, 182, 273, 289–90
adolescents, 50–51
affluent households: neighborhood effects on academic outcomes, 298–99; presence in neighborhoods as social buffer for lower-income households, 110–11; residential segregation, **109,** 111; school decision, xv, xvii, 16, 130
affordable housing, 114, 146–47, 309. *See also* public housing
African Americans. *See* blacks
Alabama State Department of Education, residential mobility–school choice relationship, 143, **145**
American Community Survey (ACS): economic residential segregation, 105–11; high-poverty neighborhoods, **125;** income measures, 110; vs. long-form census data, 100–101; Mobile neighborhood characteris-

tics, **144;** private school enrollment, 71; racial and economic segregation of school-age children, 111–14; racial differences in neighborhood quality, 33, **34, 35;** racial-ethnic identification, 101–2; racial segregation, 103–5, **106, 107;** racial segregation–economic segregation relationship, 115–21; residential mobility–school choice relationship, 143
American Recovery and Reinvestment Act (ARRA) (2009), 306
Anderson, Elijah, 41
Asian Americans: Boston population, 212; Boston Public School students, 212; census identification, 101; economic segregation, 108, **109,** 110, 111; neighborhood quality, 33–35; residential preferences, 39, 41, 44, 45; residential segregation trends, 1–2, 28–36, 98; segregation of children, **112,** 113; stereotyping of blacks, 39
Asian-black dissimilarity index, 105
Asian-Hispanic dissimilarity index, 105
Asian-white dissimilarity index, 1, 28, 105, 128
asthma, 298
Atlanta, Ga.: residential segregation, 105; social class and residential preferences study, 46; white neighborhood preferences, 43
attitudinal studies, 54
audit studies, 46–47, 54–55
AYP (adequate yearly progress), 14, 182, 273, 289–90

315

study, 171–75; urban public school choice in Chicago, 239–43; urban public school choice study, 273–75. *See also specific data sources*
day care centers, 15, 278
decennial census, 71, 76
de facto segregation, 7
de jure segregation, 6, 9
Delale-O'Connor, Lori, 237, 262
DeLuca, Stefanie, 52, 53, 130, 137, 163n8, 177, 240
Denton, Nancy, 28, 114
Detroit, Mich.: poverty concentration, 126; racial differences in residential preferences, 45; residential segregation, 2, 105; school choice studies, 17; social class and residential preferences study, 46; white neighborhood preferences, 43
Digest of Educational Statistics (2011), 201n4
discipline, 156
discrimination: audit studies, 46–47, 54–55; economic factors, 46–47; in housing market, 2–3, 37–38, 40–44, 46–47, 53–54, 97; and residential preferences, 40–44
dissimilarity indices: Asian-Hispanic, 105; Asian-white, 1, 28, 105, 128; black-Asian, 105; black-Hispanic, 105; black-white, 1, 5, 28, 29, 103–4, **106, 107,** 128; definition of, 1–2, 102; Hispanic-white, 1, 28, 105, 128
diversity, 2, 200, 224–26, 284

East Lake Foundation, 307–8
East Side Housing Opportunity Program, 306–7
economic explanations, for residential segregation, 36–37, 44–47, 170
economic segregation, 97–136; data collection and methodology, 99–103, 105–7; by economic status, 105–11; educational equity implications, 128–31; introduction, 97–99; and poverty concentration, 98–99, 121–28; and racial segregation, 114–21; results of study, 103–28; of

school-age children, 111–14; and school decision, 199; in suburbs, 169; trends, 2, 36–37, 105–11, 200
Education, U.S. Department of, 307
educational achievement gap, 36
educational attainment: measurement of, 72–73; and neighborhood poverty concentration, 121, 124; and residential segregation, 2, 37; and school decision making, 271
educational equity, 128–31, 195
educational goals, 244–45
education decision process. *See* school decision process
Elementary and Secondary Education Act (1965), 6, 14, 308
elementary schools, school decision process, 218–20
Ellen, Ingrid, 298–99, 302
Emerson, Michael, 4
employment, 300
England: community use of school resources, 307; school choice studies, 272
environmental hazard exposure, 28, 35, 36, 37
ethnicity, segregation by. *See* racial-ethnic segregation
ethnocentrism, benign, 3
Evans, Lorraine, 9
Ewert, Stephanie, 68
extracurricular activities, 222–23, 299

Fair Housing Act (1968), 3
Fairlie, Robert, 9
families with children, residential segregation of, 111–14
family networks, 151, 153–54. *See also* social networks
Farley, Reynolds, 3, 40, 42–43
Farrie, Danielle, 45
Fasenfest, David, 29
financial challenges, 149–50, 245–46
Fischer, Mary, 47
Fitzpatrick, Jody, 272
Flint, Mich.: Genesee Scholars Program, 306
food, 35

foreclosures, 38
foster children, 248, 252–55
Freely, Joshua, 45
friendships, 299–300

Galster, George, 40
Garboden, Phillip, 163*n*8
Garrity, W. Arthur, 212
Gary, Ind.: poverty concentration, 126
Gautreaux, 51
gender differences, in discrimination, 47. *See also* women
Genesee Scholars Program, 306
gentrification, 16, 201*n*8, 207, 223, 283–85
geographic units, residential segregation changes by race and class study, 99–100
GeoLytics, 29, **30, 32**
Georgia: East Lake Foundation, 307–8
ghetto stereotype, 41–42
Gini index, 102
GIS (Geographic Information Systems), 75
Glaeser, Edward, 27, 31
Gleason, Phillip, 238, 242
Goldring, Ellen, 16
Goyette, Kimberly, xi, 1, 45, 65, 97, 131*n*3, 201*n*1
Great Recession, 35
Greatschools.org, 271–72, 279, 283, 290
Guest, Avery, 11

Hanley, Caroline, 64, 132*n*8
Hanushek, Eric, 297
Harker, Lisa, 298
Harris, David, 4
Hastings, Justine, 292
health issues, 35–36, 298
helicopter parenting, 217
Hennigan; Morgan v., 212
high school drop-out rates, 9
high schools, school decision process, 219–20, 228
Hispanic-Asian dissimilarity index, 105
Hispanic-black dissimilarity index, 105

Hispanics: black stereotypes, 39; Boston population, 212; Boston Public School students, 212; census identification, 101–2; economic segregation, 108, **109**, 110, 111; neighborhood quality, 33–35; real estate steering, 46; residential knowledge, 48; residential preferences, 39, 41, 44, 45; residential segregation trends, 1–2, 28–36, 98, 104–5; school segregation, 8, 9–10; segregation of children, **112**, 113
Hispanic-white dissimilarity index, 1, 28, 105, 128
Holme, Jennifer Jellison, 16–17, 201*n*3, 207
Homelessness Prevention Program, 306
homeownership rate, **34, 35**
homeschooling, 17
homework, 297
Honolulu, Hawaii: residential segregation, 2
HOPE VI, 51–52, 140, 308
household income: distribution in metropolitan areas, 109; measurement of, 73; in Mobile, Ala., 144; racial differences in neighborhood characteristics, 33, **34, 35**; and residential mobility, 11, 46; and residential segregation, 2, 36–37; and school decision, 15
Housing and Urban Development, U.S. Department, 43
housing assistance, 51–52, 140, 147–48, 305–7, 308. *See also* public housing
housing characteristics: and academic outcomes, 296–98; measurement of, 73; in Mobile, Ala., 143, 149, 150–51, 152
Housing Choice Vouchers, 161–62
housing decision. *See* neighborhood decision process
Housing Discrimination Studies (HDS), 43
housing–education relationship, 295–314; conclusions, 310; housing unit's impact on children's